Andrew J. Wilson was born in Dungannon, County Tyrone. He studied at Manchester Polytechnic and Queen's University Belfast, and later earned his Ph.D. in European history from Loyola University of Chicago, where he now teaches. His writings have appeared in a number of journals, including *Eire-Ireland*, *The Recorder* and *The Irish Review*.

IRISH AMERICA
AND THE
ULSTER CONFLICT
1968–1995

Andrew J. Wilson

THE
BLACKSTAFF
PRESS

BELFAST

First published in 1995 in the European Union by
The Blackstaff Press Limited
3 Galway Park, Dundonald, Belfast BT16 OAN, Northern Ireland
with the assistance of the
Cultural Traditions Programme which aims to encourage
acceptance and understanding of cultural diversity

Published simultaneously in the United States of America by
The Catholic University of America Press

Typeset by Books International, Norcross, Georgia

Printed in the United States of America by
Thomson-Shore, Inc., Dexter, Michigan

A CIP catalogue record for this book
is available from the British Library

ISBN 0-85640-563-9

To Barbara, in gratitude,
and Rachael and Charlotte, in hope

CONTENTS

PREFACE

On November 11, 1992, a heavily armed squad of FBI agents stormed the Phoenix Bar in the Bronx and arrested its owner, Thomas Maguire from Fermanagh. As Maguire was taken at gunpoint, the Gárda Special Branch, in keeping with their longstanding cooperation with US authorities, simultaneously raided his holiday cottage in Donegal. Maguire and five others were later charged with transporting nearly three thousand bomb detonators from Tucson to New York and then shipping them to Ireland. Prosecutors claimed that a number of these devices were recovered from defused IRA bombs in 1991. Some of the defendants were also implicated in a conspiracy to acquire Stinger surface-to-air missiles for use against British helicopters in South Armagh.

Federal authorities had devoted extensive resources to the Tucson investigation. During the subsequent trial, prosecuting attorneys produced more than one thousand exhibits and hours of secretly taped conversations. They also called one hundred and twenty-five witnesses, many of whom were brought to Arizona from Britain and Ireland. Yet on April 26, 1994, a jury found the six defendants not guilty on all counts. The verdict was a shattering blow to US law-enforcement agencies and their counterparts across the Atlantic. To militant Irish-American nationalist groups, however, the release of the "Tucson Six" was a major boost to morale and renewed their commitment to the republican cause in Ireland.

In October 1993, Gerry Adams, president of Sinn Féin, was a pall-bearer at the funeral of Thomas Begley. Begley had died while planting a bomb at a fish shop on the Protestant Shankill Road in Belfast. Nine innocent shoppers were killed in the explosion, including thirteen-year-old Leanne Murray. Adams was accused of sanctioning the murder of children and became an international pariah. Shortly afterward, President Bill Clinton reaffirmed an earlier decision to deny Adams entry to the United States because of his links to terrorism.

Just eighteen months later, during Congress's annual St. Patrick's Day luncheon, Clinton welcomed Adams with a handshake. The Sinn Féin president's metamorphosis from blacklisted sponsor of terrorism to honored guest came despite strong British objections. Prime Minister John Major was livid and refused to accept a telephone call from the American president for five days. Some British media commentators denounced Clinton's "betrayal" and characterized his handshake with Adams as "America's biggest snub to Britain in recent history and the lowest point in a special relationship sustained for half a century by ten presidents."

The "Tucson Six" case and the "Adams Affair" are the latest manifestations of a continuous transatlantic influence on the Ulster conflict. From the outbreak of the Troubles in 1968, small, clandestine cells of Irish Americans developed gunrunning networks which, at certain periods, played a key role in sustaining the IRA's "armed struggle." Others formed organizations such as the Irish Northern Aid Committee (Noraid), which sent important financial aid to the republican movement. These groups also launched publicity campaigns designed to focus attention on Britain's "repression and discrimination" against the nationalist community.

Despite the attention given to gunrunning and Noraid, the majority of Irish Americans remained apathetic and largely uninterested in Northern Ireland. Those with an opinion generally tended to endorse the goals of constitutional nationalism and condemn IRA violence. Their views were represented by prominent Irish-American politicians in the congressional Friends of Ireland. The Friends tried to discourage support for Irish-American republicanism and to use their power on Capitol Hill to influence British policy in Northern Ireland. They strongly encouraged political initiatives designed to enhance the role of the Irish government and the Social Democratic and Labour Party.

This analysis concentrates on the development and achievements of both the militant and the constitutional wings of modern Irish-American nationalism. Consideration is also given to the role played by the United

States government, the activities of reconciliation and investment groups, and the way Northern Ireland has been presented in the American media. The study of these issues is intended to provide historical context to the crucial role Irish America has played in the IRA cease-fire of September 1994, and the ongoing peace process in Ulster.

ACKNOWLEDGMENTS

This book is based on research originally completed at Loyola University of Chicago. I am indebted to Professor Lawrence McCaffrey for his encouragement and advice throughout the research and writing of the dissertation on which the book is based. My committee members, Professors Janet Nolan and Jo Hays, also made invaluable contributions through their insightful comments on the original manuscript. I am grateful to Loyola University for awarding me a dissertation fellowship, which provided the financial resources to complete the initial stages of research.

My deepest thanks to Robert Bell, who provided me with documents, collections, and contacts from the LinenHall Library, Belfast, without which this book could not have been completed. Thanks also to Vanessa Crouther of Loyola University's interlibrary loan department, who helped track down the most obscure documents and articles.

I am extremely grateful to all those who gave me access to their personal collections, especially Sean Prendiville, Paul Brosnahan, and Nancy Heaney, and to Adrian Bannister, Joesph E. Wilson, and Ray O'Hanlon for their research assistance.

My thanks to Anne Tannahill of The Blackstaff Press and David McGonagle of The Catholic University of America Press for making publication of this book possible. My manuscript also benefitted enormously from the editorial direction and advice of Susan Needham of The Catholic University of America Press. And finally, my sincere thanks to all those who took time to talk and correspond with me and offer their personal experiences.

IRISH AMERICA AND

THE ULSTER CONFLICT, 1968–1995

CHAPTER I

◆

IRISH-AMERICAN NATIONALISM,

1800–1968

◆

In order to grasp fully the Irish-American dimension to the Ulster conflict, it is important to outline the background that shaped the nationalism of Irish immigrants. From the 1830s onward, Irish Americans played an increasingly important role in the political development of Ireland. The tactics they developed to help liberate their homeland set precedents that would be copied by almost all the current Irish-American support groups. The following brief synopsis of the achievements and characteristics of Irish-American nationalism is intended to place the main body of work in historical context.

The Irish-American community has its origins in the wave of Roman Catholic immigrants leaving Ireland due to the adverse economic conditions following the Napoleonic Wars. Many were comparatively well off and left to seek better opportunities in the New World. Some were small tenant farmers who were evicted as landlords tried to stabilize profits through consolidation of their property. Between 1815 and 1845, more than one million Irish immigrants crossed the Atlantic. They began a pattern that developed into a mass exodus during and after the Great

3

Famine. From 1845 to 1854, starvation and poverty drove over one and one-half million people to America and institutionalized emigration as a permanent feature of Irish life. Further lack of economic opportunity, as well as despair, led to an average of fifty thousand Irish immigrants per year entering the United States between 1860 and 1900.[1]

Such large-scale emigration created an Irish diaspora which became an integral part of the historical development of their native land. Nurturing an intense anglophobia, they vowed revenge for the suffering they had to endure. Nationalists in Ireland soon realized the potential of this vast immigrant population in America and began to tap its power and wealth to sustain the drive against British rule.

Daniel O'Connell was the first Irish leader to exploit the potential of Irish America. In the late 1820s, Friends of Ireland organizations and Hibernian Relief Societies were formed in the US to aid his campaign for Catholic Emancipation. Similarly, in the early 1840s, O'Connell's Irish-American supporters established Repeal Associations to agitate against the Act of Union. These support groups were often led by United Irishmen who had fled to the US after the 1798 rebellion. They sent thousands of dollars to finance O'Connell's activities and first established the diaspora as an important source of funding for political movements in Ireland.[2]

The American Repeal Associations held mass demonstrations and organized two national conventions, which were attended by thousands of delegates. They used their voting power to obtain support from congressmen and secured endorsements from such prominent figures as President John Tyler, the future president and Senator James Buchanan of Pennsylvania, the former president Martin Van Buren, and Governor William Seward of New York.[3] Optimistic members of the Repeal Movement believed that such strong support in Washington could prove decisive in forcing Britain to grant some measure of autonomy to Ireland.

The vitality and unity of the American Repeal Association shattered, however, when O'Connell began to make pronouncements on US po-

1. L. J. McCaffrey, *The Irish Diaspora in America* (Bloomington: Indiana University Press, 1976), 60.

2. Thomas F. Moriarity, "The Irish-American Response to Catholic Emancipation," *Catholic Historical Review* (July 1980).

3. Tom Fleming, "The Green Flag in America," *American Heritage* (June/July 1979): 52.

litical issues. In 1842, he asked Irish Americans to support the abolitionist movement and announced that the Repeal Association would not accept money or assistance from those who accepted slavery. This statement enraged many Irish immigrants who detested abolitionism and feared that freeing slaves would threaten their livelihood by increasing competition for manual labor.[4] The Repeal Movement in America was virtually annihilated by mass defections and the dispute over slavery became the first of many instances in which the views of Irish nationalist leaders often clashed with their counterparts in America.

The immigrants who fled to the United States from 1845 onward had a major impact on the character of Irish-American nationalism. Those who were forced to emigrate during the Great Famine brought with them a burning sense of injustice. They believed the British had driven them from their country through a calculated policy of genocide, and they longed for revenge. Their intense hatred was fused into Irish-American nationalism and made it more prone to extremism.

This bitterness toward England was exacerbated by the harsh conditions Irish immigrants suffered in America. In the squalor of the urban ghettoes they had to endure exhausting physical labor, discrimination, loneliness, and Anglo-American nativism. Many developed an intense nostalgia for their former lives in Ireland. They constructed a highly romanticized and sentimental image of their homeland, which contrasted sharply with their situation in the United States. Their frustration and anger at having been removed from this "idyllic" past were naturally channeled toward England and contributed to the growth of a belligerent nationalism.

Following the demise of Daniel O'Connell's constitutional efforts to repeal the Act of Union, militant Irish Americans began working for the revolutionary Young Ireland Movement. Despite transatlantic support, however, the uprising of 1848 collapsed in dismal failure. Many Young Irelanders, such as Thomas Meagher and John Mitchell, fled to the United States and helped reinforce the romantic and revolutionary strands of Irish-American nationalism. Their influence kept the diaspora committed to physical force in an era in which the Irish at home concentrated on parliamentary politics.

4. O'Connell further alienated Irish Americans when he later stated that if the Act of Union were repealed, it would make the Irish so loyal they would fight England's enemies throughout the world, including Americans in the dispute over control of Oregon.

In 1858, John O'Mahony and Michael Doheny, both Young Ireland émigrés, founded the Fenian Brotherhood. They committed the new organization to violent revolution and soon forged links with the Irish Republican Brotherhood (IRB) in Ireland. The Fenians devised a strategy whereby the IRB, with financial and material support from America, would encourage violent uprising in Ireland to end British rule and establish an independent republic.

In 1861, the Fenian Brotherhood achieved one of its major successes by engineering a patriot funeral to encourage popular support for their cause. When Terence Belew McManus, another Young Ireland veteran, died in San Francisco, the Fenians decided to send his body back to Ireland for a triumphal burial. Before the coffin was shipped out of New York, thousands attended a funeral Mass in St. Patrick's Cathedral conducted by Archbishop John Hughes.

While the coffin was enroute across the Atlantic, Paul Cardinal Cullen, a fierce opponent of revolutionary nationalism in Ireland, fought bitterly to ensure the funeral would not become a Fenian-engineered celebration. Despite Cullen's attempt to undermine the IRB's strategy, however, fifty thousand people followed the coffin through Dublin, while hundreds of thousands lined the route to Glasnevin Cemetery. At the graveside, Fenian leaders delivered highly emotional orations lambasting Cullen and constitutional nationalism. Historians thus characterize the McManus funeral as a major psychological victory for Fenianism and some suggest it was the zenith of the movement.[5]

The outbreak of the American Civil War disrupted plans for rebellion in Ireland, as many Fenians enlisted in both armies. The war did, however, increase the Brotherhood's potential to drive the British from their homeland. They recruited volunteers from both armies and by the end of the war had more than fifty thousand members. Many of these men were well-trained soldiers who could use their experience to lead the Irish rebellion. In 1865, groups of these combat veterans began arriving in Ireland to drill and instruct the IRB. The Fenians in America had also built up a large war chest to buy arms and ammunition. They collected $228,000 in 1865 and the figure soared to $500,000 one year later.[6]

Just as the Fenians were making final preparations for the uprising in Ireland, a series of internal feuds seriously weakened the movement. The

5. McCaffrey, *The Irish Diaspora in America*, 120.
6. Charles C. Tansill, *America and the Fight for Irish Freedom, 1866–1922* (New York: Devin-Adair, 1957).

conflicts first emerged at the 1865 Fenian Convention in Philadelphia. One group, led by Colonel William R. Roberts, advocated a diversionary military attack on the British Empire. Instead of supporting a rebellion in Ireland, Roberts proposed that the Fenians send an army to capture part of Canada. After this had been achieved, Roberts planned to return the territory to Britain in exchange for Irish freedom. John O'Mahony strongly opposed this scheme, and a serious rift developed within the Fenian movement. James Stephens, head of the IRB, went to America to resolve the dispute, but his own abrasive personality only exacerbated divisions.[7]

Roberts and his faction were encouraged by the attitude of the US government. Relations between America and England had deteriorated after the Civil War, as a result of Secretary of State William Seward's attempt to make the English pay for damages inflicted on US shipping by the British-built warship *Alabama*. In 1865, Seward refused to prevent the Fenians buying guns and ammunition from US arsenals and allowed them to drill and recruit openly.

In 1866, Colonel John O'Neill led a force of about eight hundred Fenians across the Canadian border. On June 2 they won an initial skirmish at Ridgeway, Ontario. The invaders, proclaiming themselves the Irish Republican Army, hoped to receive assistance from the US government. This was a grave miscalculation, however, as Washington did not want to see a major escalation of their dispute with England. American forces closed the border to Fenian reinforcements, seized their weapons, and arrested the leaders. In 1870, after the Gladstone government agreed to pay the *Alabama* claims, President Ulysses S. Grant made it clear his government would no longer tolerate Fenian activities.

In 1867, when the Fenians eventually did launch a rebellion in Ireland, it was a complete fiasco. Despite the participation of Irish-American Civil War veterans, the whole affair lacked coordination. The authorities made military preparations well in advance, after receiving plans of the uprising from informers within the Fenian movement. Irish soldiers serving in the British army and stationed in their native land were transferred throughout the Empire. Fenians in New York sent the *Erin's Hope*, carrying more than five thousand Spencer rifles and three cannons, to assist the rising, but by the time the ship arrived in Sligo Bay the rebels had already been

7. William D'Arcy, *The Fenian Movement in America* (Washington: Catholic University Press, 1947).

defeated. After twenty-eight crewmen were arrested by Crown forces, the remainder escaped across the Atlantic.

Following the ignominious collapse of the 1867 rising, those defeated rebels who escaped British forces and prison sentences again fled to the United States. John Devoy, one of the most important of these exiles, emerged as the chief figure in Clan na Gael, the new militant nationalist organization that superseded the Fenians. In 1876 Devoy and his associates acquired the whaling ship *Catalpa*, which was used in a spectacular rescue of Irish revolutionaries held prisoner in Australia. In 1877 the Clan forged a formal alliance with the IRB in Ireland and established a joint revolutionary directory to coordinate rebellion against British rule.

Leaders of Clan na Gael began formulating an important new strategy designed to encourage revolution. They were impressed by a militant element in the Irish Parliamentary Party led by Charles Stewart Parnell, emerging as the new hero of Irish nationalism through his obstructionist policy in the House of Commons. Parnell's confrontational and dynamic campaigns coincided with an agricultural recession in the United Kingdom. Ireland, particularly the West, suffered most from bad weather, poor harvests and the competition of American and Canadian grain. The Clan tried to exploit the growing discontent in Ireland with a New Departure strategy, originally suggested by Patrick Ford of *The Irish World*, which aimed at combining Parnell's activities in Parliament with peasant bitterness against the landlord system. Devoy, Ford, and their associates hoped that, through agitation over the land issue, Irish peasants would become radicalized and rise up against British rule.

The New Departure aimed at politicizing the Irish masses through a campaign for tenant rights and, ultimately, peasant proprietorship. As soon as the peasantry was aroused, the Clan wanted Parnell to demand Home Rule. When the British rejected this demand, the rebels would establish an independent parliament in Dublin. Devoy and company proposed that this new Irish government would be defended by the peasant masses armed with weapons sent from America.[8]

Clan leaders contacted Irish MPs to seek support for the New Departure. When Parnell heard details of the strategy, he remained evasive and refused to give a specific commitment. He needed Irish-American financial support but did not want to sacrifice his independence or become openly associated with revolutionary nationalism. Parnell did, however,

8. Kerby Miller, *Emigrants and Exiles* (Oxford: Oxford University Press, 1985), 442.

give his full support to the agrarian agitation associated with the New Departure.

Clan na Gael supported Michael Davitt as the leader of the agrarian campaign. Davitt, an ex-Fenian who had served a jail sentence in Britain, traveled to America and formulated a plan of action after discussions with Devoy and other Irish-American leaders. When he returned to Ireland in 1879, he laid the foundations for the National Land League, which demanded the abolition of landlordism. The Land League soon attracted widespread support from the Irish peasantry and also from Parnell and his parliamentary supporters.

In 1880, after Parnell became leader of the Land League, he conducted a ten-week fund-raising tour of the US. He spoke to huge crowds of Irish Americans and urged them to support the struggling Irish tenant farmers with money and to publicize the issue to American politicians. In Washington, Parnell gave a rousing address to a joint session of Congress and was received at the White House by President Rutherford B. Hayes.

Following discussions with Parnell in New York, John Devoy greatly assisted the land war by helping to establish a front organization called the Irish National Land League of America. Despite continual conflict within the organization between constitutional nationalists and revolutionaries, it sent a steady stream of dollars to help tenant farmers resist threats of eviction.

Eventually the sustained agrarian unrest in Ireland forced the British government to accept reform. In 1881, Prime Minister Gladstone introduced legislation that guaranteed Irish farmers stable tenure at fair rents. This Land Act initiated a process of reform that eventually secured peasant land purchase and proprietorship by the early twentieth century. The destruction of the landlord system is one of the most significant events in Irish history and owes much of its success to the influence and support of the Irish-American diaspora.

In the early 1880s Parnell was the undisputed national leader of both the Irish in Ireland and those in America. From this position, he felt confident enough to lead a concerted campaign to achieve Home Rule. In the US, a reconstituted Irish National League of America channeled its funds into support for parliamentary activity. The Clan continued to play a dominant role in the INLA; consequently, more moderate Irish Americans founded their own Irish Parliamentary Fund Association in 1885. The IPFA was patronized by prosperous members of the diaspora and was committed to supporting constitutional campaigns. Despite their differences, both groups sent financial aid that played an important role by underwriting election costs and the living expenses of Home Rule MPs in London.

Thomas N. Brown, in *Irish-American Nationalism*, suggests that the Home Rule campaigns in the later decades of the nineteenth century help illustrate another important characteristic of Irish nationalism in the US. He contends that second- and third-generation Irish Americans who had achieved some social and economic mobility believed that an Irish nation state could earn them respectability. They felt that British control of their mother country was a symbol of Irish inferiority and encouraged the contempt of Anglo-Americans. Only when this "stain of degradation" was removed could the diaspora achieve respect in American society. Brown consequently sees Irish-American nationalism as a means whereby immigrants could be assimilated in the US. Irish self-government was thus only a secondary objective, which served the psychological and social needs of the diaspora.[9]

During all the constitutional agitation for Home Rule, the Clan never abandoned plans to drive Britain out of Ireland by force. Between 1876 and 1881, its central executive spent more than $60,000 on the development of a submarine, the *Fenian Ram*, to attack British ships. A faction within the Clan, led by Alexander Sullivan of Chicago, also masterminded a campaign of dynamite attacks against English cities in the early 1880s. John Devoy and his supporters condemned the bombings, and a bitter rift developed in the organization. Dr. Patrick Cronin, one of Sullivan's foremost critics, was murdered in Chicago in 1889 as part of this feud. The dynamite campaign itself was a desperate failure and brought strong condemnations from the Catholic church, prominent US politicians and newspapers. This would not be the last time the cause of Irish nationalism in America would be damaged by the bomb attacks of militant irredentists.[10]

The problems faced by physical-force nationalists in the late 1880s, however, seemed minor in comparison to the devastating consequences caused by the public revelations of Parnell's affair with Katherine O'Shea. This issue split the Irish Parliamentary Party into a Parnellite mi-

9. Thomas N. Brown, *Irish-American Nationalism* (Philadelphia: Lippincott, 1966).

10. K. R. M. Short, *The Dynamite War: Irish-American Bombers in Victorian Britain* (New Jersey: Humanities Press, 1979).

nority and an anti-Parnellite majority. In the US, the Irish National Federation remained loyal to Parnell, while anti-Parnellites formed the Irish National Federation of America. Throughout the 1890s, bitter personal antagonisms led to constant conflict between these groups and greatly weakened constitutional nationalism.

The split within the Irish Party eventually led to a sharp decline in financial contributions from the United States. It was partly from the need to restore confidence among its Irish-American benefactors that constitutional nationalism was reunited. In 1900, John Dillon, chairman of the anti-Parnellites, stepped down and, in the interest of unity, accepted the Parnellite, John Redmond, as leader of the new party.

Almost immediately Redmond helped establish the United Irish League of America (UILA) to collect funds and lobby US politicians for support. It persuaded President William Howard Taft and former President Theodore Roosevelt to endorse Home Rule. UILA financial contributions also covered most of the Irish Party's expenses during the general elections between 1906 and 1910 and played an influential role in bringing Home Rule to the center of British politics.[11]

The British general election of 1911, held on the issue of the People's Budget, left an even balance between Liberals and Conservatives in Parliament. Consequently, the Liberals were forced to rely on Irish support to form a government. In return for their allegiance, Irish MPs persuaded the Liberal government to curb the power of the House of Lords because it had continually blocked Home Rule. Despite a major political crisis, the Liberals passed the Parliament Act of 1911. Under this law the veto power of the House of Lords was effectively eliminated if a piece of legislation passed through the Commons in three consecutive votes.

With the power of the Lords effectively cut, the Irish Party convinced Prime Minister Herbert Asquith to introduce a third Home Rule Bill in 1912. Its inevitable passage in 1914 precipitated an intense crisis as Ulster Unionists, backed by British Conservatives, preferred to forcibly resist. Both factions in Ireland armed themselves for the ensuing conflict, which was avoided only by the outbreak of World War I in August 1914.

---

11. Alan Ward, *Ireland and Anglo-American Relations, 1899–1921* (Toronto: University of Toronto Press, 1969), also shows that Irish Americans played an important role in preventing closer diplomatic relations between Britain and the US in this period by working against a series of free trade agreements.

At the beginning of the Great War, John Redmond decided to support Britain in its hour of need and encouraged Irishmen to enlist. His action infuriated Irish Americans; within the space of a few months, the United Irish League collapsed through lack of support. Clan na Gael exploited this situation and joined the National German-American Alliance in working to keep the US out of the war. John Devoy also kept in close contact with the IRB and encouraged rebels, such as Thomas Clarke, to return from New York and plot insurrection. Clan leaders helped plan the Easter Rising of 1916, sent vital funds to the IRB, and consulted with the German ambassador in New York to arrange arms shipments to supply the rebels.[12]

In March 1916 Clan na Gael helped form a new Irish-American nationalist group called the Friends of Irish Freedom. The FOIF conducted vigorous campaigns to publicize the British executions following the Easter Rising. To generate popular outrage at British policy, it organized nationwide tours by rebel leaders Diarmiud Lynch and Liam Mellows. At its peak, the FOIF claimed more than 250,000 members.[13]

After the First World War, the FOIF began working for Irish recognition at the Versailles Peace Conference. In February 1919, it sponsored an Irish Race Convention in Philadelphia attended by more than five thousand delegates. The convention achieved a degree of Irish-American unity unmatched for decades, as politicians, bishops, and members of the Clan joined in demanding Irish independence. An Irish Victory Fund, which was launched by the convention, received immediate pledges of over one million dollars. In March 1919, the US House of Representatives voted 216 to 45 that the peace conference should consider Ireland's claim to self-determination. The Senate also endorsed a resolution supporting Eamon de Valera, leader of the Irish provisional government, in his attempt to attend the negotiations at Versailles.

In April 1919, a delegation from the American Commission on Irish Independence arrived in Versailles to win Woodrow Wilson's support for Irish self-determination. The President, however, refused to pressure Britain to recognize the Irish provisional government. Wilson's actions infuriated many Irish Americans, who determined to make him pay. They

---

12. F. S. L. Lyons, *Ireland Since the Famine* (London: Fontana, 1973), 350.

13. The FOIF greatly declined after America entered the war in 1917. Most Irish Americans held primary allegiance to the US and remained unconcerned when the organization was suppressed by federal authorities for unpatriotic activities.

worked closely with Senator Henry Cabot Lodge and helped prevent ratification of the League of Nations in the Senate.

In June 1919, de Valera traveled to America in an attempt to gain US recognition for the Irish government and to raise funds for the IRA. Despite the crisis in Ireland, a bitter feud developed with John Devoy and Daniel Cohalan of the Clan over their different opinions about the League of Nations. De Valera supported the League and believed it could help Ireland gain independence. He also wanted to use all Irish-American funds for the War of Independence. Cohalan and Devoy wanted to keep the money in America to continue anti-League agitation during the 1920 presidential election. The two Clan leaders were also incensed by de Valera's suggestion that Ireland would accept a degree of independence from Britain similar to the relationship between the United States and Cuba.[14]

De Valera eventually broke with Devoy and Cohalan and formed the American Association for the Recognition of the Irish Republic in 1920. Within a year this organization recruited nearly 750,000 members and eclipsed the Friends of Irish Freedom. De Valera also launched an Irish Bond Certificate drive, which raised $5.5 million to support the War of Independence. Later, the American Committee for Relief of Ireland raised an additional $5 million to help victims of the conflict. This financial support helped the IRA conduct military operations against the British and was an important factor in the success of their campaign.

Irish Americans supplemented their financial support for the War of Independence with extensive publicity campaigns, which bombarded the public with stories of British atrocities. The high-water mark of this effort was the investigation carried out in 1920 by the Committee of One Hundred Fifty on conditions in Ireland. The Committee elected a smaller commission of prominent Americans to conduct a public inquiry into British brutality. It held hearings and issued a report containing descriptions of the terror tactics of the Black and Tans. The work of the Commission kept events in Ireland before American public opinion and increased pressure on the British government to reach an agreement with the rebels.

In the War of Independence the IRA never aimed at achieving a military victory over the British. They hoped that through a series of guerrilla actions they could wear the enemy down. Essential in this strategy was

14. Because of the feud between de Valera and Clan leaders, attempts to get an Irish platform at the Republican and Democratic conventions in 1920 were both dismal failures.

the battle for international public opinion, especially that in America. IRA leaders believed that hostile opinion would pressure the British to make some concessions on Irish independence. In *American Opinion and the Irish Question*, Francis Carroll expresses his belief that the rebels succeeded in this goal. He contends that adverse American public opinion toward the British position, combined with the prospect of a continued flow of dollars to the IRA, was an important element in Lloyd George's decision to negotiate the Anglo-Irish Treaty.[15]

The Treaty was a watershed event in the history of Irish-American nationalism. After it was signed, commitment to the nationalist cause greatly diminished. Most Irish Americans accepted the Treaty as a first step toward eventual independence. The viciousness of the Irish civil war sickened many and caused them to disengage from nationalist activities. As the Irish Free State evolved into a republic, the diaspora, most of whom came from the twenty-six counties, lost interest in the politics of their homeland. Partition was not the same burning issue as British subjugation of the whole island.

Only a small minority of Irish Americans rejected the Treaty and clung to the republican ideal. In the 1920s and 1930s their activities were sustained by IRA militants who fled to America after the Civil War. These men left Ireland with an intense bitterness toward the Irish Free State and were among the most militant group of nationalists ever to leave Ireland. They kept Irish republicanism alive in America despite all the odds. Many of them also provided leadership for the groups that formed in response to the outbreak of the current Troubles in Ulster.

Joseph McGarrity emerged as the dominant figure within Clan na Gael in the 1920s. He had emigrated from County Tyrone at the turn of the century and made a fortune through a series of business ventures in Philadelphia. During the War of Independence, McGarrity sent much of his money to the IRA and provided the rebels with supplies of modern weapons. He supported the irregulars during the Civil War but later attacked de Valera's formation of Fianna Fáil and entry into constitutional politics.

In the 1930s, McGarrity continued to send Thompson submachine guns to the IRA and encouraged militarism. He joined Seán Russell in pushing for a violent campaign on the British mainland and promised strong financial backing. McGarrity's influence prevailed and his sup-

15. F. M. Carroll, *American Opinion and the Irish Question, 1910–1923* (New York: St. Martin's Press, 1978).

porters began bombing English cities in 1939, killing and maiming a number of innocent civilians. De Valera, recognizing the threat this posed to Irish neutrality, outlawed the IRA and interned many of its leaders. Public opinion reacted strongly against republicanism and the campaign ended in abject failure.[16]

Despite the adverse effects of the bombing campaign in England, Irish Americans did help secure one important victory in the early months of World War II. British Prime Minister Winston Churchill sharply condemned de Valera's insistence on Irish neutrality. He was particularly concerned that Britain regain control of naval bases they had surrendered to Ireland in 1938. After the fall of France in 1940, Churchill offered de Valera an end to partition if he opened the Irish ports to the Royal Navy. When prospects of this deal collapsed, the British government considered a military expedition to retake the ports by force.

De Valera looked to Irish America for support and encouraged formation of the American Friends of Irish Neutrality in November 1940. The AFIN began a campaign of political lobbying to ensure that President Roosevelt would pressure the British not to invade. After a warning from Secretary of State Cordell Hull, Churchill was persuaded to postpone military action. The threat of Irish-American political agitation during the upcoming presidential election helped preserve Irish neutrality in a period when it was under most threat.[17]

Ireland's neutrality throughout World War II caused serious problems for Irish-American nationalism. For over a century, the diaspora had maintained that an independent Ireland would be a strong ally of the United States. Yet, while American troops by the thousands were dying fighting the Nazis, de Valera made formal complaints about the presence of G.I.s in Northern Ireland. David Grey, US minister in Ireland, was strongly critical of de Valera and supported allegations that the German and Japanese embassies in Dublin were being used to spy on allied military operations. The image of the Irish government further plummeted in American opinion when the Taoiseach sent an official message of condolence to the German ambassador after Hitler's death.

The damage done to Irish-American nationalism by de Valera's neutrality was further exacerbated by social changes in the post-war era. As

16. Seán Cronin, *The McGarrity Papers* (Tralee: Anvil, 1974).

17. T. Ryle Dwyer, *Strained Relations: Ireland at Peace and the U.S.A. at War, 1941–45* (Dublin: Gill & Macmillan, 1988).

more and more Irish Americans experienced upward social mobility, concern for events in Ireland grew even weaker. The flight to the suburbs gradually led to a demise of old Irish neighborhoods and eroded ethnic solidarity. As Irish Americans became increasingly concerned with improving their position in the United States, their support for nationalism continued to decline. In the 1950s the American League for an Undivided Ireland failed miserably in an attempt to generate public outrage against partition. Similarly, the IRA's Border Campaign between 1956 and 1962 received virtually no assistance from the diaspora, save for a few isolated gunrunning schemes.

By the mid-sixties, therefore, it seemed that the long history of Irish-American involvement in the political destiny of their homeland had finally ended. Stricter immigration laws reduced the number of Irish entering the United States. Militant republican organizations like Clan na Gael were virtually extinct, while the fraternal and social societies experienced a steady decline in membership. No one could have predicted that the outbreak of the Ulster Troubles in 1968 would lead to a reversal of this trend and present some Irish Americans with the opportunity to play again an important role in Irish affairs. New groups emerged, which adopted traditional methods of supporting both branches of nationalism in Ireland. Their activities continue to have a major impact on political developments in Ulster.

◆

CHAPTER 2

IRISH AMERICA AND THE NORTHERN

IRELAND CIVIL RIGHTS MOVEMENT,

1967–1970

◆

In the early 1960s in the US, only a few small Irish-American groups and individuals worked to keep the nationalist cause alive. They conducted ineffective publicity campaigns against partition and tried to heighten Irish-American awareness of anti-Catholic discrimination in Ulster. It was not until the emergence of the Northern Ireland Civil Rights Association (NICRA) in 1967 that larger numbers of Irish Americans again began to take notice of political events in their ancestral homeland.

The NICRA was an umbrella organization for a variety of groups working to end anti-Catholic discrimination under the Stormont regime. From 1921 government was controlled by the Ulster Unionist Party, which monopolized political power and generally catered to the needs of the Protestant majority. While Catholics had many grievances against the central administration, discrimination was most blatant in local government. Unionists gerrymandered electoral boundaries and maintained a ratepayer's franchise to ensure their control of many district councils. These local authorities became associated with a wide range of discriminatory practices, particularly in the distribution of jobs and public housing.[1]

In 1963 Captain Terence O'Neill, the new Stormont prime minister, recognized the need for political change within Northern Ireland. He pioneered a policy of reforms designed to remedy some Catholic grievances and launched an energetic program of attracting new industries to the province. As part of this initiative of modernization and reconciliation, O'Neill tried to improve relations with the Republic of Ireland through a series of meetings with Taoisigh Seán Lemass and Jack Lynch.

Although there were some signs that O'Neill's policies improved relations between Stormont and the Catholic community, they were instituted at a time of heightened demands for change. British educational reform after World War II significantly increased the number of Catholics attending university. As the Catholic middle class expanded, pressure to end discrimination in Ulster intensified. Many saw O'Neill's reforms as coming too slowly and too late. Through the NICRA, Catholics demanded, not a series of gradual changes, but a complete dismantling of the system of discrimination.

The NICRA was a highly amorphous organization composed of traditional nationalists, republicans, progressive unionists, and trade-union activists. Although its campaigns and activities followed traditional nationalist forms of protest, deeply rooted in Irish history, the organization was in some ways influenced by current international political movements. Students from Queen's University Belfast were a major force within the civil rights association. Many claimed inspiration from worldwide student protests, particularly the campus demonstrations that spread to colleges all over America by 1968.[2]

NICRA leaders and political analysts also stress the inspirational effects of Dr. Martin Luther King's campaign for African-American civil rights in the United States. Throughout the sixties, African-American demonstrations were widely reported in Ireland and had some influence

1. Bob Purdie, *Politics in the Streets: The Origins of the Civil Rights Movement in Northern Ireland* (Belfast: Blackstaff Press, 1990).

2. Some civil rights leaders claim greater inspiration from the international student protests than others. Michael Farrell, a leader of People's Democracy, claims student activism in America acted as a spur to action among his Queen's University colleagues. Bernadette Devlin, on the other hand, maintains that events like the 1968 student demonstrations in Paris had little impact on her.

on the tactics and goals of the NICRA. Early civil rights activists tried to draw a direct parallel between the condition of African Americans in the Deep South and Catholics in Northern Ireland. The example provided by demonstrations in America partly influenced the NICRA to escalate its protests in the summer of 1968 to include sit-downs and street marches. In all these demonstrations, Irish civil rights campaigners incorporated African-American protest songs such as "We Shall Overcome" and "We Shall Not Be Moved."[3]

Dr. King's inspiration is acknowledged today by leaders of the Social Democratic and Labour Party (SDLP) who took part in the civil rights movement. John Hume, for example, claims that his party's philosophy comes directly from the African-American civil rights leader. In a commencement address at the University of Massachusetts in 1985 he acknowledged:

> The dream which Dr. King proclaimed of a glorious opportunity for a new America, transformed by the moral energy of its minorities, was for me and others of my generation in Northern Ireland the inspiration for our search for justice and equality. The American civil rights movement gave birth to ours. The songs of your movement were also ours. Your successes were for us a cause of hope. We *also* believed that we would overcome. Most importantly, the philosophy of non-violence, which sustained your struggle, was also part of ours.[4]

Perhaps ironically, Irish republicans also acknowledge inspiration from the African-American civil rights campaign. Gerry Adams, president of Sinn Féin, says it encouraged many forcibly to resist the Stormont regime. Speaking of the American protest marches and the Black Panthers he said, "Courtesy of television we were able to see . . . that you didn't just have to take it. You could fight back!"[5]

Although Martin Luther King acted as an inspiration to NICRA activists, there is little evidence to show there was a systematic attempt to

3. Bob Purdie, *Politics in the Streets*, 157.

4. Congress, Senate, John Hume's commencement address at the University of Massachusetts, 99th Cong., 1st sess., *Congressional Record* 131, no. 67 (21 May 1985): 3.

5. Gerry Adams, *The Politics of Irish Freedom* (Kerry: Brandon Books, 1980), 10. Adams continues to draw parallels between Irish republicanism and the African-American campaign for civil rights. During a visit to the US in October 1994, he held a widely publicized meeting with Rosa Parks, the heroine of the Montgomery bus boycott. Adams has also tried to establish close ties with the Congressional Black Caucus on Capitol Hill.

use the African-American civil rights movement as a model. In *Politics in the Streets*, Bob Purdie expresses the belief that most Irish activists had only a limited and simplistic impression of what was happening across the Atlantic and were much more influenced by conditions in Northern Ireland. He concludes:

> Although the Black civil rights movement in the US had been an inspiration, strictly speaking it was not a model. There is no evidence that any of the founders or leaders of NICRA ever visited the Southern United States, consulted with any of the Black civil rights organizations, or even undertook a thorough study of the movement. Their information came from the media and, inevitably, their application of the lessons of the American movement was patchy and reflected their own pre-occupations and experiences.[6]

Despite Purdie's minimalist assessment of the impact of the African-American civil rights movement in Ireland, he does acknowledge that the demonstrations in the US influenced NICRA leaders to adopt more confrontational street protests in the summer of 1968. The most important of these demonstrations occurred in Derry on October 5. Civil rights activists defied a government ban on public rallies and held a protest march against discrimination in the city. The ensuing conflict between protestors and the Royal Ulster Constabulary (RUC) erupted into severe rioting. During the disturbances, police officers indiscriminately used their truncheons on the crowd. Bernadette Devlin, a young activist in the civil rights movement, later compared events in Derry with one of the milestone incidents in the African-American campaign:

> I think the impact on public opinion was something like what happened after Dr. King's people were beaten by "Bull" Connor's cops in Alabama. Suddenly fair minded people everywhere could see us being treated like animals. In retrospect, I realized the police had actually done us a great favor. They dramatized our plight to the world. The civil rights movement had started out as a small middle-class pressure group, but it took only one day of police violence to transform it into a mass movement.[7]

The Derry riots inspired Devlin, along with other radicals at Queen's University, to form the People's Democracy (PD). More militant than the

6. Bob Purdie, *Politics in the Streets*, 244.
7. Interview with Bernadette Devlin, *Playboy Magazine* 19 (September 1972): 57.

NICRA, PD aimed at the formation of a socialist republic in Ireland. The group also wanted direct confrontation with the Stormont government. In January 1969, it organized a march from Belfast to Derry to pressure Prime Minister O'Neill into greater reform. Michael Farrell, an organizer of the protest, claims it was directly inspired by Dr. King's march from Selma to Montgomery in 1965.[8] A loyalist mob attacked the marchers at Burntollet Bridge in County Londonderry. Many were injured by stones, while some were beaten with spiked clubs. When the protestors reached Derry on January 4, 1969, prolonged rioting erupted in nationalist sections of the city. This unrest culminated in a police invasion of the Bogside district, during which officers assaulted residents and wrecked their homes.

Like the riots in Derry on October 5, 1968, these incidents received considerable international media coverage. This was especially true in the United States, where the growing political crisis in Ulster was widely reported for the first time. The three main national television networks relayed footage of the RUC wading into peaceful civil rights protestors, cracking heads with their batons and blasting others with high-powered water cannon. Major newspapers carried front page headlines describing the riots in detail and outlining incidents of police savagery.

Most of the American coverage of Northern Ireland was based on reports sent by international wire services and newsreel from the British Broadcasting Corporation. A recurring characteristic of these news reports was the comparison of events in Ulster to the racial problems in the United States. In order to make the Irish situation more comprehensible to the American audience, newspaper and television reports constantly made analogies with the African-American civil rights campaign. For example, anchorman Chet Huntley of "NBC Nightly News" finished a broadcast with the following analysis:

> The Catholics in Ulster are the same as the Blacks in the United States; they've been deprived of their rights, harried into slums, and denied jobs, hurt and slashed, ever since the Battle of the Boyne. And like Blacks they've revolted; and like Blacks they've burnt down the very ghettoes that were built to contain them; and like Blacks they've been shot down.[9]

8. Michael Farrell, *Twenty Years On* (Kerry: Brandon Books, 1988), 57.
9. *NBC Nightly News*, 15 August 1969.

American newspapers and current affairs journals carried numerous reports describing Ulster Catholics as "White Negroes."[10] Others compared the attitude of Ulster Protestant extremists with the racism of poor whites in the Deep South, while the Orange Order was presented as an organization similar to the Ku Klux Klan. An article by Joan Wyatt in *Commonweal* observed:

> Small favors to the Protestant poor give them one small "up" over their poor Catholic neighbors, much as "whiteness" was the only status symbol of poor Whites in the American South and inflamed them to maintain the ruling group where it was—on top![11]

This simplistic comparison ignored the fundamental differences between the political situation in Northern Ireland and racism in America.[12] Yet the analogy was continuously used in the deluge of reports that appeared in the US media after the Derry riots and Burntollet attack. Partly because of the media identification of Ulster loyalists with Southern racists, reports generally criticized the Stormont government and supported the campaign for Catholic civil rights.

The response by the US media to events in Ulster convinced NICRA leaders that they could benefit from expanded publicity in America. Some hoped it would increase pressure on the Unionist government to initiate wider reforms, while others saw the United States as a potentially lucrative source for funds.

The American Congress for Irish Freedom and the National Association for Irish Justice

Although there had been a gradual decline in Irish-American nationalism since the War of Independence, 1919–21, certain factors offered prospects for a revival. In *Irish Blood*, Dennis Clark points out that frequent and relatively inexpensive airline service across the Atlantic gave

10. Robert Korengald, "The White Negroes," *Newsweek* (2 December 1968), 45.

11. Joan Wyatt, "Battle of the Boyne II," *Commonweal* (23 April 1971), 162. For a good analysis of the American news coverage in this period see Ken Ward, "Ulster Terrorism: The U.S. Network News Coverage of Northern Ireland, 1968–1979," in Y. Alexander and A. O'Day, eds., *Terrorism in Ireland* (New York: St. Martin's Press, 1984), 201–12.

12. For an assessment of the differences between the condition of Catholics in Ulster and African-Americans in the Deep South see Frank Wright, *Northern Ireland: A Comparative Analysis* (Dublin: Gill & Macmillan, 1988), 165.

thousands of Irish Americans the opportunity to see the land of their fore-bears. Most were satisfied with bus tours, tourist shops, and kissing the Blarney Stone. Others, however, developed a deep concern for Irish affairs and tried to publicize the abuse of civil rights in Northern Ireland.[13]

A network of fraternal organizations, ranging from IRA veterans groups to the Loyal League of Yiddish Sons of Erin, still survived despite years of decline after World War II. Irish-American radio programs were broadcast in many cities, while newspapers like the *Irish Echo*, the *Irish World*, and the *Irish Advocate* continued to circulate. When the civil rights demonstrations erupted in Northern Ireland, Irish-American activists revived this decaying network to generate publicity and support. Groups like the Ancient Order of Hibernians, Irish Counties Associations, Friendly Sons of the Shillelagh, etc., provided membership for the new organizations that formed in response to the political developments in Ulster.[14]

In the winter of 1968, a number of small NICRA support groups emerged in Irish-American communities throughout the United States. The Committee for Justice in Northern Ireland was one of the most active of these groups and established chapters throughout New England. The Boston chapter produced its own newspaper, *The Rising of the Moon*, and held weekly fund-raising dances in Jamaica Plain. By the end of 1969, the CJNI had sent more than $6,000 to Northern Ireland.[15] Eventually these small groups amalgamated with larger organizations that had national memberships. From 1967 to 1970, the American Congress for Irish Freedom (ACIF) emerged as the most active and widely supported group working to publicize the Ulster conflict.

The ACIF had its origins in the enthusiasm generated during celebrations in New York for the fiftieth anniversary of the 1916 Easter Rising.

13. Dennis J. Clark, *Irish Blood: Northern Ireland and the American Conscience* (Port Washington, N.Y.: Kennikat Press, 1977), 13.

14. The Ancient Order of Hibernians, formed in 1836 partly as a response to nativism, is the largest Irish-American organization in the US, claiming 80,000 to 100,000 members. In 1968 it supported the NICRA by issuing a series of statements attacking anti-Catholic discrimination and calling for intervention in Northern Ireland by the Pope and the United Nations. The AOH also established a "Freedom for all Ireland Committee" to raise funds and work for a united Ireland. In 1970 it sent $100,000 for "social and economic aid" and $10,000 to Cardinal Conway to help Catholic riot victims. Some journalists allege that a substantial amount of this cash was diverted to the IRA. See David Anable, "How U.S. Aid Filters to the I.R.A.," *Christian Science Monitor*, 17 August 1972.

15. Figure from CJNI chairman Dr. Donald McGaughan's letter to Boston chapter, dated 15 September 1969.

All the Irish societies had organized memorial banquets, socials, and parades. A few small groups, such as the United Irish Publicity Committee (UPIC), formed to exploit this heightened awareness. The UPIC tried to publicize the issue of partition, and it organized protest demonstrations against Unionist and British politicians when they came to New York.[16]

In early 1967, James Heaney, a lawyer from Buffalo who had been agitating for civil rights issues in Northern Ireland, called a meeting of these groups and individuals at the Irish Institute in New York. Heaney managed to get those present to coordinate their activities and agree to concerted action. The ACIF was formed for this purpose on February 26, 1967, and began its operations well before the outbreak of violent street battles in Ulster.[17]

James Heaney was a Protestant whose family had immigrated to the United States from Derry during the Famine. As a lawyer, he was particularly interested in the legal provisions of the Special Powers Act and made numerous trips to Northern Ireland to investigate Catholic complaints against it. During these visits, Heaney met with prominent civil rights advocates and built up a strong friendship with Dr. Conn McCluskey, the leading figure in the Campaign for Social Justice.[18]

Heaney, as national president, molded the ACIF into a highly structured organization. It worked to expose the Stormont regime's civil rights abuses and to build American pressure in support of reform.[19] To further these objectives the group produced a monthly newspaper, the *Irish-American Reporter*, which gave details of discrimination in Ulster and

16. Tom Enright, former National Treasurer of the ACIF, recalls that when Terence O'Neill made a private visit to New York in 1966, the UPIC picketed his speaking engagements and burned Union Jacks outside his hotel. Some activists petrol bombed British business offices and organized round-the-clock protests outside the residence of Lord Caradon, British representative at the United Nations. Tom Enright, correspondence with author, 4 December 1989.

17. Andrew J. Wilson, "The American Congress for Irish Freedom and the Northern Ireland Civil Rights Movement, 1967–70," *Eire-Ireland* (Spring 1994).

18. The Campaign for Social Justice was one of the first groups to publicize civil rights issues in Northern Ireland. From the early sixties it worked to expose anti-Catholic discrimination in the allocation of public housing. James Heaney used CSJ material to heighten American public awareness of abuses in Ulster. In 1969 he also sent money which helped enabled the group to publish *The Plain Truth*, a stinging critique of the Stormont regime. Information provided by Paul Brosnahan, former ACIF executive in Massachusetts.

19. *A.C.I.F. Constitution*, approved at a Board of Directors meeting on 28 December 1968.

provided information on the latest activities of the NICRA. James Heaney sent copies to international delegations at the United Nations and to prominent members of the United States Congress and British Parliament.

Although the ACIF was genuinely concerned about civil rights in Ulster, Heaney and most of the membership saw the issue primarily as a vehicle for achieving Irish unification. They hoped that unfavorable publicity over anti-Catholic discrimination would push the British government into severing its ties with Northern Ireland. At one point, Heaney even tried to persuade NICRA activists they should establish an exile Ulster government in New York.[20] The organization also paid little regard to the wishes of unionists and implied that those who didn't want to be part of a new united Ireland could return to England. In 1968 Heaney wrote:

> Our ultimate objective is the expulsion of Britain from Northern Ireland. The present civil rights movement is merely one step in that direction. I am in almost daily contact with the leaders of that movement and I can assure you that the present agitation is aimed at the expulsion of British authority. Those supporting the British government in Belfast are actually Englishmen who were planted in Ireland 300 years ago. They're neither Irish in blood or outlook.[21]

Though some aspects of the ACIF's program were based on a rather crude nationalistic interpretation of events in Ulster, the group did become adept at publicizing its message. James Heaney organized continuous letter-writing campaigns to major American newspapers. In June 1968 he appeared on the nationally syndicated Alan Burke Show in New York, which reached over eighty million viewers. His attacks against the Stormont regime were widely reported in Northern Ireland and caused the Unionist government to send John Taylor, MP, across the Atlantic for a second show on July 6, 1968.

The ACIF also sponsored lecture tours to the US by leading civil rights activists. In March 1969 it helped arrange for Gerry Fitt and Austin Currie to address Irish-American gatherings in Boston, New York, Chicago and Los Angeles. Fitt, in particular, helped raise American

20. This suggestion was made by Heaney to Conn McCluskey in correspondence dated 6 May 1969.

21. From correspondence between Heaney and the Spanish ambassador in Washington dated 19 December 1969.

awareness of events in Northern Ireland following meetings with Senator Edward Kennedy and Hubert Humphrey, the Democratic presidential candidate in 1968.[22]

James Heaney believed he could generate international condemnation of the Stormont government by exposing the draconian provisions of the Special Powers Act. In cooperation with Conn McCluskey, he initiated a legal suit before the European Commission on Human Rights in Strasbourg on April 5, 1968. The suit was filed on behalf of six Northern Ireland residents and maintained that the British government, by tolerating the Special Powers Act, was violating the human rights guarantees of the Council of Europe.

After reviewing the case, the Court in Strasbourg accepted its legitimacy and requested that Britain answer the charges. This decision generated substantial publicity in Ireland and forced the British government to launch a legal initiative designed to stall the Court's proceedings. Eventually, however, Heaney and McCluskey were forced to drop the case because they could not afford the expense of sending witnesses to France or cope with the massive workload in preparing the suit.[23]

Despite its eventual collapse, the Strasbourg case did have important repercussions. Several British newspapers described it as an embarrassment to the government and in May 1968, Prime Minister Harold Wilson was forced to condemn the civil rights situation in Ulster. Publicity surrounding the case contributed to the mounting pressure on the Labour administration to demand meaningful reform from Stormont. A number of civil rights activists also recall that the Strasbourg case gave them hope and inspiration that their campaign would eventually draw international attention and support. Harry Diamond, former MP for West Belfast, maintained:

> The lesson of the case is that the nationalist people of the Six Counties are no longer alone in their uphill struggle. It is encouraging to them in the desperate fight they're waging to know that the terrible sacrifices they have made have not gone unnoticed in the world.[24]

22. *Belfast Telegraph*, 18 March 1969.

23. Conn McCluskey, *Up Off Their Knees: A Commentary on the Civil Rights Movement in Northern Ireland* (Dublin: Conn McCluskey and Associates, 1989), 51.

24. Harry Diamond, "Human Rights Case Against Britain," *Irish Weekly*, 8 August 1970.

Publicity generated by the litigation in Strasbourg encouraged Heaney to seek the support of European governments for his activities. He made a number of unsuccessful appeals to French officials in Washington, suggesting that the ACIF's campaigns could indirectly help Charles de Gaulle's efforts to keep Britain out of the EEC. Spanish officials were initially more responsive. During a visit to Belfast in July 1968, he established contact with V. Ramirez-Montesinos, the Spanish consul in Liverpool. The consul was impressed by Heaney's legal suit at Strasbourg and felt anti-British publicity could aid his government's position in the conflict over Gibraltar. Heaney convinced the Spanish that there were many similarities between Northern Ireland and Gibraltar, claiming both were the last outposts of British imperialism in Europe.[25]

When Heaney returned to America, he held a series of meetings with the Spanish Ambassador and members of the Spanish delegation at the United Nations. He tried to convince them that anything to further expose the problems in Ulster would be certain to shed light on the situation in Gibraltar. Heaney suggested an arrangement whereby the ACIF would escalate its publicity campaigns against Britain in return for financial assistance from Spain.[26]

Heaney worked out details of this arrangement with Adolpho Gomero, the Spanish consul in New York. In the summer of 1969, Gomero returned to Madrid and apparently persuaded officials in the Foreign Ministry to support the ACIF for a trial period of one year. Gomero gave an oral promise to supply $50,000 in assistance and offered Heaney the opportunity to use Spanish broadcasting stations to present anti-British propaganda.

In September 1969, the Spanish government paid for Heaney to visit Ireland and promised delivery of the $50,000 on his return. In October, however, Ramon Bravo was appointed as the new Spanish foreign minister. Bravo adopted a less hawkish attitude toward Gibraltar and consequently refused to send the promised financial assistance to the ACIF.[27]

Heaney was infuriated by the Spanish government's reversal and immediately began a legal suit to recover the promised financial aid. The

25. From correspondence between James Heaney and V. Ramirez- Montesinos, dated 7 May 1969.

26. Correspondence between Heaney and the Spanish ambassador in Washington dated 30 August 1968.

27. From correspondence between Heaney and Senator William Fulbright, dated 4 August 1970.

Spanish did not deny their contacts with the ACIF or the promised financial assistance, but instead claimed diplomatic immunity. Judge Friendly of the Circuit Court of Appeals in New York wrote to the US State Department requesting a ruling on the legitimacy of this Spanish claim. The State Department declined to answer and, consequently, the case was dropped.[28]

Despite the embarrassing end to their Spanish initiative, the ACIF attempted to win the support of other European governments throughout the early seventies. The principal focus of their activities, however, centered on the Nixon administration. Heaney firmly believed that if the US government was made aware of the nature of Unionist rule in Northern Ireland, it would apply pressure on the British to implement reforms. As part of this process, the ACIF launched a vigorous campaign to tarnish Britain's image in Washington by "exposing" Britain's links with North Vietnam. He wrote letters to the main American newspapers alleging that British merchant ships were transporting vital military supplies to Haiphong. These supplies, he claimed, were being used to kill US troops.[29]

Members of the ACIF began lobbying congressmen to win support for these allegations. Through their contacts on Capitol Hill, the group secured a meeting with State Department officials on April 22, 1969. James Heaney and Robert McCann, director of the ACIF chapter in Yonkers, met Undersecretary of State Elliot Richardson to present their case. They pleaded with the undersecretary to threaten economic sanctions against Britain unless it ended assistance to Hanoi and pushed the Stormont government into reform. Richardson curtly refused the request and told Heaney that British ships entering Haiphong were taking food not military supplies.

While Heaney's attempts to secure State Department intervention in Ulster were hopelessly quixotic, given the "special relationship" with Britain, he did succeed in generating interest on Capitol Hill. In June

28. In October 1971 Heaney obtained State Department documents under the Freedom of Information Act. They show that in August 1970 the Spanish government met State Department officials to get support for its claim to diplomatic immunity. The officials advised the Spanish that their contract with Heaney was "commercial" and because of this, diplomatic immunity did not apply. Despite this decision, the State Department did not provide the information to the Circuit Court in New York. Heaney tried to win the intervention of Senator William Fulbright to force the State Department to acknowledge this ruling, but his effort failed. From correspondence between Heaney and Secretary of State William Rogers dated 8 September 1972.

29. *How Britain Aids the Commies*, undated ACIF leaflet.

1969, after incessant lobbying, Heaney helped persuade Thomas "Tip" O'Neill and a group of one hundred congressmen to write to President Nixon expressing their "concern that intolerance and discrimination are encouraged by and rooted in the laws of Northern Ireland."[30] The Nixon administration responded by sending a request for information on recent political developments to the US consul-general in Belfast. This initiative, however, had no effect on the State Department's position that the Ulster conflict was an internal problem for the British government.[31]

Undeterred by their failure with the Nixon administration, the ACIF also tried to pressure the Stormont government by discouraging American companies from investing in Northern Ireland. They targeted letter-writing campaigns to corporations with holdings in the province, maintaining that their continued presence was a tacit support for discrimination.[32] James Heaney also printed notices in Ulster newspapers asking workers to inform the ACIF of discriminatory policies employed by American companies. He warned the presidents of these firms that if they were found to be practicing discrimination, he would take legal action against them.

The ACIF never got significant information on discrimination by US companies, but the campaign did elicit criticism from the Unionist government. In April 1969, Robert Porter, Minister of Home Affairs, launched a severe attack against the ACIF. He alleged they were completely ignorant of conditions in Ulster and that the anti-investment campaign would bring hardship to both communities. Shortly after this, Prime Minister James Chichester-Clark announced he would fly to America to combat the ACIF campaign in early September.[33]

The sustained activity of the ACIF throughout 1968 and 1969 led to a rapid expansion of the group. When the organization formed in 1967 its strength revolved around the activities of small chapters in New York, Boston, and Chicago. By August 1969, however, it claimed twenty-five chapters nationwide from Birmingham, Alabama, to Dayton, Ohio. Many

30. *The Times* (London), 26 June 1969.

31. Seán Cronin, *Washington's Irish Policy, 1916-1986* (Dublin: Anvil Books, 1987), 294.

32. One undated ACIF leaflet entitled, *If You Are Looking For Trouble Invest in Northern Ireland*, described Ulster as an economic desert in which employment discrimination was all pervasive. It advised US companies to pull out of Ulster and relocate in the Republic of Ireland.

33. "Ulster in Shambles—U.S. Claim," *Belfast News Letter*, 16 July 1969.

of the small independent civil rights support groups merged with the ACIF because of its well-publicized campaigns. Heaney eventually claimed a dedicated core of three thousand members, with several thousand sympathizers.[34]

The National Association for Irish Justice (NAIJ) grew as the second most prominent group working in America to support the Irish civil rights movement. One of the original founders of the NAIJ was Brian Heron, a grandson of James Connolly. Heron inherited his grandfather's political ideals and was active in leftist organizations in California. His efforts on behalf of human rights in Ulster began as an organizer of pro-NICRA demonstrations in San Francisco. Following this, Heron moved to New York in April 1969 and helped form the NAIJ.[35]

Heron later met with NICRA executive members in Belfast, and they named his association as their official branch in America. The NAIJ established headquarters in Manhattan with a small permanent staff under the supervision of a national coordinator. It soon began producing the *Irish Activist*, a six-page, bi-monthly newspaper, which printed articles on Irish socialism and publicized campaigns of action. The NAIJ also ran fund raisers; by 1970 they had sent $160,000 to Ulster.[36]

The NAIJ grew rapidly in New York City around its largest and most active chapters in Flatbush and Bay Ridge. Eventually branches formed in other East Coast cities until the group claimed thirty-one affiliates by August 1969. It also tapped the radicalism on American campuses by establishing college groups called the Students for Irish Justice at Columbia and Fordham Universities in New York.[37]

Despite working in support of civil rights in Ulster, the NAIJ aroused the antagonism and suspicion of the ACIF. The majority of ACIF members viewed the growing tensions in Ulster from a strongly nationalist perspective and believed the street battles were part of the historic struggle between Irish patriots and British oppressors. On American political issues they tended to be, but were not exclusively, conservative. Some

34. Tom Enright, former ACIF treasurer, interview with author, 14 November 1989.

35. Brian Heron, "National Group Underway," *The Felon: Newsletter of the Irish-American Action Association* (June 1969).

36. NAIJ statement on funding in *Irish-American Review* (New York), 19 September 1970. Some newspapers and individuals also claim the NAIJ were involved in sending funds to Cahal Goulding and the Official IRA.

37. Linda Charlton, "Irish Americans are Aroused by New Troubles," *New York Times*, 16 August 1969.

condemned the anti-Vietnam war movement and supported Catholic social policy. A number, ironically, opposed Martin Luther King's civil rights campaign and failed to appreciate similarities between African Americans and Catholics in Ulster. Since its membership included many younger left-wing activists, the NAIJ wanted to present the Irish struggle as part of a worldwide, anti-imperialist, Marxist revolution. They hoped to ally the civil rights campaign in Ireland with the struggle for African-American equality in the United States and the anti–Vietnam War movement.

Ideological conflicts between the ACIF and NAIJ were exacerbated by the activities of People's Democracy. The NAIJ executive supported PD and began sending small financial donations; James Heaney, on the other hand, criticized them as communist agitators and tried to encourage more traditional nationalist elements. In July 1969 he condemned PD leader Michael Farrell as a "Red Fascist," and he described Kevin Boyle as a "Johnny-come-lately to the civil rights movement who, as a law lecturer at Queen's University, has been part of the Unionist establishment for years." Heaney assured Irish Americans that the vast majority of activists in Ulster "seek a just society, not a red society."[38]

Bernadette Devlin and Irish America

While the conflict between the NAIJ and the ACIF was intensifying, both groups were bringing prominent Irish activists to America in an effort to reinforce their respective positions. When Bernadette Devlin announced she would tour the United States in August 1969, some believed she could end the growing divisions between Irish-American groups and give them a unity of purpose. As events unfolded, however, this hope proved illusionary. Rather than heal divisions, Devlin's visit only served to sharpen antagonisms.

In 1969, when she was elected to the British Parliament at the age of twenty-two, Bernadette Devlin became the Irish politician most recognized in America. In the United States, the media focused on her as someone the public could identify with and gave her celebrity status. Newspaper articles presented her as a courageous and feisty leader battling against an unjust system. Reports continually referred to her as the "Irish Joan of Arc" but failed to provide a systematic analysis of her

38. *Irish-American Reporter* (Buffalo), July 1969.

political ideals. Most stories were blatantly sexist, concentrating on her "modern and with it" dress style, while her socialist political views were hardly mentioned.

A typical example of the coverage given to Devlin appeared in a 1969 *Newsweek* magazine article. After describing her "striped mini-dress" and referring to her as a "folk hero," the report summarized Devlin's maiden speech to Parliament:

> The proceedings began lightly enough. When Bernadette was introduced to the Speaker of Commons, Dr. Horace King, the subsequent handshake lasted so long that the MPs burst into loud laughter. And the laughter redoubled when King, with mock dignity, declared,: "I have said before that it is out of order for the House to be jealous."

After this humorous introduction, Bernadette went on to deliver a rousing speech and the article concluded,

> When Bernadette had finished, the greats of Parliament vied in singing her praises. One after another, MPs hailed her maiden speech as one of the best in the history of Commons.[39]

The adulation of the American press increased when Devlin arrived in New York on August 21, 1969. Mayor John Lindsay presented her with a golden key to the city and the two were photographed in an embrace. Devlin persuaded him to issue a statement attacking discrimination in Ulster and he later told the *New York Daily News* that "it was love at first sight."[40] One journalist covering the first stage of Devlin's trip commented:

> Coming straight from the barricades, yet holding a seat in Parliament, she was every reporter's dream story. The mass media, which constantly demands a new subject to talk about, lunged at her with undisguised passion, falling on her every word.[41]

When Bernadette met with Secretary General U Thant of the United Nations, the *New York Times* played up the fact that she eschewed normal procedure and had arranged the meeting by simply giving him a phone call. During the conference the newspaper marvelled at her "cool confi-

39. "Song of Bernadette," *Newsweek Magazine*, 5 May 1969.
40. *New York Daily News*, 23 August 1969.
41. Philip Tracy, "Soapbox U.S.A.," *Commonweal* (26 September 1969), 583.

dence and diplomatic stature." She conveyed the same image during television appearances on "Meet the Press" and "The Johnny Carson Show."

This media hype boosted Devlin's fund-raising efforts. Major American newspapers covered all her rallies and reported how vast amounts of
money were collected in plastic buckets. These reports were soon conveyed back to Ireland and Bernadette boasted she would easily raise $1
million. Journalist Seán Cronin wrote in the *Irish Times*:

> Without a doubt, Bernadette is the best envoy Ireland ever sent to
> America. She has taken over the city and her cry for justice has come
> across loud and clear. Not even Eamon de Valera in 1920 commanded
> the audience she has. She is young and articulate and her mini-skirts
> help too. All consider her the brightest, the freshest, and of course the
> prettiest Irish politician to come to these ports in living memory.[42]

Although Devlin's first few days in New York were a great success,
the longer she stayed, the more she challenged traditional Irish-American
nationalists. Groups like the ACIF, the Ancient Order of Hibernians, and
the Irish Counties Association wanted Devlin to concentrate on purely
Irish issues and deliver rousing nationalist speeches. Many of their members were strongly conservative and opposed African-American civil
rights. The latent racism of these Irish Americans was later epitomized
during demonstrations against busing in Charlestown, Massachusetts,
when the chant of "Niggers out of Boston, Brits out of Belfast" was frequently heard.[43]

The more contact Devlin had with these Irish Americans, the more she
recoiled at their narrow-mindedness and racist attitudes. With full encouragement from the NAIJ, she resolved to condemn their lack of support for African Americans and to emphasize her socialist ideals and
criticisms of the Catholic church.

Devlin's focus on social issues alienated large sections of the Irish-
American support network. This process intensified when she embarked
on the second half of her tour to California and the Midwest. In Los Angeles, against the advice of local Irish societies, she paid a highly publi-

42. Seán Cronin, "Away from the Barricades, Bernadette hits the U.S.A.," *Irish Times*
(Dublin), 1 September 1969. Such reports greatly alarmed Unionists in Northern Ireland.
They sent a "Truth Squad" to New York, composed of Stormont and Westminster MPs,
which made little impact in trying to expose Devlin as "Fidel Castro in a mini-skirt."

43. From Laura Flanders, "Principles at Stake in Duke's Bush War," *Fortnight Magazine* (July/August 1988), 11.

cized visit to Operation Bootstrap in Watts. Later, at a rally in MacArthur Park, she addressed a crowd composed of Irish Americans holding small green flags and members of the American Young Socialist Movement. Scuffles broke out between the two factions after the Young Socialists performed a skit in which a man was beaten for not singing the American national anthem. Groups of Irish Americans heckled Devlin when she spoke of African-American civil rights, while others simply left in disgust.[44]

In Detroit, leaders of the Irish Associations tried to exclude African Americans from attending Devlin's rally in Ford Hall. When she heard of this, she refused to speak until they were admitted. This greatly infuriated officials from the Ancient Order of Hibernians. They had presented Bernadette with a large sum of money. However, after press photographs captured the event, they took it back and sent it to the Catholic church in Ireland.[45]

The most publicized conflict between Devlin and conservative Irish Americans came with her visit to Chicago. Before her arrival, Leonard Glazer of the NAIJ telephoned Mayor Richard Daley's office and told staff that Devlin did not want to meet the mayor because he was "a racist pig."[46] Devlin and Irish civil rights activists had given the Chief of the RUC in Derry the nickname "Mayor Daley"—"because of his fondness for beating people off the streets." Some of the tour organizers, however, realized that a clash with Daley would damage fund-raising efforts in Chicago. They tried to downplay the conflict, but Daley issued a statement saying that money should be donated to the Irish Red Cross instead of to Devlin. When she arrived he didn't try to meet her and left to spend the weekend at his summer home in Michigan.[47]

44. Sara Davidson, "Bernadette Devlin: An Irish Revolutionary in Irish-America," *Harpers' Magazine* 240, no. 1463 (January 1970): 83.

45. Bernadette Devlin, interview with author, 31 May 1989. Devlin says that the check, presented by Michael Flannery, was for $1 million. The AOH was incensed by her radical views, particularly the attacks on the Catholic church. They sent the money to Cardinal Conway and the Irish Red Cross.

46. *Chicago Daily News*, 28 August 1969.

47. This conflict between Mayor Daley and Devlin endured. During a later visit to Chicago, the mayor tried to repair their differences by sending a limousine to collect Bernadette at O'Hare airport. When she found out the motorcade was taking her to a reception hosted by Daley at City Hall, she stopped the car and refused to attend. See Bernadette Devlin, "A Peasant in the Halls of the Great," in Michael Farrell, ed., *Twenty Years On*, (Kerry: Brandon Books, 1988), 87.

In Chicago, Devlin took the opportunity to launch a scathing attack on the mayor and delivered her strongest indictment of conservative Irish Americans. She told a rally of the Irish Societies that by opposing African-American civil rights they were guilty of the same oppression enforced by Orangemen in Ulster.[48] Devlin also tried to convince the groups that only through a socialist republic could Ireland be truly free. She later lampooned the reaction she received:

> In America the word socialist is a smear you apply to other people. You never get up and say you are a socialist yourself. All the men in the big green suits cheered and roared when I mentioned James Connolly, until I started quoting what he actually said.[49]

There was a radical change in the US media perception of Devlin as reports of her attacks on conservative Irish Americans made headline news. Editorials strongly condemned her views, claiming she was unrepresentative of the majority of Catholics in Ulster. The *Detroit News* ran an editorial describing her as a "rabble rouser" and a "mini-skirted Danny the Red."[50] After the donnybrook with Mayor Daley, the *Chicago Tribune* commented:

> Instead of aligning herself with the Irish Catholic establishment, she appeared on stages with the barefoot bluejean brigades. Whatever her personal appeal, Miss Devlin has shown herself to be more anti-establishment than pro-Irish. And if this is the course to be followed by Catholics in Ulster, then the outlook is grim for everyone except Communists and other subversives who regard the religious conflict as a pretext for turning all of Ireland into Britain's Cuba.[51]

Devlin's problems intensified when she also began criticizing the activities of the NAIJ. She had continually told American reporters that the money she raised would be used to help needy families in Northern Ireland and not for the purchase of weapons. While she was in Los Angeles, however, she began to suspect that Brian Heron was sending part of the money to the IRA. In a subsequent interview with Mary Holland in the

48. "Bernadette Likens Civil Rights Struggle Here to Irish Struggle," *Chicago Tribune*, 31 August 1969.
49. *Irish Times* (Dublin), 8 September 1969.
50. "Siren Song of Bernadette," (editorial) *Detroit News*, 28 August 1969.
51. *Chicago Tribune*, 4 September 1969.

Observer, Devlin said she was opposed to this because she felt the IRA would use the money to buy guns. To guard against this possibility, she contacted leaders of People's Democracy in Belfast and began setting up bank accounts in her own name from which only she could transfer cash to Ireland.[52]

Devlin now says that the issue wasn't so much that the money would go for weapons but that she was not specifically told either way. This caused a bitter dispute between her and the NAIJ as they fought for control of the funds. The antagonisms and bickering reached such intensity that Bernadette returned to Belfast prematurely and canceled an invitation to address both Houses of Congress.[53]

Devlin's dispute with the NAIJ continued when she returned to Ireland. She insisted that all the money raised should be sent to her, and she instigated legal proceedings against the group. She eventually recovered the money deposited under her name. However, the NAIJ insisted on holding $93,000. In response, Bernadette publicly ridiculed Brian Heron and some of the NAIJ's young radical activists. She said they were totally ignorant of Irish affairs and sarcastically remarked that within the association, "the only qualification needed for being an expert in Northern Ireland was to have been involved in the California grape strike."[54]

Many conservative Irish Americans welcomed Devlin's conflict with the NAIJ, but hopes that she would now conform to their image of a modern Kathleen ni Houlihan were misplaced. In subsequent visits to America in the early 1970s, she continued to push her socialist views and

52. Devlin interviewed by Mary Holland, *Observer* (London), 7 September 1969.

53. The NICRA, when it heard Devlin was going to cut short her tour, sent out Chairman Frank Gogarty to patch things up with the Irish-American groups. Devlin says the final incident that convinced her to leave America occurred at a dinner party in New Jersey attended by leading members of the Democratic Party. During the evening she willingly had her photograph taken with the guests. She later discovered the people were being charged $30 per photograph. She says this reminded her of being photographed with the monkeys at the zoo as a child. She stormed out of the party and borrowed money from Paul O'Dwyer for the flight home.

54. *Observer* (London), 7 September 1969. Because of the controversy surrounding the money raised in America, Devlin had a public audit of the $19,564 she was able to get back to Ireland. A Northern Ireland Emergency Relief Fund allocated $5,000 to help rebuild Bombay Street in Belfast—a Catholic block of houses that had been burned down by a loyalist mob. The rest of the money was taken by the NICRA, and a small portion was used to pay the bills of families on electricity strike in Derry. The NAIJ retained $93,000 for use in America.

support African-American civil rights. In March 1970 she authorized Eamon McCann to present the golden key of New York City that she had received from Mayor Lindsay to leaders of the Black Panthers. Devlin sent an accompanying message stating her action was "a gesture of solidarity with the Black liberation and revolutionary socialist movements in America."[55] In February 1971, Bernadette visited Angela Davis in Marin County Jail. Davis, a communist and African-American separatist, had been arrested for buying the guns used in a shootout during a courtroom escape attempt in which a judge and three other persons were killed. Bernadette praised the Black Panthers after the meeting and described Davis's treatment as scandalous.[56]

These two actions infuriated many Irish Americans, and a number of groups attacked Devlin. The *Irish Echo* and the *Irish Advocate* ran editorials describing the "key incident" as a flagrant act of discourtesy. James Heaney was particularly strong in his attacks and issued statements calling her a "communist subversive" with no support in Ireland. After the meeting with Angela Davis, he ran the following editorial in the *Irish-American Reporter*:

> Red Bernie told Americans they were racist bigots and capitalists of the worst sort. Britain is using Miss Devlin to convince the world that Irish agitation for freedom is a Communist plot. Many have concluded the best thing the English government has going for it is Bernadette Devlin. She couldn't serve England better if she were on the payroll![57]

Despite such strong attacks, a number of leading ACIF activists refused to accept Devlin's commitment to socialism and African-American civil rights. They believed her actions were a result of the malignant influence of the NAIJ. Many were convinced that Brian Heron used Devlin to push issues that were unrelated to the Irish struggle. The divisions this caused meant that a great opportunity for uniting Irish Americans was lost. One activist typically lamented:

> I am heartbroken at the utterances of Miss Devlin. This brilliant young woman had the potential to do so much good. Because of her, hope

55. "Irish Give Key To City To Black Panthers As Symbol," *New York Times*, 3 March 1970.

56. "Miss Devlin on Coast, Assails Jail Treatment of Miss Davis," *New York Times*, 22 February 1971.

57. "Joan of Arc or Mao's Maiden," *Irish-American Reporter* (Buffalo), July 1971.

sprang high in the hearts of the Irish people that here perhaps was someone whom they could rally around and provide leadership in the last great fight to attain the unity and freedom of our homeland. But this dream has been shattered because she has listened to the wrong people and been misled. . . . I hope and pray that she will see the light and realize that the direction she has taken can bring nothing but ill for the Ireland we all love.[58]

The perceived corruption of Devlin by the NAIJ led the ACIF to launch a sustained campaign designed to destroy its activities. James Heaney began a publicity barrage in the Irish-American press claiming the NAIJ was exploiting the civil rights issue for its own political ends. He claimed the group was collecting money from unsuspecting Irish Americans to support left-wing agitation in the United States. Heaney also tried to publicize Brian Heron's links with communists, the Black Panthers and Students for a Democratic Society.

James Heaney combined this attack on the NAIJ with a campaign against leftist elements in the civil rights movement in Ireland. He intensified his earlier denunciations of People's Democracy and encouraged moderate members of the NICRA to distance themselves from the group. The ACIF supported Conn McCluskey and Brid Rodgers in their disputes with People's Democracy and encouraged them to take complete control of the NICRA executive.

Leaders of People's Democracy responded strongly to attacks from the ACIF, accusing Heaney of financing a right-wing takeover of the NICRA. In America, the NAIJ described Heaney and his supporters as "reactionary bigots" who were "blinded to the social realities of Ireland by their hazy, romantic nationalism."[59] Yet despite this strong counterattack, the NAIJ did suffer from the ACIF's successful campaign to tarnish its image among Irish-American activists. Some members of the NAIJ who had joined purely to campaign on behalf of Irish civil rights left the group after the attacks from Heaney and the dispute with Bernadette Devlin.

The NAIJ also experienced serious internal disputes between its diverse and often hostile affiliate groups. The organization contained mem-

58. Letter to the editor from Seamus MacQueney, *Irish-American Review* (New York), 6 March 1971.

59. From NAIJ flyer, "James Connolly and our Irish-American Leaders," dated 10 October 1969.

bers who were also variously associated with the Communist Party, Trot-
skyite groups, the Black Panthers, the American Young Socialists, and
Students for a Democratic Society. These members argued over whether
to support Bernadette Devlin, whether to support the NICRA or IRA, and
whether to retain funds for political campaigns in America or send all donations back to Ireland.

In early November 1969, the NAIJ held its first national convention in
New York, with IRA leader Cahal Goulding as guest of honor. Brian
Heron hoped the meeting would bring cohesion to the association. Delegates from all over the United States came to formulate a constitution and
to issue policy resolutions. A group from People's Democracy, led by
Frank Gogarty and Kevin Boyle, also attended and held widely publicized
meetings with the Black Panthers. They infuriated ACIF activists by
claiming to be the true leaders of the civil rights movement. They also emphasized that the NAIJ had been voted the official arm of the NICRA in
America.[60]

The convention delegates reached a consensus on some resolutions
and wrote a new constitution. They supported the rights of Catholics to
forcibly resist "Orange bigotry," established an Irish Defense Fund to
secure freedom of political prisoners, and announced a boycott of British
automobiles in the United States. In an attempt to minimize internal conflicts, the convention voted that the NAIJ executive should not issue
statements on American political issues but should rather allow individual chapters to formulate their own policies.[61]

Despite this attempt at compromise, the infighting and bickering within
the NAIJ persisted as each group continued to support its own particular
political perspective on American and world affairs. There was also a continuing conflict over Brian Heron's leadership. Many delegates considered
his control to be dictatorial and in defiance of the wishes of affiliate
groups. Some NAIJ executive members were incensed by Heron's actions
during the convention. He installed a huge portrait of his grandfather
behind the speakers' podium and insisted on dominating the proceedings.[62]

60. For a description of the activities of the People's Democracy delegation in America
see Eilis McDermott, "Law and Disorder," in Michael Farrell, *Twenty Years On*, 152–53.

61. *N.A.I.J. Constitution and Policy Statements*, 9 November 1969.

62. Robert St. Cyr, former member of NAIJ executive, correspondence with author,
26 May 1990. St. Cyr also recalls that many members of the NAIJ were infuriated by
Heron's disposition to suspect everyone of being an FBI informant. Some were also sickened
by Leonard Glazer's implicit threats of violence against opponents within the organization.

James Heaney informed his friends in Ulster of the NAIJ convention and the "provocative" actions and statements of the PD delegation. In response, Conn McCluskey and a group of moderates within the NICRA denounced Kevin Boyle and Frank Gogarty. He claimed their support for the Black Panthers while in New York had infuriated many Irish Americans and destroyed an opportunity for positive publicity. McCluskey and his associates also accused PD of imposing a dictatorship within the Irish civil rights movement.[63]

Antagonism over the American network was just one of many conflicts between PD and moderates within the civil rights movement. These irreconcilable differences greatly contributed to the NICRA's eventual dissolution and produced major realignments within the nationalist political spectrum. On August 21, 1970, the more moderate majority of civil rights activists joined with Gerry Fitt to form the Social Democratic and Labour Party, dedicated to the goals of constitutional nationalism. Many of the more militant NICRA activists supported the IRA, particularly with the rise of the Provisional wing in late 1969.

These developments had important consequences for the Irish-American support network. As the civil rights movement declined, the NAIJ increasingly lost its relevance. More and more of its affiliates began to withdraw their support, while traditional Irish-American nationalists continued to attack the organization. In the winter of 1970 the NAIJ collapsed as new leftist groups emerged in response to changes in Ireland.

The ACIF also suffered from the political changes in Northern Ireland and their repercussions in America. New organizations emerged which specifically supported the Provisional IRA These groups proved extremely appealing to most traditional Irish-American nationalists. As many of Heaney's associates left to join new IRA groups, the ACIF's influence sharply declined.

The Irish Republican Clubs and Noraid

In December 1969, a conflict developed within the IRA between those who wanted to launch a military campaign and others who felt they should concentrate on achieving a socialist republic through political

63. Information from correspondence between Heaney and Conn McCluskey dated 20 November 1969.

action. Consequently, the IRA split into leftist "Official" and militant "Provisional" wings. The Provisionals soon became the main guerrilla force opposing the British presence in Northern Ireland. The Officials carried out a short campaign of bombings and shootings but declared a cessation of operations in 1972.

In the early seventies, both the Officials and the Provisionals needed financial support and publicity for their respective causes. They inevitably turned to the traditional avenues of support among the Irish diaspora in America. In 1970, a small Official IRA network formed in America around a nucleus of James Connolly Clubs in New York and Boston. Many of these groups were composed of old IRA veterans with a socialist inclination and of younger militants who joined because of the demise of the NAIJ. In May 1971, Official Sinn Féin leaders Seán Kenny and Dennis Cassin traveled to America to coordinate the activities of these groups. They met with supporters in New York, Boston, and San Francisco and in May formed the Irish Republican Clubs of the United States and Canada (IRC).

The Irish Republican Clubs' main strength was in New York City, where five units quickly emerged. Eventually it managed to form chapters in other cities including Chicago, Boston, Philadelphia, and Baltimore. The group also had Canadian branches in Toronto, Winnipeg, and Montreal. All these chapters were coordinated by a national executive committee, which ran publicity campaigns and joint fund-raising ventures.[64]

The IRC followed the political line of Official Sinn Féin and supported the establishment of a socialist republic in Ireland. The group also endorsed African-American civil rights and strongly attacked American imperialism. As such, it condemned the war in Vietnam and expressed solidarity with liberation movements in the Third World. To publicize these views, individual IRC chapters produced their own newsletters and distributed copies of the *United Irishman*, Official Sinn Féin's monthly newspaper. The group also collected funds for the Official Republican Prisoners Fund in Dublin.[65]

64. For a brief history of the IRC see Michael Funchion, ed., *Irish-American Voluntary Organizations* (Westport Conn: Greenwood Press, 1983) 210–12.

65. There is extensive information on the activities of IRC in FBI files FOIPA. No. 270, 097, which were compiled during an investigation under the FARA.

A similar new leftist Irish-American group was the National Association for Irish Freedom. It was formed in New York in the spring of 1971 by former members of the NAIJ who wanted to continue their work in Irish affairs. The NAIF had links with the Irish Republican Clubs but still maintained that its official association was with the NICRA.

Like the Irish Republican Clubs, the NAIF attacked the capitalist system in Ireland and supported socialist causes throughout the world. It organized demonstrations and ran fund-raising events for "political prisoners" in Irish jails. The most successful of these was a folk concert at Carnegie Hall in April 1971, which raised $40,000.[66]

The IRC and NAIF both remained small organizations and attracted only a few hundred supporters. Most Irish-American activists were repelled by their leftist orientation and were naturally inclined to support the Provisional IRA. The Provos, through formation of the Irish Northern Aid Committee (Noraid), appealed to Irish Americans by avoiding wider political issues and concentrating on the national question. Their presentation of the Ulster conflict as one between Irish patriots and British invaders appealed more strongly to the traditional nationalism of Irish-American activists.

Michael Flannery was the driving force behind the formation and growth of Noraid. At the age of fourteen, he had joined the Irish Volunteers in his native Tipperary and later fought against the Black and Tans in the War of Independence. After the Treaty, he supported the "irregulars" in the Civil War. He was captured by Free State forces, interned, and later participated in the 1923 hunger strike at the Curragh Camp. Upon release, Flannery left Ireland for New York in 1927 to organize IRA veterans. Within two years he became the leading figure in what remained of Clan na Gael.[67]

For forty years Flannery pursued a relatively peaceful career with the Metropolitan Life Insurance Company and worked for a variety of Irish-American social groups. When the Troubles erupted in Ulster he resumed his militant activities and joined the ACIF for a short period. The political maneuvering of the group frustrated Flannery, and he left to form the Irish Action Committee, composed of militant nationalists. One affiliate,

66. The performers included Pete Seeger, the Clancy Brothers, Mary Travers, and actress Siobhan McKenna. For information on the NAIF see FBI files FOIPA 297, 650.

67. Dylan Foley, "Rebel Without a Pause: After 76 Years Flannery Still Speaks Out for Irish," *Irish Echo* (New York), 13 May 1992.

the United Ireland Committee, tried to recruit volunteers to cross the Atlantic and fight alongside Catholics in Northern Ireland.[68]

In December 1969, Flannery traveled to Ireland for a meeting with members of the newly emerging Provisional IRA. The Provos were impressed by his revered standing in New York's Irish community. They felt Flannery would be the perfect leader of a new organization to collect financial support from Irish Americans.

After this initial contact, Provo leaders Joe Cahil and Dáithí O Conaill traveled to the United States. They met Flannery and asked him to lead a fund-raising organization to support a renewed military campaign aimed at uniting Ireland. Flannery promised to do what he could to aid the cause. In April 1970, at a press conference in New York, he announced the formation of Noraid. Also present as trustees for the new group were John McGowan and Jack McCarthy, both former IRA veterans who had left Ireland after the Civil War.[69]

These three founding members claimed Noraid's primary function was to raise cash for the families of imprisoned Provisional IRA members. They initially saw pro-republican publicity efforts in the United States as a minor part of their activities. Michael Flannery was careful to emphasize that their funds would not be used to purchase weapons. He therefore insisted Noraid's links were with An Cumann Cabhrach, Provisional Sinn Féin's prisoner relief organization in Dublin. An Cumann Cabhrach transmitted cash to the Green Cross in Belfast, which then gave weekly payments to prisoners dependents. British authorities have continually claimed that Green Cross fails to provide adequate records of the disbursement of its funds.

As required under United States law, Noraid declared its foreign principal as the Northern Aid Committee Belfast, a precursor of Green Cross. The group also named Joe Cahill as one of the chief recipients of its funds. While Noraid continued to assert its collections were for "humanitarian relief," it made no stipulation on how its funds should be spent in Ireland. British, Irish, and American authorities alleged that a large percentage of the money was used for the purchase of weapons. This controversy has continued throughout Noraid's history.

68. This call to arms was printed in *New York Times*, 16 May 1969. A later article in *The Times* (London), 16 August 1969, claimed that twenty Irish-American volunteers had arrived in Ulster.

69. Michael Flannery, correspondence with author, 18 November 1992.

Irish bars in cities throughout the United States became the focal point for Noraid activities. Some owners allowed their premises to be used for fund-raising events and for the business meetings of local chapters. Noraid volunteers held regular collections among the clientele and received substantial donations from the bar owners themselves. Some establishments, like the Four Provinces Tavern in New Jersey, were opened specifically to send profits back to Ireland.[70]

While these barroom collections were a major element in Noraid fund raising, the group also organized dinner-dance benefits and appealed for cash through direct mail solicitations. Financial statements given to the US Justice Department show that mailing campaigns were moderately successful. Noraid's headquarters in the Bronx received regular weekly donations from individual Irish Americans throughout the United States. These contributions usually ranged between $10 and $20 from each donor; only rarely were sums of more than $300 received.

The largest financial contributions to Noraid's central office came from its various chapters nationwide. There was substantial variation in the amount these branches raised, usually depending on the size of the Irish community in a particular region or city. Noraid units in Chicago, Boston, New York, Philadelphia, and San Francisco regularly raised between $3,000 and $7,000 each month. This contrasted sharply with chapters in Kansas City, Vancouver, or Rogue, Oregon, which raised barely $100 per month.[71]

Michael Flannery and the other Noraid officials used only a small percentage of these donations to finance activities in America. The bulk of Noraid money went to Ireland through money orders, bank drafts, or direct deposits. The preferred means of conveyance, however, was cash carried by trusted couriers and delivered directly to An Cumann

70. See Michael McKinley, "Lavish Generosity: The American Dimension of International Support for the Provisional I.R.A.," *Conflict Quarterly* 7, no. 2 (Spring 1987): 26. The many Irish bars in Queens, Brooklyn, and the Bronx in New York were particularly important to the Noraid network, as they provided the principal social center for many working-class Irish Americans and recent immigrants. These bars provided not only a familiar social outlet but a way in which information about accommodation and employment could be obtained by Irish immigrants. Consequently, they were prime recruiting and fund-raising sources for Noraid. See also Kevin Cullen, "Purchase of Irish Bar in Dorchester Raises Questions," *Boston Globe*, 20 June 1989.

71. Information from reports submitted under the FARA, 1976–1981.

Cabhrach. Such deliveries were virtually impossible for the authorities to trace.[72]

Noraid publicized its activities and fund-raising events in the *Irish People*. Although the newspaper was legally separate from Noraid, it operated out of the group's headquarters in the Bronx; most of its staff and editorial board were Noraid members. The newspaper reproduced material first published in *An Phoblacht/Republican News*, the weekly newspaper of Provisional Sinn Féin. It also ran virulently republican articles by its own staff writers, which encouraged the IRA to increase its campaign of violence.

Noraid soon began organizing trips to America by leading members of Provisional Sinn Féin. Seán Keenan and Ruairí O Brádaigh, in particular, conducted speaking tours in Irish-American communities to promote the formation of new INA chapters. Although there were a number of Provos who considered themselves socialists, the organization adopted a chameleon like character. They recognized the conservative nature of their Noraid supporters and adapted themselves accordingly. In *To Take Arms*, Maria McGuire, a defector from the Provos, recalled how speakers were drilled on how to appeal to Irish Americans:

> It was in the United States that our main funding efforts were conducted and visiting speakers were carefully briefed on how the audience should be played. There should be copious reference to the martyrs of 1916 and 1919-21—the period in which most of the audience would be living. Anti-British sentiment, recalling Cromwell, the Famine, and the Black and Tans, could be profitably exploited. By no means should anything be said against the Catholic Church and all references to socialism should be avoided.[73]

Many of these leading Provisionals made little secret of their desire to get weapons. Maria McGuire mentions the fund-raising activities of Sinn Féin's Billy McKee, who had a reputation for being "fond of the bottle." She claims he began by missing his flight after a hard night's drinking, and when he finally arrived in New York, McGuire reported:

72. Angus Deming, "Arming the I.R.A.," *Newsweek*, 6 March 1972, claims that some Noraid cash at this time was sent to an account in Switzerland and then transferred to the Provos.

73. Maria McGuire, *To Take Arms: A Year in the Provisionals* (London: MacMillan, 1973), 108.

As soon as he had a few drinks he would begin touting for arms in a most unsubtle way, once giving a US senator a conspiratorial elbow in the ribs and muttering, "Any hardware?"[74]

At receptions after he had delivered a speech, McKee had the habit of abusing Irish Americans with profane insults. McGuire maintains that even despite these incidents, McKee's fund-raising efforts were very successful. Republicans who toured the US at this time recall that there were many Irish-American activists who would not have donated money unless they were assured it would be used to buy guns.

Initially, the split between the Provisional and Official IRA confused most Irish Americans. One activist recalls that members of the Ireland for the Irish Club in New York sent cash and weapons to both factions in early 1970.[75] Irish groups in Boston tried to encourage members of both Official and Provisional Sinn Féin to attend their functions. As Noraid grew in strength, however, this momentary confusion soon ended.

Just as the Provisionals attacked the Officials in Ireland, so Noraid began a series of bitter conflicts with the Irish Republican Clubs and members of the National Association for Irish Freedom. When Official Sinn Féin sent Seán Kenny to America to coordinate the activities of the IRC, Noraid began distributing leaflets which described him as a "raving communist agitator intent on deceiving Irish Americans."[76] The IRC responded to this campaign and issued statements describing Noraid as "Green Fascists" and ignorant of the real social needs of Ireland. One IRC activist complained:

> Northern Aid puts on a holier-than-thou attitude to give the impression that they're the sole custodians of the Irish revolution and the republican ideal. They appeal to emotions rather than to logic. . . but ask them what sort of republic they want, and they wouldn't have a clue.[77]

74. Ibid., 110.

75. R. H. Brown, *I Am of Ireland* (New York: Harper and Row, 1974): 100–103.

76. Jack Deacy, "The I.R.A. New York Brigade." *New York Magazine*, (13 March 1972): 43. Another article which deals with the conflicts between Noraid and the IRC is Ken Botwright, "Can the Irish Dump the British?," *Washington Post*, 16 January 1972.

77. Roger Williams, "American Aid: Lifeblood for the I.R.A.," *World Magazine* (24 April 1973), 30. Williams also gives an account of the case of Pat Purcell, an IRC supporter who was caught sending guns to the Officials in 1973. IRC members were enraged when Noraid leaders publicly gloated over the conviction of Purcell and suggested he was a communist infiltrator.

Eventually these animosities between Noraid and the IRC went beyond a war of words. Fist fights began erupting between both factions at anti-British demonstrations in New York. Journalist Jack Deacy relates how Noraid supporters jeered IRC and NAIF members at a demonstration outside Madison Square Garden. The Noraid delegation asked the police on duty to erect a barricade between them and the "bloody Reds." This led to a physical confrontation between the two factions, during which a number of IRC supporters were injured. One demonstrator reported:

> I was carrying a sign supporting a Socialist Workers Republic in Ireland. And, Jesus, all of a sudden this man has me by the back of the neck, shoving me and shouting I'm not one of theirs and to go to your own group, the Commies![78]

The traditional nationalist majority of Irish-American activists welcomed Noraid's attacks on the leftists associated with the IRC and NAIF. Consequently, Noraid emerged as the strongest, most active, and most widely supported militant Irish-American group. The NAIF and the IRC remained small and largely ineffective. Dennis Cassin, one of the IRC's chief organizers, admitted:

> Our philosophy has little appeal to established Irish society in America. So we don't have much money to send to the other side; a few hundred a month, maybe . . . [which] is barely enough to pay the rent, let alone buy weapons.[79]

Noraid also capitalized on the network established by the American Congress for Irish Freedom. By the end of 1970, many ACIF mem-

---

78. Jack Deacy, "The I.R.A.," 40. Noraid supporters also conducted leaflet-distribution campaigns against bars that were sympathetic to, or linked with, the Irish Republican Clubs. A number of violent confrontations ensued between "Stickie" patrons and Noraid pickets.

79. Dennis Cassin, interviewed in Roger Williams, "American Aid: Lifeblood for the I.R.A.," 30. The Irish Republican Clubs continued to publicize Connollyite socialism in America to a very small number of supporters. They endorsed the formation of the Worker's Party in Ireland and were particularly vocal during the 1981 hunger strikes. The IRC's most active cells are on the West Coast, particularly in San Francisco, where it is alleged they control a number of bars that send profits back to Ireland. Though the relationship between Noraid and the IRC has often been antagonistic, the groups have also worked together in support of common objectives, particularly on publicity and fund raising for extradition and gunrunning cases.

bers felt that civil rights agitation had gone as far as it could and that it was time to aid the "armed struggle." James Heaney believed that any association with violence, regardless of how justified the cause, would wreck ACIF chances of winning political support in Congress. Consequently, many of Heaney's associates left to join Noraid, and the ACIF became a marginal force within the nationalist support network in America.

This process was accentuated by growing dissatisfaction with James Heaney's leadership. A number of personal disagreements developed between Heaney and other ACIF officials. Many were thus attracted by Michael Flannery, who seemed to be more responsive to the wishes of his supporters and offered dynamic leadership. Tom Enright recalls of Heaney:

> He was not an "organization" man. He was a loner, working away from the action in Buffalo. He was quick to react against criticism and sometimes he would write to people expelling them from the organization. Some of us received legal notices to account for funds which even he knew were of no substance.[80]

As growing numbers of ACIF members left to join Noraid, Heaney issued acrimonious statements about his former associates. He claimed that these defectors stole $30,000 in ACIF funds and gave them to Noraid headquarters in New York.[81] Michael Flannery strongly denied this allegation, and relations between the two organizations greatly deteriorated.[82]

The ACIF had collapsed by the end of 1970; Heaney formed a much smaller organization called the National Council of Irish Americans (NCIA). The NCIA continued to publicize human rights violations in Ulster and to concentrate on exposing the "harassment" of Irish-American activists by federal agencies. It also maintained efforts to persuade companies not to locate or invest in Northern Ireland. The NCIA remained active until Heaney's death in 1986.

The ACIF played an extremely influential role in the reemergence of a nationalist support network in America. Its campaigns were the first to publicize the Northern Ireland civil rights movement and catalyzed in-

80. Tom Enright, correspondence with author, 4 December 1989.
81. Mrs. James Heaney, correspondence with author, 6 April 1990.
82. Michael Flannery, correspondence with author, 23 July 1991.

creased Irish-American activism. Noraid exploited this renewed interest and emerged as the most prominent group supporting the IRA. In the early 1970s it would play an important role in providing material assistance to the "armed struggle." Noraid would also benefit from a succession of Unionist and British policy blunders, which further increased Irish-American sympathy for militant nationalism.

CHAPTER 3

◆

BLOODY SUNDAY AND THE GROWTH

OF IRISH-AMERICAN REPUBLICANISM,

1971-1972

◆

By 1971, the Stormont government was faced with a virtual collapse of civil order in Northern Ireland. Both the Provisional IRA and the Official IRA were waging relentless bombing campaigns throughout the province and had begun shooting British troops. In this situation, the Unionist government, headed by Brian Faulkner, initiated a series of repressive measures aimed at crushing the IRA and restoring order. These policies, rather than reducing the crisis, actually led to the intensification of nationalist bitterness toward the Stormont regime and produced even more violence.

Noraid and the other irredentist groups in America greatly benefited from these events in Northern Ireland. They publicized the repressive measures of the Stormont government and convinced Irish-American activists and some leading politicians that the nationalist community was being subjected to massive oppression and injustice. By the spring of

1972, Noraid had secured a dominant position within the Irish-American support network and substantially increased its membership and financial contributions.

One of the most important factors in the continued growth of Noraid was the introduction of internment. In August 1971, security forces arrested more than three hundred republican suspects and held them for interrogation. The IRA responded with an escalation of violence. Inter communal conflict soared as Protestant and Catholic families were intimidated and forced to flee their homes. Nearly four thousand Catholics sought refuge in military camps across the border in the Irish Republic.[1]

All these events attracted wide coverage in the American media. During the first weeks of renewed violence, reaction was mixed. Editorial comments in the *New York Times* maintained that Brian Faulkner was justified in introducing internment because of the uncompromising stand taken by extremists on both sides. The *Christian Science Monitor* stated that internment would reduce violence by removing Provo leaders and was essential to the preservation of Faulkner's "progressive administration."[2] Other newspapers, including the *Washington Post,* the *Chicago Daily News*, and the *St. Louis Post-Dispatch*, objected to internment from the outset. They attacked the denial of human rights and warned that the policy would backfire on Faulkner's government. Editorials in these papers correctly predicted that the policy was likely to increase tensions and produce more violence.

As reports began to grow of the disastrous effects internment was causing through death, destruction, and alienation of the Catholic community, even the newspapers that had initially supported the move began to adopt a more critical position. The *Christian Science Monitor* ran reports and interviews with Catholics who had fled to military camps in the Republic, describing their harsh living conditions and relating the horrors they had been forced to flee. In October 1971, the *New York Times* published reports by Anthony Lewis concluding internment was a devastating mistake that had mortally wounded the Stormont government.[3]

The reports most damaging to the British and Stormont governments began to appear after the first batch of internees were released. Allega-

1. For a detailed analysis of these events see John McGuffin, *Internment* (Dublin: Anvil Books, 1973).

2. *Christian Science Monitor*, 10 August 1971.

3. Anthony Lewis, "Tet In Belfast," *New York Times*, 11 October 1971; also, "Internment Doesn't Work Say the Dead," *New York Times*, 2 January 1972.

tions of brutality reached most newspapers and some began to print interviews with ex-internees describing torture. One of the most influential
of these appeared in a *New York Times Magazine* report by Bernard
Weinraub on conditions inside Long Kesh. The article contained horrify-
ing descriptions of the techniques of interrogation and recorded the testimony of many who had been released.[4]

One of the most important figures in getting information on internment to the American media was Dr. Rona Field, a social psychologist at
California State College in Los Angeles. In December 1971, during an
eighteen-day investigation in Northern Ireland, she interviewed more
than one hundred men who had been interned. Dr. Field maintained that
internees had been subjected to intense psychological torture. She began
publicizing these abuses in the American media. On February 16, 1972,
in her report published in the *Congressional Record*, she concluded:

> Every person in these camps has been subjected to extreme physical
> and psychological torture prior to arrival. None has any assurance of
> release nor of subjection to further torture. They suffer physical pain,
> an aftermath of hallucinations, disorientation and extreme anxiety
> symptoms. Psychological and physical torture have been applied to
> persons as young as 12 and has resulted in severe consequences. These
> effects also indicate that there is a high probability of permanent
> damage for those so treated . . .[5]

Irish-American newspapers expanded on these reports. The *Irish Echo*
contained articles describing how internees had been forced to run over
broken glass and barbed wire while being savaged by army guard dogs.
The *Irish People* printed photographs of the injuries internees had received while in custody. It also reported ghastly descriptions of British
torture techniques.

The stories of torture and ill-treatment were later confirmed not only
by independent inquiry but also by government reports. To Irish Americans they were particularly shocking. Activist groups in the United States
capitalized on the heightened emotions. A series of major demonstrations
outside British consulates and British businesses received coverage on

4. Bernard Weinraub, "Inside the Irish Internment Camps," *New York Times Magazine,*
2 August 1972.

5. Dr. Rona Field quoted in Richard Mansbach, *Northern Ireland: A Half Century of
Partition* (New York: Facts on File Inc., 1973): 145–46. See also, "Psychologist Says Detainees in Ulster Undergo Torture," *New York Times,* 9 January 1972.

the television networks. Noraid organized tours of ex-internees to inform Irish Americans of their experiences in Long Kesh. Frank McGuigan, the first prisoner to escape from detention, appeared on the circuit while he was still on the run. Because of his daring feat he attracted much publicity. His tales of beatings and torture appeared in newspaper interviews throughout America.[6]

By 1972, most newspapers and political commentators in the United States were strongly opposed to internment and correctly acknowledged that the policy was boosting the IRA support network in America. The *Chicago Tribune*, for example, summarized the situation as follows:

> Internment has contributed mightily to the bitterness of the Ulster crisis and served to cast government in the role of oppressor in many minds. Whatever the justification (real or imagined) it is a practice which would not be tolerated in England, or in this country, and is viewed by many Americans as unjust. Anger against internment has in too many cases taken the form of support for the IRA, viewed as heroic freedom fighters by many Americans.[7]

While Noraid benefited from American condemnations of internment, it also successfully exploited a US deportation order against Joe Cahill in September 1971. At this time Cahill was Ulster's most wanted man. Colorful tales of his escapes from the security forces made him an IRA hero, noted for his cockiness and daring. For his audacity, republicans in the United States had christened him the "Emerald Pimpernel."

Noraid wanted to exploit Cahill's hero status by sending him on a four-week, fund-raising tour of New York, Philadelphia, San Francisco, and Los Angeles. When arrangements were completed, he flew from Dublin to New York, arriving at Kennedy airport on September 1, 1971. As Cahill got off the plane, however, he was seized by immigration officials and taken into custody.

Cahill had been issued a four-year visa in November 1970 by the United States consulate in Belfast. At the time of its issuance, he had been a relatively unimportant figure in the eyes of the British authorities. By 1971, however, Cahill's republican activities so alarmed them that diplomats contacted the US State Department. Officials from the British Foreign Office convinced their American counterparts that Cahill's ob-

6. John MacLean, "Irish Prison Camp Horror Described," *Chicago Tribune*, 6 March 1972.

7. *Chicago Tribune*, "Justice and the I.R.A.," 23 April 1972.

jective was to organize a weapons supply network for the Provisionals. As a result of this intervention, Cahill's American visa was canceled while he was flying over the Atlantic.[8]

Cahill was imprisoned overnight and appeared the next morning at a hearing on his visa denial. Noraid had secured the services of noted Irish-American lawyer Frank Durkan. The group had also alerted the media, and they turned the hearings into an exercise in publicity and propaganda. Daily reports appeared in the *Washington Post* and the *New York Times*. During breaks in the proceedings, Cahill gave interviews defending the IRA and the campaign of violence in Ulster.

Cahill was held for one week. During this time, Noraid, the NAIF, and some American civil liberties groups organized pickets and demonstrations outside his cell. He was inundated with messages of support, and his heroic image among Irish-American republicans was enhanced. The whole episode attracted a great deal of media attention; reports and biographies of Cahill appeared in many newspapers.

Irish-American activists were particularly incensed at Cahill's treatment because they felt the State Department was acting as an agent of the British government. In August 1971, Geoffrey Johnson Smith, British undersecretary of defense, had toured America defending the role of the British Army and attacking the IRA. Noraid supporters therefore believed the US government was permitting the British point of view to be heard while stifling the Irish republican perspective.[9]

Joe Cahill was deported on September 8, 1971. The following day, however, Paddy Kennedy, Republican MP at Stormont, arrived in the United States to fulfill his speaking engagements. Political analysts such as John Ridge contend that the publicity generated by the Cahill incident increased sympathy and financial support for the republican cause among Irish-American activists.[10] Following the episode, Tom Enright, former treasurer of the ACIF who left to work in Noraid's Bronx chapter, alleged:

8. For details of the exchanges between the State Department and the British Foreign Office see *The Times* (London), 2 September 1971.

9. See Seán Sheesgreen, "Missing the Story in Northern Ireland," *Chicago Journalism Review* (20 November 1971), 12.

10. John Ridge, "The Irish Northern Aid Committee," in Michael Funchion, ed., *Irish-American Voluntary Organizations* (Westport, Conn.: Greenwood Press, 1983): 202. After this deportation, Cahill made several clandestine trips to the US before he was again apprehended in 1984. He is believed to have been a central figure in the IRA's arms procurement operations in America.

Joe Cahill giving media interviews just before his deportation from New York in September 1971. UPI/BETTMANN

Five years ago an Irish-American friend looked at me as if I was nuts when I told him I was going to picket the British Prime Minister. A year ago they would say, "Here's some money for the cause, but not for guns." But now what a turnabout. We don't have to collect outside the churches and the bars anymore. They're coming to us![11]

The Cahill case and the consequences of internment spurred the formation of another new Irish-American nationalist group, the American Committee for Ulster Justice (ACUJ). It was launched on September 23, 1971, with a seven-thousand-dollar, full-page advertisement in the *New York Times*. Under the heading "The Time Is Running Out," the adver-

11. *New York Times*, 2 December 1971.

tisement listed the group's sponsors and stated it would bring the Northern Ireland problem before the United Nations.[12]

Paul O'Dwyer was the driving force behind the organization. He
had been raised in a republican family from County Mayo, and, like
so many others in the Irish-American network, had come to the US
after the civil war. In 1929 O'Dwyer graduated from law school in
New York, and he soon developed a reputation for defending liberal
causes. In the 1950s, he represented clients accused of communist conspiracy by the House Un-American Activities Committee, and in the
1960s became active in the civil rights movement through the Mis-
sissippi Freedom Democratic Party. Many Irish Americans in New
York resented O'Dwyer's association with "radical causes." Because of
his support for militant trade union leader Mike Quill, some believed
that he was a communist conspirator. When he ran for Congress in the
Washington Heights–Inwood section of Manhattan in the late 1940s, he
received little support from Irish Americans. He was threatened with
physical violence and had to use IRA veterans as bodyguards at his
political rallies.[13]

O'Dwyer maintained a deep interest in his native land. During the
1950s he was a chief organizer of the American League for an Undivided
Ireland. After the 1968 riots in Northern Ireland, he made frequent visits
to the province to investigate civil rights abuses. In July 1971 O'Dwyer
was part of a commission, under Lord Gifford, that strongly criticized the
killing of two Catholic teenagers by British soldiers.

Since Paul O'Dwyer saw the necessity of securing the support of
American politicians for the cause of civil rights in Ulster, the primary
function of the ACUJ was as a lobbying group. It successfully attracted
the support of influential citizens. Among its members were Ramsey
Clark, former attorney general of the United States; Robert Wagner,
former mayor of New York; Charles Desmond, former chief justice of the
State of New York; and Francis Adams, former police commissioner of
New York. The ACUJ membership also boasted Matthew Guinan, president of the Transport Workers Union of America, Thomas Gleason, president of the International Longshoremen's Union, and an array of doctors,
businessmen, congressmen, and journalists.[14]

12. *New York Times*, 23 September 1971.
13. Paul O'Dwyer, *Counsel for the Defense* (New York: Simon and Schuster, 1979), 136.
14. Collected correspondence of Paul O'Dwyer. File number one, section one, at St.
John's University, New York.

From its central office in Manhattan the ACUJ kept congressmen and senators informed of political developments in Northern Ireland. It lobbied State Department officials, in the hope that the Nixon administration would persuade the British to end partition. ACUJ activists also established a news bureau, which aimed at correcting "misinformation" in the US media about Ulster.

The ACUJ, from its formation, adopted a militant nationalist perspective and gave implicit support to the IRA's right to resist "British oppression." Key members of the group were also in Noraid, and the two organizations coordinated anti-British political demonstrations in New York. Paul O'Dwyer and other lawyers associated with the ACUJ provided Noraid with free legal services throughout the 1970s.[15]

Senator Edward Kennedy and Ulster

Despite ACUJ efforts, prospects for involving significant numbers of American politicians in the Ulster conflict did not seem bright. Since 1968 groups of congressmen had periodically issued statements on Northern Ireland. In March 1970, Allard Lowenstein (D, N.Y.), Thomas "Tip" O'Neill (D, Mass.), and Edward Boland (D, Mass.) delivered a strong attack on the Special Powers Act and demanded its removal by the British government. Richard Ottinger (D, N.Y.) further endorsed this call in a policy statement issued on August 14, 1970. But these interventions were uncoordinated and had very little impact in America or Northern Ireland.

Eventually Irish-American groups persuaded some individual congressmen to travel to Ulster and see for themselves the effects of "British injustice." These visits were of limited importance and achieved very little. In early 1972, for example, Congressman Lester Wolff (D, N.Y.) organized an undercover operation to investigate conditions inside Long Kesh. He began cultivating an Irish accent and he assumed the identity of Joe Brannigan. With forged papers Wolff managed to pass through prison security after enduring a humiliating body search. He interviewed a number of internees about ill-treatment and listened to their complaints about conditions in the camp.[16] When Wolff returned to Washington, he

15. See Seán Cronin, "Northern Situation is now a Major Issue in United States," *Irish Times* (Dublin), 22 October 1971.

16. Congress, House, Subcommittee on Europe, *Report of Congressman Lester Wolff on Trip to Northern Ireland: Hearing before the Subcommittee on Europe.* 92nd Cong., 2nd sess., 18 July 1972.

testified before a congressional hearing, but failed to get support for a full-scale US inquiry into internment.[17]

Despite the general lack of impact from the intervention of American politicians in Ulster affairs, one important exception did produce significant results. Senator Edward Kennedy (D, Mass.) was by far the most famous Irish-American politician in the early seventies. Since many believed he was destined for the presidency, ACUJ activists informed him of events in Northern Ireland and encouraged him to speak out on the conflict.

Kennedy had issued a few minor statements on Ulster before the formation of the ACUJ. He supported the NICRA and in 1969 sent a telegram to its leaders praising their courage and endorsing the reforms they sought.[18] In the early seventies, however, the senator became much more active in civil rights issues, not only in America but throughout the world. He stood firmly behind the campaigns for African-American and Native-American rights in the United States. Kennedy also made controversial statements on various atrocities committed in East Pakistan, Biafra, and Vietnam.

In light of Kennedy's increased activities for worldwide human rights, the ACUJ asked him to make a major statement on Ulster. Paul O'Dwyer often contacted the senator to discuss what action he should take. As part of this process, in August 1971 Congressman Hugh Carey (D, N.Y.), a member of the ACUJ, went to Belfast to analyze the situation. On his return, the congressman met with Kennedy and discussed reports of torture during internment. Carey related cases of physical abuse endured by the internees. His information was endorsed by James King, Kennedy's personal aide, who had also collected data on internment during a recent trip to Belfast. These reports finally prompted the senator to speak out against British policy. On October 20, 1971, he issued a congressional resolution calling for a British withdrawal. Hugh Carey sponsored this resolution in the House, while Kennedy and Senator Abraham Ribicoff (D, Conn.) introduced it in the Senate.

The Kennedy/Ribicoff resolution called for the suspension of Stormont and the temporary imposition of direct rule from London. It further proposed that British troops should gradually be removed from the

17. Russell Warren Howe, *The Power Peddlers: How Lobbyists Mold America's Foreign Policy* (New York: Doubleday, 1977), 401.

18. *The Times* (London), 26 June 1969.

province before the calling of an all-party convention. Kennedy suggested that delegates at this convention could discuss their political differences and find a way to reach an agreed solution to the Ulster problem, preferably through a united Ireland.

Speaking passionately in support of the resolution, Kennedy tried to emphasize the parallel between American involvement in Vietnam and British involvement it Ulster. He contended that, like the situation in Vietnam, increased troop deployments to Northern Ireland served only to intensify the problem and made it even harder for the achievement of a long term solution. The senator also found hope in reports that the British public supported a troop withdrawal. He expressed confidence that an antiwar movement would grow and produce the same effects it had in America during the Vietnam War.[19]

One consequence of the Kennedy resolution was an increased use of the Ulster/Vietnam analogy by the American media. In an attempt to give the American public a comprehensive frame of reference, many reporters who had covered the war in Southeast Asia began to emphasize the similarities with the Ulster conflict. Political analyst Ken Ward reported that from 1971 onward the symbolism of Vietnam was in virtually every television newscast in the United States. Newspaper articles predicted that Ulster would become "Britain's Vietnam"—draining its resources, killing its troops, and turning its population against the government. Ward contended that the analogy helped convince Americans that Britain was wrong to be involved in Northern Ireland and should withdraw.[20]

Although the increased use of the Ulster/Vietnam analogy tended to help militant Irish-American groups in their appeals for support, the immediate reaction of journalists and political analysts to the Kennedy resolution was hostile. American editorial opinion generally interpreted it solely as an effort by Kennedy to hold the Irish-American vote and as a ploy in his bid for the presidency. Kennedy still passionately denies this allegation and claims his sole motivation was disgust at internment and British "misrule" in Northern Ireland.[21]

The Kennedy/Ribicoff resolution produced an immediate political controversy in Britain, Ireland, and the United States. Leading politicians

19. *New York Times*, 20 October 1971.

20. Ken Ward, "The U.S. Network News Coverage of Northern Ireland, 1968–79," in Y. Alexander and A. O'Day, eds., *Irish Terrorism* (New York: St. Martin's Press, 1984), 207–9.

21. Senator Edward Kennedy, correspondence with author, 28 March 1989.

issued extremely strong attacks. Unionist Prime Minister Brian Faulkner accused Kennedy of "playing American politics with Ulster people's lives," while British Prime Minister Edward Heath described the senator's remarks as "an ignorant outburst."[22] Both the American embassy in London and the State Department in Washington immediately denied that the Kennedy resolution was official policy. A host of critical editorials appeared in the American press and the British press. The *Daily Telegraph*, for example, commented:

> This speech, full of distortions and cliches, will not help Ulster. But it will no doubt make him a popular figure among the gunmen and saboteurs operating in the province and among the Irish Catholic voters of Massachusetts. . . . In his grotesque outburst about Northern Ireland, Senator Kennedy showed no more regard for the truth than he did after the drowning of Miss Kopechne on Chappaquidick Island. He was an untrustworthy witness then, and he is an untrustworthy guide to the realities of Ulster now.[23]

In the face of these vehement attacks, Kennedy did not attempt to change the congressional resolution. In fact he intensified his criticisms of British policy in Northern Ireland. Sir Edward Compton headed an official inquiry into the ill-treatment of internees, which concluded on November 16, 1971, that the prisoners had not been subjected to "cruelty or brutality." Kennedy sharply attacked the report, calling it a "whitewash" and "sheer hypocrisy." He also launched a strong counterattack against his critics in the American and British presses. In an open letter to the *London Times* he alleged:

> The passionate response directed against my remarks has, I think, a basis of another sort. It is difficult to believe that my proposal would have generated so much fervor if Britain, one of the great symbols of freedom and democracy to us in America, did not have a guilty conscience over Ulster.[24]

In all the statements Senator Kennedy made on Northern Ireland, he tended to ignore IRA violence. The criticisms he raised against the British were very similar to those of militant Irish-American groups.

22. *The Times* (London), 26 October 1971.

23. *Daily Telegraph* (London), 21 October 1971. See also Adam Bukshian, "Ireland on the Potomac," *Spectator*, 6 November 1971.

24. Letter from Kennedy in *The Times* (London), 25 October 1971.

Some sources even allege Kennedy actively assisted the Provisional IRA. Maria McGuire claimed he used his influence in Washington to secure visas for top Provos to enter the United States. She recalled:

> We knew that Edward Kennedy would be quite ready to play Ireland for all it was worth—if he was going to use us, we might as well use him—and we enlisted the help of the prominent civil rights lawyer, Paul O'Dwyer. Whenever there seemed to be a difficulty over obtaining a visa for a member of the Provisionals intending to go to the US to raise funds, we would phone an official of one of the Irish-American associations, Jack McCarthy. McCarthy would contact O'Dwyer; a phone call from Kennedy's office to the American embassy in Dublin would result; and all difficulties would magically disappear.[25]

These claims were never substantiated and Kennedy still maintains that the allegations are false.[26] Nevertheless, the strong criticisms launched by Kennedy against British policies in Ulster, and the resultant publicity, did assist the militant nationalist cause in America. Although Kennedy did not necessarily wish to promote republicanism in the United States, many Irish Americans could not perceive a difference between his statements and the policy positions issued by Noraid. The *Irish People* strongly endorsed the congressional resolution and praised Kennedy's attacks on the British. The political storm unleashed by the senator thus boosted the appeal of extremist groups among Irish-American activists.

Bloody Sunday

The growing support for Irish republicanism in America reached a peak following Bloody Sunday. Worldwide criticism of Britain after the incident led to an unprecedented rise in financial contributions and activism by Noraid. The group effectively exploited the emotions raised by the deaths in Derry to strengthen its organization and recruit previously apathetic Irish Americans.

25. Maria McGuire, *To Take Arms: A Year in the Provisionals* (London: MacMillan, 1973), 36, 108. *New York Times*, 28 November 1972, printed a report that Seán MacStiofain, chief of staff of the PIRA, received a telegram of support for his hunger strike from Robert and Joseph Kennedy. The article alleged that one telegram signed "From Bob Kennedy" said "Up the Republic. Good luck Seán!" The Kennedy family immediately denied this report.

26. Senator Edward Kennedy, correspondence with author, 28 March 1989.

The events of Bloody Sunday began during a demonstration in Derry on January 30, 1972, to protest internment. Trouble started at a meeting place where Bernadette Devlin was due to address the rally. As demonstrators and British paratroopers confronted one another, the officer in command ordered two hundred additional reinforcements. Some of these troops began storming the crowd and arresting protestors, while others took up firing positions. In the midst of the confusion and disorder, live ammunition was fired and thirteen demonstrators were killed. British commanders claimed that over two hundred rounds were fired in their direction during the thirty-minute incident and that they had returned fire only at identifiable targets. The marchers completely denied the army statements, claiming troops had not been provoked and that the deaths were outright murder.

The House of Commons met the next day, and Home Secretary Reginald Maudling announced a judicial inquiry into the incident. He also defended the action taken by the paratroops. Bernadette Devlin, who had earlier been denied permission to give her eyewitness account of the shootings, was so enraged at these remarks she pounced on Maudling—punching, scratching, and kicking the home secretary while cursing him as a "murdering hypocrite." On February 2, 1972, an angry mob in Dublin burned down the British embassy, while the Bloody Sunday killings initiated a hail of criticism throughout the world.

No previous Irish event had received as much media coverage in America as did Bloody Sunday. All three major television networks provided extensive reports, showing footage of Father Edward Daly attempting to get medical aid for one of the victims while brandishing a bloodstained handkerchief and being harassed by soldiers. The incident was front-page news in American national and regional newspapers. Editorial comments ranged from demands that Stormont be suspended to condemnations of the paratroops as murderers.

The *New York Times*, as usual, provided the greatest coverage of the incident. In an editorial on February 1, 1972, it suggested that rule from Westminster was now the only viable option to take. The *Times* did, however, conclude that the demonstrators had deliberately set out to create a confrontation and seriously provoked the troops. It also carried false reports that eight of the dead were IRA suspects and that several had been found with weapons.

These reports in the *New York Times* infuriated Irish-American groups, and they all united in a mass picket of the newspaper's offices on February 5, 1972. Demonstrators handed out leaflets attacking the newspaper's editorial position. A group of delegates later met with editors and argued the newspaper was printing pro-British propaganda.

Most American newspapers, however, were strongly critical of the British paratroops and called for drastic changes in policy. The *Boston Globe*, the *Philadelphia Inquirer*, and the *Baltimore Sun* offered editorials challenging the army's claim that they had been fired upon first. These newspapers also severely criticized internment and suggested the only way toward a solution of the Ulster problem was the unification of Ireland. One of the strongest editorials was in the *St. Louis Globe-Democrat*, which stated:

> The British government must stand before the court of world opinion as guilty of massacre in Northern Ireland, or at the very least plead failure to maintain law and order in the tragic enclave it pretends to rule . . . Sundays' bloody slaughter in Londonderry, in which 13 unarmed civilians were slain by British paratroops, is inexcusable. Disciplined soldiers do not run amok with automatic weapons, mowing down little children because a few bullies on the fringe of a crowd have thrown rocks. . . . Mistakenly, the English have abandoned all concept of law. They have rounded up and detained hundreds of people without charge. . . . When will the British learn that Ireland should be one country—with justice for all.[27]

The Irish-American press naturally contained the severest criticisms of the British paratroops. The *Advocate* described Bloody Sunday as "Ulster's Sharpville" while the *Irish Echo* and the *Irish People* condemned British troops as "Savage Murderers." The various editors of these publications all reported they were inundated with telephone calls from furious Irish Americans asking how they could help the IRA.[28]

When Paul O'Dwyer received news of Bloody Sunday, he immediately contacted prominent members of the ACUJ, encouraging them to pressure their political representatives to condemn the killings. This grassroots activism proved quite successful. On February 2, 1972, a group of senators led by James Buckley (R, N.Y.) strongly attacked the paratroops' actions in Derry and called on the United States to urge Britain to withdraw its troops from Northern Ireland. Mayor Richard Daley of Chicago caused an uproar in the British media when he compared the parachute regiment to

27. *St. Louis Globe-Democrat*, 2 February 1972.
28. *Advocate* (New York), 5 February 1972.

Nazi stormtroopers and announced he would send $75,000 to the families of the victims in Derry.[29] When a march was held in Newry on February 6 to protest the "Derry Massacre," Congressman Mario Biaggi (D, N.Y.) participated as a sign of disgust at the atrocity.[30]

The Irish government encouraged these American denunciations of the Bloody Sunday killings and tried to get the Nixon administration to pressure Britain. On February 2, 1972, Foreign Minister Patrick Hillery traveled to the United States and met with Secretary of State William Rogers. The strong anglophile tradition in the State Department, coupled with the fact that the Irish government had failed to develop a network of influential political connections in Washington, meant that this diplomatic initiative was doomed to failure from the outset. Rogers maintained that the Ulster crisis was Britain's "internal affair" and, in light of the cold war alliance, refused to contemplate any action that might damage the Anglo-American "special relationship."

Despite the refusal of the Nixon government to get embroiled in Ulster, American politicians continued to criticize British policy. The climax of this campaign came when the US Foreign Affairs Subcommittee on Europe held hearings on the Kennedy/Ribicoff resolution between February 28 and March 1, 1972. Senator Kennedy opened the testimony with his previously stated demand for the dissolution of Stormont and the unification of Ireland. He also criticized the Widgery Report, the official British investigation into Bloody Sunday that largely exonerated the paratroops. The senator extended his Vietnam analogy by drawing a parallel between Bloody Sunday and the My Lai massacre:

> Just as the injustice of internment was compounded by the torture of the men imprisoned, so the slaughter at Londonderry is being compounded by the arbitrary limits of the scope of the inquiry being held by Lord Widgery. Just as Ulster is Britain's Vietnam, so Bloody Sunday is Britain's My Lai.[31]

29. *Chicago Tribune*, 1 February 1972. Father Edward Daly, the priest who had been shown on television during the Bloody Sunday incident, received most of this money and gave it to the families of the victims. Bishop Edward Daly, information supplied to author, 11 October 1990.

30. Richard Mansbach, *Northern Ireland*, 162. On 18 November 1971, Biaggi had introduced a bill to provide for 25,000 emergency refugee visas for those trying to escape the violence in Northern Ireland.

31. Congress, House, Committee on Europe, *Northern Ireland: Hearings Before the Committee on Foreign Affairs, Subcommittee on Europe.* 92nd Cong., 2nd sess., (28 Febru-

Thirteen congressmen followed Kennedy and issued statements universally critical of British policy in Ulster. Another twenty-two congressmen, who could not be at the hearings to testify, submitted written statements condemning everything from the Widgery Report to the Orange Order.

Just before the Congressional Hearings began, more than two hundred members of the ACUJ traveled to Washington to lobby for political support for the Kennedy/Ribicoff resolution. During the proceedings, representatives from Noraid, the NAIF, and the Republican Clubs submitted statements espousing their political perspective. They also paid for a number of Irish politicians and activists to come to Washington and give testimony. These included Father Dennis Faul, Father Edward Daly, Dr. Conn McCluskey, and Austin Currie. Father Daly was particularly effective. He conducted a whirlwind publicity tour describing the events of Bloody Sunday and presenting first-hand testimony that the paratroops had fired indiscriminately on the protestors in Derry.[32]

There were many political differences between the Irish and the Irish-American groups. However, they managed to present a united front during the hearings by concentrating their attacks on British policy. While the proceedings again failed to shift the Nixon administration from its position of nonintervention, the hearings were widely reported in the American media and served to publicize the militant nationalist perspective.

From the beginning of the Ulster Troubles, the Roman Catholic Church in America had generally remained silent on the issue. The Bloody Sunday killings changed this and the church got more actively involved in charitable relief work for the province. Some clergy even joined with American politicians in condemning the British government. Masses were held all over the country for the thirteen victims of Bloody Sunday. In New York, Terence Cardinal Cooke issued a statement that was read at all services calling on parishioners to "pray for all those who have been imprisoned in Ulster, for civil rights reforms, and for new and far-reaching

---

ary to 1 March 1972): 6. Kennedy was supported in his attack on the Widgery Report by Professor Samuel Dash, a lecturer in law at Georgetown University. In late February 1972, Dash traveled to Derry in an attempt to collect the evidence of people who were present when British paratroops opened fire. From his research, the professor strongly criticized the conclusions of Lord Widgery and accused the army of murder. See *Washington Post*, 25 April 1972.

32. Bishop Edward Daly, information supplied to author, 11 October 1990.

initiatives."[33] The cardinal, along with Archbishop Humberto Medeiros of Boston, also announced the creation of an Irish Relief Fund to send cash to the victims of violence in Ulster. Although these church leaders were careful not to endorse republicanism, a number of priests openly sympathized with the IRA and allowed Noraid to use parish buildings for fundraising events.[34]

Three thousand worshipers were present at St. Patrick's Cathedral in New York for the largest Bloody Sunday service. Irish Foreign Minister Hillery attended, along with many prominent Irish-American politicians, businessmen, and trade union leaders. During the sermon, former president of Fordham University, the Reverend Robert Gannon, strongly condemned the Bloody Sunday killings as "vicious and unprovoked." Father Gannon told the congregation:

> British bungling has made matters worse. Only stupid soldiers and stupid politicians would attempt the pacification of a country in 1972 by imprisonment without trial, torture of prisoners for information, and by hysterical shooting of innocent civilians who dared to march in their own ghetto.[35]

These critical reactions, coupled with the extensive coverage given to Bloody Sunday, greatly increased Irish-American concern and activism. Noraid and the other militant groups channeled growing outrage into anti-British demonstrations. In the first few days after the killings in Derry, republican activists organized protest marches outside British government offices and business premises in most cities on the East Coast. However, these demonstrations were not well attended, because of severe winter weather in the first few days of February. Also, because Bloody Sunday was a spontaneous incident, republicans had not made the usual preparations to publicize and coordinate a large protest.

Nevertheless, after the first disappointing efforts, militant nationalists began to synchronize their activities and organize much more effective demonstrations. At one protest outside the British consulate in New York, a mini-riot developed after police tried to arrest a man for burning a Union Jack. One group invaded the office of the British consul general,

33. *New York Daily News*, 7 February 1972.

34. Some of the more prominent priests associated with Irish-American republicanism include Father Maurice Burke, Father Pat Moloney in New York, and Father Walter Martin of Our Lady of Good Voyage chapel in Boston.

35. *Irish Echo* (New York), 12 February 1972.

John Ford, and destroyed official documents. The British ambassador in
Washington was inundated with abusive phone calls and death threats
from Irish activists. In San Francisco, Noraid demonstrators pelted the
British consulate with bricks and dumped thirteen symbolic coffins outside the entrance. The American media covered all these incidents and
were further attracted by the presence of rock star John Lennon at Bloody
Sunday demonstrations in New York.[36]

A Labor Committee for Justice in Northern Ireland formed to coordinate the anti-British activities of the Transport Worker's Union and the
International Longshoremen's Union. On March 1, 1972, both unions
combined to impose a twenty-four-hour embargo on the unloading and
transportation of British goods. Other groups handed out leaflets at department stores urging customers not to buy British products.

The campaign of public demonstrations peaked during the St. Patrick's
Day parades throughout the United States in 1972. In New York, where
the parade had traditionally been nonpolitical, the theme was "Get England Out of Ireland." One band from Iona College in New Rochelle, an
Irish Christian Brothers College, was told it could not march because it
had participated in a concert given by the British Army's Grenadier Guards.

Noraid, the NAIF, ACUJ, and Irish Republican Clubs formed a large
segment of the New York parade and chanted pro-IRA slogans while
marching up Fifth Avenue. Many participants, including Mayor Lindsay,
wore black armbands, while others carried placards displaying photographs of the thirteen victims. The whole event was widely reported on
both sides of the Atlantic and was presented as yet another publicity victory for militant nationalism.

To add to their successes at home during the early spring of 1972,
Irish-American republicans further benefited from events in Ulster. After
Bloody Sunday the IRA greatly intensified its campaign of bombing and
shooting. The violence was maintained at such an incessant pitch that it
became an important factor in persuading the British government to suspend Stormont and impose direct rule from Westminster.

36. In 1972 John Lennon recorded the album "Some Time in New York City," which included the tracks, "Sunday Bloody Sunday" and "Luck of the Irish." Both songs attacked the
British presence in Ulster; all royalties from the album were donated to the NICRA. Later in
the year, Lennon tried to hold a concert in Belfast to raise money for the dependents of internees, but drug charges against him in Britain prevented from doing this. Recent reports
also allege that Lennon directly contributed to the IRA through groups in New York; see
Anne Caborn, "Lennon's Secret Cash to the I.R.A.," *Today*, 9 December 1988.

The escalating disorder in Ulster forced General Sir Harry Tuzo, commander of British forces, to conclude that the IRA could be defeated only by the transfer of all powers of law and order from Stormont to the British Parliament. As the intensity of violence in Ulster increased, Prime Minister Edward Heath became convinced that Tuzo's analysis was correct.

On March 22, 1972, Heath summoned Brian Faulkner to London and told him of Westminster's desire for complete control of security forces and the courts in Northern Ireland. Faulkner naturally refused to accept this demand. The British prime minister responded by proroguing Stormont and transferring all its powers to Westminster. To control and implement British policy in the province, Heath created a new post, secretary of state for Northern Ireland, and appointed William Whitelaw as its first holder.

The suspension of Stormont, however, did not lead the IRA to slacken its military operations. Attacks reached unprecedented heights and gradually produced a war weariness in the nationalist ghettoes. Residents began to exert pressure on the Provos to ease their campaign and work toward some kind of truce with the British. While this pressure mounted, William Whitelaw was considering all possible options in the search for a settlement in Ulster.

On June 13, 1972, the Provisionals responded to the wishes of their supporters and announced they would cease operations for a week if Whitelaw agreed to talk with them. Although the secretary of state publicly rejected the offer, secret contacts almost immediately occurred between the Provos and British officials. Following these meetings, the IRA announced a cessation of its military operations beginning June 26, 1972. The British then informed the Provisionals that the security forces would reduce activity in republican areas.

As part of the truce, a team of IRA leaders flew to London on July 7 to meet with Whitelaw. They warned him that the cease-fire would last only if the British government announced a declaration of withdrawal and an amnesty for political prisoners.[37] The British negotiating team said they would reply to the IRA proposal in one week. But on July 9, an in-

---

37. For an analysis of the truce, see Tim Pat Coogan, *The I.R.A.* (Dublin: Fontana, 1981), 490–96. One of the first indications that the IRA was seeking a cease-fire came during a "peace mission" by American evangelist Billy Graham. During a crusade to achieve Christian reconciliation, Graham met with IRA leaders and told a subsequent news conference they wanted talks with the British. Reported in *Los Angeles Times*, 3 June

cident involving the relocation of Catholic families in the Lenadoon
estate in West Belfast led to the resumption of hostilities between republicans and the British Army.[38]

The events between March and mid-July of 1972 marked a watershed
in the prestige of the IRA. Its leaders believed their campaign of violence
had toppled the Stormont regime and forced the British into negotiations.
The IRA's success helped to inspire American republican groups. Noraid
activists were greatly encouraged by the fact that British officials had negotiated with representatives of physical force nationalism for the first
time since the Anglo-Irish Treaty. They redoubled their work for the
cause, as many believed that an IRA victory was imminent and that a
united Ireland would soon be achieved.

From the beginning of 1971 to the end of spring 1972, militant Irish-
American groups were able to increase their support and effectiveness.
The introduction of internment, torture of detainees, and Bloody Sunday
enabled republicans to present Ulster Catholics as victims of brutal
British oppression. A significant number of Irish-American activists were
convinced that the only way to help was to support the IRA.

All militant organizations reported substantial growth in the first six
months of 1972. The Irish Republican Clubs claimed new chapters in
New York, Boston, and San Francisco. Hugh Murray, a member of the
N.A.I.F. executive committee, claimed that his organization was inundated with financial donations after Bloody Sunday. The group sent
$2,000 to NICRA in February, hired three fulltime officials, and began
producing a monthly newspaper.[39]

Journalists who reported on Irish-American affairs increased their
coverage of developments after Bloody Sunday. Almost all the articles
they produced supported claims that militants were receiving increased
support from Irish-American activists throughout the United States. In a
detailed analysis of Irish republican activity on the East Coast, Frank
Donovan of the *Washington Post* concluded:

> The shooting deaths of thirteen Catholics by British troops in Lon-
> donderry swept away the apathy that Irish Americans have had toward

1972. See also "He Put it Over With Love: Billy Graham in Ireland," *Christianity Today* 16
(July 1972), 951–54.

38. For details, see Patrick Bishop and Eamonn Mallie, *The Provisional I.R.A.* (London:
Heinemann Press, 1987), 179.

39. Hugh Murray, "The Green and Red Unbending: The National Association for Irish
Freedom from 1972–1975," *Journal of Ethnic Studies* (Summer 1975), 13.

their native land. In Boston and New York, where there are large populations of Irish Americans, the money is beginning to pour in and rival rebel factions are beginning to draw together for the first time in years.[40]

Noraid was the principal beneficiary of increased Irish-American concern for events in Northern Ireland. In *The American Connection*, journalist Jack Holland reported that, from the group's formation until August 1971, it had five chapters in New York with an estimated total of two thousand members. There were eleven Noraid chapters in other cities from Buffalo to St. Louis. After the introduction of internment, Noraid expanded rapidly and reached a peak after the collapse of Stormont. By July of 1972, Michael Flannery claimed there were over one hundred chapters with a combined membership of 80,000.[41] Irish diplomats and most nonpartisan observers contend that this figure is greatly inflated and estimate Noraid had between seventy and eighty chapters by 1972 and around seven to ten thousand members and supporters.[42]

In 1971, Noraid was forced to register under the Foreign Agents Registration Act (1938). It began to file six-month reports on its finances and activities. Although the validity of these documents has constantly been challenged by the Justice Department, they do give an indication of Noraid's rise up to 1972. In the six month period ending on July 29, 1971, just before the introduction of internment, it spent a total of $16,075, of which $11,500 was sent to Belfast. From August 1971 to January 1972, the group spent $140,837 and reported delivering $128,099 specifically to Joe Cahill and veteran republican Joe Clarke. This money was carried to Ireland by couriers who took cash packages of up to $11,000. Noraid's largest single fund-raising effort came after Bloody Sunday in the period

40. Frank Donovan, "Derry Killings End U.S. Apathy," *Washington Post*, 16 March 1972.

41. Reported in Michael McKinley, "Lavish Generosity: The American Dimension of International Support for the Provisional I.R.A., 1968–1983," *Conflict Quarterly* 7, no. 2 (Spring 1987): 25.

42. Roger Williams and Jack Holland both agree that there were seventy Noraid chapters by 1972, but an article in the *New York Times*, 17 July 1972, tended toward Flannery's figure and said there were ninety-three units. It is difficult to check the accuracy of these figures, because Noraid did not divulge information about its chapters or give official figures on its national membership at this time. The weekly circulation of *Irish People* (New York) was about 10,000 copies, and this probably marked the solid core of Noraid membership.

ending July 29, 1972. It spent $25,440 on its US operations and sent $312,700 to Ireland.[43]

Ideology and Structure of Noraid

Analysts who have studied the rise of Noraid in the early seventies conclude that a significant number of new recruits were third- or fourth-generation Irish Americans. In 1981, Andrew Greeley suggested this was a consequence of a desire to find an identity in America's pluralistic society. He says that decades of economic success had left many Irish Americans alienated from their ethnic roots. Greeley contends that involvement with nationalist groups such as Noraid gave them an opportunity to express their cultural identity and achieve a sense of solidarity.[44]

Professor John McCarthy of Fordham University later refined aspects of Greeley's thesis by suggesting that support for militant nationalism reflected a reaction to the declining Irish dominance of certain urban neighborhoods and occupations. He contends that modern Irish-American nationalism is a reflection of a superiority complex over more recent immigrants who have encroached on traditional areas of Irish control. According to McCarthy, Noraid attracts its support from Irish Americans

> whose dominance in certain urban neighborhoods and labor markets, like public transportation, construction, the police, and public utilities has disappeared. They are wound up about Northern Ireland not so much by a close understanding of it, but as a badge of Irish identification necessary amidst the pressure of various other activist ethnic groupings in the United States.[45]

Journalist Pete Hamill wrote a number of articles on New York's Irish community in the early seventies and found evidence for both Greeley's and McCarthy's views. Hamill distinguished between an "Old Irish" group and the "New Irish." He characterizes the "Old Irish" as mostly middle-class Irish Americans who sustained their sentimentality for Ireland in a cosmetic way by organizing corned beef and cabbage dinner parties and drinking green beer on St. Patrick's Day. The "New Irish"

43. FARA reports No. 2239 to 29 July 1972.
44. Andrew Greeley, *The Irish Americans* (New York: Harper and Row, 1981), 98–99.
45. John P. McCarthy, *Dissent from Irish-America* (New York: University of America Press, 1993), 89.

were mostly young, third-generation Irish Americans rebelling against the meaningless traditions they had grown up with and also against their socioeconomic success in America. Hamill contends that this group brought a new vibrancy to the New York Irish centered around political agitation for Ulster's Catholic minority. Involvement in nationalist groups gave them a cause through which they felt they could do something positive for Ireland. This political activism also generated a renewed interest in Irish cultural traditions and history.[46]

In an extensive 1973 analysis of Noraid in Philadelphia, Mike Mallowe also found that younger, third-generation Irish Americans were getting involved in the republican cause. Unlike Pete Hamill, however, Mallowe minimized divisions between generations of Irish Americans and said all age groups were uniting behind Noraid. He showed that parents were joining their children in republican activities because, "they were discovering a more meaningful way to spend their week-end than on the golf course or at the country club."[47]

Like Pete Hamill's study in New York, Mallowe concluded Noraid had led a full-fledged Irish renaissance in Philadelphia. This involved not only political activism over Ulster but a revival of interest in Irish music, literature, and the Gaelic language. He asserted:

> The civil war in Ulster has cut across Irish class differences in Philadelphia and it is rapidly becoming impossible these days to remain a self-respecting Irish-American and insulate one's self against the forces that are re-shaping the community. . . . There is little doubt

46. Pete Hamill, "Irish America—Origins and Irony," *Irish Voice* (New York), 19 March 1988. Richard Brown, in *I Am of Ireland*, 79–80, offers some insight into the reasons why Irish Americans became involved in the Northern Ireland problem. He joined an Irish republican group in New York and eventually participated in a gunrunning scheme to the IRA. He says he got involved as a form of rebellion against his comfortable middle-class existence and the lack of ethnic identity it brought. He says, "I took up the Irish cause against the respectability of raising a family and the conformity of an office routine in a job I did not like. . . . I knew little about Ireland but I had a romantic idea that by declaring myself an Irishman I was somehow asserting myself against the fact I was doing well in a meaningless position."

Some Irish Americans like P. Michael O'Sullivan went to Northern Ireland and wrote about the IRA. In *Patriot Graves: Resistance in Ireland*, he described taking part in IRA activities and he actually photographed some operations. The book was dedicated to C Company of the Belfast Brigade and was naturally very pro-republican.

47. Mike Mallowe, "My Life and Times With The I.R.A.," *Philadelphia Magazine* 64, no. 3 (3 March 1973): 108.

that their [Noraid] organizing and cajoling has renewed the passion of being self-consciously and belligerently Irish.[48]

Mallowe's research also discovered interesting differences between Philadelphia's six Noraid chapters based on class and politics. The oldest and largest Noraid unit had its offices in the Philadelphia Irish Center. Mallowe described it as cosmopolitan and composed of Irish Protestants as well as Catholics. Its members tended to be ambivalent toward the IRA's bombing campaign and emphasized that its activities were for charitable work in Northern Ireland. The Main Line unit adopted a similar political stance and comprised mostly doctors, teachers, lawyers, and other professionals. In contrast, the Olney and Upper Darby units were almost entirely working class and developed a reputation for uncompromising support for the IRA and involvement in gunrunning to Ireland.

Despite the significant rise in support for Irish-American republican groups between 1970 and 1972, it must be emphasized that those who became involved in the Ulster conflict were only a very small minority. Irish Americans are not a homogenous ethnic group; they are divided along class, political, generational, and geographic lines. It was still the case that the vast majority of the forty-four million Americans who now claim some Irish descent remained uninterested and disengaged.[49]

It was also true that, despite the increased participation of younger, third-generation Irish Americans, militant nationalist groups were still dominated by those born in Ireland. Although the support from third-generation Irish Americans injected new life into Noraid and rejuvenated its fund raising, the Irish-born activists provided the dedication and commitment basic to the group's success.

Irish-born activists in Noraid were generally working-class immigrants who had resisted assimilation into American society. Some gravitated toward nationalist groups in the United States because they provided a social network with which they were familiar. Others had strong republican connections and naturally continued their support for the IRA.

48. Ibid., 105.

49. In the 1970 census, 16 million Americans said their parents or grandparents were born in Ireland. In 1980, 40.7 million claimed their ethnic background was Irish. It is also important to note that both census data and reports from the National Opinion Research Center have shown that the majority of those claiming Irish heritage are Protestants. See Barry Kosmin, *One Nation Under God: Religion in Contemporary American Society* (New York: Harmony Books, 1993).

Old republicans who had been forced to leave Ireland after the Civil War constituted a very important segment of Noraid's membership. Many IRA men who immigrated to the United States in the 1920s and 1930s retained an extreme bitterness because of their treatment by the Free State government. They rose to prominent positions within the major Irish-American fraternal societies and maintained a burning commitment to republicanism, which they passed on to their children and grandchildren.

In the late sixties, when the Troubles erupted in Ulster, many of these old republicans took the lead in establishing support groups for the Catholic community and were instrumental in the formation of Noraid. The militant views of this generation are characterized by one eighty-year-old veteran from Mayo, who gave the following perspective on the Provisional IRA's campaign of violence:

> That pack of self-righteous jackals that ruled with fascist tyranny in Belfast for 50 years deserves every bit of blasting that they get. Not only should the English soldiers be shot on sight, but their Orange dogs into the bargain. If there is no way to cripple that black crowd, then the whole of Ulster should be laid waste.[50]

The staunch views of these old IRA veterans were also dominant among the small number of Catholics from Northern Ireland who immigrated to the United States in the 1950s and 1960s. Many were forced to leave because of reduced employment opportunities, which they directly attributed to Unionist discrimination. The burning hatred these immigrants held, because of their experience of the sectarian system in Ulster, made them natural recruits for Noraid. They were later joined by Catholics who left Northern Ireland as a result of the present Troubles. Many brought with them direct experience of loyalist intimidation and harassment by the security forces. Some had links with the Provisional IRA and continued their republican activities in the US.

Another segment of Noraid supporters was composed of post–World War II immigrants from the Irish Republic. A significant number became involved in Irish-American fraternal societies because of the social activities they provided. Some supported Noraid, not because they were deeply committed republicans, but because the group provided another opportunity to socialize with their fellow countrymen. There were others,

50. Quote from Peter F in Dennis Clark, *Irish Blood*, 54.

however, particularly from the border counties, who came from families in which there was a long republican tradition. These people became associated with Noraid because of a firm commitment to the republican cause for which their relatives had fought and died.

Each Noraid chapter contained members from all these various groups and usually had between twenty-five and fifty persons. Within each unit, a small group of five to ten individuals made up the active nucleus. They were almost entirely Irish born, but not necessarily from Northern Ireland. A typical example of these hard-core activists is Maureen O'Looney, an immigrant from County Mayo who now lives in Chicago. She was born into a staunchly nationalist family and immigrated to the United States in the 1950s. O'Looney became involved in many of Chicago's Irish fraternal societies and began selling Irish products at her "Shamrock Imports" store.

When the Ulster Troubles erupted, O'Looney helped form a chapter of the ACIF and used her house to entertain visiting civil rights activists. In 1970, she amalgamated her ACIF chapter with Noraid, because she felt the time was right to support more direct action against the British. Since then, O'Looney has used her import store as a center for republican activities in Chicago. She organizes Noraid fund raisers; hosts Sinn Féin and IRA activists passing through the city; distributes the *Irish People* and republican literature; and broadcasts information about Noraid activities on her local radio program.[51]

It was activists like O'Looney who, through their dedication and unending work for the republican cause, formed the backbone of Noraid. They kept the organization alive when it experienced a steep decline in the mid and late seventies. O'Looney and others like her maintained their fierce loyalty while other, less committed members, who had joined in the emotional wave created by internment and Bloody Sunday, withdrew their support.

51. Maureen O'Looney, interview with author, 21 July 1990.

CHAPTER 4

CHALLENGES TO IRISH-AMERICAN

REPUBLICANISM: From Direct Rule to Formation

of the Irish National Caucus, 1972–1975

◆

In the early 1970s, the IRA's ability to wage a sustained campaign of violence against the British security forces attracted Irish-American activists to revolutionary nationalism. These militants saw the Provisionals as heirs of the 1916 heroes, guided by the same principles and objectives. Yet following the suspension of Stormont, the new British administration began a series of far-sighted political initiatives. These policies attracted substantial support from moderate nationalists in Ireland and also received strong endorsement in America. Consequently, support for the Provos began to decline on both sides of the Atlantic. This process was further accentuated by the IRA's campaign of bombing civilian targets. The carnage of these attacks led many Irish Americans to reassess their image of rebel gunmen.

The Stormont government's civil rights record had been a focal point of nationalist discontent for decades. Internment and the events of

Bloody Sunday only served to increase condemnations of the regime. In America, this translated into sharp criticisms of the British government for not curbing the abuses of the provincial administration. American politicians and leading newspapers supported the direct transfer of power from Stormont to Westminster. Press comments at the time are epitomized by this March 1972 editorial in the *Philadelphia Inquirer*:

> Politically threatening as it may be, it is far past the time that Heath should have moved to suspend the Ulster parliament. . . . An end to internment and a beginning of real political equality seem absolutely minimal necessities. The violence is clearly self-regenerating, and muddling and hesitant responding have contributed. The alternative to courage in Westminster is civil war in Ulster.[1]

Hostile international opinion toward Britain's failure to take decisive action against Stormont increased pressure on the Heath administration. This seems to have been at least one of the factors that finally persuaded the British prime minister to impose direct rule in March 1972. In a 1984 article in *Irish Studies*, Adrian Guelke accepted that internal factors, such as the escalating violence after Bloody Sunday, were of primary importance in explaining Britain's decision to suspend Stormont. He did, however, conclude that the Heath administration was also influenced by hostile opinion in America, especially the constant criticism emanating from Senator Edward Kennedy.[2]

The assumption of full governmental control of Northern Ireland by the Heath administration produced a significant change in the American press perception of British policy. Direct rule was almost universally praised as a positive and necessary step toward the achievement of a political solution. The *San Francisco Chronicle* described Britain's move as one of "courageous responsibility," while the *Washington Post* held that "rule from London is a promise to the Roman Catholics of fair treatment that they never got from Stormont."[3] The *Los Angeles Times* commented:

---

1. *Philadelphia Inquirer*, 24 March 1972.

2. Adrian Guelke, "The American Connection to the Northern Ireland Conflict," *Irish Studies in International Affairs* 1, no. 4 (1984): 29.

3. Editorials in *San Francisco Chronicle*, 28 March, and *Washington Post*, 27 March 1972.

Whatever the past sins of the British government, London is trying, decently and honestly, to tip the scales to the side of peace and justice. It deserves the world's sympathy and understanding in that enterprise.[4]

In the US Congress, former critics of British policy strongly praised the initiative. Senators Edward Kennedy and Abraham Ribicoff commended the British government for implementing an important element of their congressional resolution. In New York, the ACUJ similarly welcomed the suspension of Stormont and applauded the actions of Prime Minister Heath.

The Sunningdale Agreement

After the establishment of direct rule, the new secretary of state, William Whitelaw, began searching for political options to reach a settlement in Ulster. His abortive negotiations with the Provisionals in July 1972 convinced him that the best way forward was to work for a political formula that would gain the support of constitutional nationalists and moderate unionists.

On the nationalist side, Whitelaw concentrated on winning over the SDLP, which had persisted in a boycott of talks with the British because of the continued use of internment. He also appealed to former Stormont Prime Minister Brian Faulkner and his moderate supporters. After negotiations and concessions from both sides, the British government published a White Paper on March 20, 1973. This document proposed a seventy-eight member parliament, elected by proportional representation, which would choose a prime minister and cabinet. The cabinet was to include a proportion of members from the leading opposition parties. As a link between the new parliament and the government of Ireland, the White Paper recommended the establishment of a Council of Ireland.

The SDLP and moderate unionists cautiously welcomed the White Paper, while the hard-line loyalists of Ian Paisley and William Craig rejected it as a British "sell out" to nationalists. The IRA similarly dismissed the proposal and maintained its uncompromising position that only a complete British withdrawal would bring a solution.

4. *Los Angeles Times*, 27 March 1972.

Following elections for the new assembly on June 13, 1973, the SDLP, moderate unionists, and the nonsectarian Alliance Party began to discuss formation of a government. These parties finalized details of a power-sharing executive during talks held at the British Civil Service training college in Sunningdale, England. The three Ulster parties were joined at this conference by representatives of the Irish and British governments. After extensive negotiations, the parties finally reached agreement. They announced that a power-sharing government would assume office in Northern Ireland on January 1, 1974.

In the United States, the power-sharing initiative attracted sustained media coverage. It was presented as a momentous breakthrough and a great step toward peace. The new governmental system received lavish editorial praise for its ability to balance carefully the aspirations of Ulster's two communities. Newspapers singled out William Whitelaw for his great political diplomacy and skill, while commentators presented the British government as a positive force for reconciliation.

Reports on US network television complemented this praise from the American press. Newscasters couldn't resist a story in which previously vicious and implacable enemies seemed to be caught up in a tide of moderation and collaboration. The major American networks carried reports that reinforced the assumption that political dialogue was at last providing hope for a peaceful solution to Ulster's problems. This belief was also supported by numerous American politicians, who competed with each other in the amount of praise they heaped on the Sunningdale agreement.

The power-sharing initiative deeply concerned Irish-American republicans. Media attention devoted to the agreement led to wide exposure of the SDLP's political program. It was the first time that many Irish-American activists realized there was an alternative to the republican creed. In contrast to the IRA activities in 1973–74, which seemed moribund and locked into senseless violence, the SDLP offered a peaceful alternative that was achieving significant results.

In April 1974, John Hume, one of the leaders of the SDLP and minister for commerce in the power-sharing government, conducted a ten-day tour of the United States. He gave a whirlwind series of press conferences and speeches to Irish-American organizations in order to promote the new government in Ulster. He recalls that the reception he received was extremely enthusiastic. Large numbers of Irish Americans expressed their support for power sharing and the efforts of constitutional nationalists.[5]

The initial euphoric praise of the Sunningdale agreement, however, ignored the degree of suspicion with which many Ulster Protestants viewed the Council of Ireland. When the new executive convened in January 1974, the Council became a rallying point for their opposition. Loyalists felt that it was too powerful and would be used to increase the influence of the Irish government in Ulster. Opposition grew until a split developed in the ranks of the Faulkner's moderate unionists. An alliance of anti-executive parties formed to contest the British general election of February 28, 1974. This coalition of hard-line loyalists won 51 percent of the votes and eleven out of twelve seats at Westminster.

The election result greatly encouraged the opponents of power sharing, and on May 15, 1974, they organized a strike designed to cripple the new executive. A coalition of loyalist trade unionists, politicians, and para-militaries called the Ulster Workers Council (UWC), began running the strike. The UWC concentrated its efforts on the province's key utilities and industries, particularly the power stations. Soon gangs of loyalists in paramilitary uniforms took to the streets to erect barricades and threaten those who carried on working. By May 20, they had cut essential power supplies and brought Ulster to a standstill.

Faced by this massive show of resistance, Brian Faulkner began frantic negotiations to dilute the powers of the Council of Ireland. This produced a series of conflicts with nationalist members of the executive who wanted to maintain or perhaps extend the Council's area of jurisdiction. In the midst of this political impasse, Faulkner resigned on May 27, 1974, and the power-sharing executive collapsed.

In the United States, newspaper editorials strongly condemned the loyalist strike and the demise of the executive. The *Boston Globe* attacked loyalist "intransigence" and "narrow mindedness," while the *Chicago Tribune* described the strikers as "idiots."[6] Irish-American republicans, however, greeted the collapse with some relief and lost no time in using it to reinforce their assertion that the only viable solution was a British withdrawal. Noraid and the NAIF emphasized the fact that troops were not used against loyalist strikers. They concluded that this showed the British would always succumb to Orange intimidation.

5. John Hume, interview with author, 3 January 1989.
6. *Chicago Tribune*, 29 May 1974.

IRA Bomb Attacks

Any benefit militant nationalists hoped to get from the collapse of power sharing was undermined by IRA militarism. In 1972, the Provos began a campaign of bombing "commercial targets" as part of the escalation of violence after Bloody Sunday. Due to incompe- tence and bloody mindedness, many of these bombings resulted in civilian casualties. The most devastating attack of the campaign came on Bloody Friday, July 21, 1972. The Provisionals planted twenty-two bombs in Belfast's city center, which killed nine people and left others horribly mutilated.

The initial reaction of the American media to these bombings was one of shock and horror at the savage disregard for civilian casualties. An editorial in the *Dallas Morning News* typified the comments of many newspapers:

> The latest demonstration of calculated, cold blooded beastliness in Belfast is such that it must shock even the most news-jaded American. Any man who claims to be civilized must look on the bloody work and wonder about the future of the human race. . . . There are no words to express the revulsion that such an act provokes. . . . Certainly there is no justice here on earth that can deal with its perpetrators. It was an act made more monstrous by the fact that it was committed not by monsters but by men who claim to be fighting for justice, freedom and tolerance.[7]

Such expressions of horror at the maiming and killing of innocent civilians soon developed into severely critical attacks against the IRA. Throughout the summer and autumn of 1972, each act of IRA violence was greeted by editorials that vehemently castigated the organization. The *San Francisco Chronicle*, for example, characterized the IRA as "a cowardly band of terrorists who bomb pubs, hotels, and barracks, shoot down men at night in the quiet of their own homes and beat up women."[8]

Incessant attacks against the IRA in the US media caused great alarm to militant nationalists. Provo bombing atrocities alienated potential sympathizers in the Irish-American community and undermined the fervor for republicanism that had grown after Bloody Sunday. Journalists de-

---

7. *Dallas Morning News*, 22 March 1972.
8. *San Francisco Chronicle*, 21 November 1972.

tected this change in many cities. Jim Williard, for example, concluded that in Boston, by the summer of 1973,

> the battle cry of "Unite Ireland" once rallied Irish Americans throughout New England—but not anymore. Irrational murders in Northern Ireland have confused and repulsed Irish Americans. . . . In Boston, tattered "Free Ireland" posters weather in the changed Irish-American climate. Political spirit rarely stirs an Irish pub in Cambridge, once boiling over with anti-British outrage. Extremist fund raisers lack an audience.[9]

The realization of this trend eventually prompted Noraid officials to contact Seán MacStiofáin and tell him that the IRA bombing campaign was severely affecting republican fund raising and destroying its image in America. Similar feelings of discontent were aired by the residents of the republican ghettoes in Belfast and Derry. In light of this information, Provo leaders were inclined to launch a campaign against a more recognizable enemy, the English.[10]

In early 1973, the IRA Army Council approved a bombing blitz on the British mainland. Provo leaders hoped to shatter public morale and create a "war weariness," which would lead to increased calls for a withdrawal from Ulster. Some IRA strategists also believed that attacks in Britain, the "old enemy," would be more appealing to Irish-American republicans and help to revitalize their support base.

From March 1973 to the summer of 1974, the IRA carried out a spate of attacks throughout England. Undercover republican units planted numerous car bombs and launched a letter-bomb campaign in London. They mailed a series of explosive devices to major department stores in Oxford Street, as well as to Harrods, the Stock Exchange, and the residences of prominent politicians.

On August 27, 1973, a letter-bomb similar to those sent in London, arrived at the British embassy in Washington, D.C. The device was opened by Nora Murray, a secretary in the building. It exploded in her face, blowing off her left hand and inflicting serious injuries to her chest.[11]

9. Jim Williard, "Irish Americans Soften Unification Rallying Cry," *Christian Science Monitor*, 13 July 1973.

10. *Los Angeles Times*, 9 September 1972.

11. For more details on this incident see, "Letter Bomb Rocks British Embassy," *Los Angeles Times*, 28 August 1973.

At the time of this letter-bomb campaign, Seán MacStiofáin denied the IRA was responsible and accused British intelligence of involvement in the explosion. The American media dismissed this claim and laid the blame squarely on the Provisionals. The *Washington Post* accused the IRA of "mental incompetence" and "a lunatic disregard for human life." The *Chicago Tribune* maintained that, far from being attracted to the cause, the bomb would repulse and sicken the vast majority of Irish Americans:

> What possible justification could anyone claim for this cruelty? What patriotic or political goal is achieved by so mutilating an innocent person? . . . In this country the IRA will find itself with few friends. Americans are sometimes given to simplistic idealism, but they will not countenance this savagery, no matter how much its perpetrators claim idealistic motives.[12]

Republicans in America realized that such attacks undermined their efforts to justify the cause of militant nationalism. A spate of letters soon appeared in the same newspapers that had attacked the Provisionals, pointing out there was no evidence linking the IRA to the explosion. These letters generally castigated the American media for printing "British propaganda" and claimed the security forces were purposely ignoring bomb warnings so that the subsequent explosions would damage the IRA's image.

In an effort of give credence to their viewpoint, Noraid officials contacted republicans in Belfast, suggesting an official denial of involvement in the Washington bombing would greatly help their argument. The IRA, therefore, released a statement that was published in *Triumph*, a Roman Catholic magazine distributed in America. The statement reiterated the Provo's claim that they hadn't sent the letter bomb and severely criticized the *New York Times* and the *Washington Post* for their lack of, "independent investigative integrity in slavishly and obsequiously publishing handouts from British propaganda."[13]

This denial, however, held little weight with opinion makers in America, especially as the IRA intensified its bombing of English cities. In July 1974, a bomb in the Tower of London exploded amongst a group of tourists, killing one woman and severely injuring more than forty

---

12. *Washington Post*, 29 August, and *Chicago Tribune*, 28 August 1973.
13. *Triumph Magazine*, September 1973.

children. In November of the same year, the IRA bombed two pubs in Birmingham. The explosions killed twenty-one people, while hundreds were injured. The major American network news stations carried grisly footage of policemen collecting parts of the victims in plastic bags.

Such incidents intensified media condemnations of the IRA, and Irish-American republicans increasingly became the focus for derision. After almost every IRA bombing in 1974, editorial writers heaped scorn on Irish Americans who continued to support revolutionary nationalism. They accused militant nationalists of equal responsibility for the carnage. For example, the *New York Times* related to its readers that after the Tower of London bomb the legs of two children were completely severed and the rescuers found a child's foot beneath a displaced cannon. The editorial then continued:

> These children are the enemy against whom the brave terrorists of the IRA are waging their heroic war. These are the civilians whom the fierce freedom fighters, well hidden and well out of any possible danger to themselves, are savagely maiming and murdering for the pleasure of making a political point. . . . The fanatics who set off those bombs that injure and kill defenseless innocents are not heroes but cowardly criminals. The misguided people in this country who believe they are helping achieve a political goal by contributing funds that find their way into the hands of such assassins are simply accessories to crime—the blood of the innocent is on their hands too![14]

Such outright condemnations in the American media continued to erode sympathy for the IRA. Republicans found it increasingly difficult to present the Provos as heroic freedom fighters. The negative effects of such adverse media coverage was further compounded by a major increase in the surveillance of Irish-American republicans by US government agencies.

The FARA Investigation

By 1970, the activities of Irish republican groups in America had begun to alarm the British government. Intelligence reports showed America was a prime source of IRA financial support and weapons procurement. The British secret service consequently began a campaign of

14. *New York Times*, 19 July 1973.

disinformation aimed at discrediting the IRA.[15] In Washington, diplomats also pushed the Nixon administration to take action against the republican support network. Partly because of this pressure, US law enforcement agencies began covert investigations against all militant Irish-American groups.

In the summer of 1970 the FBI, greatly assisted by agents of Irish descent, launched a comprehensive surveillance and infiltration operation. Under the Nixon administration, these agents were given wide latitude to collect information on groups and individuals throughout the United States. Posing as Irish rebels, they observed republican demonstrations, took photographs and head counts at meetings, and monitored "subversive" conversations in bars believed to attract IRA sympathizers. The FBI later questioned a number of Irish-American republicans about fund raising and gunrunning.[16]

One of the principal objectives of this investigation was to force militant Irish-American nationalist groups to register under the Foreign Agents Registration Act (FARA). Registration would require a group to report details about the relationship with its "foreign principal." This included six-month statements on fund raising and detailed accounts of activities. Registration also permitted the authorities to conduct unannounced searches, without warrant, of the group's financial records and correspondence.

The Justice Department believed that registration under the F.A.R.A. would enable federal agencies to monitor militant Irish-American groups tightly. Noraid, as the largest single organization, was at the center of the investigation. FBI agents hoped that court cases would link the group to gunrunning and deter many of its less-dedicated members.

Michael Flannery and other Noraid leaders immediately saw the threat that registration under F.A.R.A. posed. With the legal assistance of Paul O'Dwyer and attorneys from the ACUJ, Flannery fought a bitter legal battle against registration. Despite their efforts, however, Noraid was eventually forced to register on January 14, 1971.

This decision merely continued litigation, as the Justice Department fought to make Noraid adhere to the provisions of the FARA and provide

15. Paul Foot, *Who Framed Colin Wallace?* (London: MacMillan, 1989).

16. The large extent of this investigation is clearly shown by Freedom of Information files on Noraid, the NAIF (FOIPA no. 297, 650), and the Irish Republican Clubs (FOIPA no. 270, 097).

greater information on its overseas connections. When Noraid registered, it continued to name the Northern Aid Committee Belfast as its principal and denied links with the IRA. The Justice Department claimed this information was false and later fought a prolonged legal battle to force Noraid's acknowledgement of the Provos as its true foreign principal.

FBI agents conducted an investigation of Noraid activities in order to secure the group's registration under the FARA. During the investigation, some less-committed Noraid members were actually shocked that they might be underwriting violence in Northern Ireland. Jack Holland quotes FBI memos that claimed some members became inactive because of the federal scrutiny. He relates how in 1973 agents interrogated members of Noraid's Bergen County chapter and told them that the $10,000 they had recently raised would be used for violent purposes and not to help impoverished families. The investigation produced a split in the chapter, as members who opposed violence left. In 1973 another Noraid unit in New Jersey and one in Portland, Oregon, completely collapsed after being investigated by the FBI.[17]

Michael Flannery disputes the extent of these defections and downplays the adverse effects of the FARA investigation. He claims that government surveillance operations actually strengthened Noraid. Its members were given concrete evidence that their activities were having an impact and, consequently, their commitment to the republican cause was strengthened.[18]

Gunrunning

At the outbreak of the Troubles in 1969, the Provos were extremely badly equipped. Their obsolete arsenal consisted mainly of World War II rifles, vintage Thompson submachine guns, and even a few shotguns. The IRA Army Council realized they had to acquire modern weapons, so they turned to traditional sources in America. As the volume of US arms flowing to Ireland increased, the Justice Department, in conjunction with the FARA investigation, initiated a large-scale undercover operation to crack the gunrunning network.

Jack Holland's research into Irish-American gunrunning shows that one of the main IRA arms suppliers in the early 1970s was George Har-

17. Jack Holland, *The American Connection* (New York: Viking, 1987), 38–39.
18. Michael Flannery, correspondence with author, 18 September 1992.

rison. Like so many of the key figures in the republican network, Harrison had come to America after the Civil War in Ireland, full of disillusionment at the actions of the Free State government. In New York, he kept his contacts with the IRA and organized a gunrunning cell, which supplied weapons for the Border Campaign between 1956 and 1962. Harrison responded to the riots of 1968 in Ulster by sending $8,000 to help rejuvenate the IRA. He followed this by shipping an assortment of seventy rifles, pistols, and hand grenades. This consignment was the first batch of American rifles to reach Belfast during the Troubles. They were used in the IRA's defense of republican areas during the bloody sectarian riots in August 1969.[19]

Patrick Bishop and Eamonn Mallie allege that in November 1969 the IRA sent Seán Keenan to America to coordinate the purchase of arms. He contacted a group of Irish Americans in Philadelphia, who supplied the first large consignment of Colt AR-15 and AR-180 Armalite rifles to the Provisionals. The Armalite soon became the IRA's ideal weapon because of its suitability for guerrilla warfare. It weighs only seven pounds, is accurate up to 300 to 400 yards, is easily hidden because of its folding stock, and will not rust when buried. Bishop and Mallie contend that this shipment of Armalites was crucial to the Provos because it modernized their firepower and gave them the means to conduct their fight against the security forces.[20]

Jack Holland maintains that eventually George Harrison also delivered consignments of Armalites to the Provisionals. He constructed an arms network, which sent continuous supplies of rifles and pistols to Northern Ireland throughout the 1970s. An essential link in this supply chain was George De Meo, who bought the weapons from the US Marine base at Camp Lejeune, North Carolina. Marines smuggled guns and ammunition out of the camp and sold them to local arms dealers who then delivered them to De Meo. These weapons were then usually transported to New York in the trunk of De Meo's automobile and sold to Harrison.[21]

19. Holland, *The American Connection*, 80.

20. Patrick Bishop and Eamonn Mallie, *The Provisional I.R.A.* (London: Heinemann, 1987), 233. The authors do not mention just how many rifles were involved in this shipment but show that over 420 of them have been recovered by security forces.

21. In March 1974, the IRA conducted an arms raid on the armory of the US naval communications station in Londonderry. Four hooded volunteers broke into the base in a hijacked truck, took a number of hostages, but fled when the alarm was raised. *New York Times*, 18 March 1974.

This plunder of US military weapons was eventually exposed in an investigation by naval intelligence. A subsequent report, first made public by Congressman Les Aspin in 1975, uncovered the theft of weapons from the Marine Corps base at Camp Lejeune and also at Fort Bragg in North Carolina. The report found that between 1971 and 1974, over 6,900 weapons and 1.2 million rounds of ammunition were stolen and that many of these had ended up in the hands of the IRA. The document also alleged that the Provos tried to recruit members of the Marine Corps as instructors in the use of heavy machine guns and advanced communications equipment.[22]

Though the naval report led to a tightening of security on US military bases and the court martial of a number of soldiers, it did not end the supply of weapons to the IRA. In 1976 a gang of criminals, the Roxbury Rats, raided a National Guard armory in Danvers, Massachusetts, and stole a large consignment of weapons which included M-60 heavy machine guns. Soon after the raid, George Harrison bought six of these machine guns and sent them to Ireland. Although M-60s were unsuitable for the majority of Provo operations, they did provide a psychological boost and were useful for publicity. The weapons were first proudly displayed to journalists during the 1978 Bloody Sunday commemoration in Derry.[23]

In addition to weapons stolen from the US military, the IRA also obtained supplies from registered gun dealers. In 1972 there were over 160,000 gun shops in America. Weapons could be purchased in most states by merely producing some form of identification. An investigation by David Anable of the *Christian Science Monitor* showed that in the early 1970s, republicans were obtaining large consignments of weapons with false identifications and sending them to Ireland.[24]

Republican gunrunners used a variety of methods to deliver their weapons to the IRA. The favored mode of transport was cargo ships sailing out of East Coast ports. George Harrison usually packed his weapons

22. In one incident, an Army lieutenant tried to organize a scheme to steal guns from a base at Fort Meyer, Virginia. The lieutenant planned to blast into the armory, kill the officer in charge, and then sell the weapons to the IRA. A psychiatrist at the soldier's court martial described him as "living in a constant fantasy land," *New York Times*, 11 March 1975.

23. Before all of the M-60s were recovered in 1982, they had been used in ten killings and a number of attacks on British Army helicopters. J. Bowyer Bell, *The Irish Troubles* (New York: St. Martin's Press, 1993), 326.

24. David Anable, "American Rifles in I.R.A. Hands," *Christian Science Monitor*, 16 August 1972.

in crates labeled as machine parts; he received full cooperation from sympathetic longshoremen. Peter McMullan, an IRA defector who organized a gunrunning scheme from New York in 1972, confessed his favorite method was to pack the weapons in household and office furniture; they would "strip the furniture down and fill it with weapons. Guns would go inside everything—cabinets, beds, sofas, chairs—everything!" After this he put the furniture inside a sealed container on a ship bound for Dublin. McMullan and others claim that a network of republican supporters called the "Emerald Society" existed within the US Customs Service. They ensured that weapons shipments would pass through government inspectors without complications.[25]

Another way in which IRA supporters transported weapons from America was on board the passenger liner Queen Elizabeth II. Bishop and Mallie allege that two republicans worked as crew members on the ship. Throughout the early seventies they regularly carried small consignments of guns and explosives. These weapons were usually transported in suitcases or hidden behind wall panels.[26] On several occasions British and Irish agents uncovered these arms caches. On October 6, 1971, Irish customs officials in Cobh discovered six large suitcases containing rifles and hand grenades. The cases were unloaded during a short stop on a journey from New York to France. The IRA was informed of the discovery and aborted plans to collect the weapons.[27]

Irish-American republicans, with the cooperation of sympathizers in the travel industry, also delivered weapons to the IRA in air freight containers via Shannon airport. Some individuals even carried guns on passenger flights during vacations to Ireland. In 1974, author Richard Brown recalled one woman who flew into Dublin with four revolvers strapped to her body by two belts of ammunition. She covered the weapons with a pillow and succeeded in convincing airline staff she was pregnant.[28]

25. Interview with Peter McMullan in *Chicago Sun-Times*, 4 September 1979.

26. Bishop and Mallie, *The Provisional I.R.A.*, 234.

27. The IRA also received substantial amounts of explosives from America. According to Tim Pat Coogan, Provo sympathizers working on the construction of the New York City water tunnel diverted sizable quantities of gelignite to Ireland in the course of the project: *The I.R.A.* (Niwok, Colorado: Roberts Rinehart Publishers, 1993), 476. James Adams, *The Financing of Terror* (New York: Simon and Schuster, 1986), also alleges that large amounts of explosives were transported on the *Q.E. II* and on cargo ships to the English port of Southampton. There it was unloaded and stored by IRA supporters working on the docks.

28. Richard H. Brown, *I Am of Ireland* (New York: Harper and Row, 1974), 98.

Republicans also claimed they hid weapons in the fake coffins of "dead patriots" being returned for burial in the "ould sod." As security greatly tightened in the mid-seventies, however, the airlines ceased to be a major route for arms delivery.[29]

These supplies from Irish-American republicans modernized the IRA's weaponry and established an important arms source which helped sustain the organization throughout the seventies. Inevitably the American weapons began constituting a large percentage of the arms caches recovered by the security forces in Northern Ireland. There is considerable dispute over just how many American weapons were reaching the IRA in this period.

In his book *The IRA: A History*, Tim Pat Coogan maintains that the US was the principal source of weapons for the Provos.[30] British Army sources agree with this assertion and claim that between 1970 and 1972 almost 80 percent of the IRA's new arms supplies came from America. By 1975, Stan Orme, minister of state for Northern Ireland, told reporters that the figure had risen to 85 percent.[31] The RUC later provided information claiming 90 percent of the IRA's firepower came from the US and over 75 percent of all killings committed by the group were carried out with American weapons.[32]

Despite their concern over the illegal flow of weapons, American law enforcement agents challenged these figures. One chief of the Bureau of Alcohol, Tobacco, and Firearms, Don Zimmermann, said the British arms estimates were a "ridiculous exaggeration." Later Don McGorty, head of the international terrorism section of the FBI, claimed that 50 percent was a more realistic figure.[33] One of the most detailed studies of weapon recovery in Ulster seems to confirm the American figures. Staff Sergeant R. D. Jones of British Army Intelligence, provides figures that show that between 1971 and 1975 a total of 4,974 weapons were seized by security forces in the province. Of these, 1,581 (approximately 30 percent) were of American origin.[34]

29. Desmond Fisher, "Exporting Death to Ireland," *Commonweal* (June 1977), 357, and Bell, *The Irish Troubles*, 323.

30. Tim Pat Coogan, *The I.R.A.: A History* (Colorado: Roberts Reinhart, 1993), 543.

31. *Daily Telegraph* (London), 10 January, 1976.

32. Information from an RUC document reported in *Belfast News Letter*, 14 April 1980.

33. *The Times* (London), 2 November 1975. See also Warren Richey, "How the I.R.A. Ships Arms to Ulster," *Christian Science Monitor*, 15 January 1985.

34. R. D. Jones, "Terrorist Weaponry in Northern Ireland," *British Army Review* (April 1978): 24. In *The Financing of Terror*, James Adams claims the British exaggerated the

Irrespective of the dispute over the exact percentage of American weapons in the IRA's possession, the transatlantic arms network became of intense concern to British, Irish, and US law-enforcement agencies. When security forces captured American guns, they compiled lists of serial numbers that had not been obliterated. These records were sent to the US authorities, who could then investigate the origin of the weapons. By the end of 1972, a whole range of guns and ammunition were traced to arms dealers throughout the United States. The Justice Department used this information to conduct a number of covert operations against the illegal shipment of arms to the IRA. These investigations, like the FARA drive, pressured the Irish republican support network and contributed to its general decline in the mid-seventies.

The first major attempt by US authorities to prosecute IRA gunrunners collapsed, however, and actually gave Irish-American republicans a significant publicity victory. In May 1972, United States Attorney General Richard Kleindienst established a grand jury investigation into an alleged arms conspiracy in Texas. The grand jury convened at Fort Worth and immediately subpoenaed twelve Irish Americans from New York to give testimony. Government attorneys later canceled seven of the subpoenas, but five individuals were told to remain in Texas and give evidence on the alleged gunrunning scheme. The five witnesses—Kenneth Tierney, Mathias Reilly, Paschal Morohan, James Laffey, and Daniel Crawford— were all born in Ireland and were involved with republican groups in New York. Their supporters christened them the "Fort Worth Five."

When the men appeared before the grand jury, federal prosecutors questioned them about Armalite rifles they allegedly bought from a Yonkers arms dealer named Edward Agramonte.[35] They were also asked about their connections with republican organizations in New York. On the advice of Paul O'Dwyer, who gave them free legal assistance, the five refused to answer questions. They were then offered immunity, which comes with an obligation to testify, but chose to remain silent. Judge Leo

---

weapons figures to ensure US authorities would continue vigorous prosecution of gun-running.

35. Edward Agramonte was a gun dealer with a long history of federal offenses involving the illegal sale of weapons. In the early seventies a number of Armalite rifles recovered in Ulster were traced to his store. During the Fort Worth investigation, a federal grand jury in New York indicted him on nineteen counts of violating gun laws. Most of these involved selling proscribed weapons, submachine guns and grenades, without government authorization.

Brewster responded by sending the men to Tarrant County jail in Fort Worth for contempt of court. He also refused their bail request, even though the men had no previous convictions and it was customary even for those charged with serious crimes to be released pending appeal.[36]

Paul O'Dwyer defended the men's silence by alleging their testimony could lead to extradition to Britain. He also pointed out that because the five were offered immunity, the real objective of the grand jury was to bring charges against more influential members of the Irish republican network and link Noraid to the illegal supply of weapons.

As the "Fort Worth Five" remained in jail, activists soon used their plight as a rallying point to build up support and publicity. The case incensed many Irish-American groups because they felt that the Nixon administration was carrying out a vindictive "witch hunt" against their community at the request of the British government. They concentrated on winning support from politicians and the press. Paul O'Dwyer and the ACUJ began lobbying in Washington. Their first success came when eight congressmen from New York sent a telegram of protest to Attorney General Kleindienst urging him to "wrap up this apparently trumped up proceeding promptly and allow these men to return to their homes and families."[37]

Paul O'Dwyer also secured the intervention of Senator Edward Kennedy, who accused the Justice Department of abusing the grand jury system by using it for harassment rather than law enforcement. Kennedy said the case was a flagrant abuse of human rights and urged the prompt release of the five men on bail. Following this, Senator George McGovern added his support to the Fort Worth Five and demanded their release from "arbitrary and capricious detention."

With this political support, Paul O'Dwyer appealed to Supreme Court Justice William Douglas to intervene in the case. Douglas, noted for his liberal inclinations, agreed to take action. On September 20, 1972, he approved release of the Forth Worth Five on bail, despite opposition from federal attorneys and Judge Leo Brewster.

The five men spent four months in uneasy freedom until they were forced to return to jail again on January 31, 1973. This occurred when the

36. For details see Paul O'Dwyer, *Counsel for the Defense* (New York: Simon and Schuster, 1979), 260.

37. James Markham, "Gun-Running Case in U.S. Embitters I.R.A. Supporters," *New York Times*, 17 July 1972.

US Supreme Court refused to hear an appeal of the case. Consequently, bail was revoked and Judge Leo Brewster's decision to incarcerate the men remained in force.

Irish-American activists resumed their efforts to free the men. New York Congresswoman Bella Abzug began working on the case after visiting the men in Seagoville jail. She initiated a hearing before the House Judiciary Committee aimed at highlighting the Justice Department's "abuse" of the grand jury system.

The hearing took place on March 13, 1972. Assistant Attorney General A. William Olson gave evidence of the alleged gunrunning plot in Texas. Bella Abzug complained that the men were being victimized and made to suffer great hardships. Senator Edward Kennedy reinforced this point and asserted:

> From the beginning, the circumstances of this case have strongly suggested it had nothing to do with Texas and a great deal to do with a thinly veiled attempt by the Department of Justice, at the request of the British government, to harass Irish Americans in the New York City area engaged in peaceful protest against British policy in Ulster.[38]

Supporters of the Fort Worth Five used the publicity surrounding the hearing to increase public awareness of the case. Paul O'Dwyer continued to petition the Supreme Court until he again persuaded Justice William Douglas to release the men. O'Dwyer remains convinced that Douglas's decision was made easier by the revelations that were then being uncovered by the Watergate investigation. He believes that the exposure of the Nixon administration's dirty tricks enhanced the allegations of grand jury abuse in the Fort Worth case.[39] After the five men were released, the government investigation in Texas collapsed through lack of evidence. No formal charges were ever filed against them.[40]

The Fort Worth Five case was a setback in the Justice Department's attempt to stifle American gunrunning to the IRA. Republicans successfully used the investigation to win support in the press and from influential politicians. Dennis Clark points out:

38. Mary Russell, "U.S. Defends Texas Gun Running Case," *Washington Post*, 14 March 1972.

39. Paul O'Dwyer, correspondence with author, 21 June 1989.

40. All five men continued their involvement with republican groups after their release and went on publicity tours to tell of their persecution by U.S. authorities.

The case gave the American support network a needed symbol. Symbols of suffering and repression were numerous in Ireland. In the United States the Fort Worth Five provided a counterpart. The flagrant and abusive federal handling of the case, so malicious legally, gave the Irish much needed allies in liberal circles.[41]

Despite the adverse effects of the Fort Worth investigation, federal agents continued to infiltrate IRA gunrunning schemes and succeeded in getting a number of important prosecutions. In June 1972, British police discovered a trunk full of machine guns, rifles, pistols, telescopic sights, and ammunition at London's Heathrow Airport. The trunk, enroute to Shannon airport, was addressed to a fictitious location in Galway. British agents replaced the weapons, let them continue to Ireland, and set a trap with the aid of Gárdaí detectives. Though no one appeared to collect the trunk, police traced a serial number on one of the rifles to Charles Malone, a prominent republican activist in San Francisco.

In February 1973, Malone pleaded guilty to illegally exporting weapons to the IRA.[42] He received a one-year, suspended sentence with two years probation and was fined $1,000. As part of the probation, Malone was ordered to sever his links with Irish republican groups and all social activities connected with Ireland.[43]

In 1973 federal authorities also traced arms discovered in Ireland back to James O'Gara, a Noraid activist from the Bronx. He escaped charges of conspiracy but was given a five-year, suspended sentence for using

41. Dennis Clark, *Irish Blood: Northern Ireland and the American Conscience* (New York: Kennikat Press, 1977): 66.

42. After his sentence, Malone, christened the "Golden Gate Gunrunner" by his supporters, organized a branch of Na Fianna Éireann in San Francisco. One of its most active members was William Quinn, who would later be the first American extradited to Britain and imprisoned for IRA activities. In 1990 Malone was again convicted in a conspiracy to send weapons to the IRA and subsequently served two years in federal prison.

43. *Los Angeles Times*, 24 February 1973. As part of the investigation into the Malone case, a grand jury convened in San Francisco during October 1972. A number of witnesses appeared from Butte, Montana, because Charles Malone received some of his weapons from there. All the witnesses had connections with Irish groups in Butte and they included a sheriff, city attorney, and two police lieutenants. The judge asked them about plans to rob the National Guard in Butte and about fund-raising activities they conducted with Malone. All these witnesses denied links with the gunrunning scheme and were later released. The key link in the case, Robert Meisel, refused to testify. He was accused of traveling to New York with Malone in August 1972 and delivering guns for export to Ireland. Meisel served more than six months in prison before the grand jury expired in 1973.

false identification to purchase arms for the IRA.[44] Soon after this, the Irish navy intercepted the *Claudia*, a West German cargo ship, while it was delivering weapons to the IRA in Waterford Bay. Joe Cahill was on board with five tons of military equipment, including machine guns, Kalashnikov automatic rifles, and hand grenades. Irish authorities seized the weapons, and Joe Cahill went to jail for illegally supplying arms to the Provos.

The *Claudia* affair was a particularly significant blow to Noraid because Cahill was the chief recipient of its funds. As the group's official representative in Ireland, he was in charge of distributing thousands of dollars. Cahill immediately denied that any of Noraid's money was used to buy the weapons and maintained the IRA got its funds from secret sources outside the group. Federal authorities in America, however, used the circumstantial evidence in the Claudia conviction to support their contention that Noraid was funding gunrunning.

On September 21, 1973, a major interagency meeting took place between officials from the State Department, Justice Department, Treasury Department, and the FBI to coordinate their work against IRA gunrunning. Subsequently, in February 1974, federal agents secured a significant breakthrough: an undercover operation cracked a gunrunning scheme based in Baltimore. The case involved four men: James Conlon, an Irish citizen who owned a bar in New York; Francis Larkin, a US citizen from Maryland; Henry Hillick, from Belfast; and Kieran McMahon, a US citizen born in Ireland. They conspired to send 158 Armalite rifles, seven handguns, and more than 10,000 rounds of ammunition to the IRA.

Undercover Treasury agents and a Washington police detective infiltrated the gunrunning operation. One posed as an artist interested in helping the republican cause. He established a friendship with Henry Hillick and tried to gain his confidence. Hillick asked the agent to contribute some of his sketches to Noraid and said the money they fetched would go to help widows and orphans. The agent later testified that when the two became more friendly, Hillick told him about their gunrunning project and that Noraid money was used in its financing.[45]

Using information from this undercover agent, the FBI seized James Conlon and Francis Larkin in New York on February 14, 1974. They had

44. When Irish officials discovered the six suitcases full of weapons on the *Q.E. II* in October 1971, some of the rifles were traced to O'Gara. After his conviction, O'Gara became an honored member of Noraid and was co-chairman of their annual dinner in 1976.

45. *New York Times*, 16 December 1975.

a cache of seventy of the Armalites in their automobile which they intended to ship to Ireland. Federal agents had been observing the men for two days. As a result of their investigation, the authorities also arrested Henry Hillick, Kieran McMahon, and the arms dealer who supplied the weapons.

All of the accused except Hillick were released on bond. Judge Edward Northrop believed he would disappear once outside custody. Hillick immediately went on hunger strike in protest but failed to win bail.

To assist the four men, Noraid established an Irish-American Legal Aid Fund and secured the services of attorney Frank Durkan. During their trial in May 1974, Durkan instructed the accused to offer no testimony. He claimed their action was dictated by the republican tradition of refusing to contest evidence offered by state prosecutors. Durkan did, however, make statements to the press and made a final argument. He maintained that the men acted from a conviction, "not to stand by and watch British soldiers kill and trample the people of Northern Ireland" and said, "Two hundred years ago these men would have been regarded as four of the finest patriots in American history."[46]

Perhaps the principal reason that Durkan offered no defense was the overwhelming amount of evidence against the four men. United States attorneys presented thirty-five government witnesses and sixty-eight items of evidence, including the seventy Armalite rifles the FBI seized in New York. On May 24, 1974, Judge Northrop found the defendants guilty and on July 9, each received a sentence of six years' imprisonment.

Although the Noraid connection was never mentioned during trial, the chief state prosecutor accused the organization of providing funds for the gunrunning scheme. In an interview with CBS television he said:

> Raffles have been held and dances. Ostensibly the money was supposed to go for orphans. Our indication was that money raised by Noraid had been used to partially pay for the weapons. The guns were going to be sent through New York to Ireland in crates labeled as machine parts. They were to be used for what Hillick called "potting the dummies," or shooting British soldiers.[47]

46. *Washington Post*, 23 May 1974.

47. "Gunrunning to the I.R.A.," report on CBS television by Robert Schakne and John Lawrence. Kieran McMahon later gave an interview in which he described why he got involved in gunrunning. Speaking of the IRA support network in Washington D.C., he alleged, "You could go into any Irish bar in Washington and find someone who would agree

The final set of convictions in this period came in June 1975 after a joint US-Canadian operation uncovered a scheme to supply fifteen automatic rifles to the IRA. The weapons were to be smuggled from Canada over the US border and shipped to Ireland from New York. On June 6, three Canadians and one US citizen received prison sentences ranging from seventeen months to two years, after they pleaded guilty to the arms smuggling. The American involved in the gunrunning scheme was Joseph Myles from Garden City, Michigan. During the court case it was revealed that Myles was an executive officer in Noraid.[48]

Following the failure of the Fort Worth Five investigation, these successful convictions were seen as a significant breakthrough by the Justice Department. Arms prosecutions, the FARA investigation, and adverse publicity caused by IRA bombing atrocities combined to weaken the militant Irish-American network. Almost every journalist and analyst of Irish-America detected a decline in support for republicanism after 1972. The turnout at protest demonstrations was sharply reduced and financial contributions declined. By the end of 1974 Dennis Clark observed:

It was almost five years since the North exploded, and the Irish supporters had been at their tasks for the whole time. Resolution flagged. Turnouts diminished. Apathy reconquered the spirits of many . . . the support and opinion that could be mobilized to picket, rally, collect funds, and present the Irish case was eroding.[49]

Indications of weakness greatly alarmed the leaders of militant Irish-American groups. They soon launched initiatives to bolster dwindling support and finances. Noraid installed a telex machine in its Bronx headquarters to improve communications and publicity. The machine was linked to the Irish Republican Publicity Bureau in Belfast to receive reports on all the latest developments in Ulster. Noraid also established an Irish information radio program in New York and other cities to publicize its activities and present the republican perspective on news items from Ireland.[50]

---

to accept money and see to it the right people received it," *Washington Post Magazine*, 12 March 1978.

48. *Irish Times* (Dublin), 7 June 1975. Also in 1974 two San Diego men were convicted and given suspended sentences for an amateurish attempt to buy semi-automatic rifles for the IRA. See *Los Angeles Times*, 2 February 1981.

49. Dennis Clark, *Irish Blood*, 69.

50. Noraid also employed more unconventional methods of publicizing their case. During an ABC television broadcast by Howard Smith in Washington, a group of four re-

To restore depleted finances, Noraid introduced a whole range of new fund-raising techniques. It began to raffle automobiles and vacations in the Caribbean, organize sponsored walks and cycling events, auction craft work produced by republican prisoners, and run benefit concerts and festivals of Irish folk music featuring groups such as the Wolfe Tones.[51] There are also reports that Noraid employed the unconventional scheme of auctioning weapons that had been used in IRA attacks in Ulster. In the late seventies, it obtained a Kalashnikov rifle used in the killing of at least twenty members of the security forces. The rifle had a notch carved on its stock for every victim and was eventually sold for $30,000.[52]

Noraid projected its fund-raising appeals to the Irish-American fraternal societies and succeeded in getting larger donations from branches of the Ancient Order of Hibernians and Gaelic Athletic Association. It also made successful appeals to smaller groups such as the Patrick Pearse Council in Chicago and the Robert Emmet Society of Philadelphia.[53] Various branches of the Teamsters, Carpenters, and Longshoreman's unions also increased their donations to Noraid. Eventually, trade union supporters formed an amalgamated group called American Labor for Irish Freedom, which made large quarterly contributions of $16,000.[54]

The most ambitious new method of fund raising was the initiation of the annual Noraid dinner in New York, the first of which was held in 1973. Delegations and supporters from all over the country came to discuss tactics and listen to Sinn Féin representatives from Ireland. Guests paid a fixed fee per plate, while raffles and collections were taken up during the night's proceedings. FARA documents show that the event usually netted between $13,000 and $16,000. Soon Noraid units throughout the United States began holding their own smaller dinners and sent the profits to national headquarters in New York.[55]

---

publicans, one in clerical garb, disrupted the show by shouting protests about the treatment of Irish political prisoners in Long Kesh.

51. Reported in R. W. Howe, *The Power Peddlers* (New York: Doubleday, 1977) 390.

52. Chris Ryder, *The R.U.C.: A Force Under Fire* (London: MacMillan, 1989), 176.

53. Information from Noraid reports under the FARA July 1977 to July 1980.

54. From Noraid reports under the FARA December 1980. Bishop and Mallie, *The Provisional I.R.A.*, 235, contend that there were close links between the Longshoreman's Union and the IRA. They allege that members of the Provos who were on the run were always given a job and protection on the docks.

55. Tom Dolan, "North Irish Group Stirs Controversy," *Los Angeles Times*, 25 December 1976.

Noraid dinners also generated positive publicity for the republican cause because of the presence of congressmen, local politicians, trade union leaders, and media personalities. In 1975, for example, author Len Deighton and actor Richard Harris were honored guests at the national dinner held in the Astoria Manor, Queens. The presence of the two celebrities, along with the wife of IRA leader Dáithí O Conaill, attracted wide media attention, especially when reports surfaced that Harris gave large sums to the Noraid collectors and ended the night singing Irish rebel ballads.[56]

These Noraid dinners were frequently reported in the British tabloid and "quality" press and infuriated readers. When Peter Stafford of the *London Times* reported on a republican fund-raising dinner on Long Island, he mentioned how participants prominently displayed IRA badges "and made it quite clear that if some of their money went to arm the Provos, they had no objections." Stafford interviewed Liam Murphy, editor of the *Irish People*, who said his only regret was that the IRA did not have better weapons to inflict more casualties on the British Army.[57]

Formation of the Irish National Caucus

The most concerted effort of militant Irish-American organizations to revive their effectiveness was the formation of a new congressional lobbying group. The ACUJ's work in Washington had faded as it increasingly concentrated on defending republicans under government investigation. Noraid leaders in particular realized the damage that adverse publicity and government investigations had caused to the republican network. They hoped the formation of a new pressure group would improve its public image, get better press coverage, and deflect Justice Department pressure.

In late 1973 Michael Flannery discussed with a variety of Irish-American organizations the idea of launching this new group. The Ancient Order of Hibernians responded very enthusiastically and contacted other societies to gauge their support. This process accelerated when the AOH elected John "Jack" Keane as its national president in the spring of

56. Reported in R. W. Howe, *The Power Peddlers*, 388.

57. Peter Stafford, "$14 Dinner Tickets Help the I.R.A.," *The Times* (London), 19 March 1975.

1974. Keane was an outspoken republican and strongly supported the drive to establish a new lobbying group. To advance the cause, he organized a meeting of more than thirty Irish-American and labor associations in New York on September 28, 1974.

At this meeting the Irish-American associations present endorsed the suggestion that an organization called the Irish National Caucus, active since February 1974, should function as an umbrella group to represent their interests. The delegates decided the INC should have an overlapping membership with every Irish-American group present. It was intended to be the only Irish-American organization that would lobby the US government, presenting a militant nationalist perspective to Congress and the American media. The initial ethos of the INC was strongly republican and supportive of the IRA's campaign in Northern Ireland.

The two most prominent members of the Irish National Caucus were Father Seán McManus and Dr. Fred Burns O'Brien. Father McManus, a Redemptorist priest, was the brother of Frank McManus, nationalist MP for Fermanagh/South Tyrone. Their brother Patrick, an IRA volunteer, had been killed during the border campaign in 1958.[58] Father McManus became an activist for Catholic civil rights in the late sixties. His political views were strongly republican and he soon became an outspoken supporter of the IRA. After being arrested for disorderly behavior at a nationalist demonstration in Fermanagh, he refused to recognize the court, and made the following declaration from the dock:

> I will be immediately suspected of being in sympathy with the IRA. Well, let's clear up this "suspicion." I want to state publicly and unequivocally that I am in sympathy with the IRA, indeed sympathy is too weak a word. . . . The oppressors of Irish freedom call the IRA terrorists and murderers, but I call them by their proper titles; I call them freedom fighters, I call them heroes, and I venerate their dead as martyrs for Ireland. . . . I abhor the deceit and hypocrisy that condemns these men and women who are sacrificing their lives for the freedom of Ireland.[59]

Father McManus became quite prominent within republican circles and he established a close friendship with Seán MacStiofáin. During the

58. Father Seán McManus, interview with author, 11 July 1991.
59. *An Phoblacht/Republican News* (Belfast), October 1971.

IRA chief's hunger strike in 1972, McManus faithfully visited his cell. MacStiofáin's condition deteriorated after his tenth day without food or water, and McManus persuaded him to end the hunger strike on November 28.[60]

McManus says that his activities for the republican cause embarrassed the Roman Catholic hierarchy. After pressure from the British government, Church officials told him he had to end his political activities or leave England. Faced with this pressure, he decided to go to America and work in a parish in Baltimore.[61]

In the United States, McManus soon reestablished his links with republicans and became a prime organizer of Noraid social events and protest demonstrations.[62] He also continued to support the IRA's right to "armed resistance" and criticized the Roman Catholic church for not supporting the republican movement. In 1974 he was arrested for staging a sit-in at the British embassy in Washington, during which he splattered the lobby with blood.[63]

Dr. Fred Burns O'Brien established a close friendship with McManus as soon as he arrived in Baltimore. As a third generation Irish American, O'Brien claimed his interest in Ireland arose when he learned his grandfather had fled to the United States after killing a British soldier. He became active in the republican network in America, contributing weekly articles to the *Irish People*, which supported the IRA bombing campaigns in England.[64]

After the September 1974 meeting, McManus became the National Coordinator of the newly formulated INC, while Fred Burns O'Brien began directing information. They were joined by Seán Walsh, a prominent republican, who became the group's executive director. Jack Keane became the INC's chairman; Paul O'Dwyer was vice chairman. To forge a link with the labor movement, Teddy Gleason, Matthew Guinan, and George Meany, president of the AFL-CIO, were made directors. Later,

60. Seán MacStiofáin, *Memoirs of a Revolutionary* (Edinburgh: Gordon Cremonesi, 1975), 354.

61. Father Seán McManus, interview with author, 11 July 1991.

62. McManus played a prominent role in organizing the annual Noraid dinner and coordinating protest demonstrations. In October 1973, for example, he led an Irish Freedom March from Baltimore to Washington. See *Washington Post*, 6 October 1973.

63. *Irish Echo* (New York), 5 January 1985.

64. Fred Burns O'Brien, "Americans Dare Not Criticize the I.R.A.," *Irish People* (New York), 6 October 1973.

the AFL-CIO officially endorsed the Caucus at its national convention in Florida in 1975.[65]

The objective of the Caucus was to lobby Congress and persuade politicians to take up the cause of human rights in Northern Ireland. It would present a militant nationalist perspective to the American media and attract support from the Irish-American community. Some members of the INC leadership initially hoped they could build their organization into a force as powerful as the Jewish-American lobby for Israel.

In order to present itself as a more "respectable" organization than Noraid, the INC did not list a foreign principal and used the money it raised to sustain its activities in the United States. The Caucus began soliciting Irish Americans through direct mail appeals. Father McManus became extremely adept at appealing to their sentimentality, patriotism, and concern for human rights violations.[66]

The Caucus was very successful and by 1978 had established a national office near Capitol Hill in Washington. To coordinate its activities, the group employed Rita Mullen as director. Cofounder of the Association for Legal Justice in Northern Ireland, Mullen came to the US in 1977 and soon became a central figure in the Caucus. She forged contacts with human rights groups in Ireland and accompanied McManus on his frequent trips to Belfast.

The INC expanded quickly and by 1979 claimed thirty-four chapters in twenty-four states. These chapters had considerable overlapping membership with other Irish-American societies, especially Noraid. They had a very loose structure but were held together by telephone and fax communications from Father McManus in Washington. The Caucus also distributed its official newsletter, the *Irish Lobby*, to every chapter and subscribing member. In the mid-seventies, it concentrated on two principal issues; securing visas for republicans to enter the United States on fundraising tours and getting congressional hearings on British human rights violations in Ulster.

In the spring of 1975, after representations from the Irish and British governments, the US State Department refused to issue visas to five top

65. Father McManus, through his friendship with Meaney and Gleason, got the AFL-CIO to issue calls for a British withdrawal at successive annual conventions between 1975 and 1977. The Caucus also held joint fund-raising events with the labor organization.

66. The Caucus was able to obtain extensive mailing lists from records of subscribers to various Irish-American newspapers and publications.

republicans who applied to enter America on a "speaking tour." The Caucus immediately championed their cause and lobbied congressmen to speak out against the action. They persuaded Mario Biaggi (D, N.Y.) to attack the State Department and lead a team of Caucus officials to Ireland. At the end of April 1975, Biaggi, accompanied by Fred Burns O'Brien and Seán Walsh, flew to Dublin to investigate visa denial and to press the American embassy for an explanation.

This visit caused a major controversy among Irish government officials. Conor Cruise O'Brien, the Minister for Posts and Telegraphs, accused Biaggi of helping IRA propaganda in America. When Biaggi tried to visit prisoners at Port Laoise prison, the government denied him access.[67]

Indignant at this rebuff by the Irish authorities, Biaggi appeared at a Sinn Féin news conference with the five Provos who were denied visas. Sitting between Ruiarí O Brádaigh and Joe Cahill, Biaggi condemned the US State Department and defended the IRA's cause.[68] When the INC delegation returned to America, they persuaded Joshua Eilberg (D, Pa.) to host a congressional committee investigation into the visa issue. Eilberg had sent a letter of inquiry to the State Department asking for an explanation for its policy. In reply, government officials said they refused visas to the men because they were members of a terrorist organization that aimed to overthrow a legitimate government.

At the hearings of this congressional committee, Eilberg sharply criticized the State Department. Mario Biaggi and Lester Wolff (D, N.Y.) both testified in favor of granting visas and stressed that British ministers continually came to America to present their "prejudiced" view of the Irish question. They argued that Sinn Féin leaders could counterbalance this perspective and present an alternative opinion. Despite this pressure, the State Department refused to grant visas to the IRA men and continued the exclusionary policy throughout the 1970s and 1980s.

The second issue on which the INC concentrated was the violation of human rights in Ulster's prisons. The Caucus worked feverishly to convene formal congressional hearings to draw attention to the subject. They planned to bring a number of witnesses from Northern Ireland

67. Apparently Fred Burns O'Brien got around this ban by posing as a journalist. He deceived warders at Port Laoise prison and was able to talk with Dáithí O'Conaill. See R. W. Howe, *The Power Peddlers*, 395.

68. *Irish Press*, 1 May 1975.

to testify against British cruelty. The ultimate hope was that this evidence would persuade the US government to condemn the abuses. Throughout their campaign to launch these hearings, the Caucus was constantly opposed by the British and Irish governments. Officials from both countries claimed that such hearings would be exploited by republicans in America and serve merely to propagandize the IRA's campaign. Therefore, Irish government officials, through their contacts with House Speaker Carl Albert, continually blocked attempts to convene hearings in Washington.[69]

In face of this powerful opposition, the INC encouraged Lester Wolff to hold an ad hoc congressional forum on Northern Ireland. Its purpose was to gather testimony for the proposed formal hearings in Washington. The forum met at the Federal Building in Manhattan on October 15, 1975. Its panel included Mario Biaggi, Benjamin Rosenthal, Leo Zeferetti, Ben Gilman, and Norman Lent—all congressmen from the New York area. They heard statements from a variety of republican groups and from representatives of the AFL-CIO.[70]

The testimonies covered a whole range of contentious issues as many republicans from America and Ireland castigated British policy in Ulster. Dennis Cassin, a former internee and IRC official, described how he had suffered continual torture at the hands of British interrogators. Paul O'Dwyer maintained that the US should immediately intervene in the Ulster crisis to prevent a cataclysmic civil war, while Matthew Higgins of Noraid claimed the CIA was training British troops for guerrilla warfare in Ireland.

This ad hoc forum received considerable media attention in America and Britain, but it did not lead to formal congressional hearings. British and Irish diplomats in Washington continued to convince the leaders of Congress that such hearings would achieve nothing and would merely provide republicans with a platform to air their views.

Despite their lack of success in working for visas and congressional hearings, the Caucus did emerge as an effective lobbying and publicity group. In the late seventies they achieved a number of propaganda victories by making influential contacts in Congress and presenting the human rights issue very convincingly. Yet the achievements of the INC would be

69. Garret FitzGerald, interview with author, 19 December 1990.
70. See Godffrey Barker, "Arms for Ulster: The Irish American File," *Spectator* (29 November 1975), 689.

greatly undermined by the intense pressure exerted by constitutional nationalists throughout this preiod. Militant Irish-American nationalism would also be impeded by the emergence of reconciliation groups, offering an alternative to support for violence, and by continued infiltration and surveillance from US authorities.

CHAPTER 5

◆

CONSTITUTIONAL NATIONALISTS AND

THE CARTER STATEMENT, 1975–1977

◆

The attempt by militant Irish-American nationalists to rejuvenate their activities made some progress. From the mid-1970s onward, Noraid became more systematic in its fund-raising efforts, while the Irish National Caucus emerged as a well organized lobbying group in Washington. Despite these achievements, however, political developments in Northern Ireland tended to increase Irish-American dissatisfaction with republicanism.

In 1975 the IRA entered into another truce with the British. The effects of this action nearly destroyed the Provisionals and produced a series of internal feuds. These internecine conflicts led to disillusionment within Noraid and other militant irredentist groups. While Irish-American republicanism continued to decline, constitutional nationalists and reconciliation groups made increasingly successful appeals for support.

Following the collapse of the Northern Ireland power-sharing executive in 1974, political developments again produced an atmosphere conducive to talks between the Provisionals and the new Labour government of Harold Wilson. By the mid-seventies, the IRA was exhausted by its sustained military offensive. Top Provisionals gradually reached the conclusion that the organization needed a rest, to regroup and revitalize its campaign.

Concurrently, the British secretary of state, Merlyn Rees, was trying to establish a constitutional convention at which he hoped the main political parties in Ulster would come together. The objective of this convention was to work out an agreed political framework to run the province. Rees felt this process would be enhanced if the level of violence dropped. Therefore, he gradually accepted the idea of compromising with the IRA. As a reward for reduced levels of violence, he increased the pace of freeing republican internees.

A line of communication was established between the Provisionals and British officials. These contacts blossomed after a delegation of Protestant churchmen met with prominent republicans at Feakle, County Clare on December 9, 1974. Following this meeting, the IRA Army Council declared a Christmas truce from midnight December 22 to January 2, 1975. In response, Merlyn Rees reduced the size and frequency of army patrols in nationalist ghettoes and increased the numbers of internees being released.

The IRA responded by extending their Christmas cease-fire for a further two weeks. Rees then announced he would stop issuing interim custody orders, phase out internment, and reduce civilian screening in republican areas. These moves appealed to the Provisionals. On February 9, 1975, the Army Council announced an indefinite cease-fire. The British government then established a series of incident centers to monitor the truce. All were equipped with a direct line through which Sinn Féin could contact British officials.

Initially, Irish republicans were encouraged by the fact that they were again negotiating with the British. Sinn Féin president Ruairí O'Brádaigh felt the truce was a prelude to British withdrawal and the unification of Ireland. This assessment was soon shown to be illusory. The cease-fire caused such intense problems that Provo leaders now admit the organization almost collapsed.[1]

Without the British Army for targets, the IRA increased its attacks on loyalist paramilitaries and on ordinary Protestants. In July 1975, the Provos exploded a bomb in the Bayardo Bar on the Shankill Road,

1. Patrick Bishop and Eamon Mallie, *The Provisional I.R.A.* (London: Heinemann, 1987), 217.

killing five patrons. When five Catholics were killed in South Armagh, they responded by shooting ten Protestant workmen near the village of Bessbrook. Some disgruntled Provos also joined an internal feud within the Official IRA which left eleven republicans from various factions dead.

By the late autumn of 1975 it was obvious that there would be no political progress through the constitutional convention and the British saw no further use for a cease-fire. Rees announced he would release all detainees by the end of the year as part of a new security initiative. Although republicans in Ireland generally welcomed this, in America Noraid realized it would remove an inflammatory issue that was a key ingredient in their fund-raising pitch. In November Rees closed the incident centers, and open hostilities with the Provos resumed.

The effects of the cease-fire presented great problems for Irish-American support groups. Internal feuds, coupled with the increase in sectarian attacks, tended to undermine the traditional republican presentation of the Ulster conflict. To some Irish-American activists, it seemed like the various factions of the IRA were acting like gangsters rather than leading a rebellion to drive the British out of Ireland.

Another problem arose from the fact that the existence of a cease-fire had not ended IRA attacks. The Provos' continued campaign of assassinations and bombings caused outrage and revulsion in the American media. Specific atrocities were given in-depth coverage both in the press and on television; they severely damaged the IRA's image.

On September 29, 1975, an IRA bomb exploded at an Italian restaurant in London's Mayfair district. Among the many tourists injured was an Irish-American attorney from Philadelphia. He gave numerous interviews to US reporters in which he attacked the viscousness of the IRA. The man told how he had previously supported the republican cause in America but now realized the brutal nature of the IRA and the true use to which Irish-American money was put.

The American press and television networks also focused on an IRA car bomb attack on October 23, 1975, which nearly killed Caroline Kennedy, daughter of the slain American president. The bomb was intended for Conservative MP Hugh Fraser, but it exploded prematurely and killed the eminent leukemia specialist Doctor Gordon Hamilton Fairley. Caroline Kennedy was staying as a guest of Fraser and he had intended to drive her to art college that morning. Reports in America described how Kennedy missed death by seconds. The incident created extremely adverse publicity for the IRA.[2] Editorial writers used Kennedy's position as a member of one of the most famous Irish-American families in order to discourage contributions to republican groups. The *Chicago Tribune* advised readers:

> There are reports that the recent wave of violence in England—which nearly killed Caroline Kennedy—was a last ditch effort by the IRA to goad the British government into retaining internment. Irish Americans who don't want to be part of this shabby act should resist whatever temptation there is to contribute to Irish organizations that may be fronts for the terrorists.[3]

The British Information Service

British government agencies in the United States encouraged the American media to publish anti-republican viewpoints and sustained an incessant campaign to discredit the IRA. The most important of these agencies was the British Information Service (BIS), in New York. The BIS developed a number of sophisticated techniques to ensure British policy was presented to Americans in the best possible light. They maintained a large mailing list of individuals and groups interested in Ireland and sent out weekly updates on political developments in Ulster. British officials sponsored public forums, encouraged British diplomats and MPs to tell Americans about IRA atrocities, and stressed the links between Irish republicans and world terrorist and communist groups.[4]

The BIS increased in sophistication during the mid-seventies and grew to a full-time staff of forty-five with an annual budget of $1.6 million. In 1975, journalist John Weisman showed how they had become particularly adept at influencing the American media. BIS officials began using public affairs consultants and public relations firms. They held informal

2. After this incident, Jackie Onassis discussed the safety of her daughter with officials at the US embassy. Caroline eventually moved to a Mayfair apartment of family friends and received a police bodyguard. See *New York Times*, 6 November 1975.

3. *Chicago Tribune*, 10 December 1975.

4. Paul Foot in *Who Framed Colin Wallace?* (London: MacMillan, 1989), 23, also claims that British Intelligence conducted a campaign codenamed "Clockwork Orange" aimed at feeding disinformation about the IRA to the international media. Part of the objective was to undermine Irish-American support for the Provos.

dinner receptions for newspaper editors, news executives, and television anchor people at which the British viewpoint was explained.[5]

The agency established a direct satellite link to the Central Office of Information in London. With this technology, one head of the BIS claimed he could pump British ministerial policy statements into six thousand local radio stations throughout the United States. The BIS also perfected the technique of producing government "news spots," which presented British policy in a favorable light, and getting them aired on network television news programs.[6]

The climax of early British propaganda initiatives against republicanism in the United States came in December 1975, when Prime Minister Harold Wilson organized a conference for the Association of American Correspondents. He called this gathering in response to escalating IRA violence. Many British politicians and newspapers had voiced their indignation that IRA atrocities were financed by Irish Americans. After the bombing of London's Hilton Hotel in September 1975, the *Sunday Times* printed the following editorial:

> There is one clear set of culprits who can be identified for outrages on innocent people—the Americans who maintain the terrorists and pay for the bombs and guns. . . . Some are stirred to help the victims of so-called British atrocities, tales of which are credulously disseminated by some American radio and television stations. The US government has done something to cut down on the illegal traffic in guns; it could do more to inhibit the collection of blood money. The darkest burden is on the consciences of individual citizens who, from the comfort of their homes, nurture the vilest terrorism.[7]

Acting from this feeling of disgust toward republican sympathizers in America, Prime Minister Wilson hoped to influence US journalists to reflect and support a similar attitude at home. At the conference he specifically singled out Noraid and stated:

> Those who subscribe to the INAC are not financing the welfare of the Irish people, as they may delude themselves, they are financing

5. John Weisman, "Foreign Lobbyists: How They Try to Manipulate U.S. Television," *T.V. Guide*, 18 November 1978.

6. Stuart Simon, "How Britain is Losing the Irish Argument," *Listener* (2 December 1982) 108.

7. *Sunday Times* (London), 7 September 1975.

murder. It should be understood by subscribers to Noraid that the million or more dollars that have flowed from America to Ireland since 1971 have financed murders and maiming. When they contribute their dollars for the old country they are not helping their much loved shamrock to flower. They are splattering it with blood![8]

Wilson then pleaded with the journalists to convey this message to their readers and show them that the IRA "killers" of the present had nothing to do with the "patriots of 1916." His tactic proved successful, as the major national newspapers and television channels reported the speech in detail and endorsed his views in news commentaries and editorials.

Although influential American opinion makers did support Wilson, it seems extremely doubtful that tactics such as his changed the minds of Irish-American republicans. Ironically, militant irredentist groups used British condemnations to enhance their campaigns and exploit the latent anglophobia of their supporters. Michael Kilian, a journalist with the *Chicago Tribune*, correctly pointed out,

> British attempts to sway Irish-American opinion to their views have proved clumsy, futile, and increasingly counter-productive. Irish Americans tend to believe just the opposite of what the British say—especially concerning the North.[9]

Irish government officials and leaders of the SDLP also felt that British statements criticizing Irish Americans served little useful purpose. They believed that condemnations from Westminster gave unnecessary publicity to Noraid and presented the group with an opportunity to strike back. Irish diplomats also frequently complained of having to fight a two-front war in the US, against BIS propaganda on the one hand and militant republicanism on the other. John Hume continually tried to get these points across to British officials. He recalls:

> I told successive British ministers that it was foolish going to America and saying to people not to support Noraid because all they did was provide them with publicity. What they should have said was they were satisfied the vast majority of Irish Americans were peaceful people and did not want to promote violence in Ireland.[10]

8. *Survey Magazine* (January 1976), 4.
9. *Chicago Tribune*, 1 June 1977.
10. John Hume, interview with author, 3 January 1989.

Senator Edward Kennedy and Constitutional Nationalism

At the outbreak of the Troubles, the Irish government had shown uncertainty in its response to the IRA. There are allegations that prominent
Fianna Fáil politicians supplied money for weapons and that Irish Army
officers helped train republicans.[11] This tacit support was extended to the
United States, where Irish diplomats did nothing to counteract the formation and expansion of Noraid activities.

By 1972, the Irish government's ambiguous policy toward the IRA
had changed. The campaign of bombing and shooting by the Provisionals after Bloody Sunday, eroded the reluctance of the Dublin government
to take strong measures. The Lynch administration introduced special
criminal courts and increased police powers to act against the IRA.

This clampdown was also extended to militant nationalist groups in
America. In October 1972 Desmond O'Malley, minister for justice,
made a publicity tour to counteract Irish-American republicanism.
Shortly after this effort, Taoiseach Lynch conducted a similar tour, in
which he emphasized that Noraid money was not used to help "widows
and orphans" but to "create them!" His trip had mixed results. The most
widely reported incident on the campaign occurred when republican
demonstrators in New York showered the Taoiseach with rotten eggs.
This attack was front-page news back in Ireland. Newspaper articles
helped Noraid by exaggerating the incident and creating the impression
that all Irish Americans were hostile to Lynch's anti-republican policies.[12]

Despite initial setbacks, the Irish coalition government, which took
office in 1973, continued and intensified anti-IRA campaigns in the
United States. Garret FitzGerald, minister for foreign affairs, personally
directed the government's anti-republican initiatives. He was strongly
supported by the Irish diplomatic and consular services in New York and
Washington. The Labour Party also wanted to show its abhorrence of the
IRA. Consequently, Conor Cruise O'Brien began playing a key role in
the drive against republicans on both sides of the Atlantic.

Conor Cruise O'Brien was particularly alarmed at the activities of
Irish-American republicans. During his period in office, he made a
number of visits to the US and concentrated on attacking the IRA. He
took every opportunity to appear on television and radio, to advise the

11. Tim Pat Coogan, *The I.R.A.: A History* (Colorado: Roberts Rinehart, 1993), 253–54.
12. *Irish Times* (Dublin), 11 January 1973.

editorial boards of newspapers, and to tell Irish-American gatherings that money donated to republicans was bringing death and destruction to the Irish people.[13]

O'Brien tried to convey this viewpoint to Irish-American delegations visiting Ireland. He also made a number of public criticisms of Paul O'Dwyer for his republican views. In 1975, for example, O'Brien addressed a delegation from the US Chamber of Commerce in Dublin. He urged the representatives to do everything in their power to stop support for the IRA in America and later told them that Paul O'Dwyer's views were similar to those of Adolf Hitler.[14]

Garret FitzGerald also made frequent publicity trips to the United States. He carried on a similar campaign of publicizing constitutional nationalism and proved particularly adept at getting his views across to the American media. Frequent editorials in a variety of newspapers quoted FitzGerald in order to persuade Irish Americans not to fund the IRA. As foreign minister, FitzGerald remained in contact with influential leaders in Congress and played a key role in blocking republican attempts to get hearings on Northern Ireland through his friendship with House Speaker Carl Albert.[15]

Republicans in the United States singled out FitzGerald and O'Brien for continual attack because they assumed that noncommitted Irish Americans would be inclined to listen to elected Irish representatives. In republican publications the two ministers were lambasted as "traitors." Conor Cruise O'Brien was continually satirized as the archetypal "West Brit" and accused of hypocrisy for presenting himself as a supporter of democracy while enforcing the Section 31 broadcasting ban against members of the IRA in the Republic of Ireland.

Irish-American republicans tried to stifle the attacks from Irish ministers at every opportunity. During a speaking engagement in New York in 1974, Noraid supporters heckled FitzGerald. The foreign minister so infuriated republicans in the audience that they rushed the platform and forced him to flee the hall. FitzGerald later bitterly condemned these protestors for having a "simplistic and frozen-in-aspic concept of Irish nationalism."[16]

13. Dr. Conor Cruise O'Brien, correspondence with author, 1 November 1989.

14. *New York Times*, 23 April 1975.

15. Garret FitzGerald, interview with author, 19 December 1990.

16. Garret FitzGerald, *All in a Life* (Dublin: MacMillan, 1991), 180.

Despite republican attempts to silence and lampoon the Irish ministers, constitutional nationalists continued to present a serious challenge to the support base of militant nationalism in America. The SDLP also assisted the Irish government. John Hume, in particular, made frequent trips to the US to explain his party's political position and to campaign for funds to support social schemes and economic development in Northern Ireland.

One of the first major publicity drives Hume undertook was the April 1974 visit to win support for the power-sharing executive. He tried to encourage American investment in Ulster, but he also took every opportunity to criticize Irish-American financing of the IRA.[17] During subsequent visits, Hume tried to establish contacts with important politicians. He realized the chief asset of the IRA support groups was their permanent presence among Irish-American activists. Because of this problem, Hume admits:

> Talking to grassroots Irish Americans in the early 1970s, I discovered that they listened to and supported my views. However, when someone else came along and presented them with a republican perspective, they changed again. Getting one's point across took a lot of time, energy, and effort, which I couldn't afford. Because of this I began to concentrate my efforts in talking to influential American politicians.[18]

Increasingly, Hume focused his efforts on Washington and nurtured political connections in order to win support for his position. The most important contact he made was with Senator Edward Kennedy.

Edward Kennedy had earlier become the darling of militant irredentist groups when he proposed British withdrawal in his congressional resolution and campaigned for the Fort Worth Five. The Irish government and the SDLP, however, regarded the senator's actions as harmful and lending credence to the republican perspective on Ulster. In an interview with the *Washington Post* in March 1972, Jack Lynch criticized Kennedy and said, "I don't think he understands the situation as fully as we do. It requires some period of time before the soldiers can be pulled out to dampen down and reconcile feelings."[19] Political analysts reported that within the Irish government there was a growing "irritation with Ameri-

17. *Christian Science Monitor*, 27 April 1974.
18. John Hume, interview with author, 3 January 1989.
19. "Lynch Raps Kennedy over Ulster," *Washington Post*, 3 March 1972.

can politicians who see this island's troubles against an outdated Abbey Theater backdrop of Britain against Ireland."[20] A leading member of Fine Gael commented, "He [Kennedy] is a bloody nuisance and I wish he would shut up!"[21]

John Hume shared some of these feelings and felt that, although Kennedy was acting out of a genuine desire to help the situation in Ulster, his comments were inopportune and somewhat naive. Hume hoped to meet the senator and discuss his own views of the problem in Northern Ireland.

In *Statesman of the Troubles*, Barry White described how this hope materialized in November 1972. While Kennedy was attending a conference in Germany, he telephoned Hume and said he would like to talk about Northern Ireland. The two met at the Irish embassy in Bonn and had a long political discussion. Kennedy maintains he was immediately impressed by Hume's politics and from this point on they became close friends.[22]

Barry White contends that through Hume's influence, Kennedy moderated his perspective on Irish politics and moved to the constitutional nationalist position. Hume himself does not acknowledge this influence, while Kennedy maintains British policy changes were more important in his "conversion." Kennedy states, "I have great respect for John Hume's leadership and insights, but my more moderate tone was a reaction to Great Britain's more moderate policy toward Northern Ireland."[23]

The moderate British policies Kennedy refers to were the abolition of Stormont and the phasing out of internment. The senator responded to each of these moves by issuing statements in support of British policy. When Secretary of State William Whitelaw began the process of constructing a power-sharing government, Kennedy warmly welcomed the initiative and increased his praises of the secretary of state. In February 1973, Kennedy held a private meeting with Prime Minister Edward Heath at the British embassy in Washington. The press reported that he assured Heath of his full support for the British initiative and told the prime minister he would "try to take a more positive attitude toward

20. C. L. Sulzberger "Ireland's Long Term Hope," *New York Times*, 11 July 1972.

21. *Chicago Tribune*, 11 March 1972.

22. Barry White, *John Hume: Statesman of the Troubles* (Belfast: Blackstaff Press, 1984), 186.

23. Senator Edward Kennedy, correspondence with author, 16 April 1989.

Ulster."[24] The senator lavished particular praise on William Whitelaw after the Sunningdale agreement and even suggested his nomination for the Nobel Peace Prize.[25]

Kennedy outlined his changed attitude to the Northern Ireland conflict in an essay entitled "Ulster Is an International Issue," which appeared in the political journal *Foreign Policy*. In this article, he restated his belief that the US government could perform a useful role in solving the Ulster problem and returned to his old analogy with Vietnam. He did, however, greatly praise the power-sharing policy as "Britain's most constructive initiative in nearly four years of bloodshed." Kennedy also emphasized his support for political dialogue and made a forthright condemnation of violence. He criticized the work of Irish-American republicans and said, "I categorically condemn the flow of arms or any funds for arms from the United States."[26]

Kennedy considered the collapse of power sharing a great tragedy. He suggested the British should have used the army against loyalist strikers. Yet the senator did not revert to his former position of calling for a British withdrawal. He was careful to temper his statements, and he worked to strengthen his connections with John Hume and Irish government officials. Kennedy, characterizing the IRA as a "cut-throat terrorist gang," thus emerged as a primary exponent of constitutional nationalism in America.[27]

The FARA and Gunrunning

The success of the SDLP and Irish government in winning the most prestigious Irish-American politician to their cause was a major blow to republicans in America. Compounding this loss was US Justice Department's increased harassment of Noraid under the Foreign Agents Registration Act.

In early 1976, the State Department, Justice Department, Treasury Department, and FBI held another high-level interdepartmental conference

---

24. Fred Emery, "Kennedy said to have Assured Heath of Positive Attitude on Ulster," *The Times* (London), 3 February 1973.

25. *The Times* (London), 11 December 1973.

26. E. M. Kennedy, "Ulster is an International Issue," *Foreign Policy* 57 (September 1973). For a detailed critique of Kennedy's article, see Brian Mawhinney and Ronald Wells, *Conflict and Christianity in Northern Ireland* (Detroit: Eerdmans, 1975), 55–72.

27. "Interview with Senator Kennedy," *Irish-America* (May 1991), 24–31.

to discuss their strategy against Irish-American republicans. They determined to forge even closer links with their British and Irish counterparts. On a visit to Northern Ireland in April 1976, the American ambassador to Britain announced that a team of US Customs agents would travel to Belfast to discuss more effective ways to stop the arms flow.[28] Later that year, US Customs officials organized a series of meetings with agents from the FBI and Bureau of Alcohol, Tobacco and Firearms (BATF) to discuss the feasibility of a joint "task force" to counteract IRA operations in the United States. Although the agents did not endorse this proposal, they determined to strengthen the supply of information between agencies and to coordinate their activities against gunrunning.[29]

Following the 1976 interdepartmental meeting, US officials decided to make Noraid declare the IRA as its foreign principal and force the *Irish People* to register as an agent of Noraid. In April, the Justice Department conducted an extensive investigation and compiled a vast collection of evidence to support their objective. Federal agents continued to assume that if Noraid was forced to acknowledge the IRA as its foreign principal, that would dilute the group's claim to be helping the families of prisoners. They still believed that this would weaken Noraid's fund-raising appeal.

This US government offensive initiated a long series of court battles in which Noraid and the *Irish People* received legal representation from Paul O'Dwyer, Frank Durkan, and attorneys from the American Civil Liberties Union. The litigation dragged on for years and eventually ended in a government victory.[30]

The United States law enforcement agencies combined this legal battle with a revamped campaign to smash the IRA gunrunning network. In 1976 they uncovered a major arms supply line working out of Philadelphia. The subsequent prosecutions were a serious blow to the republican network and further increased the circumstantial evidence that Noraid was linked to weapons procurement.

---

28. *New Orleans Times-Picayune*, 5 April 1976.

29. FOIA files on the FBI and the IRA, 5 November and 10 December 1976. No. NY 100–7828.

30. The *Irish People* was forced to acknowledge a legal connection to Noraid and, under the FARA, its management was opened to intense federal scrutiny. In 1986, the newspaper won an appeal against this. The *Irish People* is now legally separate from Noraid, despite the fact that the group's executive has a significant influence over the newspaper's operations.

In 1973, Daniel Cahalane, a key member of the Philadelphia gun-running cell, was the subject of a grand jury investigation. He spent more than six months in jail for refusing to testify but was later released due to lack of evidence. The FBI continued to investigate Cahalane's activities after his release and in 1975 they infiltrated the group. Bureau agents uncovered an attempt to send more than four hundred rifles and 140,000 rounds of ammunition to the Provisionals. After a grand jury investigation, Cahalane and Neil Byrne, both members of Noraid, were convicted along with three accomplices. In a separate court case, Frank Grady, a co-conspirator, received a two-year, suspended prison sentence. Grady was the founder and chairman of the Yonkers chapter of Noraid.[31]

Cahalane and Byrne appealed their convictions. A Pennsylvania court upheld the original decision and ruled that

> Noraid engaged in various fund-raising activities and was also the center of the armament purchase and transportation efforts. A Noraid member testified about his work in picking up, crating, and transporting weapons for the organization. . . . Telephone records disclosed innumerable conversations . . . to Noraid headquarters by both Byrne and Cahalane. Byrne also negotiated with a government for the purchase of rifles, machine guns, armour-piercing ammunition, rocket launchers and mortars.[32]

The increasing conviction rate of Noraid members for gunrunning led important Irish-American associations to distance themselves from the group. Michael Flannery insisted his organization was not involved in supplying arms, nor was it responsible for the activities of its members in these schemes. Despite denials, however, there was a widespread impression that Noraid was heavily involved in the arms supply business. This feeling intensified after a series of detailed investigations of the organization by the *New York Times*, the *Washington Post* and the *Los Angeles Times* in the winter of 1975–76.[33]

---

31. For details of this case see *Sunday Independent*, 14 March 1976.

32. "The Noraid Involvement in Gunrunning," British Information Service document, 14 December 1981.

33. See Bernard Weinraub, "I.R.A. Aid Unit in the Bronx Linked to Flow of Arms," *New York Times*, 16 December 1975; Charles Powers, "New York Irish Aid: The Collecting o' the Green," *Los Angeles Times*, 12 January 1976; William Claibourne, "Cash is for the Bairns 'tis said, Not for Guns," *Washington Post*, 25 January 1976.

These investigative reports all implied that Noraid was an important link in the supply of weapons to the IRA. They supported British and US government charges that 75 percent of the money sent to the group went to buy guns. From the evidence produced in these reports, all three newspapers issued editorials attacking Irish-American republicans and alleging that money given to Noraid was funding violence and murder in Ireland.[34]

These newspaper investigations were supported by special features on network television. In early 1976, the three major channels ran carefully prepared documentaries on Noraid's link to gunrunning. ABC produced their report on February 2 and 3, NBC on April 9, and CBS on St. Patrick's Day. All tried to expose Noraid's subversive activities. They suggested a clear connection between the military effectiveness of the IRA and financial support from the United States.[35]

Constitutional Nationalists and Reconciliation Groups

The forces working against the republican position in America coalesced and intensified in 1976. As part of the Bicentennial celebrations, Irish Taoiseach Liam Cosgrave traveled to the US for an official visit in March. He toured the country extensively and met formally with President Gerald Ford. Cosgrave's diplomatic staff convinced him that he had a perfect opportunity to cut Irish-American funding for the IRA. Cosgrave agreed; the forum he chose was an address to both houses of Congress on St. Patrick's Day. The tactic was a publicity coup, as his speech was widely reported in the press and broadcast by the network news stations on their evening reports. CBS evening news showed footage of the Taoiseach delivering the following section of his address:

There are in this country some people who contribute in the most direct way possible to violence in Ireland by sending guns and bombs for use in Northern Ireland. A large number have contributed, thoughtlessly or otherwise, to organizations nominally engaged in relief work which have used that money to buy arms and explosives. What they are doing, whatever their motives, with every dime or dollar they give

34. *New York Times*, 24 December 1975.

35. See Ken Ward, "Ulster Terrorism: The U.S. Network News Coverage of Northern Ireland, 1968–79," in Y. Alexander and A. O'Day, eds., *Terrorism in Ireland* (New York: St. Martin's Press, 1984), 210.

thoughtlessly, is helping to kill and maim Irish men and women of every religious persuasion.[36]

Political analysts considered this appeal, launched by the Irish Taoiseach on St. Patrick's Day, to have had a significant impact on Irish Americans who were interested in Northern Ireland. They believed the speech, which was reinforced by a joint communique from Cosgrave and President Ford, persuaded substantial numbers of Irish-American activists to reconsider their support for the IRA and cut their contributions to republican groups.

Irish diplomats also tried to cut Noraid funding by encouraging the Ireland Fund. This organization was founded in 1976 by groups of influential Irish Americans and Irish people living in the United States. The driving force behind the new organization was Tony O'Reilly, former Irish rugby star and president of H. J. Heinz Company. O'Reilly had been involved in supporting charitable projects in Ireland and wanted to establish an organization similar to the United Jewish Appeal.[37] He was joined by other business and professional people including Daniel J. Rooney, president of the Pittsburgh Steelers; Charles Daly, president of the Joyce Foundation; and the Reverend Theodore Hesburgh, president of the University of Notre Dame.

Through mail soliciting and $500-per-plate dinners, the Ireland Fund developed into a huge money-raising organization. By 1992 it had raised a total of $50 million and supported hundreds of development initiatives, cultural projects, and charities.[38] One of the Ireland Fund's major goals was the encouragement of reconciliation schemes in Ulster. It continuously supported integrated education, the Corrymela Community, and cross-denominational business enterprise.[39]

The directors of the Ireland Fund insisted it was a nonpolitical organization with the sole objective of achieving reconciliation in Ireland. Tony O'Reilly, while encouraging Irish Americans not to support violence,

36. *CBS Evening News*, 17 March 1976.

37. For a biography of Tony O'Reilly see Donal O'Donovan, *Dreamers of Dreams: Portraits of the Irish in America* (Bray: Kilbride Books, 1984), 163–67.

38. *Connections*, Newsletter of the American Ireland Fund, December 1993.

39. In 1987 the Ireland Fund merged with the American Irish Foundation, which was formed in June 1963 by President John F. Kennedy. The organization changed its name to the American Ireland Fund and established branches in Australia, Canada, France, Germany, Britain, and New Zealand.

continually denied it directly competed with Noraid.[40] The Irish government, however, supported the organization principally because they felt it could offer Irish Americans a legitimate channel to donate for "the good of Ireland."[41] Political commentators and academics highlight this aspect of the Ireland Fund and claim it has weakened republican fund raising. In *The Pale Green Internationalists*, Bernard Crick concluded:

> Since 1976 the Ireland Fund has, with the public support of the Irish government, steadily drawn off the bulk of American donations into peaceable, legitimate, and above all accountable projects throughout Ireland. Wryly, Irish diplomats point to the correlation between the rise of the Fund and the rise of IRA bank robberies.[42]

Other political analysts were more sceptical about the Ireland Fund's impact on republican fund raising. In *Northern Ireland: The International Perspective*, Adrian Guelke pointed out that such claims need to be treated cautiously because the Ireland Fund operates in a very different social milieu than the Irish bars and clubs that are the main republican sources.[43] Ireland Fund dinners are traditionally lavish affairs, attended by the wealthy and famous, business leaders and politicians. O'Reilly said that it is not uncommon for one dinner to raise more than half a million dollars. This contrasts sharply with republican fund raisers. Noraid leader Matthew Higgins commented:

> The Ireland Fund is not a competitor because it's not money that would have come to us in the first place. They're what you might call fat cats—or lace curtain Irish. They have no use for republicans like us. When we raise $12,000 at a dance, why that's big money. It's peanuts to them.[44]

Even if the Ireland Fund did not seriously encroach on the traditional sources of republican donations, it did provide a forum for Irish ministers and British officials to meet and issue severe attacks against Noraid.

40. See Kevin O'Neill, "An Irish Peace Plan," *Boston Globe*, 31 March 1985.

41. Garret FitzGerald interview with author, 19 December 1990.

42. Bernard Crick, "The Pale Green Internationalists," *New Statesman* 96 (7 December 1979): 888.

43. Adrian Guelke, *Northern Ireland: The International Perspective* (Dublin: Gill and MacMillan, 1988), 137.

44. Donald McNeil, "Three Year Old Ireland Fund Grows With Peace Movement," *New York Times*, 21 May 1978.

Because of this, Ireland Fund dinners became prime targets for republican demonstrations. Militant Irish-American republicans also realize that, as one Irish official stated, "The Fund acts in a positive way, because it gets 700–800 people together to hear the Irish government and constitutional nationalist point of view."[45]

Irish Americans also began to get involved in the peaceful venture of sponsoring summer holidays for children from Northern Ireland. In the summer of 1974, the Rotary Club of Hibbing, Minnesota, organized a fund-raising scheme to provide an American vacation for children from troubled areas of Belfast. Members of the Rotary Club raised $47,000 and brought 120 teenagers over, half of the group being Protestant and the other half Catholic. The children stayed in the homes of host families in Minnesota who had volunteered to participate in the scheme.[46]

The Minnesota venture caught the imagination of Irish Americans and others concerned with promoting reconciliation in Ulster. In 1975, a number of new schemes emerged to bring Irish children to the US for a holiday away from violence. These included the *Ulster Project*, based in the Midwest, the *Cape Cod Irish Children's Program*, and the *Irish Children's Summer Program* in Greensboro, North Carolina. One of the most successful of these new organizations was the New York–based *Project Children*. The scheme was launched by Dennis Mulcahy, a bomb disposal expert with the New York Police Department. In 1975, he organized a series of fund-raising events and collected enough cash to bring six Irish children to upstate New York. Since then, the organization has flourished and now raises hundreds of thousands of dollars to provide holidays for 800 to 900 children annually.[47]

Initially these organizations merely wanted to give Ulster children a break from sectarian violence. But as the groups expanded, they extended their objectives to include the fostering of reconciliation between Protestant and Catholic children through their shared experiences in the United States. In the initial schemes, children stayed with host families of the same religion and met the other participants only on their journey to and from America. Gradually, groups such as the *Children's Friendship Pro-*

45. Peter Gunning, former Irish consul-general in Chicago, interview with author, 13 July 1989.

46. See Judy Klemesrud, "For Belfast Children, a Summer of Tranquility in Minnesota," *New York Times*, 10 July 1974.

47. See report on Project Children in *Los Angeles Times*, 21 September 1986.

ject began organizing joint activities to bring all the children together. They placed both Protestants and Catholics in the same household. Some also organized reunions for children who had participated in the scheme when they returned to Belfast. The aim was to enable the continuance of cross-religious friendships formed in America.[48]

Leaders of the children's holiday schemes strongly believed that contacts and relationships developed in the United States would help the process of peace in Ulster. They continually cited examples of children who maintained friendships despite intense pressure within their respective communities. This optimism was epitomized by Vaughan Nesslar of the *Ulster Project*, who maintained, "None of our kids have joined the IRA or UDA. When they get on that plane, we have 20 friends going back, not 10 Catholics and 10 Protestants."[49]

Despite these lofty claims, there is scepticism about the level of reconciliation actually achieved by the American holidays. Dr. Liz McWhirter, a psychologist at Queen's University, conducted research that found basic sectarian attitudes unchanged in the children despite their experience in the United States. Some journalists and political analysts contend that the holidays are merely a welcome break for the children and have no effect whatsoever on cross-community relations.[50]

John Morrow, a director of the Corrymela Community, also criticized the holiday scheme and said that Americans could do more good by sending funds to support reconciliation projects in Northern Ireland. He said the short vacations actually had the effect of alienating some of the younger participants from their home environment. Morrow described how some children were extremely frustrated at having to return to the ghettoes of Belfast after spending time in the affluence of suburban America. There have also been suggestions that immigration rates among children who have been to the US is high, thus depriving the province of individuals who were a potential force for reconciliation.

Although there are contradictory views of the effects of American holidays on children from Ulster, the schemes have had an important effect on Irish Americans. The various groups provide an outlet for individuals who want to do something for Northern Ireland. The leaders and

48. Kevin McHugh, "Coppin' an Attitude," *Irish Echo* (New York), 13 October 1993.

49. *Chicago Tribune*, 18 November 1993.

50. See Bob O'Connor, "Ulster Children's Getaway to U.S. Draws Scepticism," *Chicago Tribune*, 22 July 1985.

supporters of these projects workenthusiastically to raise funds and publicize their activities.[51] Like the Ireland Fund, the children's schemes provide Irish Americans with a means to project their concerns for Ulster
into peaceful programs.

The growth of reconciliation groups in America coincided with the
emergence of a women's peace movement in Northern Ireland in 1976.
The Peace People caused serious problems to the IRA and also to Noraid.
The women attracted extremely favorable media coverage and widespread support in the United States, which further undermined republican publicity efforts.

The incident that gave rise to the formation of the Peace People occurred on August 10, 1976. As Anne Maguire was walking with her four
children in Belfast, a speeding car approached, pursued by a convoy of
British army vehicles. Troops fired on the car and killed the driver, a
member of the IRA from Andersonstown. The vehicle careered off the
road, killing three of the Maguire children and seriously injuring their
mother.

After this incident, Anne Maguire's sister, Mairead Corrigan, collapsed in tears during a television interview. Betty Williams, another
Belfast housewife, was so moved she contacted Corrigan; the women decided to form the Peace People. They organized a series of emotional rallies and marches, which attracted impressive support from women in
both communities. Williams and Corrigan became international celebrities and won the 1976 Nobel Peace Prize for their efforts.

In America, the Peace People received euphoric support. The press
and television presented Williams and Corrigan as great heroines, praising their courage and fearlessness. The peace movement was presented
as a great sign for change in Ulster and an expression of mass disgust at
violence.

The adulation in support of the Peace People redoubled when the two
women were awarded the Nobel Peace Prize. Publicity increased as leading American politicians registered their support and were joined by personalities from the entertainment world. Folk singer Joan Baez became
an active supporter of the Peace People and sang at some of their major
rallies.

51. The commitment of those working in holiday schemes has been greatly strengthened
by the death of Leanne Murray, a thirteen-year-old Protestant who was killed in the Shankill
Road bombing of October 1993. Murray had spent the previous summer in Chicago as part
of the *Irish Children's Fund.*

At the end of September 1976, Betty Williams and Mairead Corrigan announced they would visit the United States to publicize their movement, raise funds, and persuade Irish Americans not to contribute to the violence in Northern Ireland. In response, republicans in Belfast asked Noraid to use all available means to discredit the two women.

Republicans learned in advance that one of the women's engagements was to tape an interview at the studios of WNED Television in Buffalo. They made threatening phone calls to the station, claiming the women would be killed if they appeared for their broadcast. Executives of the television station decided to cancel the show, but Williams and Corrigan insisted on going ahead with their original plans. After some negotiation, they agreed to tape the show in New Orleans. This venue was considered safer than Buffalo, where there was significant republican support both in the city and just across the Canadian border in Toronto.

The two leaders of the Peace People arrived in New Orleans on October 4, 1976, and fulfilled their television engagement. They then embarked on a hectic round of press conferences, radio broadcasts, and television appearances. Betty Williams typified the message they presented during an interview on the *MacNeil/Lehrer NewsHour*:

> Americans send money over to Ireland and they think that they are sending us help. They're sending us death. They're killing us with groups like Noraid. Third generation Irish Americans think they are helping orphans and widows but they are killing our people.[52]

Irish-American republicans tried to counteract the support and publicity the Peace People generated but were singularly unsuccessful. Noraid leaders accused the two women of being "British stooges and collaborators"; a series of scathing editorials in the *Irish People* referred to them as "Dangerous Clowns."[53] These attacks seemed particularly unjust, even to some noted republican activists such as Paul O'Dwyer. When Williams and Corrigan announced they were afraid to go to New York during their tour, O'Dwyer tried to persuade them they would not be harassed and their safety would be guaranteed.[54]

After the triumph of their first tour, Williams and Corrigan made many more visits to America and continued to pressure the republican support network. On each successive visit they gathered support from American

52. From interview reported in *New Orleans Times-Picayune*, 6 October 1976.
53. *Irish People* (New York), 11 June 1977.
54. *New York Times*, 7 October 1976.

politicians. On a visit to the US in June 1977, Betty Williams held extensive talks with Edward Kennedy, Hugh Carey (governor of New York), and Andrew Young (US ambassador to the United Nations). Afterwards, these politicians promised to increase their efforts to cut Irish-American support for the IRA. They also made a commitment to help establish Peace People support groups in America, which would raise funds and distribute the movement's newspaper, *Peace by Peace*. President Jimmy Carter also expressed his admiration for the peace movement and sent them a telegram to say, "We are 100 percent behind you in your courageous efforts."[55]

The Four Horsemen

The US publicity campaigns organized by the Peace People increased the groundswell of opinion building against Irish-American republicans. Noraid leaders, therefore, were greatly relieved when the peace movement suffered a series of internal divisions that severely weakened its effectiveness.[56] These developments, however, did not ease the problems faced by militant Irish-American nationalism. In the late seventies, the Irish government and SDLP greatly intensified their efforts against the republican network in the United States. One of the principal factors behind this renewed constitutional nationalist campaign was a publicity victory staged by the Irish National Caucus during the 1976 presidential campaign. The INC, with the support of many republican groups, tried to get politicians to speak out against British policy in Ulster. Father Seán McManus concentrated on the Democratic primaries and emphasized the importance of the "Irish vote" for electoral victory.

The Caucus and other Irish-American groups had some success: they persuaded Jimmy Carter to walk in the St. Patrick's Day parade in New York. As the then-governor of Georgia was marching down Fifth Avenue, someone stuck an "England Get Out of Ireland" badge on his lapel. Press photographers captured Carter in a wide grin with the political statement pinned to his coat. Almost immediately, the photograph appeared in the

55. *The Times* (London), 14 June 1977.
56. The Peace People were sharply criticized for keeping the money they received for the Nobel Peace Prize. Some suggested the women should have used the cash to finance reconciliation projects. Personal antagonisms also grew between the leaders of the group and Betty Williams left in 1980.

Irish Americans demonstrating against Prince Charles during a royal visit to San
Francisco in 1977. UPI/BETTMANN

British tabloids with a series of hostile commentaries attacking the governor for "exploiting the tragedy in Ulster to win votes."[57]

The publicity this incident generated encouraged militant irredentist
groups to campaign for an Irish policy in the Democratic Party's manifesto. After intense lobbying by Father McManus and Paul O'Dwyer,
they succeeded, but the resulting statement was a major disappointment.
The policy was jointly written by Mayor Richard Daley of Chicago and
Carter staff members. It was extremely vague and did not include a criticism of British policy. The Irish National Caucus, therefore, determined
to persuade Jimmy Carter to adopt a much harder line on human rights
abuses in Ulster.

57. See Kevin Kelley, *The Longest War: Northern Ireland and the I.R.A.* (Westport
Conn: Lawrence Hill and Co., 1982), 227.

At this time, Jimmy Carter, in the final stages of his presidential campaign, was trying to sell himself to East Coast ethnic groups. To impress Irish Catholics, he held a much-publicized conference with Cardinal Cooke in New York. He then flew to Pittsburgh on October 27 to meet with delegates from eighteen Irish-American political groups. The meeting was engineered by Father McManus, who used his friendship with State Senator Joe Timulty to convince Carter aides of the political benefits the Irish lobby could deliver. Despite efforts of the Irish and British government to stop McManus, Carter decided to go ahead with the meeting.

McManus made the introductory speech at the conference, issuing a fiery condemnation of British human rights violations. Carter, exhausted from continuous campaigning, overlooked controversial sections of the opening statement and said he supported McManus's views. In his speech, Carter remained purposely vague and made ambiguous references to civil rights and achieving peace in Ireland. Despite this, the British media characterized Carter's statements as endorsing the militant nationalist position.[58]

These media reports on Carter's speech caused a political storm across the Atlantic. A group of British MPs, supported by the Northern Ireland Secretary Roy Mason, tabled a House of Commons motion strongly condemning Carter and his unwelcome interference. In Belfast, James Molyneaux, the leader of the Ulster Unionist Party, attacked the "irresponsible opportunism of this peanut politician."[59]

Carter was alarmed at reaction his comments had generated. He immediately instructed his staff to cable both the Irish and British governments and inform them of the inaccuracy of the press reports. Carter aides then released an official statement which read, "I do not favor violence as part of a solution to the Irish question. I favor negotiations and peaceful means of finding a just solution which involves the two communities."[60]

Despite Carter's attempt to distance himself from militant nationalism, Irish-American republican groups claimed he supported their cause. They formed an "Irish American Committee for the Election of Carter and Mondale," with Paul O'Dwyer, Frank Durkan, and Matthew Higgins as

58. Seán Cronin, "What Carter said that day in Pittsburgh," *Irish Times* (Dublin), 10 November 1976.

59. *Belfast News Letter*, 29 October 1976.

60. *The Times* (London), 29 October 1976.

chief officials. The *Irish People* ran a banner headline encouraging its readers to vote democratic because "Jimmy Carter Doesn't Dodge the Issue of Northeast Ireland."[61]

The claim by Irish-American republicans to have influence with Carter was soon dispelled. In 1977 Dr. Fred Burns O'Brien supplied the new administration with ten documented cases of torture by British security forces. The cases were compiled by the Association for Legal Justice in Ireland and received support from Amnesty International. When the State Department released its annual report on human rights violations in 1978, there was no mention of the cases. The Irish National Caucus protested vehemently but was ignored by White House officials. Carter's administration thus continued the traditional policy of cautious impartiality on the Ulster question.[62]

The Carter incident had a major impact on constitutional nationalists. They realized that republican claims to have leverage with the president were insubstantial, yet they were greatly alarmed at the publicity the incident caused. They initiated a concerted lobbying campaign to show that militants had no real power in Washington and that all the important American political leaders supported moderation and reconciliation through dialogue.

Garret FitzGerald coordinated this policy from the Irish Foreign Affairs Department in Washington and was joined by two key figures— Seán Donlon, the former consul general in Boston, and Michael Lillis, the former press officer at the New York consulate. This triumvirate set out to increase the influence of constitutional nationalists in Congress by forging stronger ties with the most influential Irish-American politicians. They hoped that closer cooperation with politicians like Edward Kennedy and Tip O'Neill could nourish a strong support network, which would be used to crush republicans.

John Hume provided an essential link in this renewed strategy. He was a close friend of Seán Donlon from their student days at Maynooth College. In 1976, Hume accepted a fellowship at Harvard University's Center for International Relations. While staying in Boston, he kept in close contact with Donlon in Washington. Hume also renewed his friendship with Edward Kennedy and began using his influence to mold major Irish-American politicians into a cohesive unit that would work against the republican network. Michael Lillis also played a vital role in this

61. *Irish People* (New York), 30 October 1976.
62. See article by Jack Anderson, *Washington Post*, 17 June 1978.

process. From his 1976 appointment to the Irish embassy in Washington, he developed an extraordinarily close personal relationship with the leading Irish-American politicians on Capitol Hill.[63]

The Irish government and British politicians had long believed that if prominent Irish-American political leaders would speak out against the IRA, this would seriously impair republican groups in America. Calls for such a statement of repudiation, from Kennedy in particular, were issued from a variety of sources throughout the mid-1970s. When the senator expressed his "disgust" after the IRA killing of Professor Gordon Hamilton Fairley, the *London Sunday Times* issued an editorial that was reported in a variety of influential American political publications. It stated:

> The senator could do more than this. He could put his name at the head of a campaign of education in the United States to alert its citizens, especially those of Irish origin, to the consequences of their continued support for republicanism. . . . Edward Kennedy has a matchless glamour and influence in America. With a large Irish constituency, he has been critical of British policy in the North for many years. But he has never approved of violence. Now is the time for him to take a very practical step toward its elimination.[64]

Irish-American political leaders had traditionally been reluctant to issue outright condemnations of the republican tradition. For concrete political reasons, they typically supported Irish unity and strategically adopted an ambiguous position on the use of violence. Irish-American republican groups have always been active in the Democratic Party, trade unions, and police and fire departments. The temptation for politicians not to tangle with these groups was considerable. Few Irish-American leaders believed that anything they said could change committed republicans, so they believed there was little to be gained from speaking out against them.

The Irish diplomatic corps and John Hume worked to break this traditional reluctance among Irish-American political leaders. Hume used his friendship with Senator Edward Kennedy to establish contacts with the most influential Irish-American Democrats—Speaker of the House Thomas "Tip" O'Neill, Senator Daniel Moynihan, and Governor Hugh Carey of New York. Together with the Irish embassy in Washington,

63. Michael Lillis, interview with author, 20 January 1994.
64. *Sunday Times* (London), 25 October 1975.

Hume began to champion the idea that these "Four Horsemen" should coordinate their efforts on Ireland and issue a joint condemnation of IRA supporters in America.

Initially these political leaders followed the traditional Irish-American reluctance to condemn the militant nationalist tradition. Some had even utilized the republican network in their political campaigns. As a congressman during the early Troubles, Tip O'Neill issued belligerent statements on Northern Ireland. He once told Marvin Kalb of CBS television, "I always gave to the cause of the IRA because I thought it was the right thing to do."[65] He was influenced by growing up in the mostly Irish, working-class neighborhood of North Cambridge, Massachusetts, and remembers:

> We had a tremendous hatred for the English. In addition to our fierce Irish pride, there was our American heritage as well. Kids in other cities were playing cops and robbers, or cowboys and indians, but with us it was patriots and redcoats. . . . Each year on Easter Sunday, men of our neighborhood would go from door to door, collecting for the IRA. On the front window of almost every house you would see a sticker: "I gave to the Army."[66]

During his career in Congress, Hugh Carey had also been willing to follow the traditional line and back the republican cause. This inclination increased when he became governor of New York in 1974. In his gubernatorial campaign, he was supported by all the leading Irish republican associations and had Frank Durkan as head of his "Irish for Carey" group. In 1974, he attended a memorial service in New York for Michael Gaughan, a republican who died on hunger strike in England. At the service he delivered a strongly republican eulogy.

Daniel Moynihan first ran for the Senate in 1976 and, like Carey, used the support of the Irish-American republican groups. He published a campaign statement in the *Irish People* in which he endorsed congressional hearings on Ulster, condemned "British torture," and demanded Irish unity. The *Irish People* responded with an editorial that strongly endorsed Moynihan and O'Neill for political office.[67]

65. Report on *CBS News* by Mike Lee and Martin Kalb, 23 October 1977.

66. Tip O'Neill, *Man of the House: The Life and Political Memoirs of Speaker Tip O'Neill* (New York: Random House, 1987), 8.

67. *Irish People* (New York), 30 October 1976.

Despite this willingness to use the Irish republican network at election time, Moynihan, Carey, and O'Neill were increasingly impressed by the arguments of John Hume, Edward Kennedy, and the Irish diplomatic corps. In the winter of 1976, Hume and Lillis launched a concerted effort to persuade the Four Horsemen to issue a joint statement condemning Irish-American support for the IRA. Edward Kennedy was immediately receptive. He contacted the other three politicians and they all agreed. Hume then drafted an outline of the proposed statement and submitted it to the four politicians for amendments. Hume suggested the statement should not be released until St. Patrick's Day 1977, so that it would have maximum effect and receive full publicity.[68]

The Four Horsemen acknowledged the primary influence of Irish diplomats and Hume in their decision to issue a joint statement. They also claimed inspiration from the Peace People. Kennedy, O'Neill, and company expressed hope that their repudiation of Irish-American support for violence would help open the way to constructive dialogue between constitutional nationalists and unionists.

The Four Horsemen released their statement on March 16, 1977, and sent copies to the American press and television networks. They also delivered copies to the British government and to both unionist parties in Belfast. The most significant section of the statement read:

> We appeal to all those organizations engaged in violence to renounce their campaigns of death and destruction and return to the path of life and peace. And we appeal as well to our fellow Americans to embrace this goal of peace and to renounce any action that promotes the current violence or provides support or encouragement to organizations engaged in violence.[69]

In order to increase the impact of the statement, Garret FitzGerald traveled to America to meet with President Carter and senior members of his administration. During this conference, FitzGerald says that Carter fully supported the campaign to cut Irish-American support for the IRA. He also told reporters that the president had no links with the Irish National Caucus and would not be influenced by its lobbying on Capitol Hill.[70] Seán Donlon, elated over this diplomatic success, later stated,

68. John Hume, interview with author, 3 January 1989.

69. *New York Times*, 17 March 1977.

70. Dick Walsh "Carter Concerned Over I.R.A. Funds," *Irish Times* (Dublin), 17 March 1977.

The harnessing of the real Irish power in the US was now accomplished and the task from 1977 was of maintaining and oiling the machine so that, whenever needed, it could be brought into play.[71]

The Four Horsemen took every subsequent opportunity to reiterate their St. Patrick's Day message. Hugh Carey, while on a visit to Ireland in April, held meetings with Prime Minister Cosgrave and government officials. At public engagements and news conferences, he attacked the IRA, and he offered a solution to Irish-American activists who were confused by the organization's two separate wings:

> If the Provisionals were simply called the Irish killers and the Officials the Irish marxists, people would see what they stood for and they wouldn't receive a nickel's worth of support in the United States.[72]

At dinners for the Ireland Fund and the Democratic Party in the spring of 1977, Edward Kennedy and John Hume issued further condemnations of Irish-American funding of violence in Ulster and defended Hugh Carey's earlier remarks. Senator George McGovern further echoed these sentiments after undertaking a fact-finding mission to Ireland during September. In a report to Congress, McGovern said the efforts of the Four Horsemen were having positive results and stressed:

> Both the American government and private individuals who are concerned about Ireland should make every practical effort to avoid support or encouragement for extremist groups. Those who wish to make private contributions should take special care to assure that their funds will be used to alleviate suffering, not inflict it.[73]

The statements of the Four Horsemen received almost universal praise in the American press and were warmly welcomed by most Irish newspapers, including the pro-unionist *Belfast News Letter*. The *Irish Times* caught the impact and significance of the St. Patrick's Day message in the following editorial:

---

71. Seán Donlon, "Bringing Irish Diplomatic and Political Influence to Bear on Washington," *Irish Times* (Dublin), 25 January 1993.

72. *New York Post*, 22 April 1977. Hugh Carey continued these anti-republican statements when he returned to America. At his first weekly news conference in Albany, he added "Maoism" and "Trotskyism" to his list of IRA offenses.

73. Congress, Senate, Committee on Foreign Relations, *Ireland in 1977: A Report by Senator George McGovern to the Committee on Foreign Relations*, 23–24.

Few more welcome gestures could have been received on St. Patrick's Day than the call by four of the most distinguished and powerful Irish American leaders for an end to violence in Ireland. . . . It has been necessary to overcome the weight of much history, to suppress emotionalism, to spurn opportunities to make local political capital out of the situation in Northern Ireland—opportunities still eagerly garnished by too many American politicians. But when their own most respected leaders add their voices so firmly to those of the Irish and US governments and the SDLP, it is at least reasonable to hope that this may mark the beginning of the end of American support for the campaign of murder and destruction.[74]

Predictably, Noraid characterized the pronouncements of the Four Horsemen as despicable acts of betrayal. Condemnations were particularly intense because the political issue combined with class antagonisms toward the "lace curtain Irish." To the working class majority of Noraid members, the Four Horsemen epitomized middle-class, suburban Irish Americans who had forgotten their roots. Many republican activists resented the abandonment of allegiance to "turf and tribe" for material prosperity. This festering bitterness was directed at Kennedy and company as representatives of the "traitors" who had forgotten their heritage and become "British lackeys."[75]

Militant Irish Americans reserved particular hatred for Hugh Carey, who they felt had used them in his rise to political office and then completely abandoned them. Noraid picketed his election offices, he was inundated with abusive mail, and reports circulated that the Ancient Order of Hibernians had suspended his membership. Old political allies turned against him: Mario Biaggi led a demonstration outside his residence in New York; Paul O'Dwyer walked out of an Israel Bonds dinner rather than appear with the governor.[76]

The Four Horsemen remained undaunted by these attacks and continued their discussions with Irish government officials and John Hume. Edward Kennedy and Tip O'Neill wanted to give their calls for peace a

74. *Irish Times* (Dublin), 18 March 1977.

75. For an excellent statement of this feeling, see Alice McGoff's opinions about Ted Kennedy during the Boston busing crisis in J. Anthony Lukas, *Common Ground* (New York: Random House, 1986), 469.

76. Francis Clines, "Carey Angers Irish Leaders in New York," *New York Times*, 26 April 1977.

practical orientation. They increasingly felt it was time the British launched a new political initiative in Northern Ireland. They envisioned a new move toward dialogue between the SDLP and Unionist parties and began looking for practical measures to further this process.

John Hume, during a visit to America in May 1977, proposed that political change in Ulster could be encouraged by a statement from President Carter. He suggested to the Four Horsemen that Carter could offer the inducement of large-scale American financial aid and industrial investment if a political agreement was reached. Edward Kennedy and Tip O'Neill responded enthusiastically and were convinced the Carter administration would be well disposed to breaking the traditional American policy of nonintervention in Northern Ireland.

The Four Horsemen were encouraged by Carter's attempt to implement a "moral" foreign policy that incorporated a high regard for human rights. The president characterized himself as a peacemaker, having achieved the considerable success of securing an agreement between Egypt and Israel at the Camp David summit. The Four Horsemen and John Hume believed that Carter would be more than willing to take on the role of encouraging both sides in Northern Ireland to come together.[77]

Tip O'Neill took the lead in pressing for a presidential statement and made sustained representations to government officials. Traditionally the State Department had given a cool reception to such requests and recoiled from any action which might adversely effect relations with Britain. However, Tip O'Neill, as Speaker of the House, was an essential ally of the Carter administration, which relied on him to get its legislation through Congress. Because of his political clout, the State Department reacted immediately to his request. On June 9, O'Neill, Kennedy, and Moynihan met with Secretary of State Cyrus Vance. They discussed a blueprint of the proposed presidential statement, and Vance responded positively. The secretary of state told them to send a draft of the statement to the British and Irish governments for amendments and then pass the document on to Carter.

In 1977, journalist Mary Holland reported that the first draft of the presidential statement set a figure of $100 million in US government aid if a political solution was reached in Ulster. It also stressed that the Irish government would have to be represented at any political discussions. The British foreign office in Washington immediately rejected these propos-

77. John Hume, interview with author, January 3, 1989.

als. They did not like the idea of taking direct financial aid from America and insisted that the encouragement of investment by private companies was more acceptable. British officials also wanted to dilute the influence of the Irish Republic in any proposed political solution for Ulster.[78]

The US State Department, faced with this hostile British response, was wary of forging ahead with the presidential statement. Mary Holland alleged that when the new Fianna Fáil government of Jack Lynch took office in June 1977, State Department officials tried to use the change of administrations as a pretext for postponing the whole initiative.

Despite these developments, Tip O'Neill refused to abandon his efforts on behalf of the presidential statement. He was helped by the fact that the British were working to secure landing rights for Concorde in America. British government officials realized that in order to get these rights at Washington and New York airports, they needed the support of Tip O'Neill and Hugh Carey. They were thus obliged to maintain an interest in the presidential statement and not dismiss it outright.[79]

British opposition to the Carter statement was further diminished by the arrival of Peter Jay, the new British ambassador, in July 1977. Jay was very impressed with the statements of the Four Horsemen and recognized their significance in countering IRA supporters in America. He realized the four politicians had put themselves out on a limb and that the British could assist them by making some concessions. Through Jay's influence the British Foreign Office became more pliable and, after arduous diplomatic negotiations, an agreed statement was passed on to the White House for approval.

On August 30, 1977, President Carter delivered his message. Its most significant element was the offer of US economic aid. The draft suggestion that $100 million would be given in the event of a solution was omitted. Instead, Carter promised to encourage private investment:

> It is still true that a peaceful settlement would contribute immeasurably to stability in Northern Ireland and so enhance the prospects for increased investment. In the event of such a settlement, the US Government would be prepared to join with others to see how additional job-creating investment could be encouraged, to the benefit of all the people of Northern Ireland.

78. Mary Holland, "Carter, Kennedy, and Ireland: The Inside Story," *Magill*, 1 October 1977.

79. Jack Holland, *The American Connection*, 126.

The statement concluded by attacking the Irish-American republican network and promised increased federal action against gunrunning:

> I ask all Americans to refrain from supporting with financial or other aid organizations whose involvement, direct or indirect, in this violence delays the day when the people of Northern Ireland can live and work together in harmony, free from fear. Federal law enforcement agencies will continue to apprehend and prosecute any who violate US laws in this regard.[80]

Although the participants in the negotiations leading up to Carter's statement tried to keep its contents secret, there were frequent leaks to the press. Throughout the summer of 1977, there was extravagant speculation in British and Irish newspapers. In July, the *Observer* ran numerous articles claiming Edward Kennedy would visit Belfast and launch a peace initiative. Later, on the eve of a visit by Queen Elizabeth II to Northern Ireland, the *Daily Telegraph* reported she would be protected by FBI agents. The alleged reason for this was a fear that American weapons would be used in an attack on the Queen.[81]

These rumors intensified speculation about the presidential statement. Reports of a US government initiative appeared in the *Sunday Times* on July 24, 1977. The article fueled allegations that Carter was contemplating a radical move aimed at achieving a solution in Ulster. In Washington, Carter's press secretary, Jody Powell, emphatically denied such reports but this only heightened press curiosity.

Media speculation had produced such exaggerated expectations that when Carter's diluted statement finally appeared, the reaction was largely unenthusiastic. Many newspapers and political commentators characterized it as a predictable list of pious platitudes and insubstantial endorsements of peace. The statement was described as "a model of caution," "a generalized endorsement of virtue," and "olymian and innocuous."[82]

Other newspapers, such as the *New York Times* and the *Christian Science Monitor*, while acknowledging the blandness of Carter's statement,

80. "President Carter States Policy on Northern Ireland," *Department of State Bulletin* (26 September 1977), 410.

81. *New York Times*, 24 August 1977.

82. Editorials in *The Guardian* (Manchester), 6 September, *Washington Post*, 2 September, and *New Orleans Times-Picayune*, 6 September 1977.

correctly showed that it was a historic step. They pointed out that Carter's action marked a significant departure from the silence of previous presidents and established publicly that the US now had an official interest in Ulster and a continuing role in determining what happened there. The *Washington Post* further urged Carter to be more specific about the aid he was offering and to present a blueprint for economic assistance and investment.[83]

In order to give Carter's statement some immediate relevance and importance, Senator Edward Kennedy told reporters that US aid could take on the dimensions of a mini-Marshall Plan and implied it would provide grants and subsidies to American firms willing to locate in Ulster. In Ireland, John Hume called for the formation of a joint SDLP/unionist delegation to travel to America and seek investment in the province. He hinted that such a team would be well received and could win important economic benefits.[84]

Secretary of State Roy Mason went to the US in October 1977 in order to test John Hume's claim that there was great potential for securing new investment. He had meetings with government officials and businessmen. After his discussions with Edward Kennedy and Tip O'Neill, reports circulated that they had told him they would work to secure new investment if the British embarked on a policy designed to encourage dialogue between the SDLP and unionist parties.

Apparently Mason was convinced of the power of the Four Horsemen after the American firm Du Pont announced it was going to modernize its plant in Londonderry. When he returned to Northern Ireland, he began a round of meetings with Ulster political leaders to test the possibility of a political structure acceptable to both moderate nationalists and unionists. The discussions proved fruitless, but political analysts contend that the

83. For an excellent analysis of the motivations within the US government that shaped Carter's statement see Ronan Fanning, "Carter's First Words About Northern Ireland," *Washington Post*, 4 September 1977. Fanning shows that the major issue dividing Britain from Ireland between 1921 and 1970 was partition. Because of the sensitivity of the issue, the American government had traditionally kept clear of the Ulster problem. After the power-sharing executive in 1974, the British and Irish governments both agreed that the major issue in Ulster was to find a governmental structure that both countries could support. With this consensus, the American government was able to back a political solution to the problem, because both the British and Irish government shared the same goal. This consensus, and the realization that both governments would not be offended, led to Carter's willingness to make a statement on Ulster.

84. *The Times* (London), 1 September 1977.

hope they would encourage increased American investment was an important motivation for the exercise.[85]

The Carter statement marked the culmination of a process that had many detrimental consequences for militant Irish-American nationalism. Despite the limited success republicans achieved through the formation of the Irish National Caucus, the period from mid-1972 to 1977 witnessed a steady decline in support and positive publicity for Noraid and other militant groups.

To some extent this can be seen in the drop in contributions to Noraid. Despite attempts to revitalize its fund raising, reported subscriptions fell steadily from the peak reached after Bloody Sunday, when the group sent $312,700 to Ireland. In the period from July 1972 to January 1973, Noraid raised a total of $172,000 while the figure for the following six months dropped to $159,617. During the power-sharing initiative of William Whitelaw, the group's income continued its decline, going from $129,968 in January 1974 to $121,822 in July of the same year. By January 29, 1975, Noraid's total six-months' income was $115,522 and rose only slightly to $130,852 in the financial report in July.

As the pressure on Irish-American republicanism intensified due to the campaigns of constitutional nationalists and surveillance from the US government, Noraid managed to raise a total of only $161,463 in 1976. This figure fell to $152,730 in 1977, after the St. Patrick's Day statement of the Four Horsemen and the Carter initiative.[86]

Even allowing for claims by the Justice Department that Noraid financial reports were understated, these figures do indicate a significant decline in the group's fortunes. Similarly, documents filed under the FARA in 1976, when Noraid made its first official statement on membership figures, report fifty-four chapters and 2,055 members. These figures were significantly smaller than the claims made by Michael Flannery in 1972 that the group had more than one hundred chapters and a membership of 80,000.[87]

William V. Shannon, author and former American ambassador to Ireland, expressed the change in attitude that he and other Irish Americans experienced in the mid and late 1970s:

85. Ibid., 20 November 1977.

86. All figures from Noraid reports under the Foreign Agents Registration Act, July 1972–January 1978.

87. Noraid statement on national membership, FARA file July 31, 1976. British and Irish officials claim that it was partly because of the decline in American financial aid that

Senator Kennedy is typical of most Irish Americans, and myself, in his change of views about the problem in Northern Ireland. When it started in 1969 the civil rights issue burst into flames, and Irish Americans tended to think of it as the final act of the drama which began in 1916. There was an instinctive desire to rally behind the Irish, kick the British out, and reunite the country. . . . But as the guerrilla war dragged on, people have become much more conversant with the realities and complexities of the situation. Now Irish Americans realize that if the British withdraw it would be nothing like the withdrawal from Dublin in 1922. On the contrary, if Britain was to withdraw now, there would be more violence.[88]

The decreased effectiveness of and support for the republican position suggests William Shannon's transformation was typical of significant numbers of Irish-American activists from 1972 onward. Gradually, through the combined efforts of John Hume, the Irish government, and finally the American president, constitutional nationalism emerged as a viable alternative. The traditional republicanism, which had dominated Irish-American perceptions of Northern Ireland, was shattered in the mid-1970s, when constitutional nationalism emerged as the most widely accepted political alternative. As one contemporary political analyst correctly pointed out, "This represents a shift in ethnic political thinking about as momentous as any that has happened in recent memory."[89]

---

the Provisionals were forced to use cheaper incendiary bombs in this period. See *Irish Times* (Dublin), 17 October 1977.

88. William Shannon, "Change of Heart Among Irish Americans Over Ulster," *The Times* (London), 27 September 1977.

89. David Murray, "An Irish-American Shibboleth is Laid to Rest," *New Times*, 13 August 1977.

◆

FORMATION OF THE AD HOC

COMMITTEE ON IRISH AFFAIRS TO

THE ATKINS INITIATIVE, 1977–1979

◆

The St. Patrick's Day statement by the Four Horsemen infuriated Irish-American republican activists, and they determined to launch a counteroffensive. The leaders of Noraid and other militant groups became convinced that the best way to advance their political agenda was to establish a committe of sympathetic congressmen in Washington. This committee could challenge the Four Horsemen, raise Irish human rights issues through congressional hearings, and work to secure US visas for prominent Irish republicans.

Initial moves toward establishing this new congressional group were begun when a joint delegation from the Irish National Cuacus and the Ancient Order of Hibernians approached likely supporters on Capitol Hill. Jack Keane, outgoing president of the AOH and also a chairman of the INC, played a key role in this process. He contacted Mario Biaggi (D, N.Y.) and asked him to establish the new group. Biaggi responded enthusiastically and on September 27, 1977, announced the formation of an Ad Hoc Congressional Committee for Irish Affairs.[1] Militant Irish-American groups immediately hailed it as a major breakthrough.

Mario Biaggi became the first chairman and began working on an Irish agenda on Capitol Hill. During his long service with the New York Police Department, Biaggi had been wounded ten times and received numerous decorations. These and the interest in Ireland he had developed during his police service endeared him to his militant supporters. He recalls that one of his colleagues, an Irish-American policeman named Pat McMahon, had passed on an encyclopedic knowledge of Irish history. The two would discuss Irish affairs while on patrol. This background pushed Biaggi to condemn British policy in Ulster and participate in the Newry protest demonstration against Bloody Sunday on February 6, 1972.[2]

From his first associations with the Ulster conflict, Biaggi's critics accused him of merely playing for the Irish-American vote. The Italian-American congressman was always angered by this suggestion and repeatedly stated that he desired to see human rights in Northern Ireland. Biaggi emphasized that his constituency was mainly Italian-American; further, that he was regularly re-elected with large majorities proved that his concern for Ulster was not merely a ploy to win votes. The congressman's opponents could, however, point out that he had run for mayor of New York in 1973 and aspired to a seat in the Senate—both ambitions that would benefit from Irish-American political support.[3]

Whatever the motivations behind Biaggi's involvement in the Ulster conflict, he was able to recruit congressmen to the Ad Hoc Committee. Its membership rose from seventy in October 1977 to one hundred thirty in 1979. Constitutional nationalists claimed that these numbers were misleading and that the Ad Hoc Committee was basically a "paper organization"—many congressmen who joined were not active members; it met infrequently; it achieved very little. Critics of the group, such as Garret FitzGerald, further claimed that new congressmen were "joiners" and

1. Father Seán McManus, interview with author, 11 July 1991.

2. Dylan Foley, "The Old War Horse: Biaggi Has Never Forgotten the Irish," *Irish Echo* (New York), 20 November 1992.

3. In October 1973 Biaggi ran for Mayor of New York City against Abraham Beame. His campaign collapsed after he was questioned by a grand jury investigating sponsorship of private immigration bills in Congress in 1971. Newspapers reported some politicians were taking bribes and hinted Biaggi had links with the Mafia.

signed up as members partly to oblige a colleague and partly to create an impression of involvement in a wide variety of issues.[4]

Members of the Ad Hoc Committee encompassed the entire ideological spectrum of American politics. However, most were Democratic representatives from eastern constituencies, particularly New York. The core of the Committee consisted of Mario Biaggi, Hamilton Fish, Jr. (R, N.Y.), Benjamin Rosenthall (D, N.Y.), Lester Wolff (D, N.Y.), Benjamin Gilman (R, N.Y.) Norman Lent (R, N.Y.) and Joshua Eilberg (D, Pa.). The fact that none from this activist core were Irish American increased constitutional nationalist accusations that the Ad Hoc Committee was merely a vehicle for Italian and Jewish congressmen to win Irish votes.[5]

Prominent members of the Ad Hoc Committee began sponsoring bills on Northern Ireland and publicizing alleged violations of human rights.[6] They also condemned the State Department's increasingly restrictive visa policy against Irish republicans. In August 1978, Joshua Eilberg and Hamilton Fish traveled to Britain and Ireland to investigate the issue. During their week-long visit, they met with US consular officials and interviewed leading republicans who had been refused visas.

When they returned to Washington, Fish and Eilberg presented their official report to the Committee on the Judiciary. They concluded that the State Department was acting "unfairly and unjustifiably in denying or revoking visas" and that officials "dealt with applicants in an unsympathetic and high-handed manner." The two congressmen also urged the State Department to reevaluate all the cases in which it had denied visas to republicans.[7]

Although the Carter administration ignored Fish and Eilberg's report, the two did create a substantial amount of publicity for the human rights and visa issues. Their criticisms of the British government and the State Department were given extensive media coverage that embarrassed officials in London and Washington.

The Irish National Caucus encouraged and financed similar "fact finding" trips to Ireland by American politicians. Caucus leaders also con-

---

4. Garret FitzGerald, interview with author, 19 December 1990.

5. Paul Artherton, "Irish-American Lobbies Reflect Splits at Home," *Fortnight Magazine* (Belfast) (18 March 1985), 13.

6. The Ad Hoc Committee worked on the cases of Damian Eastwood and Pearse Kerr, both US citizens who were arrested for alleged terrorist activities in Northern Ireland.

7. Hamilton Fish and Joshua Eilberg, *Northern Ireland: A Role For The United States?* Report before the House Committee on the Judiciary (August/September 1978), 219.

ducted "investigative" trips themselves. In 1979 a delegation led by Father Seán McManus, Fred Burns O'Brien, and Rita Mullen toured Northern Ireland. During the visit, McManus infuriated unionist politicians and the Northern Ireland Office by his accusations that the Royal Ulster Constabulary (RUC) was being used as a training force for loyalist paramilitaries.

While in Ireland, McManus held extensive discussions with Seán McBride, a founder of Amnesty International and a recipient of both the Nobel Peace Prize and the Lenin Peace Prize. McBride agreed to become chairman of a new group called the Irish National Caucus of America Liaison (INCAL), to be based in Dublin. The INCAL's function was to provide information on Ulster to the Caucus and the Ad Hoc Committee. It would also publicize the activities of American republican groups to the Irish public. In October 1979 the INC *Newsletter* announced that former Irish cabinet minister Kevin Boland would be included in the INCAL, as would Michael Mullen, general secretary of the Irish Transport and General Worker's Union. Neil Blaney, a member of the Irish parliament, was also associated with the group and in December 1979 conducted a tour of America to promote the Caucus and the Ad Hoc Committee.[8]

The formation of the INCAL and the support given it by these prominent Irish politicians brought added publicity and prestige to militant nationalists working in Washington. It increased the INC's ability to receive information on Ireland and created a transatlantic link through which Britain's human rights record could be attacked.

Biaggi's Peace Forum

The most ambitious and optimistic initiative taken by the Ad Hoc Committee and the INC was the attempt to form a "peace forum" for Northern Ireland. In October 1978, a delegation composed of Caucus officials and leaders of Irish-American societies met with Mario Biaggi. They suggested he could organize a peace forum on Ulster by calling on all the antagonists to come together and discuss their differences. Father Seán McManus originated the concept of this peace forum. He envisioned Biaggi performing the role of "honest broker" between unionist and nationalist representatives. Biaggi, convinced the scheme could be successful, agreed to lead the initiative and began exploring ways to bring Ulster's contending factions together. The congressman insisted that his motiva-

8. Father Seán McManus, interview by author, 25 April 1995.

tion for taking on the role of mediator came from a humanitarian desire to try any scheme that might achieve peace in Northern Ireland. Some critics, however, contend he was trying to emulate President Carter's breakthrough at the Camp David agreement between Egypt and Israel.[9]

The growing politicization of Ulster loyalist groups created hope that a peace forum could succeed. In the mid-1970s, loyalists began supporting the establishment of an independent Ulster. They envisaged an important role for the United States in this new political formula. Consequently, their traditional attitudes toward American involvement in the Ulster conflict were significantly altered.

In the early 1970s, Ulster loyalist groups had condemned American politicians and Irish-American groups active in supporting the nationalist cause. Both the Ulster Volunteer Force (UVF) and Ulster Defence Association (UDA) attacked Irish Americans as anti-Protestant bigots who were financing a war of genocide against them. They reserved particular scorn for Senator Edward Kennedy and Tip O'Neill, who were generally characterized as carrying a deep, malicious hatred for Ulster loyalists. These verbal criticisms became physical threats. When Congressman Lester Wolff visited Northern Ireland in 1972 he reported that a group of loyalists told him they would kill Ted Kennedy if he ever came to Belfast.[10] The UVF also held news conferences at which they produced lists of Noraid members and warned the individuals concerned that they were legitimate targets for assassination.[11]

The concept of Ulster independence had its origins in the mid-1970s, when the UDA formed a "think tank" to formulate political policy. The group called itself the New Ulster Political Research Group (NUPRG) and gradually proposed that Ulster should be an independent state. One of the major problems of independence was how the new state could survive economically. In an attempt to solve this problem, members of the NUPRG went to Libya in 1974 in order to secure the promise of financial aid from Colonel Muammar Qaddafi.[12]

9. See Linda Charlton, "Biaggi, a Bronx Power, Has a Second Constituency in Northern Ireland," *New York Times*, 7 May 1978.

10. Congress, House, Subcommittee on Europe, *Report of Congressman Lester Wolff on Trip to Northern Ireland: Hearing Before Subcommittee on European Affairs* (18 July 1972), 23.

11. Sally Belfrage, *Living with War: A Year in Northern Ireland* (London: MacMillan, 1987), 237.

12. Steve Bruce, *The Red Hand: Protestant Paramilitaries in Northern Ireland* (New York: Oxford University Press, 1992), 103–5.

This mission to get Libyan financial assistance failed and, from 1975 onward, the NUPRG increasingly concentrated on the possibility of American aid. Loyalists suggested that the political institutions of an independent Ulster should be modeled on America, with a president, a Bill of Rights, and a congressional-style committee system drawn from an elected legislature. Some even suggested that the United States could provide external defense and that the administration of justice could be supervised by a Supreme Court Justice. The NUPRG felt that this provision would instill confidence in the legal system from both communities.[13]

With such a key role proposed for the United States in their political scheme, the NUPRG began to reassess their traditional contempt for Irish America. Some felt that if contacts were made with Irish-American groups, such as the Irish National Caucus, they could win support in Congress for Ulster independence. Fortunately for the loyalist plan, the INC was concurrently working for the peace forum at which all sides in the Ulster conflict could come together to discuss their differences. The Caucus was thus receptive to the possibility of talks with loyalists.

In late 1977, after initial contacts were made, a group from the Ulster Independence Association, led by George Allport, met with Fred Burns O'Brien in Washington. The loyalists were enthusiastic about O'Brien's suggestion of a peace forum, and both agreed it could be used to explore the conditions under which independence would be acceptable to nationalists. Later in the spring of 1978, Andy Tyrie, leader of the UDA, publicly supported the idea of a peace forum. In a reversal of earlier attitudes, he suggested Edward Kennedy would be a good mediator because of his "integrity and credibility."[14]

On their tour of Ireland in August 1978, Hamilton Fish and Joshua Eilberg met NUPRG leaders Andy Tyrie, John McMichael, and Glen Barr in Belfast. They told the congressmen that they were tired of being manipulated by Unionist politicians such as Ian Paisley. They outlined their proposal for Ulster independence and said that if conditions were right they would sever the link with Britain.

Throughout these discussions, Glen Barr, the NUPRG's most articulate spokesman, adopted a conciliatory tone. He attacked sectarian violence and continually emphasized that Catholic rights would be guaranteed in an independent state. He also told the congressmen his organization would

13. See Chris Walker, "The American File," *The Listener*, 3 February 1979.

14. *New York Times*, 26 May 1978. See also, "Barr Plans For Northern Ireland to Include United States," *Irish Times* (Dublin), 22 February 1978.

welcome the opportunity to participate in a peace forum organized from America.

Hamilton Fish and Joshua Eilberg were greatly impressed by the loyalist delegation and concluded that their proposal was "a most significant change and the best possibility of progress there has been for some time." The two politicians met with Mario Biaggi in Washington and convinced him that the NUPRG's attitude

> demonstrated clearly that the loyalist paramilitaries were disenchanted by continued British domination and were actually seeking a political solution by negotiation with the republican groups, independent of Britain.[15]

Encouraged by these reports, Biaggi decided to travel to Ireland and test support for a peace mission. In November 1978, he and Congressman Ben Gilman met with more than twenty-five different groups. They were impressed by the enthusiasm of the loyalist paramilitaries and the positive response from Sinn Féin. When Biaggi returned to the United States, he announced that the peace forum would convene in Washington on May 14, 1979.

Militant Irish-American groups were divided in their attitude to the loyalist political program. Most of the leading figures in Noraid refused to accept negotiations with people they regarded as bigots and sectarian murderers. Others, principally members of the INC, were very enthusiastic and wanted to explore the possibility of an independent Ulster. They were especially attracted by the loyalist willingness to cut their ties with Britain. Consequently, support grew for a loyalist tour of America that would allow the NUPRG to discuss their political views and would give impetus to Biaggi's peace forum.

In December 1978, the Minnesota Irish National Caucus invited NUPRG leaders to come to the United States. The group accepted, and on January 18, 1979, a loyalist delegation embarked on a two-week tour. The most prominent members of the group again included Glen Barr, Andy Tyrie, as well as Tommy Little and Harry Chicken. They held numerous of public lectures, discussions with political groups, and media appearances.[16]

---

15. Fish and Eilberg, *Northern Ireland*, 47.

16. Alf McCreary, "Ulster Protestants Promote Plan to Cut British Ties," *Christian Science Monitor*, 18 January 1979. The NUPRG's itinerary was organized by Harold

The tour was one of the most unusual events of the Troubles. The loyalists, noted for their traditional militancy and association with sectarian killings, impressed nearly everyone they met with their willingness to accommodate the aspirations of the nationalist community. The group held discussions about the status of Catholics in an independent Ulster with Archbishop John Roche of Minnesota and Monsignor Frank Lally, head of the Catholic International Conference Center. Afterwards both clergymen praised the NUPRG for their progressive political ideals. They were similarly acclaimed after discussions with Senator George McGovern and the chief aides of Tip O'Neill and Edward Kennedy.[17]

One of the most unexpected supporters of the loyalist tour was Paul O'Dwyer. He hosted the NUPRG delegation in New York and they all became instant friends over shots of Bushmills whiskey.[18] O'Dwyer was so impressed by the loyalists that he provided them with free legal service to draft a constitution for an independent Ulster. The loyalist group published this constitution in a pamphlet entitled *Beyond the Religious Divide*. It contained numerous provisions to safeguard minority rights and was widely praised by political analysts as a sincere and thoughtful attempt to break the logjam of Ulster politics.[19]

The success of the loyalist tour, however, did not help rising problems faced by the peace forum. Mario Biaggi had hoped to fund the forum with cash contributions from US corporations and peace foundations. This money never materialized, and Biaggi could not afford to bring the various Ulster groups to Washington. The peace initiative was also scuttled by the refusal of all constitutional parties to participate. British and Irish government officials, along with nationalist and Unionist parties, flatly refused to get involved in discussions with "terrorists." Biaggi was therefore forced to postpone the initial meeting date of the peace conference.

After a futile attempt to get President Carter involved, Biaggi, in a last desperate attempt to save the peace initiative, decided to go to Northern

---

Alexander, registered under the FARA as American representative of several loyalist groups.

17. From *Ulster*, newspaper of the UDA, February 1979. Glen Barr recalls his disbelief during a radio phone-in when an Irish American alleged that the British were holding on to Ulster because there was gold and coal in the Mourne mountains.

18. Ed Maloney, "The U.D.A. Roadshow Returns Home," *Hibernia Magazine* (Dublin), 22 February 1979.

19. Seán Cronin, "O'Dwyer Plays Host to Top Loyalists," *Irish Times* (Dublin), 19 February 1979.

Ireland and bring the conflicting groups together. He arrived in Belfast with INC officials and immediately sent out invitations for all political factions to attend a conference in the Europa Hotel. The NUPRG was the only loyalist group to attend—it continued to believe the meeting might further plans for Ulster independence. Although republicans were extremely sceptical of the initiative, Sinn Féin agreed to participate and sent Gerry Adams, Dáithí O Conaill, and Ruairí O Brádaigh as representatives.

When the two delegations arrived at the Europa Hotel, they occupied separate conference rooms. Mario Biaggi attempted "shuttle diplomacy" between the groups and tried to persuade them to call a cease-fire. Despite four hours of moving between the republican and loyalist delegations, he achieved no agreements. Biaggi maintains that while Dáithí O Conaill and Ruairí O Brádaigh were flexible, Gerry Adams was intransigent and completely refused suggestions of an IRA truce. The conference eventually disintegrated; hope for a Camp David–style settlement in Northern Ireland ended.[20]

The failure of Biaggi's peace forum was a serious blow for the NUPRG. It represented the end of American interest in their scheme for Ulster independence. In addition, the NUPRG's proposal never received significant support within the unionist community. The vast majority of Protestants believed that an independent Ulster would not be economically viable and that breaking the link with Britain would only lead to absorption by the Republic of Ireland.

The collapse of peace negotiations exacerbated conflicts festering between the INC and Noraid. When the Caucus formed in 1974, Father Seán McManus made clear that the group sympathized with the IRA's right to resist British forces in Ireland. He soon realized, however, that congressmen were reluctant to be associated with an organization that appeared to support violence. Consequently, McManus stressed that the Caucus had no links with the IRA, retained all financial contributions for use in America, and adopted the dove of peace as the group's emblem.[21]

Noraid condemned the INC for not sending cash to "alleviate the suffering of Ulster Catholics." Personal animosities also grew between

20. Father Seán McManus, interview with author, 11 July 1991.
21. Joseph E. Thompson, "The Irish National Caucus," in Michael Funchion, ed., *Irish-American Voluntary Organizations* (Westport, Conn.: Greenwood Press, 1983), 178–83, and Father Seán McManus, interview with author 11 July 1991.

McManus and Michael Flannery, who was incensed by what he called INC attempts to encroach on Noraid fund raising. In 1978, just before the annual Noraid dinner, McManus organized his own function and began soliciting republican supporters for $25 donations. Flannery strongly condemned this action, believing it reduced potential donations Noraid would have collected.[22]

Noraid leaders also condemned the Caucus for maintaining dialogue with Ulster loyalists. After Fred Burns O'Brien met leaders of the Ulster Independence Association in 1977, Michael Flannery accused him of being an agent for the American government. The Noraid chief conveyed this suspicion to Provisional Sinn Féin in Belfast, which then issued a statement accusing Burns O'Brien of scheming with the CIA to undermine Irish-American groups. They declared him persona non grata with the republican movement and warned him to keep out of Ireland.[23]

Fred Burns O'Brien denied the accusations against him. He was supported by Father Seán McManus, who alleged Sinn Féin was trying to destroy the INC's power. This conflict with the leadership of the republican movement in Ireland alarmed some members of the Caucus who had opposed McManus's more moderate line. Irish National Caucus chapters in New Jersey, Illinois, Connecticut, and Pennsylvania condemned the central leadership in Washington. These chapters attacked the discussions with Ulster loyalist groups and eventually broke away to form independent organizations.[24]

The feud between Sinn Féin, Noraid, and the Caucus increased after the failure of the "peace forum" conference at the Europa Hotel in 1979. The INC accused the republican delegation of inflexibility and issued an article in the *Andersonstown News* attacking Sinn Féin for wrecking "a great opportunity for political progress."[25]

Sinn Fein responded by accusing the Caucus of furthering the aims of British propaganda. Gerry Adams stated that, because the peace forum did not include British officials, it gave credence to the perception that the Ulster conflict was purely sectarian. An article in *An Phoblacht/ Republican News* outlined this view and concluded:

22. Michael Flannery, correspondence with author, 18 November 1992.
23. Kevin Kelley, *The Longest War: Northern Ireland and the I.R.A.* (Westport, Conn.: Lawrence Hill and Co., 1982), 280.
24. *Irish People* (New York), 18 August 1979.
25. "M. Dawson Attacks P.S.F.," *Andersonstown News* (Belfast), 18 August 1979.

The British government for the last decade has justified its presence in the six counties as one of security forces keeping religious communities apart. For republicans to sit down and talk with loyalists (in a peace forum which by definition means a meeting of the antagonists) positively helps the British in projecting their role as a peace-keeping force instead of an occupation force.[26]

Noraid fully supported Sinn Féin and intensified its own condemnations of the Caucus. In October 1979, a series of articles in the *Irish People* personally attacked Father Seán McManus and accused the Caucus of fomenting divisions within the militant nationalist network in America.[27]

Journalists reporting on the conflict between Noraid and the Caucus concluded the feud had detrimental effects on militant Irish-American nationalism. Bernard Weinraub of the *New York Times* produced an extensive analysis of the split, in which contended that fund raising for both groups had been seriously impaired. Publicity efforts also declined as Noraid and the Caucus devoted their energies to mutual criticism.[28]

Apart from the adverse effects of internal squabbling, Irish-American republicanism also continued to suffer from the actions of the IRA. In February 1978, an active service unit detonated a fire bomb at the La Mon House Hotel near Comber, County Down. The bar was packed with people who were engulfed in a sheet of blazing petrol. The explosion killed twelve, while twenty-three received appalling burns. The incident produced front-page reports in the main American newspapers and editorials describing the IRA as "savage monsters." NBC television news broadcast pictures of the charred remains of victims and implied this was the consequence of donating money to Noraid.

In 1979, the Provos also launched a number of attacks on British politicians and members of the "establishment." In March, an IRA team assassinated Sir Richard Sykes, the British ambassador to Holland. Eight days later, the INLA planted a bomb that killed Airey Neave, Conservative Party spokesman on Northern Ireland, as he drove out of the House of Commons parking lot. These killings increased American criticisms of Irish republicanism, but the condemnations reached unprecedented levels after the republicans attacked Lord Louis Mountbatten.

26. *An Phoblacht/Republican News* (Belfast), 1 September 1979.

27. *Irish People* (New York), 18 October 1980.

28. Bernard Weinraub, "Split Among Irish Americans Said to Cut Funds to I.R.A.," *New York Times*, 7 September 1979.

On August 27, 1979, the IRA detonated a bomb on Mountbatten's fishing boat off the west coast of Ireland. The explosion killed Mountbatten, his grandson Nicholas, and a local boat boy. The elderly dowager Lady Bradbourne, a passenger on the boat, died of her injuries the next day; Lord and Lady Bradbourne were both seriously injured.

The killing of Lord Mountbatten created an international wave of revulsion against the IRA. The attack was seen as particularly callous against a figure whose long and distinguished military career had never brought him near Ireland. During the Second World War, many American troops had served under Mountbatten, and he had earned admiration and respect. Throughout the United States, the attack became the primary news item; hundreds of editorials described the IRA as everything from "fanatical terrorists" to "psychopathic murderers."[29] Typical of the response in the United States media was the commentary given by the *Atlanta Constitution*:

> It is tempting to describe the IRA terrorists who killed Lord Mountbatten as animals, but that's demeaning to animals. It would be more accurate to describe them as savages, but at least savages can be excused because of ignorance. . . . It is a terrible shame that a man of such talents and achievements can be killed by cowards so low. They are truly the dregs of humanity.[30]

The Four Horsemen and the Atkins Initiative

The continued activities of constitutional nationalists, however, provided the greatest challenge to militant irredentist Irish-American groups during this period. The Irish government solidified its links with the Four Horsemen and joined them in condemnations of republican groups. Irish diplomats also encouraged these leading Irish-American politicians to pressure the British government into political change. Eventually this activity produced results which enhanced the prestige and influence of the

29. For a collection of these commentaries, see *Editorials on File* "The Murder of Lord Louis Mountbatten," August 1979.

30. *The Atlanta Constitution*, 30 August 1979. Mountbatten's murder became a catalyst for more concerted and intensive efforts by US law-enforcement agencies against the IRA's transatlantic weapons pipeline.

"Big Four" and eclipsed the relatively unsuccessful attempts of republicans to influence political events in Ulster.[31]

After their 1977 St. Patrick's Day statement, the Four Horsemen had hoped the British government would launch a major new political initiative in Northern Ireland. They believed they had made a bold and imaginative move in attacking the republican network in America and felt they deserved a reward—a renewed effort by the British to construct a political framework that would give the nationalist community real power.

Although the British government warmly welcomed the 1977 St. Patrick's Day statement, it did not want to take any new political initiatives in Ulster. The dismal failure of the constitutional convention in 1976 had convinced Prime Minister James Callaghan that the best way to govern the province was to continue direct rule for an indefinite period. The British had also introduced the twin policies of Ulsterization and Criminalization and believed their success would depend on there being a long period of political stability.[32] Thus they opposed new political initiatives likely to increase conflict and tension in Ulster.

In contrast, the Four Horsemen felt that a fresh political initiative was the minimum reward they deserved for attacking IRA supporters in America. When the "Big Four" realized that the British were not going to make any major move in Ulster, they became increasingly critical of the Callaghan administration. Their growing anger and frustration was compounded by a series of official reports in 1978, which confirmed the British had committed serious human rights violations in the province.

The origins of these official reports dated back to December 1971, when the Irish government had filed complaints with the European Commission on Human Rights. They alleged that British troops had used five illegal interrogation techniques on internees, sensory deprivation techniques that included exposing suspects to continuous "white noise" and covering their heads with hoods for extended periods of time. In September 1977, the European Court on Human Rights found Britain guilty.

31. In February 1978, Irish Taoiseach Jack Lynch sent an open letter to Mario Biaggi in which he attacked the congressman's, "public identification with supporters of violence in Ireland." This letter was sent to every member of Congress in the hope it would discourage membership of the Ad Hoc Committee and embarrass Biaggi in the American media.

32. Ulsterization involved the transfer of security from the British Army to the RUC and the Ulster Defense Regiment (UDR). Criminalization involved the categorization of republican and loyalist prisoners as common criminals.

The judges concluded that the five techniques, while not constituting torture, were "inhuman and degrading."

The leaders of constitutional nationalism in America responded to the verdict of the European Court and the lack of political activity in Ulster by sharply criticizing the British in their 1978 St. Patrick's Day statement. Fourteen major politicians including Senators Joe Biden, Gary Hart, and George McGovern, joined the Four Horsemen in their condemnation. The joint statement continued to criticize Irish Americans who supported the IRA, but it also attacked the British government and unionists for blocking political progress.[33]

The criticisms of British political inactivity in Ulster increased throughout 1978. Tip O'Neill, speaking at an Ireland Fund dinner in May, alleged that the Callaghan administration's lack of commitment to a political settlement was contributing to the continued death and destruction in Northern Ireland.[34] Senator Edward Kennedy concentrated on the abuse of human rights and on June 11 called for the appointment of a special prosecutor to investigate allegations of brutality by the RUC.[35] Hugh Carey showed his displeasure at British policy by refusing to attend a dinner honoring Prime Minister Callaghan in New York.[36]

In December 1978, Senator Daniel Moynihan traveled to London in an attempt to assess the effects of this increased criticism on British officials. He met with Roy Mason and Foreign Secretary David Owen. The senator told them that the campaign of constitutional nationalists against republican groups in America would be ineffective unless there was political progress in Ulster. Mason and Owen explained that a new political initiative, in a situation in which there was no basis for consent, would only make the problem worse and intensify violence. This casual attitude infuriated Moynihan, who told reporters:

> I came away absolutely dazed; he [Mason] had no intention of doing anything about Northern Ireland except keeping British troops there. The question of Northern Ireland never even came up at conferences of

33. "St. Patrick's Day Statement Critical of Britain," *New York Times*, 16 March 1978.
34. Full text of this speech is printed in *Irish Times* (Dublin), 12 May 1978.
35. "Call for Independent Special Prosecutor to Investigate Charges of Police Brutality in Northern Ireland," statement by Senator Edward Kennedy, 11 June 1978.
36. Jack Holland, "Hugh Carey's Problems in New York Elections," *Irish People* (New York), 4 November 1978.

the two leading British political parties. There is no political will to settle.[37]

When Moynihan returned to the United States, he gave details of the London meeting to his constitutional nationalist colleagues. They were similarly outraged at the British attitude and determined to increase their efforts for a political initiative in 1979. Their resolve was further heightened by the continued evidence exposing misconduct by Ulster's security forces.

In the summer of 1978, Amnesty International conducted an inquiry into allegations of police brutality during the interrogation of terrorist suspects. The Amnesty report provided strong evidence of seventy-eight cases in which suspects suffered serious physical injury while being held at the RUC interrogation center at Castlereagh.

The British government responded to these findings by calling an independent inquiry to examine interrogation procedures. Harry Bennett, an English Crown Court judge, led the investigation in early March 1979. The subsequent Bennett Report confirmed that RUC detectives physically mistreated suspects during questioning; it recommended the installation of closed-circuit televisions to monitor interrogations. The report also called for regular physical examinations to be carried out on suspects in order to detect physical abuse.

The Bennett Report's findings of RUC misconduct contributed to the severity of criticisms contained within the 1979 St. Patrick's Day statement by the Four Horsemen. The message accused the British government of "negligence" and "acquiescence" in the face of "gross violations of human rights." It called for a more extensive investigation into the ill-treatment of suspects and renewed the demand for a fresh political initiative in Ulster.

John Hume encouraged the Four Horsemen to increase their pressure on the British government and suggested to Tip O'Neill that he could lead a political delegation to Ireland. Hume felt that such a trip, timed to coincide with the British general elections in April, could convince both the Conservative and Labour parties to give more consideration to a political solution in Northern Ireland.[38]

Convinced by Hume's suggestion, Tip O'Neill led a delegation of fourteen leading Democrats and Republicans to Ireland in the spring of

37. "Irish Americans Switch, Chide U.K.," *New York Times*, 8 April 1979.
38. John Hume, interview with author, 3 January 1989.

1979. He held discussions with leaders of the SDLP, as well as Harry West of the Official Unionists and Ian Paisley. He was reportedly very impressed by the sincerity of the two Unionist leaders; he was optimistic about new attempts to establish political dialogue.

O'Neill also traveled to London to meet leaders of the main political parties. Although Prime Minister Callaghan suggested there might be a new Ulster initiative if the political climate changed, O'Neill felt there was no real intent for such a move. He was further infuriated by a political deal Callaghan had reached with the Unionist MPs at Westminster. The prime minister, leading a minority government, had agreed to increase Unionist representation in exchange for continued support of Labour policies in the House of Commons.

O'Neill condemned the Labour/Unionist deal and accused both British parties of using Ulster as a "political football." On April 20, he issued his strongest attack on British policy:

> I have been deeply concerned by the lack of political progress in Northern Ireland over the last few years. . . . Together with all sides in Ireland we insist that Britain bears a heavy responsibility for the failures of recent years on the political front. We have been concerned that the problem has been treated as a political football in London or has otherwise been given a low priority. . . . We insist on an early, realistic and fresh initiative on the part of the incoming British government, so as to get negotiations moving quickly.[39]

This statement caused intense controversy in Britain. Shirley Williams, Labour's Secretary of Education, attacked O'Neill's "ignorant immigrant attitudes." Margaret Thatcher endorsed these criticisms, while Robert Adley, MP, condescendingly remarked, "There are few more nauseating sounds than ignorant Irish-American politicians visiting Dublin and grubbing around for votes in the United States by venting their spleen on Britain."[40]

British television and newspapers carried O'Neill's statements as the lead story on April 20, 1979. The major tabloids ran banner headlines advising the house speaker, "Keep Your Nose Out of British Affairs!" The "quality press" issued editorials that were equally abrupt. The *Daily Telegraph* commented:

39. *Irish Times* (Dublin), 20 April 1979.
40. *Daily Telegraph* (London), 21 April 1979.

Mr. O'Neill's observations were both brief and confused, and probably intended primarily for the Irish electorate in America, but Americans would be best advised to do their electioneering at home. . . . What makes Mr. O'Neill's speech a scandal rather than a trivial impertinence is the effect which it is likely to produce in Ulster itself. There it will both encourage the IRA in its new campaign of murder and harden Protestant militancy.[41]

This critical reaction from British politicians and the media was strongly condemned by constitutional nationalists in Ireland. Both the Irish government and SDLP defended O'Neill. Garret FitzGerald sent a beligerent letter to the *Daily Telegraph* attacking its editorial line and describing the house speaker as

. . . a man of outstanding political courage and statesmanship. A man who has shown that his only concern with our affairs is to work for peace in Ireland, regardless of what it may cost him in votes from Irish-American extremists.[42]

On April 22, Vice-President Walter Mondale met with Irish Foreign Minister Michael O'Kennedy in Washington. After hearing his views, Mondale defended Tip O'Neill and said the house speaker had acted out of a genuine concern felt at the highest levels of the United States government about what was happening in Northern Ireland. O'Kennedy implied that Jimmy Carter fully supported O'Neill's remarks. One day later, however, White House aides distanced the president from the controversy and said the house speaker's statements did not necessarily reflect the views of the Carter administration.[43]

Hugh Carey delivered the strongest reaction to the British attacks on Tip O'Neill. The New York governor issued a joint article with Dr. Kevin Cahill, his adviser on Northern Ireland. The article appeared in major newspapers throughout America and defended O'Neill's remarks. It reemphasized the call for a new political initiative and proposed that if Britain refused to act it should be made an "international outcast" and the United States should impose economic sanctions.[44]

41. *Daily Telegraph* (London), "More Than Impertinent," 21 April 1979.

42. "Tip O'Neill on Northern Ireland," letter from Garret FitzGerald to *Daily Telegraph* (London), 23 April 1979.

43. "Mondale Backs O'Neill," *Daily Telegraph* (London), 23 April 1979.

44. Hugh Carey and Kevin Cahill, "A Life Before Death for Northern Ireland," *New York Daily News*, 22 April 1979.

Despite this American pressure, the new Conservative government, headed by Margaret Thatcher, gave no indications that it would change the Ulster policy that had been followed by the Callaghan administration. Constitutional nationalists, therefore, re-doubled their efforts. In May 1979, Taoiseach Jack Lynch met Margaret Thatcher in London and expressed his strong desire for a fresh political move. In America, Senator Kennedy gave a detailed interview to the *Belfast Telegraph* in which he renewed assurances that the American government would give extensive financial aid to support an agreed political framework in Northern Ireland. He also warned that if a new political initiative was not taken, this would strengthen republican groups in America and undermine the ability of the Four Horsemen to block funding for the IRA.[45]

The Thatcher government reacted to these renewed criticisms with traditional dismissals of Irish-American ignorance about Ulster. Conor Cruise O'Brien supported the British response. The former Irish cabinet minister wrote an open letter to Daniel Moynihan which appeared in the American press. O'Brien stated that Irish-American pressure would achieve nothing except to make unionists more intransigent and encourage the IRA. Further, he attacked Moynihan's lack of knowledge about Ulster and accused him of being motivated by "ethnic anglophobia."[46]

This letter led to an exchange of criticisms between O'Brien and the Four Horsemen in the press and in periodical journals. The conflict grew so intense that Tip O'Neill was reported as describing the former minister as "a silly son of a bitch."[47] Although members of the Irish government and SDLP did not articulate similar opinions in public, they made it clear that they fully welcomed Irish-American political support. In *Foreign Affairs*, John Hume criticized O'Brien's views and pointed out:

> The support for violence from the United States has been contained
> and has in fact dropped. That this should have been maintained during
> the past years of political vacuum in Northern Ireland is an extraordi-
> nary achievement. There are many men, women and children who are

45. "Edward Kennedy, His Views, His Life," interview with Barry White in *Belfast Telegraph*, 9 May 1979.

46. Conor Cruise O'Brien, "An Irishman's Open letter to Senator Moynihan," *Christian Science Monitor*, 18 July 1979.

47. *Daily Telegraph* (London), 25 September 1979.

alive today, I am convinced, because of the political courage and concern of these men [Four Horsemen].[48]

Constitutional nationalists were increasingly frustrated by the lack of
British response to their calls for political change. The Four Horsemen
concluded that only punitive measures would provide their appeals with
serious consideration. The opportunity for such action presented itself in
the summer of 1979.

Throughout the 1970s, the Royal Ulster Constabulary had purchased
a significant number of weapons from American arms manufacturers. In
1979, it placed an order for 3,000 Magnum pistols and 500 rifles with the
Connecticut arms manufacturers Sturm, Ruger and Company. Following
previous government policy, the US State Department had permitted the
sale of arms to the police in Northern Ireland.

The Irish National Caucus received information about this arms ship-
ment. Father Seán McManus pushed Mario Biaggi to work for a reversal
of State Department policy. Biaggi attacked the arms sale on two grounds.
He contended that, by permitting the sale of United States weapons to the
RUC, the State Department was supporting one particular faction in
Northern Ireland and could not claim its policy was neutral and impartial.
The Bronx congressman also pointed out that both Amnesty International
and the European Court had found the RUC guilty of human rights abuses.
He contended that it would be a massive contradiction for the Carter administration to claim its foreign policy was guided by a desire to protect
"human rights," yet supply weapons to a proven violator. Biaggi announced that when the annual appropriations bill for the State Department
went through Congress in July, he would sponsor an amendment designed
to halt further arms sales to the Ulster police.[49]

In June, Tip O'Neill released a statement supporting the weapons ban
to the RUC. He hoped that the threat of his support for such an amendment would persuade the Thatcher government to take the call for a new
political initiative seriously. Instead, the new Secretary of State for
Northern Ireland, Humphrey Atkins, condemned O'Neill. He said the
speaker was irresponsible in criticizing the sale of weapons which the

48. John Hume, "The Irish Question: A British Problem," *Foreign Affairs* (Winter
1979/80), 312.

49. For details see Adrian Guelke, *The International Dimension* (Dublin: Gill and
MacMillan, 1988), 140.

RUC would use "to defend the community and themselves from attacks by mindless assassins." In Washington, the deputy British ambassador met with O'Neill and conveyed his government's regret and displeasure at the speaker's remarks.[50]

In response to Biaggi's amendment to the appropriations bill, the State Department announced, in August 1979, the suspension of its license for arms sales to the RUC, pending a review of policy. Tip O'Neill played a vital role in this decision. He could easily have blocked Biaggi's amendment. As speaker of the house, he regulated the flow of legislation in Congress. But on this occasion, he did not intervene. Instead, he was prepared to let the amendment carry—an indication to the British government of the kinds of problems it could expect if calls for a fresh move on Northern Ireland continued to be ignored and met with derision.

Although the State Department had supported the sale of guns to the RUC, the Carter administration was facing increased criticism of its domestic political agenda. The president relied on Tip O'Neill's support to get legislation through Congress and could not afford to criticize such a powerful and essential ally. The administration felt that maintance of good relations with O'Neill was more important than the risk of offending the British. Therefore, the RUC arms sales were suspended.[51]

Irish-American weekly newspapers from New York to San Francisco all hailed the arms suspension as a great victory. Editorial comment in the metropolitan and national newspapers was generally favorable. The *New York Times*, however, criticized the suspension, while the *Washington Post* gave it qualified support. The *Chicago Tribune* strongly praised the decision:

> When Tip O'Neill criticized the State Department for licensing sales of weapons to the police in Northern Ireland he was exactly right. The sales should be stopped immediately. . . . If the RUC really needs the weapons [and we question the wisdom of introducing 3,000 handguns and 500 automatic rifles to an already over-armed environment] there are plenty of other countries that can provide them [other than America].[52]

In Northern Ireland, the reaction from unionists was swift and hostile. On August 2, Ian Paisley delivered a strong protest to the American am-

---

50. "Tip O'Neill in Fresh Ulster Row," *Daily Telegraph* (London), 2 June 1979.
51. Lawrence Halley, *Ancient Affections* (New York: Prager, 1985), 166.
52. "A Senseless Irish Arms Sale," *Chicago Tribune*, 7 June 1979.

bassador in London; Alan Wright, chairman of the Northern Ireland Police Federation, accused the Carter administration of "tacitly supporting terrorism in Northern Ireland."[53] The *Belfast News Letter* ran an editorial that attacked the conduct of United States police forces and described the RUC as one of the most professional in the world. It claimed the State Department not only "denied arms to the force that keeps this country in some semblance of order, but also gave an almighty boost to the killers. A powerful propaganda weapon has been placed in their hands."[54]

In Britain, these attacks were echoed by an assortment of Conservative MPs, including Mrs. Jill Knight and Mr. John Stokes. Among government ministers and those directly involved with Northern Ireland, however, reaction was uncharactericly muted. The arms sale suspension came as a profound shock and brought home the power of the Irish-American lobby. Humphrey Atkins refrained from the customary attacks on the Four Horsemen and tried to mimimize the importance of the arms ban. He said that the RUC had no pressing need for new weapons, which could be obtained from other countries in the future.

British Defense Minister Francis Pym, a former Northern Ireland Secretary, supported Atkins's restrained reaction. He said that the efforts of Irish-American politicians had been misinterpreted in Britain and their concern for Ireland was positive and genuine. Merlyn Rees, another former Ulster secretary, supported Pym and praised the Four Horsemen for their work against the IRA network in America. Almost immediately, the British press interpreted this changed attitude as an indication the government had yielded to Irish-American intimidation and was about to make new political moves in Ulster. The *Daily Telegraph* warned:

> The government should realize, before it is too late, that any proposal for Ulster bearing the marks of American sponsorship would be foredoomed to failure, the price of which might well be counted in the lives of UK soldiers and civilians.[55]

A further indication of the shift in British policy came just five days after the RUC arms ban. Hugh Carey, on his return from vacation in Europe, met with Humphrey Atkins in London. There were reports that

53. *Belfast News Letter*, 2 August 1979.
54. "A Shocking Decision," *Belfast News Letter*, 3 August 1979.
55. *Daily Telegraph* (London), 7 August 1979.

Carey was accompanied by a State Department official at this meeting and they discussed the possibility of holding a peace conference in New York. Atkins said he would consider the proposal but maintained that Ulster's political future could not be negotiated. When Carey returned to New York, he announced he would host talks between Atkins and Irish Foreign Minister O'Kennedy in September. He said he had received strong indications that the Thatcher government would make significant policy changes in Ulster.[56]

In Britain, while some newspapers and political commentators dismissed the "Carey initiative," others reacted quite positively. The *Guardian*, for example, ran an editorial that concluded:

> Humphrey Atkins should follow his first thought and accept Hugh Carey's invitation to take part in informal talks, in New York, on the future of Northern Ireland. He should not be deterred by the mist of diplomatic protocol and Anglo-Irish suspicion which have swiftly enveloped the Governor's suggestion.[57]

Throughout August, press speculation about the proposed "Carey initiative" increased as Edward Kennedy, Tip O'Neill and the Irish government gave their support. On August 21, A. McIlroy, New York correspondent for the *Daily Telegraph*, reported that "an authoritive American diplomatic source" told him there were extensive unofficial consultations between Whitehall and Dublin over the agenda of the New York talks. McIlroy claimed the main elements of the discussions would be the prospect for political progress in Ulster, an exchange of views on cross-border economic cooperation, and joint measures to combat the IRA.[58]

It appears, however, that plans for these discussions between British and Irish officials collapsed because of the opposition of Margaret Thatcher. She discussed the feasibility of the Carey initiative with Humphrey Atkins but remained unconvinced the exercise could produce significant benefits. Consequently, Atkins wrote to Carey on August 23 that he would not be attending the proposed discussions. He was careful,

56. *Irish News*, 8 August 1979.

57. *Guardian* (Manchester), 8 August 1979. Although the majority opinion within the British press had been critical of the Irish-American intervention in the Ulster crisis, there was a growing body of opinion which adopted a different perspective. See Mary Holland, "Kennedy's New Irish Policy," and Bernard Crick, "The Pale Green Internationalists," in *The New Statesman* 11 May and 7 December 1979.

58. A. McIlroy, "Agenda Ready For Ulster Summit in New York," *Daily Telegraph* (London), 24 August 1979.

however, to praise the governor for his actions against IRA fund raising. He referred to their meeting in London as "invaluable and enjoyable and looked forward to seeing him again."[59]

That the British government even contemplated talks in New York was indicative of the changed perception of Irish-American involvement in the Ulster question. The RUC arms ban brought home to Thatcher's administration the power of the Four Horsemen and indicated the potential trouble they could cause in Washington. British officials also feared that if they did not respond to the Irish-American lobby, the lobby would exploit the Ulster issue in the upcoming presidential race.[60]

Constitutional nationalists did not attack Atkins's refusal to go to New York because they felt the British were on the verge of making a major political initiative in Ulster. Their expectations were realized on October 25, 1979, when Atkins announced he would convene discussions aimed at finding consent among Ulster's political parties. Most significantly, the Northern Ireland secretary chose to disclose details of the new initiative before the Association of American Correspondents in London.

At this press conference, Atkins lavished high praise on President Carter and the Four Horsemen for steering the flow of Irish-American money away from the IRA. He appealed directly to the Irish-American leaders for more understanding of the British position and asked for their assistance in encouraging political dialogue in Ulster:

> I hope that as a result of speaking to this audience today more awareness will be forthcoming in the United States and that will in turn temper the attitudes and utterances and activities of some people and groups there who in their profound ignorance of the situation only play into the hands of an outcast terrorist organization whose stated aim is to destroy the democratic structure of government in Ireland, North and South, and replace it with a distinctively Marxist-oriented regime.[61]

In New York, the British Information Service quickly issued copies of the Atkins address to the media. On November 12, Margaret Thatcher gave an extensive interview to the *New York Times* in which she further

---

59. "U.S. Summit on Ulster Vetoed," *Daily Telegraph* (London), 24 August 1979.

60. British government officials feared that Jimmy Carter, because of his increasing unpopularity, could be persuaded to appeal to Irish-American support by adopting a militant position on the Ulster conflict. See Michael Leapman, "How the Presidential Race Could Prolong Ulster's Agony," *The Times* (London), 16 January 1980.

61. "Northern Ireland: Secretary of State's Address to U.S. Correspondents," British Information Service, 29 October 1979.

elaborated on the new political initiative. The State Department was very enthusiastic about the change in British policy and said it would be most pleased if the discussions produced an agreement.[62]

In late October, the British issued a White Paper on the new initiative. It excluded from consideration either the Stormont system or the Sunningdale formula. Discussion of the constitutional status of Northern Ireland was also ruled out. Within these parameters, the main political parties were free to consider any arrangements for the devolution of power from Westminster. The White Paper described the task of the conference as being "to establish the highest level of agreement between unionists and nationalists."

Ironically, in view of the role played by John Hume in working for the initiative, there was initial confusion about whether the SDLP would participate. Internal party divisions led to the resignation of Gerry Fitt as leader. He was succeeded by John Hume and in December the party finally agreed to take part in the conference. Atkins also persuaded the DUP and Alliance parties to attend but failed to secure the cooperation of the Ulster Unionist Party.

The first session of the Atkins conference took place on January 7, 1980, and the last on April 18. By the end of January, it was clear that very little basis for agreement existed among the parties. The Four Horsemen were somewhat disappointed that the British did not force the unionists into some form of cooperation. This disappointment, however, did not quench their conviction that they had made a significant contribution in persuading the British to do something in Ulster.

Analysts of the Atkins initiative almost universally agree that American pressure was the key element that finally pushed the British into action. One of the strongest proponents of this view is Adrian Guelke, who concluded:

> While the evidence of the role of the American connection is largely circumstantial, no other factor loomed as large in analysis of the initiative and it seems reasonable to conclude that American pressure was the main reason for the initiative.[63]

Despite the eventual failure of the Atkins conference, the Four Horsemen saw their campaign as a major victory. They fully believed that for

62. Seán Cronin, *Washington's Irish Policy* (Dublin: Anvil Books, 1987), 316.
63. Adrian Guelke, "The American Connection to the Northern Ireland Conflict," *Irish Studies in International Affairs* 1, no.4 (Summer 1984): 36.

the first time in the Troubles, Irish-American political pressure had actually been instrumental in bringing a new British initiative. The Big Four could now give a concrete example of the influence of constitutional agitation and persuade Irish Americans that theirs was the only way to achieve real political change in Ireland.

The "Donlon Affair"

In the summer of 1980, the leaders of constitutional nationalism in America again demonstrated their power and ability to influence Irish politics. On July 8, an article in the *Washington Star* reported that the new Irish government of Charles Haughey was planning to remove Seán Donlon as the ambassador in America. Political analysts in Ireland suggested the move was a symbolic gesture designed to win support among the militant nationalist elements in Fianna Fáil.

Haughey especially wanted to cement an alliance with Neil Blaney. In 1979, Blaney had toured the United States under the sponsorship of the Irish National Caucus. During the trip, he launched a series of attacks on Seán Donlon because of his constant attempts to undermine the Ad Hoc Committee. Donlon, since his appointment as ambassador in 1978, had continued to lead a sustained campaign against republican groups in America. When Blaney returned to Ireland he began pushing Haughey for Donlon's removal.[64]

Reports of this deal between Haughey and Blaney initiated a wave of criticism from Irish politicians. John Hume and Garret FitzGerald both called the move a classic piece of political opportunism that would weaken constitutional nationalism in America. When the Four Horsemen heard of Haughey's proposed action, they each issued statements praising Donlon for his invaluable work against IRA supporters in America.

Tip O'Neill and Edward Kennedy contacted John Hume and U.S. Ambassador William Shannon in Dublin. They instructed both men to convey their extreme displeasure to Haughey.[65] Later, O'Neill and Kennedy telephoned the Taoiseach and said they would not cooperate with his administration if Donlon was removed from Washington.[66]

64. See Mary McGrory, "Irish Envoy's Firing Stirs Up Irish Trouble," *Washington Star*, 8 July 1980.

65. Elizabeth Shannon, *Up in the Park: The Diary of the Wife of the U.S. Ambassador to Ireland* (New York: Atheneum, 1983), 278.

66. Garret FitzGerald, interview with author, 19 December 1990.

Haughey, faced with this intense pressure from America, was initially evasive but eventually backed down. On July 9, he met with his cabinet and announced Donlon would remain as the Irish ambassador.

Reports immediately circulated that the Four Horsemen had caused Haughey to reverse his decision to remove Donlon, and their intervention received praise in the American press. O'Neill and Kennedy, however, wanted Haughey to make a public condemnation of Irish-American republican groups. John Hume conveyed their feelings in this appeal:

> In order that all shreds of suspicion be removed and this unfortunate affair closed, it is necessary that it be made clear that the activities of Congressman Mario Biaggi and the organizations with which he is associated enjoy no support whatsoever among any section of Irish opinion.[67]

Haughey again acquiesced, and on July 27 he made a major policy speech at a Fianna Fáil conference in Cork. He strongly attacked Irish-American republicanism and told his audience there was "clear and conclusive evidence available to the government that Noraid has provided support for the campaign of violence and direct assistance for its pursuit." The Taoiseach also attacked the Irish National Caucus and accused it of prolonging the violence in Ulster.[68]

The "Donlon affair" was yet another example of the influence of the Four Horsemen. Their ability to affect political developments in Ireland increased the prestige of constitutional nationalism in America. The political achievements of Kennedy, Moynihan, O'Neill, Carey, and their supporters stood in sharp contrast to the failures of the Ad Hoc Committee. While Noraid and the Irish National Caucus were engaged in mutual recrimination and Mario Biaggi was still suffering from the failure of his peace initiative, constitutional nationalism was going from strength to strength.

The ACIS and Irish Forum

The political activities of the Four Horsemen were complemented at the grassroots level by the activities of Irish-American professional and

---

67. Statement by John Hume in *Irish Press*, 13 July 1980.

68. "Northern Ireland : A Positive Role for Irish Americans," address by Charles Haughey to the Fianna Fáil Organization, *Bulletin of Foreign Affairs*, 27 July 1980.

academic associations. One of the most influential of these was the American Conference for Irish Studies, founded in the early sixties as a forum for the discussion of Irish history, literature, and politics. At its regional and national meetings, the ACIS consistently hosted academics, journalists, and political analysts from both traditions in Northern Ireland. Their presentations revealed the complexity of the Ulster conflict. This generally nurtured an intellectual climate within Irish America that endorsed constitutional dialogue, rather than violence, as the only path to a lasting settlement.

In the 1980s, the work of the ACIS was enhanced by a number of regional Irish Forum groups based in Boston, Philadelphia, and San Francisco. Their purpose was to present Irish Americans with a deeper understanding of the Ulster conflict by providing a platform for representatives of all parties. The Boston group, for example, helped organize symposiums at the Kennedy Library in 1982 and 1984. At these meetings, nationalist and Unionist politicians joined with representatives of the Irish and British governments to present their particular perspective on the Troubles. Again, the general effect was to highlight the deep divisions in Ulster society and show the necessity of constitutional approaches.

CHAPTER 7

◆

IRISH AMERICA AND THE HUNGER

STRIKES, 1979–1981

◆

Support for the IRA among Irish-American activists decreased in the mid-seventies partly because of the continued success of constitutional nationalists. Political actions taken by the Four Horsemen weakened the effectiveness of republican publicity campaigns and undermined their fund raising. Reconciliation groups offered Irish Americans a peaceful alternative through which to focus their concern for Ulster, while academic and professional associations helped nurture an intellectual climate that generally endorsed constitutionalism. Noraid tried to counteract these developments by highlighting Britain's human rights record and exploiting the provisions of the draconian legal system in Ulster. They concentrated on publicizing a series of prison protests undertaken by republicans against the British penal system. Most Irish Americans remained apathetic and showed little interest in these republican maneuvers.

The lack of Irish-American concern for IRA prisoners changed dramatically, however, when the inmates launched a hunger strike campaign in 1980–81. The strike provided militant irredentist groups with a series of publicity victories which enabled them to regain the initiative lost to constitutional nationalists. The deaths of ten prisoners rejuvenated the republican network and won levels of Irish-American support far in excess of that achieved by Bloody Sunday.

Background to the Prison Protests

The key issue in the republican prison protests concerned the inmate's classification within the penal system. Convicted Irish republicans have traditionally fought to be acknowledged as prisoners of war instead of common criminals. Recognition of IRA prisoners as "political" gave them the same standing as captured soldiers in a legitimate war of national liberation. It was only natural that when republicans were convicted or interned in the early seventies, they would fight within jail for prisoner of war status.

The first protests began in Belfast's Crumlin Road Jail. On May 8, 1972, republican inmates refused penal labor and eventually rioted to demand treatment as political prisoners. Secretary of State William Whitelaw denied the legitimacy of their demand and announced there would be no change in prison conditions. Provo leaders in Crumlin Road then declared they would go on hunger strike if Whitelaw did not reverse his position. On May 15, after having received no concessions from the British, republican inmates carried out their threat and began refusing food.

Five Provos, led by Billy McKee, initiated the fast and warned authorities that they would starve themselves to death if their demand for prisoner of war status was not met. Each week, five more republicans joined the hunger strike. Eventually the protest spread to Armagh Women's Prison and to the internees in Long Kesh. At the peak of the strike, more than sixty prisoners were refusing food.

William Whitelaw ignored the hunger strike and seemed unconcerned about growing public demonstrations supporting the prisoners. Even after May 20, when Billy McKee's physical condition rapidly deteriorated, the government remained unresponsive. In June, however, British officials began contacts with Provo leaders outside the jails. These discussions eventually led to the short-lived truce between June and July of 1972.

As part of the preconditions to talks, the Provisionals asked Whitelaw to accept the demands of the hunger strikers. The secretary of state was so anxious to commence dialogue that he immediately announced a change in the prison regime and introduced a "Special Category Status."

Republican and loyalist prisoners were granted the right to wear their own clothes; to abstain from penal labor; to associate freely; to participate in recreational and educational activities; and to have full remission of sentence restored. These concessions amounted to de facto recognition of republicans as prisoners of war. The hunger strike ended with the prisoners claiming a major victory. On July 7 a delegation of Provo leaders met Whitelaw in London and agreed upon a truce.[1]

The British achieved little from the talks, and they had granted a political status to republicans, thus enhancing the IRA's claim to be conducting a war of national liberation. Worse than this for Westminster, the new prison regime became a training ground for the IRA. Inside Long Kesh, the prisoners ran their own affairs and organized themselves along military lines. Provo leaders conducted weapons training using wooden rifles, gave lectures on the use of explosives, and continually planned schemes for escape. Living conditions were among the most favorable in the entire European penal system.[2]

This situation grew increasingly repugnant to the British government, which determined to implement reforms. In 1974, Merlyn Rees, secretary of state, established an independent inquiry into the workings of antiterrorist legislation in Ulster. Headed by Lord Gardiner, the commission published its report in January 1975. It concluded that the granting of special category status had been a mistake and recommended that all prisoners be treated equally. Rees hesitated to implement these recommendations because of the cease-fire with the Provisionals in 1975. When he realized that continued contact with the IRA was fruitless, he closed the incident centers in October 1975 and announced that after March 1, 1976, special category status would no longer apply to new prisoners. They were to be classified as terrorist criminals, without a political dimension to their actions.

Republicans immediately grasped the significance of this change. Not only would it eliminate their privileges within the prisons, but it denied their claim to be captured soldiers and different from common criminals. IRA inmates naturally prepared to resist the new reforms.

One of the first measures announced by the British was that prisoners would no longer be allowed their own clothes and would have to wear

1. Padraig O'Malley, *Biting at the Grave: The Irish Hunger Strikes and the Politics of Despair* (Boston: Beacon Press, 1990), 18.

2. See Patrick Bishop and Eamonn Mallie, *The Provisional I.R.A.* (London: Heinemann, 1987), 270–74.

regulation uniforms. In 1976, the first republican to be subjected to this new regime was Ciaran Neugent, a longtime IRA activist from Belfast. When warders brought prison clothes to his cell in the newly constructed H-block compounds at the Maze Prison, Neugent refused to wear them. He remained naked in his cell until the authorities brought him a blanket. He told warders that the only way they could get him to wear prison clothes was to nail them to his back. He remained in his cell wrapped only in the blanket. This "blanket protest," as it became known, grew as each new republican came under the reformed prison regime.

To highlight the harsh conditions the blanketmen were enduring, supporters formed a Relatives' Action Committee. It organized demonstrations and tried to heighten public awareness of the dispute. The IRA also began attacks against prison officers. By the end of 1976, they had assassinated seven warders; that figure had risen to eighteen by the time the protest ended. This IRA campaign led to an intense hatred between the prison officers and the protesting prisoners and made the British government even more determined to enforce its new regime.

In 1977, while the IRA attacked prison officers, the Relatives' Action Committee organized several protest marches. These were not well attended, and the H-block dispute initially failed to raise widespread anger within the nationalist community. Republicans trying to publicize the issue in America faced similar problems. Despite sustained efforts to get media attention, the blanket protest received little coverage in the US press and television. Noraid demonstrations attracted only handfuls of supporters. The situation was so bad that the *Irish People* attacked the apathy of Irish Americans. One editorial complained:

> As we go to press, Irishmen—naked but for a blanket—have been beaten, humiliated and tortured for twelve months in H-block. I give you these details because it seems to me that so many Irish people don't want to know about it—they're too busy having a good old time for themselves . . . and that is why there is a Long Kesh and torture chambers called H-blocks. The Irish don't care! The Irish don't want to know! The Irish are selfish! And, the selfishness of the Irish has left them divided because the wily enemy caters to our selfishness and keeps us in bondage.[3]

The prisoners in the H-block escalated their protest partly in response to public apathy. In April 1978, they refused to empty their chamber pots

3. *Irish People* (New York), 17 September 1977.

and neither shaved nor bathed. Warders would not clean the prisoners' cells, and soon some three hundred republicans began smearing the walls with excrement.

This new "dirty protest" was slow to win support and publicity, as many people were revolted by it. Public demonstrations continued to be poorly attended, while media coverage was limited and generally supportive of the British position.[4] In August 1978, however, the Relatives' Action Committee finally made some headway in its campaign. The Catholic archbishop of Armagh, Tomás O Fiaich, visited the H-blocks and strongly condemned prison authorities. After describing the appalling conditions in which prisoners were living, he went on to support the demand for political status:

> The authorities refuse to admit that these prisoners are in a different category from the ordinary, yet everything about their trials and family background indicates that they are different. They were sentenced by special courts without juries. The vast majority were convicted on allegedly voluntary confessions obtained in circumstances which are now placed under grave suspicion. Many are very youthful and came from families which had never been in trouble with the law, though they lived in areas which suffered discrimination in housing and jobs. How can one explain the jump in the prison population of Northern Ireland from 500 to 3,000 unless a new type of prisoner has emerged?[5]

O'Fiaich's statement was extensively quoted in the American press. Leading US newspapers began running their first articles on the H-block protest. This encouraged supporters of the prisoners to increase their appeals to Irish Americans.

In October 1978, Father Raymond Murray, a longtime activist for the prisoners' cause, went on a publicity tour of the United States. The tour was financed by the Irish National Caucus. Murray met with American politicians and media executives to explain the protest. He distributed copies of a pamphlet entitled *The Castlereagh File*, which outlined extensive cases of alleged police brutality at the RUC interrogation center. Murray was so enthusiastic about his reception in America that he and Father Dennis Faul produced the booklet *The Sleeping Giant*. It called upon H-block activists to concentrate their efforts on a transatlantic pub-

---

4. Tim Pat Coogan, *On the Blanket: The H-Block Story* (Dublin: Ward River, 1980), 152.
5. *Irish News*, 1 August 1978.

licity campaign. The clergymen claimed that this was the best way to force the British into concessions in the prisons.[6]

In the autumn of 1978, republican supporters organized American tours for family and friends of the prisoners. The inmate's wives spoke at Irish-American gatherings and gave personal accounts of the horror both they and their husbands were experiencing. The American media covered these visits and occasionally the relatives won newspaper columnists over to the prisoner's cause. After meeting with four of the women, Chuck Stone, a reporter for the *Philadelphia Daily News*, wrote an article supporting the H-block protest. After Stone described "the stomach-wrenching rottenest of British atrocities which would make Idi Amin proud," he concluded, "The real heroes in this dirty and endless war are the prisoners in the H-blocks."[7]

The prisoner's relatives also won support from journalists Pete Hamill and Jimmy Breslin in the *New York Daily News*, but they received the greatest publicity from syndicated columnist Jack Anderson. In 1978, the Irish National Caucus persuaded Anderson to write about Northern Ireland. He met with prisoners' families in October and afterwards wrote a scathing attack on British policy. In an article supplied to more than eight hundred newspapers, he compared the H-blocks to the tiger cages in Vietnam and concluded:

> It is estimated that perhaps 70 percent of the political prisoners in Long Kesh have been convicted by uncorroborated statements or forced confessions made in Stalin-like kangaroo court procedures. Human rights violations have put Northern Ireland on an unenviable par with some of the most barbarious regimes of communist commissars or tinhorn Latin American dictators. The British are trampling on the rights of Irish citizens in a manner reminiscent of Oliver Cromwell's iron-fisted rule more than three centuries ago.[8]

This article created immediate controversy and was strongly condemned by the British government. Ambassador Peter Jay responded by describing H-block prisoners as "bloody murderers" and argued their

6. Fathers Dennis Faul and Raymond Murray, *The Sleeping Giant: Irish Americans and Human Rights in Northern Ireland* (1979), 12.

7. Chuck Stone, "No St. Patrick's Day in Belfast, Only British Terror," *Philadelphia Daily News*, 15 March 1979.

8. Jack Anderson, "A Camp David for Northern Ireland," *Washington Post*, 29 October 1978.

conditions were self-inflicted.[9] In February 1979, high-ranking officials from the Northern Ireland Office traveled to the United States. They met with British diplomats in New York and Washington and advised them on ways to present their case more persuasively. They specifically told British Information Service (BIS) officials to conduct a more sustained media campaign to counteract the effects of the H-block relatives' tours.[10]

Determined to achieve this result, British authorities allowed American reporters, photographers, and television cameramen to tour the H-blocks on March 15, 1979. They hoped this concession would help to bring the "reality" of conditions in the Maze to Irish Americans and undermine the effects of Jack Anderson's article. The correspondents were not allowed to interview the protesting prisoners. Despite this restriction, however, reports of the tour in the American press tended to sympathize with the men. Some British officials consequently believed their exercise had backfired.[11]

In October 1979, encouraged by the increasing media reports, various prisoner support groups in Ireland merged into the National H-Block/Armagh Committee. This new group revitalized the publicity battle and increased support within the nationalist community by stressing that endorsement of the H-block protest did not necessarily mean acceptance of the IRA's armed struggle. The committee established an information bureau which kept Irish Americans up to date with every new development in the prisons and shipped large amounts of literature across the Atlantic.

Militant Irish-American groups gradually became more successful at increasing awareness of the H-block issue. Noraid supporters drew widespread attention when they symbolically wore blankets during the 1979 St. Patrick's Day parade in New York. They also organized demonstrations against Royal Navy ships docking in US ports and increased protests outside British consulates.[12]

---

9. For an excellent report on the publicity battle between Anderson and the British, see Kieth Kyle, "America's Ireland," *Listener* 101 (15 February 1979): 238–39.

10. See Chris Walker, "The American Threat To Ulster," *Spectator* (3 February 1979), 11. See also Alf McCreary, "Ulster Prison Protest Fuels Propaganda," *Christian Science Monitor*, 7 December 1978.

11. Leonard Downie, "Press Tours Ulster Prison Befouled by I.R.A. Protestors," *Washington Post*, 16 March 1979.

12. *Irish People* (New York), 29 September 1978. Noraid units in San Francisco offered $500 reward for any British officer captured, painted green, and returned to ship.

Noraid became particularly adept at exploiting Roman Catholic symbolism to win support. Its handouts carried drawings of bearded, long-haired, prisoners clad in blankets and clasping rosary beads. The comparison with Christ suffering was obvious and intentional. Editorials in the *Irish People* constantly employed this imagery and told readers how the prisoners were suffering religious persecution. One of these editorials presented the allegation in the following manner:

> In the H-block concentration camp, a young Irish republican—naked but for a blanket—faces a trio of British soldiers. One hand holds his blanket around his shoulders and the other grasps the crucifix of his rosary. His rosary beads have been a great source of comfort to him all these long, cold, and dreary nights as he recited decade after decade for his parents, family, friends, and especially for his fallen comrades. Now these foreign mercenaries make fun of his religion and his dedication to the Mother of God. They use four-letter words as they grasp at his neck. The rosary beads snap in broken pieces. A part falls to the floor and one of the soldiers laughs raucously as he stamps his boot on it.[13]

Militant Irish-American groups continued to use this kind of emotive imagery throughout the prison campaign. They also sponsored US tours by ex-blanketmen designed to give Americans personal accounts of conditions in H-block. In August 1980, Ciaran Neugent entered the US illegally and conducted a hectic information tour in which he addressed crowds of supporters. He met with newspaper columnists, conducted radio talk shows, and appeared on the MacNeil-Lehrer NewsHour.

The publicity generated by Neugent's tour prompted the British to send Cyril Grey, a key official in the Northern Ireland Office, to the embassy in Washington. Although the Thatcher administration described the move as a "routine deployment," it was specifically designed to strengthen anti-republican activities in America. Grey emphasized his government's displeasure at Neugent's activities and encouraged federal authorities to have him arrested for illegal entry.[14] On August 28, Neugent was apprehended outside the British consulate in New York; he was subsequently deported.

---

13. *Irish People* (New York), 6 April 1978. For an analysis of how republicans in Ireland exploited Catholic symbolism, see Paul Bew and Henry Patterson, *The British State and the Ulster Crisis* (London: Verso Books, 1985), 120.

14. "Civil Servant to Counter I.R.A. in U.S.," *The Times* (London), 31 August 1980.

Publicity for the H-block campaign in America next covered a visit of US churchmen to Northern Ireland in August 1980, sponsored by the H-Block Committee. Relatives of the prisoners hoped the clerics would be allowed to visit the Maze prison and report on conditions themselves. Father Daniel Berrigan, S.J., longtime antiwar and civil rights activist, led the group. British officials, fearing a republican propaganda exercise, refused to allow the priest to visit the H-blocks. Berrigan reacted furiously and described the Maze compounds as comparable to Nazi concentration camps. When he returned to the US he continued to speak against conditions in the prison and wrote a series of anti-British articles for the press.[15]

Noraid capitalized on the publicity generated by Berrigan and continued financing U.S tours by former blanket protestors. In September 1980, Liam Carlin and Fra McCann entered the country illegally and gave lectures on their experiences in prison. They conducted a nationwide publicity campaign while evading immigration officers from New York to Los Angeles.

British officials condemned the apparent ease with which the two men were able to escape arrest and the political support they attracted.[16] In Boston, Fra McCann was awarded a citation from the Massachusetts State Legislature, which commended "his heroic stand in suffering over three years of torture and degradation." He met privately with Edward King, governor of Massachusetts. The Boston City Council extended its best wishes to McCann and wished him success in "educating the American people in the struggle to achieve justice." Liam Carlin received similar citations from State legislatures in California and Michigan. He also persuaded a number of city councils throughout the US to support political status for republican prisoners.[17]

Hunger Strikes

Despite the increasing publicity and support for the H-block in Ireland and America, by September 1980 the prisoners felt that they would have to intensify their campaign. After contacting British officials, the prison-

15. Father Daniel Berrigan, interview with author, April 26, 1991.

16. Eileen McNamara, "Hackles Rise Over Visitor From Belfast," *Boston Globe*, 8 October 1980.

17. Immigration agents finally arrested Fra McCann on 1 October and seized Liam Carlin one month later in Pittsburgh. Following their deportation, Rose McAllister, a former

ers were convinced that the blanket and dirty protests would not force concessions on political status. On October 27, therefore, seven prisoners, led by Brendan Hughes, began a hunger strike.

On October 29, Hughes called for an escalation of protests outside the prisons. He specifically appealed for greater efforts from the Irish-American groups and emphasized that demonstrations in New York, Boston, and Chicago would bring most pressure on the British government. In response, Noraid organized weekly protests across the US. The Irish National Caucus lobbied members of the Ad Hoc Committee and encouraged them to support the prisoners. Mario Biaggi tried unsuccessfully to get Donald McHenry, chief US delegate at the United Nations, to mediate with the British.

The caucus, in the person of Father Seán McManus, convinced Senator Alfonse D'Amato (R, N.Y.) to conduct a fact-finding tour of Ulster, which began on December 8, 1980. D'Amato was accompanied by Dennis Dillon, a Nassau County district attorney, and then–Long Island councilman Peter King. All three attended an H-block rally in Belfast and met with Sinn Fein leaders. Afterwards they issued statements condemning British human rights violations in Ulster and supporting the demand for political status.[18]

Publicity of the tour kept the hunger strike a major item in the US news. The vast majority of American newspapers did not support the IRA prisoners and denied the legitimacy of political status. Some, however, suggested that Margaret Thatcher should employ greater flexibility in the dispute. The *New York Times*, for example, believed there was room for compromise over the issue of prison clothing.[19]

The British government, hoping to prevent the American media from adopting a more favorable view of the hunger strikes, began its own series of publicity initiatives. Michael Allison, minister of state for Northern Ireland, held formal lunches with American correspondents in London to ensure adequate coverage of the British viewpoint. On November 24, Conservative MPs John Biggs-Davison and Brian Mawhinney were sent

---

inmate of Armagh Women's Prison, entered the US illegally and continued the publicity campaign.

18. William Borders, "D'Amato Ends Visit to Northern Ireland," *New York Times*, 10 December 1980. Republicans in New York later reported that the US State Department had exerted considerable pressure on D'Amato not to undertake the visit, because it would be used to boost the IRA's image.

19. *New York Times*, "Don't Let Clothes Make the Martyr," 27 November 1980.

to Washington to coordinate BIS publicity against the prisoner's demands. They distributed a new, glossy brochure entitled *H-Block: The Facts*, which described conditions in the Maze prison as the best in Western Europe and blamed the rising crisis solely on the prisoners.[20]

Britain's position received a further boost from the meeting between Margaret Thatcher and Charles Haughey on December 8, 1980, in Dublin. It was part of a series of Anglo-Irish summits, which had begun in May 1979. When the talks concluded, Charles Haughey claimed an "historic breakthrough" in Anglo-Irish affairs and that a new formalized relationship between Britain and Ireland would emerge. There ensued speculation that a solution to the hunger strike was near.

Haughey's claims of a breakthrough were greatly exaggerated and angered Margaret Thatcher. She did not, however, immediately dismiss the Taoiseach's statements, because they were politically useful. She could use Haughey's excessive appraisal of Anglo-Irish relations to dilute the expected outcry if any of the prisoners died.[21]

The American press interpreted the Haughey statement as an indication that the British were working hard to find a solution, not only to the hunger strike, but to the whole Northern Ireland problem. Articles suggested Thatcher would be giving Dublin a direct political role in the future of the province. Editorials praised the progress in Anglo-Irish affairs, and attention was deflected from Thatcher's handling of the prison dispute.

The hunger strike reached its crisis point on December 16, 1980. Seán McKenna, one of the original protestors, was near death and would receive the last rites. Within the prison, frantic negotiations were conducted between Brendan Hughes and British officials. Prison authorities presented the hunger strikers with a thirty-four-page document, which hinted that concessions could be made if the fast was ended. While the hunger strikers were wary of British promises, they decided to end their fast on December 18 and save Seán McKenna's life.

There was confusion after the end of the hunger strike, as both sides claimed victory. When republican prisoners tried to negotiate concessions, however, the British were not flexible. Hoped-for improvements in the penal regime were not granted. Author Kevin Kelley correctly observed:

20. *H-Block: The Facts*, (Belfast: H.M.S.O., 1980).
21. Padraig O'Malley, *The Uncivil Wars: Ireland Today* (Boston, Houghton and Mifflin, 1983), 29.

The Provos had been badly out maneuvered by the British in the propaganda war. Many people in Ireland and around the world were left, rightly or wrongly, with the impression that Britain had won and the IRA had lost on this key battleground.[22]

That the British did not make substantial concessions after the ending of the hunger strike embittered the prisoners. While some leaders wanted to continue negotiations in the hope of making an agreement, the majority of republicans in the H-blocks braced for another hunger strike.

There was considerable apprehension when support groups on the outside heard of the prisoners' attitude. Sections within the National H-Block Armagh Committee felt their cause had been dealt a serious blow by the ending of the first hunger strike. They believed it would be impossible to build up national and international support for another fast. Leaders of Sinn Féin advised Bobby Sands, Provo commander in the Maze, to wait and see if the British would make any new offers. Irish-American republicans, believing they could not afford to tie up resources in another protest that might end in failure, were likewise discouraged after the first hunger strike campaign and expressed similar reservations.

Despite this initial apprehension, H-block support groups gave their full support when a second fast began. The hunger strike started on March 1, 1981, when Bobby Sands refused food. Other strikers joined him at fortnightly intervals. The strategy was to allow these prisoners a reasonable time period for negotiations if Sands died and to maintain relentless pressure on the authorities.

In the first weeks of the hunger strikes the initial fears of the H-Block Committee seemed confirmed. Public demonstrations in Ireland were poorly attended and publicity was minimal. The perceived failure of the first hunger strike had also weakened Irish-American republicanism. In February, Margaret Thatcher traveled to Washington to receive an honorary law degree from Georgetown University. Despite strenuous attempts to organize a protest, only a handful of demonstrators appeared at the ceremony.[23]

To add to the problem of poor attendance at demonstrations, militant irredentist groups in America also suffered from the continued activities of constitutional nationalists. During the first hunger strike, the Four

22. Kevin Kelley, *The Longest War* (Westport, Conn.: Lawrence Hill, 1982), 327.

23. Chris Winner, "Irish Caucus Sues U.S.C.C.," *National Catholic Reporter* 17 (April 24, 1981): 38–39.

Horsemen had been criticized for not using their political influence to resolve the dispute. Noraid attacked Tip O'Neill, in particular, claiming he
was callous and uncaring. They tried to convince Irish Americans that

> a few words uttered by any of the four might have had great effect
> upon the British and prevented much of the suffering endured by the
> hunger strikes. Yet, the four were silent and did nothing. . . . They are
> shallow, self-serving politicians unworthy of our support.[24]

In response to this attack, the Four Horsemen began considering
ways to re-establish their image and leadership among Irish Americans.
In February 1981, Senator Christopher Dodd (D, Conn.), Congressman Thomas Foley (D, Wash.), and Carey Parker, chief aide to Edward
Kennedy, held a meeting with John Hume. They agreed that efforts to
counteract republican groups in America would be greatly enhanced by
the formation of a formal group in Congress. Consequently, twenty-four
of the most influential senators, congressmen and governors formed
the congressional Friends of Ireland on St. Patrick's Day 1981. They announced the group would champion the goals of constitutional nationalism and attack Irish-American support for violence.[25]

Constitutional nationalists persuaded President Ronald Reagan to endorse the new group. Seán Donlon had established good relations with
the new president following his inauguration. He convinced Reagan to
visit the Irish embassy for lunch on St. Patrick's Day, welcome the formation of the Friends of Ireland, and issue a statement obviously aimed
at Noraid:

> We will continue to condemn all acts of terrorism and violence, for
> these cannot solve Ireland's problems. I call on all Americans to ques-
> tion closely any appeal for financial or other aid from groups involved
> in this conflict to ensure that contributions do not end up in the hands
> of those who perpetuate violence.[26]

Formation of the Friends of Ireland and the Reagan statement compounded the problems faced by Irish-American republicans in winning
support for the H-block prisoners. The hunger strike campaign in Ireland

24. *Irish People* (New York), 27 December 1980.
25. The Friends of Ireland was led by Senators Kennedy and Moynihan and House
Speaker O'Neill. It also included Senator Chris Dodd (D, Conn.), Congressman Tom Foley
(D, Wash.) and Governors Carey of New York and Byrne of New Jersey.
26. *Statements by Presidents: Administration of Ronald Reagan*, 17 March 1981.

also seemed to suffer when Frank Maguire, MP for Fermanagh/South Tyrone, died suddenly in early March 1981. Maguire had been an outspoken supporter of the hunger strike and had attracted substantial publicity by his militant speeches.

Although Maguire's death was a setback, it created an unparalleled publicity coup for the prisoners: Sinn Féin, despite fear of rejection at the polls, nominated Bobby Sands as a candidate for Maguire's vacant seat. A series of political maneuvers left Sands as the sole nationalist candidate running against Harry West of the Ulster Unionist Party.

Media Coverage

During the election campaign, the H-Block Committee successfully presented their case to the nationalist electorate. They convinced many that a vote for Sands was not necessarily an endorsement of the IRA but a means to save a prisoner's life. As the election day neared, media coverage in Britain reached unprecedented levels. When Sands was elected on April 9, journalists and newsmen flocked to Belfast in expectation of a breakdown of order if he died. It was the greatest concentration of international press that Northern Ireland had ever witnessed. The battle of wills between a starving MP and the "Iron Lady," Margaret Thatcher, presented an irresistible media event. Journalist Gerry Foley caught the essence of the situation when he observed:

> The election victory brought an altogether new dimension to the hunger strike. Now, overnight, the British were dealing with not just a "convicted terrorist," but an elected MP. The issue was now front-page news throughout the world.[27]

Media coverage of the hunger strike peaked as Sands's condition deteriorated in late April. Twenty-three nations sent television crews to Belfast, while more than four hundred international journalists reported on the event. After Sands died on May 5, 1981, more than three hundred photographers provided the world with front-page pictures of his funeral.

Perhaps most significantly for groups like Noraid, American journalists composed the largest segment of the international newsmen. The three major US television networks sent sixteen camera crews to the

27. Gerry Foley, "Bobby Sands: The Making of a Martyr," *Magill*, 11 May 1981.

province and provided the American public daily news footage of the deepening crisis.[28]

Republicans and some media analysts claim that this build-up of journalists had a profound effect on the nature of news coverage from Ulster. Noraid had continually attacked the mainstream US media coverage of the conflict as pro-British. They alleged that most American reporters never went to Belfast and wrote all their reports from the comfort of London. They further claimed these journalists took their information from British sources and therefore produced reports highly unfavorable to the IRA. Irish-American republicans were particularly critical of the *New York Times*, transforming the popular slogan and accusing it of containing "All the News That's Brit to Print."[29]

These republican criticisms of the US media have been supported by journalists who worked in Ulster. Jo Thomas, who covered the province for two years with the *New York Times*, recalls how easy it was to remain in London, with its fine restaurants and excellent entertainment, and compose reports from the weekly press briefing issued by the British Foreign Office. She maintains:

> American journalists cover Northern Ireland infrequently, in short trips sandwiched between other assignments, if they go there at all. Many stories are simply written from London, with no on-the-ground reporting, even though Belfast is just an hour away by air shuttle. When reporters do go, they rarely leave Belfast. . . . Sometimes the press officers in the Northern Ireland Office will do something as blatant as arranging the visiting correspondent's entire itinerary.[30]

28. Neil Hickey, "Northern Ireland: How T.V. Tips the Balance," *T.V. Guide*, 21 September 1981.

29. See Father Maurice Burke, *A Decade of Deceit: The New York Times and the War in Ireland* (New York: Noraid Publications, 1981). For an analysis that concludes the IRA receive more favorable media coverage than other groups, see David Paletz et. al., "The I.R.A., Red Brigades and F.A.L.N." in William Adams, ed., *Television Coverage of International Affairs* (New Jersey: Cablex, 1985), 143–65. From the mid-1980s onward, some of the leading US newspapers did begin sending reporters on major assignments to Northern Ireland. Kevin Cullen of *Boston Globe*, Jim Mulvaney of *Newsday*, and Francis Clines of *New York Times* are just a few of the reporters who made a succession of investigative trips to Ulster and supplied detailed articles on major political developments. Their work has been complimented by James F. Clarity and John Darnton of the *New York Times*, who have provided insightful coverage of the current IRA cease-fire.

30. Jo Thomas, "Bloody Ireland," *Columbia Journalism Review* (May/June 1988). Roger Faligot, *Britain's Military Strategy in Ireland* (London: Zed Press, 1983), 75, sup-

Republicans claim that it was the large build-up of journalists in Belfast between April and May of 1981 that changed the nature of American media coverage of Ulster. Reporters scoured the province to report on the daily violence; they talked directly to the groups involved. Media analysts Liz Curtis and Roger Faligot contended that for the first time in years, US journalists provided information stemming from other than British sources.[31] Consequently, there was much greater criticism of the British position on the hunger strike. Lamenting this change, Phillip Knightley of the *London Sunday Times* concluded:

> The hunger strikers have rekindled a flagging interest in Ulster and its problems; as a result, world opinion has begun to shift away from the British government and in favor of the IRA. The image of the gunman has actually improved. And the general opinion is emerging that the time has come for Mrs. Thatcher to begin negotiations with Dublin leading to eventual union with the south.[32]

In America, no other event in the Ulster conflict had received as much media coverage as the hunger strikes. It became the lead item on network television news, and the column inches previously devoted to Northern Ireland in the press ran into miles. With Sands' impending death, editorial comment generally attacked the hunger strike and the IRA. Some encouraged the British to take a tougher stand. The *Chicago Tribune*, for example, suggested the British government should deny the IRA martyrdom by force-feeding the prisoners.[33] Almost all the major American newspapers denied the legitimacy of political status for republican prisoners. They backed the British government's claim that concession to this principle would only encourage terrorism. The *Detroit News* typified editorial opinion on the issue when it commented:

> Margaret Thatcher was right to refuse political status to Bobby Sands, the IRA man who died on a hunger strike at Maze Prison. Mr. Sands

---

ports Thomas and claims that when American correspondents came to Belfast, "They didn't go further than the Europa Hotel lounge" and took their reports directly from the British Army Information Unit.

31. Liz Curtis, *Ireland: The Propaganda War* (London: Pluto Press, 1984), 203, and Roger Faligot, *Britain's Military Strategy in Ireland*, 82.

32. Phillip Knightley, "Is Britain Losing the Propaganda War," *Sunday Times*, 31 May 1981. See also David Willis, "I.R.A. Capitalize on Hunger Strike to Gain Worldwide Media Attention," *Christian Science Monitor*, 29 April 1981.

33. *Chicago Tribune*, "Bobby Sands' Fast," 30 April 1981.

belonged to a terrorist organization, and no government can afford to concede that repugnant acts of violence are somehow sanctified by political aspirations.[34]

The American press maintained its lack of support for political status throughout the hunger strike but, as more prisoners died, they launched equally strong attacks against the British government. Many newspapers condemned the legal system and the process whereby most of the prisoners ended up in the H-blocks. The *Boston Globe* commented, "Britain's prison system in Northern Ireland is defective because the system of justice is a sham."[35] The *New York Times* supported this contention and renewed its earlier calls for Britain to allow the prisoners to wear their own clothes.[36]

In July 1981, after a series of independent negotiating teams failed to secure a compromise between prison authorities and the hunger strikers, the American press issued strong criticisms of Margaret Thatcher. They attacked her "haughtiness," "starchy tone," and "monumental inflexibility." The *Baltimore Sun* condemned Thatcher's "misplaced resolve" and urged President Reagan to "convince her that stubbornness, not flexibility, is the great evil to be avoided."[37] The *Chicago Tribune*, in assessing the violence after Bobby Sands's death, concluded:

> Much of the blame for this can be laid on Mrs. Thatcher and her obstinate refusal to work for reform. . . . It must be abundantly clear to her now that her policy of complacency and inactivity has failed miserably. Now that she has won her point, she should give some consideration to relaxing prison rules to accommodate some of the inmates' demands.[38]

Newspaper columnists also produced innumerable articles on the hunger strike. Many extended the editorial attacks on Margaret Thatcher's uncompromising stand and urged her to talk directly with the prisoners. In the *Wall Street Journal*, Alexander Cockburn castigated "The Bankrupt British Policy in Northern Ireland," while Dennis Shanahan, in the *Chicago Sun-Times*, described Bobby Sands as an "extraordi-

34. *Detroit News*, "America and Ireland," 5 May 1981.
35. *Boston Globe*, 6 May 1981.
36. "Britain's Gift to Bobby Sands," *New York Times*, 29 April 1981.
37. *Baltimore Sun*, 13 July 1981.
38. *Chicago Tribune*, 8 May 1981.

nary individual" in dying for a principle that "subsumes life and sets fire to the soul."[39] Coleman McCarthy, in the *Washington Post*, gave strong support to the prisoners and told his readers:

> The prisoners' demands—involving changes in political status, work rules, and privileges—are modest. The men are not seeking to be released from prison for reduced terms, even though their arrests and convictions were suspect and their sentences—such as fourteen years merely for being found in a car that had an unloaded gun in it—were extreme."[40]

American television stations broadcast background reports on the hunger strike which tended to romanticize Irish republicanism. On April 27, 1981, "CBS Morning News" presented a very complimentary biography of Bobby Sands and his republican ideals. It told viewers of Sands's poetry and political writings and how "he memorized the entire contents of *Trinity* by Leon Uris, translated them into Irish, and then tapped them out in code to his co-prisoners in other cells."[41] On May 3, CBS ran an extensive report describing the New York Irish-American reaction to the hunger strike. With republican songs playing as a background, those interviewed cursed Margaret Thatcher, praised Bobby Sands, and expressed their own willingness to die for Ireland.[42]

Many local television and radio stations broadcast similar reports and interviewed prominent Irish-American republicans. Michael Flannery and Martin Galvin, Noraid publicity director, appeared as commentators on New York's WNBC television station. They detailed the British human rights violations in Ulster and publicized the republican position.[43]

The British government was extremely concerned about the American media presentation of the hunger strike. Margaret Thatcher was convinced that one of the ways to defeat the IRA was to deprive it of Irish-

---

39. Alexander Cockburn, "The Bankrupt British Policy in Northern Ireland," *Wall Street Journal*, 7 May 1981, and Dennis Shanahan, "May Bobby Sands and Ireland Rest in Peace," *Chicago Sun-Times*, 27 May 1981.

40. Coleman McCarthy, "In Ireland Where the Struggle Continues," *Washington Post*, 26 July 1981.

41. *CBS Morning News*, 27 April 1981.

42. Ed Rabel, "The Irish Connection," *CBS Sunday Morning News*, 3 May 1981.

43. Stuart Simon, "How Britain is Losing the Irish Argument," *Listener* (2 December 1982), 5.

American support.[44] Yet diplomats at the BIS were continually reporting that unfavorable reactions to British policy was greatly increasing Noraid fund raising. British officials also dreaded the prospect of increased militancy from Tip O'Neill and Edward Kennedy and the possibility they would try to get the US government involved.

These fears increased as American media coverage of the hunger strike grew more critical of Britain. The English press carried reports of how Britain was losing the propaganda war and occasionally condemned specific views in the United States. The *London Times*, for example, attacked the *New York Times'* suggestion that the hunger strikers be allowed their own clothing. It called American media reports "prejudiced and inaccurate" and concluded:

> Advice such as that in the *New York Times* is well meaning no doubt, as well as apparently being a salve to the liberal conscience and popular in certain Irish constituencies in the US. But is very dangerous none the less![45]

Britain's *Daily Mail* focused on a report by Michael Daley, a correspondent with the *New York Daily News*, deeming it "a malevolent piece of lying propaganda" designed "to persuade American politicians to take an increasingly anti-British line."[46] Daley's article recounted the story of a British army patrol firing on a teenage boy. He told the story through the eyes of "gunner Christopher Spell," one of the British soldiers. After the allegations from the *Daily Mail*, Daley admitted that Christopher Spell was a pseudonym. He said the rest of his story was true, but, in order to spare his newspaper any further "embarrassment," he resigned on May 8, 1981.[47]

---

44. Margaret Thatcher, *The Downing Street Years* (New York: Harper Collins, 1993), 384.

45. *The Times* (London), 30 April 1981 and 10 April 1988.

46. *Daily Mail*, 9 May 1981.

47. Michael Kramer, "Just the Facts Please," *New York Magazine* (25 May 1981). British officials also criticized foreign photographers for staging riots during the hunger strike. Some freelance photographers from France apparently paid teenagers to hurl stones and petrol bombs at the security forces. One American reporter alleged, "I saw them go up and hand them money afterwards. It was disgusting but I want to make it clear no American was involved." Following these incidents, foreign journalists held a conference in the Europa Hotel and condemned the practice. See Anne Keegan, "Irish Riots On Cue," *Chicago Tribune*, 20 May 1981.

Officials at the British Information Service were particularly incensed at some of the reports on American local television and radio. They attacked specific programs they considered pro-republican. The British press joined these condemnations; one weekly journal concluded:

> In cities with big Irish-American groups, local newscasts have been appalling. Highly popular, they are not so much journalism as news-as-show business. Presenters picked for their pretty faces and ethnic mix have been let loose on the complexities of Ulster.[48]

The Thatcher administration again sent delegations to America to counteract republican publicity in the media. Senior officials from the Northern Ireland Office and prominent MPs assisted the BIS in trying to influence editorial boards and television executives. These efforts produced few noticeable results. One official lamented:

> I'm very much aware that opinion in the US is severely against us. We haven't enough resources to counter this very skillful campaign. And, American opinion is very important to us. If the US government was persuaded that our actions in Northern Ireland are wrong, or that human rights are being violated, it would effect overall policy toward Britain. But, there is no real interest in our side of the story in the US![49]

The failure of British efforts to counteract Irish republicanism in America produced continual criticism from Unionist politicians. They accused the Thatcher administration of incompetence and lack of commitment to the publicity battle. These criticisms were endorsed by a number of British newspapers, which in turn called on the government to employ private publicists and lobbyists in its campaign. There was also a demand for the appointment of a top official from the Northern Ireland Office (NIO) to head the British Information Service. The *Economist* characterized the government's efforts as follows:

> The intermittent salesmanship by such Northern Ireland ministers as Humphrey Atkins and Adam Butler has been embarrassingly patrician

48. "Blarney: A Lot of it About in American Media Coverage of Ulster," *Economist* (London), 16 May 1981, 16.

49. Neil Hickey, *Northern Ireland: How T.V. Tips the Balance*, 15, and David Blundy, "Funeral Guns Mute Ministerial Offensive," *The Times* (London), 12 July 1981.

and inept. It is an axiom of public relations that the best publicity cannot sell a bad product. But in America no publicity is conspicuously not selling a good one—especially when a worse product is being sold by one of the world's most effective techniques, ethnic loyalty backed by terrorists ready to die for the cause.[50]

Public Protests

The unprecedented media coverage of the hunger strike in the US greatly increased Irish-American concern for events in Ulster. Noraid and other groups capitalized on this heightened awareness. As the fast continued, they organized the largest and most prolonged public demonstrations of the Troubles. The biggest of these took place in New York City outside the British consulate on Fifth Avenue. Republicans held daily protests throughout May 1981. They peaked in the week after Sands's death, when several thousand people protested daily.

Initially these demonstrations were orderly, typically consisting of protestors marching up and down Fifth Avenue, led by pipers playing Irish laments, chanting pro-republican slogans. As the hunger strike reached a climax, the protestors burned effigies of Margaret Thatcher and forced British officials to take down the Union Jack outside their consulate. On July 6, 1981, six protestors broke into the consulate building and held a three hour sit-in. Consular staff claimed they broke furniture and destroyed documents in the library.[51] On August 4, an IRA sympathizer entered the British mission at the United Nations. He said he had a bomb strapped to his body and demanded to talk to Margaret Thatcher about the hunger strike.[52]

Demonstrators dressed in IRA uniforms maintained all-night vigils outside the British consulate throughout the hunger strike. They cursed and jeered at consular staff entering or leaving the building. The British embassy was forced to ask for greater police protection for its staff in New York and had to increase security at its consulates throughout the United States. One British diplomat complained to the *London Times*,

50. "The Selling of Ulster," *Economist* (London), 27 June 1981, 17.

51. "Maze Protestors Attack British Consulate in U.S.," *The Times* (London), 9 July 1981.

52. *Wall Street Journal*, 5 August 1981. The bomb turned out to be a fake but the incident was reported in Britain and reinforced the feeling that the hunger strike was getting substantial Irish-American support.

"When I go to work I am called a bastard, a murderer, a butcher, and a liar—and I suffer the same all over again when I leave."[53]

Militant Irish-American demonstrators were given an added bonus when Prince Charles visited the United States in mid-June 1981. Noraid ran a spontaneous campaign to disrupt his public engagements. As the Prince toured New York harbor in the yacht *Highlander*, a small flotilla of protestors, waving anti-British placards, followed and chanted republican slogans. Later, when the Prince attended a ballet performance at the Lincoln Center, he was greeted by thousands of jeering demonstrators. Inside, at regular intervals, protestors rose from their seats and ran down the aisle shouting obscenities at the royal box.[54]

Following these protests, the *New York Daily Post* published an article that criticized the timing of the royal visit and complained at the cost to the city of providing security for Prince Charles. Mayor Ed Koch and Mario Cuomo joined the controversy, issuing statements that condemned "the centuries-old British policy of denying basic civil rights in Ireland" and called for the withdrawal of British troops from Ulster.[55]

As a result of the demonstrations against Prince Charles, British officials advised Princess Margaret to cancel a proposed trip to Washington in July 1981. The Princess had raised the fury of Irish Americans in 1979. During a dinner party in Chicago, she reportedly referred to the Irish as "pigs." British agents convinced the Princess that her presence in the US would only act as a "royal rag to the Irish-American bull."[56] She accepted this advice and canceled her trip. Princess Anne and Captain Mark Phillips followed her lead and declined an invitation to visit Pennsylvania in August for a horse show. Irish republicans reveled in these victories and determined to escalate the H-block publicity campaign.

Noraid continued to enhance its publicity efforts with further tours of former blanketmen. Noel Cassidy, Charles Crumley, and Séamus Delaney,

53. *The Times* (London), 12 July 1981. See also the report by Michael Leapman in this newspaper entitled, "Soft Assignment a Fiery Time for Our Man in New York," 13 May 1981.

54. *Chicago Tribune*, 18 June 1981.

55. "Koch Sends the Brits a Bronx Cheer," *New York Daily Post*, 19 June 1981.

56. Princess Margaret's "Irish pigs" remark was reported by Irv Kupcinet, an esteemed journalist with *Chicago Sun-Times*. It led to an outburst against the Princess from almost every Irish-American society. When she later traveled to San Francisco, Noraid herded a group of pigs outside her hotel. Some were painted in the colors of the Irish tricolor with "Mags" printed on their backs. There were also reports that the IRA sent an assassin to kill the Princess in California.

all ex-Maze inmates, conducted lectures and press conferences in the US during late spring 1981. These former prisoners were later joined by a group of relatives of the hunger strikers, including Seán Sands, the brother of Bobby, and Oliver Hughes, brother of Francis, who died on 11 May. They visited twenty-six cities on a three-week tour and conducted numerous press interviews, television appearances, and public lectures.

The relatives enraged Irish-American audiences with tales of British brutality. Elizabeth O'Hara, sister of INLA hunger striker Patsy O'Hara, told how prison officers had tortured her brother before he died by leaving hot meals beside his bed. On July 8, Oliver Hughes told a crowd in New York that during his brother's funeral, "British thugs stopped the hearse and bashed the funeral director senseless. I heard one of them say `get the casket, we'll burn the body.'"[57]

Jack Holland contends that the relatives' tours greatly increased republican fund raising and publicity in America. He says they were, "[some] of the most successful tours ever on the Irish-American circuit" and claims they raised over a quarter of a million dollars—this despite strained relations between Noraid and Elizabeth O'Hara, who insisted on emphasizing that her brother Patsy was a member of the "Marxist" Irish National Liberation Army.[58]

Political Support

One of the most significant aspects of the hunger strike was the amount of political support the prisoners received. After Bobby Sands died, his campaign agent, Owen Carron, was elected to the vacant seat in Fermanagh/South Tyrone. During the June 1981 elections in the Irish republic, hunger striker Kieran Doherty and blanketman Kevin Agnew were elected to the Dáil. Because of these electoral victories, the British could no longer claim that the prisoners were a small group of fanatics without public support. Republicans in America emphasized the victories at the polls and tried to win support from politicians, labor leaders, and the Catholic church. They achieved some notable and widely publicized successes.

57. Reported in *Irish People* (New York), 18 July 1981. Maura McDonnell, sister of Joe McDonnell, and Malachy McCreesh, brother of Raymond McCreesh, also participated in this tour.

58. Jack Holland, *The American Connection* (New York: Viking, 1987), 52.

Two days after Bobby Sands died, the 135,000-member International Longshoremen's Association (ILA) imposed a twenty-four hour boycott of British ships. The action affected vessels from Maine to Texas and was masterminded by ILA president Teddy Gleason. Later, an Irish-American Labor Coalition was formed to coordinate trade union activities in support of the hunger strike. The new organization ran boycotts against British goods and organized a mass demonstration to greet the Queen Elizabeth II when it sailed into New York on May 9, 1981.[59]

On April 27, 1981, Terence Cardinal Cooke of New York sent a message to Mrs. Thatcher, which urged her to change prison regulations in the H-blocks. A number of other bishops and high-ranking clerics supported Cooke. Although the church did not officially support political status for H-block prisoners, it continued to press the British for concessions. As each successive prisoner died, there were large commemoration services at St. Patrick's Cathedral in New York and in churches all over America.[60]

The Irish National Caucus played a leading role in the American campaign to publicize the prison conflict. Father Seán McManus had shown solidarity with Bobby Sands by undertaking a twelve-day hunger strike outside the British embassy in Washington.[61] After this, McManus tried to get members of the Ad Hoc Committee to support the prisoners. He contacted Hamilton Fish, Jr. (R, N.Y.) in the hope that the congressman's close friendship with Vice-President George Bush would have some influence. Fish tried to get the Reagan administration to mediate in the hunger strike, but he was later told by the State Department there would be no such action.

Undeterred by this State Department response, McManus encouraged Mario Biaggi to lead a drive within Congress to rally support for the hunger strikers. Biaggi got members of the Ad Hoc Committee to endorse a series of statements sharply critical of the Thatcher administration. In April 1981, the Caucus also organized a trip by former US Attorney General Ramsey Clark to the H-blocks. When British authorities refused to let Clark meet with Bobby Sands, he reacted with bitter

59. Tom Collins, *The Irish Hunger Strike* (Dublin: Gill and MacMillan, 1986), 11.

60. For a report on Cardinal Cooke's plea to Thatcher see *The Times* (London), 27 April 1981.

61. In April 1981, former Yippie leader Abbie Hoffman, conducted a similar hunger strike in support of Sands. Hoffman held his fast in a New York prison cell, where he was serving a sentence for drug possession.

Father Seán McManus carrying the coffin of the dead hunger striker Thomas McIlwee in Bellaghey, County Derry. UPI/BETTMANN

condemnations of Margaret Thatcher. During a news conference in Belfast, he commented:

> The fact is that Margaret Thatcher—who had the power to keep Sands alive, to wear his own clothes, and to receive a letter a day in prison—permitted him to die. . . . She has destroyed any claim she may have had of moral leadership by this outrageous act. . . . People around the world will wonder what failure of character in the government there is that permits young men to die because it will not do a small thing that is right.[62]

62. Speech reported in Alan Brownfeldt, "Many Americans Unaware of I.R.A.'s Terrorists Connections," *Human Events* 41 (13 June 1981): 17.

The hunger strikers received strong support from state assemblies and city governments, particularly on the East Coast. Many issued resolutions calling for political status, while some city politicians tried to get British diplomats evicted from their consulates. The Boston City Council changed the name of Chestnut Street to "Francis Hughes Avenue" in honor of the dead hunger striker. Maire Howe, assistant majority leader of the Massachusetts House of Representatives, led a group of republican demonstrators who dumped British tea into Boston Harbor in a symbolic protest.[63] In response to Bobby Sands's death, the Massachusetts State legislature passed a resolution

> condemning the government of Prime Minister Thatcher for its insensitivity to the value of human life and the real issues of Ireland's divisive struggle, and wholeheartedly supports the ultimate objectives of the IRA.[64]

Although this local political pressure had no impact on government policy in Washington, it did increase the strains on constitutional nationalist leaders. The congressional Friends of Ireland recognized the growing sympathy for the hunger strikers among Irish Americans who were concerned with Ulster, but the Friends did not want to be associated with republican groups. In April 1981, they tried to maintain the position adopted during the first hunger strike—urging the British government to compromise on some of the prisoners' demands, but refusing to support the prison protest.

As the hunger strike progressed and the crisis deepened, constitutional nationalists were pushed into a more militant position, and their criticisms of Britain intensified. Following Sands's death, Senator Edward Kennedy made the following statement:

> I urge the British government, which has clear responsibility for prison administration in Ulster, to act on an urgent basis to end its position of

63. Howe continues to be one of the most prominent anti-British activist in Boston. In 1987 she was awarded $10,000 in a legal suit against the British government. The case arose from an incident in 1985. She was detained by security forces for five hours after taking photographs of the Maze prison. The Northern Ireland High Court ruled in favor of her charge of wrongful detention. See *Boston Globe*, 19 May 1987.

64. *Resolution on the Death of Right Hon. Robert Sands M.P., Prisoner of War and Irish Nationalist*. Commonwealth of Massachusetts, 7 May 1981.

inflexibility, and to implement reasonable reforms capable of achieving a humanitarian settlement of the hunger strike.[65]

On May 6, 1981, the Four Horsemen sent a telegram to Margaret Thatcher, which was made public in the American and British press. It strongly condemned Thatcher's "intransigence" and urged her to end the "posture of inflexibility that must lead inevitably to more senseless violence and more needless deaths."[66]

In her public response to this telegram, Thatcher was careful to acknowledge the contribution the four politicians had made to cutting Noraid fund raising. Yet, she refused to offer concessions, claiming that Britain had tried all possible ways to end the hunger strike. She bluntly stated that responsibility for continued deaths rested with the IRA for ordering the prisoners to commit suicide.[67]

Thatcher's cool response led constitutional nationalists to concentrate on securing the involvement of the American government. Edward Kennedy made initial contacts with the State Department and encouraged the Irish government to launch a direct appeal to the president. On July 15, 1981, Seán Donlon met with Reagan in the Irish embassy. He conveyed a message from Garret FitzGerald asking for American support in pressuring Margaret Thatcher. Donlon wanted Reagan to persuade the British to send an emissary to negotiate directly with the hunger strikers. On August 3, the Friends of Ireland sent a telegram to Reagan endorsing FitzGerald's request and urging him to play an active role in ending the prison protest.[68]

Reagan refused to endorse a US diplomatic initiative, estimating in this instance that it was not worth risking his "special relationship" with Thatcher. He did discuss the issue of the hunger strike at the Ottawa Economic Summit on July 20 but told Thatcher he would not be getting involved. Some newspapers, however, suggested that FitzGerald's initiative did convince the British to permit mediation by a delegation from the Red Cross, a concession they had previously denied.

65. Statement of Senator Edward Kennedy on the death of Bobby Sands, 4 May 1981.

66. "Letter From Four American Politicians to Margaret Thatcher," British Information Service, 6 May 1981.

67. "Northern Ireland: The Prime Minister Replies to American Politicians," British Information Service, 14 May 1981. Despite denials from the Thatcher administration, there were constant contacts between the British Foreign Office and the republican movement during the hunger strikes. See Padraig O'Malley, *Biting at the Grave*, 196–200.

68. Garret FitzGerald, interview with author, 19 December 1990.

The failure to get Reagan's direct intervention was a setback to the Irish government and the Friends of Ireland. It seemed to expose the limitations of their ability to influence the US government on critical issues. The "Friends" were also outmaneuvered by republicans. Their vehement attacks on Margaret Thatcher reinforced Noraid's contention that the British were responsible for the crisis in Ulster.

Many British newspapers concluded that the Friends of Ireland had given direct encouragement to Irish-American republicanism. On October 10, 1981, an IRA bomb killed two people in London. The *Daily Express* ran a front page editorial which described Moynihan, Carey, Kennedy, O'Neill, and Ed Koch as "Five Guilty Men." The newspaper claimed that, because of their statements on the hunger strike, all five were "equally responsible morally" for the bomb attack.[69]

The positive effects of the prison protests on militant Irish-American nationalism can be gauged to some extent by FARA statements from Noraid. For the six-month period prior to July 1980, Noraid received $90,056. In the following report, its collections rose to $105,124. Due to hunger strike publicity the group collected $15,424 in November, $33,395 in December, and $21,695 in January. This marked a steady increase from the $9,139 collected in October 1980.[70]

In the six-month period from January to July 1981, Noraid's fund raising leapt to a total of $250,511. The monthly figures rose from $5,088 raised in February to $42,848 in May and $84,894 in June—the period of maximum publicity for the second hunger strike. Martin Galvin further stated that in the week after Sands's death, $20,000 was sent to Noraid's Bronx office alone, compared to a previous weekly donation rate of $3,500 nationwide.[71] Noraid chapters from Los Angeles to Baltimore all reported similar increases in weekly funding. In October 1981, the group claimed it had established twelve new chapters to accommodate increased membership during the prison protests.[72]

Because of a legal dispute with the Justice Department, Noraid refused to file a financial statement after July 29, 1981, so no official documents

69. *Daily Express*, 13 October 1981.

70. All Noraid financial figures from FARA registration file 2239, 29 July 1980–29 January 1981.

71. "Money Pours in After Sands' Death," *Chicago Tribune*, 26 May 1981.

72. John Breecher, "The I.R.A.'s Angels," *Newsweek Magazine*, 18 May 1981. See also Jane O'Hara, "Going Great Guns for the Cause," *Macleans* 94 (23 November 1981), and Stanley Penn, "Ulster Pipeline: How U.S. Catholics Help Their Brethren in Northern Ireland," *Wall Street Journal*, 12 October 1981.

exist on the amount of money raised during the final phase of the hunger strike. Activists allege that the group continued to receive unprecedented levels of financial support for the next several months.

The hunger strike, consequently, rejuvenated militant Irish-American nationalism and reversed a downward trend in support and effectiveness—a trend noticeable from the mid-1970s. Not only did Noraid increase its fund raising, but it used the prison protest to achieve significant publicity victories. This success substantially damaged the work of the British Information Service. Republican activities also eclipsed the efforts of constitutional nationalists and took the initiative away from the Friends of Ireland. When the hunger strike ended on October 3, 1981, militant nationalists were determined to maintain the high level of activity sustained during the prison protest and to achieve even further breakthroughs.

◆

THE REJUVENATION OF MILITANT

IRISH-AMERICAN NATIONAOLISM,

1981–1985

◆

In January 1982 a delegation of Ulster Unionist leaders launched a major publicity initiative aimed at counteracting the support Irish-American republicans had generated during the hunger strikes. The campaign was christened "Operation USA" and was led by Ian Paisley, Peter Robinson, deputy leader of the DUP, and Official Unionist MEP John Taylor. All three had been incensed by reports of the large Noraid demonstrations in New York after Bobby Sands's death and were frustrated by BIS efforts to challenge republican publicity. They believed that with a series of speaking engagements throughout the US, they could present the unionist position and reduce support for militant nationalism.

From the outset, however, Operation USA suffered a succession of problems. The Irish National Caucus persuaded leading members of Congress to work for the withdrawal of Ian Paisley's US visa. The State Department bowed to this pressure and announced Paisley would not be allowed to enter the country. Peter Robinson and John Taylor were forced to conduct their publicity efforts alone, but they failed to raise interest in the media. Noraid staged demonstrations at most of their public appearances and claimed credit for the failure of the unionist campaign.

The collapse of Operation USA was just one of the positive developments for Irish-American republicanism in the post–hunger strike period. Noraid and other militant groups continued the high level of activism they had achieved during the prison protest. The sacrifice of ten hunger strikers in the H-blocks greatly inspired these groups and contributed to a rejuvenation in their support network.[1]

In Ireland, the hunger strike also reinforced a politicization of the republican movement which had been growing since the mid-1970s. Gerry Adams was the central figure in this reassessment of policy. He emphasized the need to "broaden the battlefield" from the IRA's traditional concentration on military action to a wider political campaign designed to win mass support throughout Ireland.

Impetus for the new republican strategy also came from an acceptance that the IRA's military campaign was not going to achieve a quick British withdrawal. Adams realized the republican movement was in for a prolonged struggle, which would have to be sustained by wider popular support. The new strategy was further influenced by the tradition of social republicanism, which traced its roots back to the writings of James Connolly, hero of the 1916 Easter Rising. Connolly and his adherents had stressed that republicanism would play a peripheral role in Ireland's development unless it championed issues vital to the daily lives of the people.

Gerry Adams hoped that, if it developed a dynamic political agenda, Sinn Féin would displace the SDLP as the main representative of northern nationalists and would also attract wider support in the Irish Republic. His group believed that increased political campaigning, combined with continued militarism, would accelerate the unification of Ireland.[2]

1. The hunger strike ended on 3 October 1981 when it became clear the British government was not going to yield and the prisoner's families began intervening to save their son's lives. In September, with the prison protest broken, Secretary of State James Prior agreed to some concessions. H-block inmates were allowed to wear their own clothes, associate freely at certain times and receive half of their lost remission.

2. For an excellent analysis of these developments see Henry Patterson, "Gerry Adams and the Modernization of Republicanism," *Conflict Quarterly* 10, no. 3 (Summer 1990): 5–24.

Adams and his supporters gradually established control over the republican movement by the late 1970s. While their appeal for greater emphasis on politics met significant opposition, the new strategy blossomed during the hunger strikes. Electoral victories of Bobby Sands and other prisoners showed that support for militant republicanism was much higher than its opponents had always insinuated. Consequently, at its 1981 Ard Fheis, Sinn Féin endorsed a new policy of achieving republican objectives with "a ballot box in one hand and an armalite in the other."[3]

Sinn Féin optimism over its new political strategy was encouraged by continued electoral success. In the Northern Ireland Assembly elections of 1982, it won 30 percent of the nationalist vote. This increased to 43 percent in the British general election of 1983, at which time Gerry Adams was elected to Westminster. For a brief period it seemed that Sinn Féin was indeed on the verge of becoming the dominant force in northern nationalist politics. These developments not only brought profound changes to the republican movement in Ireland, they also had important consequences for the US support network.

The electoral victories of Sinn Féin gave great encouragement to Irish-American republicans. Noraid publicity director Martin Galvin hoped to build upon the successes achieved during the hunger strike. He wished to increase the sophistication of Noraid publicity efforts and raise the effectiveness of its political lobbying campaign. Galvin won strong support from new Irish-American recruits who had joined the organization during the H-block campaign and who wished to sustain the heightened level of activism.[4]

Irish Northern Aid further benefited from the increase in Irish immigration to the United States in the early 1980s. The weakness of the Irish economy forced larger numbers of young people to enter America illegally in search of employment. Most of these new immigrants were solely concerned with surviving financially and keeping one step ahead of immigration authorities. They did not get involved with irredentist groups and tended to lampoon Irish-American nationalism.[5] There were others, however, who were immediately attracted to Noraid. Their involvement arose from a variety of factors. Some were bitter at the Irish

---

3. Padraig O'Malley, *Biting at the Grave: The Irish hunger Strikes and the Politics of Despair* (Boston: Beacon Hill Press, 1990), 211.

4. Martin Galvin, interview with author, 14 November 1992.

5. John P. McCarthy, *Dissent from Irish-America* (New York: University of America Press, 1993), 257–59.

government's inability to provide them with employment. They could readily project their frustrations against "the system" in Ireland through association with Noraid's vehement attacks against the political leaders of the twenty-six counties. Others, as in the past, got involved with Irish-American republicanism simply because the social events were lively, entertaining, and offered the opportunity of meeting fellow Irish people.

A significant number of new Irish immigrants worked in England before they came to America and claim this experience led to their involvement with Noraid. They felt that some English people regarded the Irish as "ignorant navies." This attitude contrasted sharply to their experience in America, where being Irish was an asset. One immigrant in New York recalls:

> I was in London for three years. After my first month an IRA bomb went off. I knew nothing about it. I'd never been interested in politics, but at my local newsagent, where I bought a paper every morning, the owner asked me not to come into his shop again. After that I felt everyone suspected me just because I was Irish.[6]

Whereas Noraid attracted fresh support from this influx of new immigrants, militant Irish-American nationalism also benefited from a radicalization of the Ancient Order of Hibernians. As the largest Irish organization in the United states, the AOH had significant influence and power. In the 1970s, it had adopted a moderate nationalist political perspective and had condemned IRA activities on several occasions. During the hunger strikes, however, the AOH bitterly condemned the British government and aligned itself with the republican position. This growing militancy was further consolidated when Joseph Roche became its President in 1982.

Roche was a fervent nationalist and sympathized with the IRA's right of armed resistance. He encouraged a more militant editorial line in the AOH newspaper, *National Hibernian Digest*, and forged closer ties between his organization and Noraid.[7] Roche also made frequent trips to Belfast to consult with Sinn Féin leaders. In 1984 he invited Gerry Adams to speak at the AOH national convention in Albany, New York. Adams accepted but was immediately refused a visa. Roche was furious

6. Quote from "Jamesy" interviewed by Mary Holland in *Sunday Observer* (London), 30 October 1988. For a detailed analysis of this attitude see Mary Corcoran, *Irish Illegals: Transients between Two Societies* (London: Greenwood Press, 1993), 116–19.

7. See biography of Joseph Roche in Donal O'Donovan, *Dreamers of Dreams: Portraits of the Irish in America* (Bray: Kilbride Books, 1984).

at this denial and became determined to circumvent government restrictions. He organized an amplified telephone link-up between Belfast and Albany through which Adams was able to address the AOH meeting. The Sinn Féin president gave convention delegates the following compliment:

> We in Ireland are familiar with the great work of the Ancient Order of Hibernians in support of Irish national freedom. We are grateful for your financial contributions to An Cumann Cabhrach and Green Cross; for your close cooperation with Irish Northern Aid; and for the invaluable efforts of President Joseph Roche.[8]

The efforts of Roche and the AOH were matched by various other Irish-American groups that had expanded their activities during the hunger strikes. These organizations had previously been overshadowed by Noraid. They were able, however, to raise their level of activity to unprecedented heights during and after the H-block campaign. The American Irish Political Education Committee (PEC), for example, had strongly criticized Britain's human rights record in Ulster since its formation in 1975. Its activities substantially increased in the early eighties through the establishment of new chapters, the financing of anti-British advertisements on local television and radio, and the publication of the monthly *American Irish Newsletter*.

Previously dormant chapters of Clan na Gael reemerged and conducted enthusiastic publicity campaigns. In Toledo, Ohio, Dr. Séamus Metress revitalized the Clan and organized demonstrations against British officials throughout the Midwest. He also ran Irish cultural awareness forums, collected funds for An Cumann Cabhrach, and pressured the Toledo media to include the republican perspective in its reports on events in Ireland.[9]

One of the more colorful organizations to achieve prominence in this period was the American Irish Republican Army (AIRA). The group was formed in 1947 and since then had worked for the republican cause. Its president, Colonel P. G. Duffy, claimed he participated in IRA raids during the Border Campaign between 1956 and 1962. He also took great pride in his inclusion in *Ripley's Believe It or Not* because of the great number of occupations he had pursued. These ranged from a shark

---

8. "Gerry Adams Addresses A.O.H. Convention," *Irish People* (New York), 21 July 1984.

9. For details on the activities of this chapter see *The American Gael* (Toledo), newspaper of the Clan na Gael, in the LinnenHall Library, Belfast.

fisherman to bodyguard for Bing Crosby. Duffy was noted for his extreme conservatism, a point reflected by AIRA membership applications, which read, "All are welcome regardless of race, sex or creed. No Communists!"[10]

After the hunger strikes, the AIRA began a sustained campaign to distribute its newspaper, the *Shillelagh*, to Irish Americans throughout the United States. It ran virulent editorials, which warmly welcomed Provisional IRA bombing attacks on the English mainland. The group raised funds for An Cumann Cabhrach by selling green bomber jackets with the AIRA logo printed on the back and auctioned oil paintings of Bobby Sands.[11]

A number of new republican groups formed specifically in response to the hunger strike. The Irish-American Fenian Society (IAFS), founded in New Jersey in 1982, soon established chapters in New York, California, Connecticut, and Massachusetts. It hosted public lectures by members of Sinn Féin who were able to bypass the State Department's visa policy. The group worked closely with Noraid in organizing fund-raisers and produced a weekly cable television news program giving the republican perspective on events in Northern Ireland.

Extradition, Deportation, and Gunrunning

The rejuvenation of the republican support network in America alarmed both the British and Irish governments. Diplomats based in Washington encouraged the Reagan administration to intensify activities against militant nationalism. Consequently, from 1980 onward, federal law-enforcement agencies increased covert surveillance operations. They concentrated on apprehending IRA fugitives at-large in the US and on infiltrating gunrunning schemes. This campaign achieved a number of major victories.

There were, however, some noted failures, which had the unintended effect of boosting republican morale and encouraging the renewed activism of militant nationalist groups. From the early 1970s the IRA occasionally used America as a "haven" for some of its members to escape

10. American Irish Republican Army membership application printed in *The Shillelagh* (Philadelphia), July/August 1983. See also P.G. Duffy, *My Struggle for Irish Freedom* (Tacoma: A.I.R.A. Publications, 1986).

11. Colonel Tommy Corbett, executive member of American Irish Republican Army, correspondence with author, 14 July 1991.

the law or recuperate after an extended period of active duty. Provos were protected by sympathetic Irish Americans, who provided new identities, employment, and housing. The British government, irritated by the situation, in the late 1970s increased the supply of information on IRA fugitives to US authorities. As each new individual was detected and arrested, British officials filed extradition requests. In most of the initial cases, however, US courts agreed with defense attorneys who classified IRA men as political refugees. These decisions were important victories for the republican movement.

The first major extradition case involving an IRA fugitive in the US was against Peter Gabriel McMullan from Belfast. In 1968 McMullan joined the British Parachute Regiment and was stationed in Belfast during the early Troubles. He became disillusioned with the British presence in Ulster and began working for the IRA, supplying information and carrying out acts of sabotage. McMullan deserted from the army, joined the Provos, and organized a number of bomb attacks against military barracks in England in 1974.

Despite his activities for the republican cause, McMullan fell out of favor with the IRA. Provo leaders accused him of abusing his position by involvement in extortion rackets for his own personal gain. McMullan's standing deteriorated to such an extent that he had to be segregated from other republican prisoners in Port Laoise jail while serving a sentence for IRA membership in 1975.

Upon completing his prison term, McMullan fled Ireland and illegally entered the US. In May 1978 he surrendered to federal authorities in San Francisco and asked for political asylum. McMullan claimed the IRA would kill him if he was sent back across the Atlantic and that he was being stalked by a Provo assassin in the US.

The British government soon issued an extradition request because of McMullan's participation in the bombing of Claro Barracks in Yorkshire. Irish-American republicans were initially inclined to leave McMullan to his fate because they saw him as a traitor and informer.[12] They soon realized, however, that any legal precedent set in his case could be used against all IRA fugitives. Consequently, lawyers from Paul O'Dwyer's office began working with sympathetic attorneys in San Francisco. Their defense was that McMullan could not be extradited because his actions

12. During captivity, McMullan gave details of his involvement in gunrunning operations from New York in 1972.

fell within a political exception clause of the 1972 treaty between Britain and the United States.

Judge Frederick Woelflen heard the case and defined the requirements for political exception before reaching a verdict. He stated that an act of violence must have occurred during an uprising, that the accused had to be a member of the uprising group, and that the action must have had political objectives. On May 11, 1979, Woelflen concluded that all of these principles applied to McMullan's case and so dismissed Britain's extradition request.

Although legal action continued against McMullan, Woelflen's decision was a significant defeat for the British government and federal attorneys. High-level meetings were arranged to discuss new legal strategies against political exception for IRA fugitives, strategies soon tested in the case of Dessie Mackin.

On March 18, 1978, Dessie Mackin, a member of the IRA from Belfast, was arrested after a gun battle with British troops. While on bail, he fled to the Irish Republic and later entered the United States. Mackin's movements were closely monitored by INS agents; he was arrested while leading a republican demonstration in New York in October 1980.

The British requested Mackin's extradition for attempted murder and tried to portray the IRA as criminals devoid of political motivation. Federal attorneys hoped their arguments against political exception would be strengthened by precedents set during the recent trial of Abu Eain, a member of the Palestine Liberation Organization. Eain had fled to the US after planting a bomb in Tiberias, Israel, which killed two children. In early 1981 his request for political exception was rejected and he was subsequently returned to Tel Aviv. During Mackin's trial, prosecuting attorneys argued the Eain decision showed that "irregular guerilla organizations" such as the PLO and IRA did not qualify for political exception.[13]

On August 31, 1981, Judge Naomi Buchwald issued a detailed decision, which concluded that Mackin's action was not a random act of terrorism directed at civilians but was directed against the British Army, a force of occupation. She endorsed Judge Woelflen's earlier opinion that the IRA were not simply criminals but were leading a political uprising in Northern Ireland. Buchwald therefore rejected Mackin's extradition. In December her decision was upheld on appeal.

13. Michael Farrell, *Sheltering the Fugitive?: The Extradition of Irish Political Offenders* (Dublin: Mercier, 1985).

Following this extradition failure, the INS began deportation proceedings. Mackin did not wish to go through a prolonged legal battle, so
he agreed to be sent to the Irish Republic on December 31, 1981. He has
lived in Dundalk since then, and no attempts have thus far been made to
extradite him to the North.

The Mackin case was a double blow for the US and British governments. Not only had the US failed to extradite a "terrorist," but Judge
Buchwald also strongly denounced the Reagan administration's view that
the executive, not the judiciary, should make decisions on the political
exception clause. Buchwald's classification of the IRA as "political" le-
gitimized its claim as leader of a war of national liberation. American
courts were recognizing the political motivations of the Provos at the
very time when the Thatcher government was trying to enforce their classification as mere criminals.

While Dessie Mackin was successfully fighting his extradition to Britain another case emerged involving William Quinn, a second-generation
Irish American from San Francisco and a devoted Noraid activist. His
commitment to republicanism led him to Ireland and membership in the
IRA in September 1971. As a sign of good faith, he brought a selection
of revolvers concealed in his luggage as a contribution to the cause.[14]

Quinn conducted bombing operations in England and served a one-
year prison sentence for IRA membership. He returned to San Francisco
in 1976 to live with his parents, at which time he was kept under surveillance by the FBI. After pressure from the British government, he was
arrested on September 30, 1981. Extradition papers charged Quinn with
sending letter bombs and with the murder of police officer Stephen
Tibble in London in February 1975.

Quinn immediately claimed political exception, but on September 29,
1982, a federal court rejected his plea. The judge accepted there was an
uprising going on in Northern Ireland but concluded that Quinn's actions
in England were too far removed from the conflict. The case was then appealed to the district court for northern California.

On October 3, 1983 Judge Robert Aguilar issued a verdict that
Quinn's letter bombs were directed not against the general public but
against members of the British establishment. He held that the bombs
were incidental to the political uprising, as they were designed to force

14. Frank Quinn, "The Shadow of the Gunmen," *Irish-America Magazine* (New York),
(January 1987), 18.

the British into negotiations. Aguilar also concluded that the killing of Officer Tibble was part of the ongoing rebellion in Ulster. The British request for Quinn's extradition was therefore rejected.

Lawyers acting for the British blocked Quinn's release on bail and brought the case before the Ninth Court of Appeals on July 11, 1984. This court took nineteen months to reach a verdict, while Quinn languished in jail. Despite the continuation of the case, Aguilar's verdict was another major boost to Irish-American republicans and another setback to the Thatcher and Reagan administrations.[15]

The most publicized and prolonged of these extradition cases involved Joseph Patrick Doherty. In May 1980 he and three other IRA men were involved in a gun battle with a Special Air Service unit in North Belfast. During the confrontation all four Provos were captured, but a British captain, Herbert Westmacott, was shot dead. Doherty and several others escaped from Crumlin Road Jail on June 10, 1981, before they could be tried.

After spending some time in the Irish Republic, Doherty fled to the US in February 1982. He was given cover and assistance by the republican network and began working at Clancy's Bar in Manhattan. Federal authorities, however, were given information on Doherty and he was arrested on June 18, 1983, and served with a British extradition warrant. During the trial in New York, an RUC assistant chief constable gave extensive testimony to help the prosecution. The Reagan administration also made clear its view that Doherty's extradition was a necessary part of the US fight against international terrorism.[16]

Judge John Sprizzo gave his ruling on December 12, 1984. Influenced by the Eain decision, he adopted a more stringent definition of political exception, but characterized Doherty's case as "the political offense exemption in its most classic form." Sprizzo also stated that the IRA had an organization, discipline, and command structure that distinguished it from other "fanatic groups" such as the Red Brigades and

15. The Irish government also pursued IRA fugitives in the US. Their most noted success came in the case of Michael O'Rourke. After escaping from Dublin's Special Criminal Court, O'Rourke fled to Philadelphia. In October 1979 he was arrested by federal agents on information supplied by Irish detectives. Following a prolonged trial, during which Irish-American republicans claim that a sympathetic judge, Ernest Hupp, was intimidated off the case by federal authorities, O'Rourke was deported back to Ireland on 21 June 1984.

16. Maire Crowe, "Confessions of a Most Wanted Man," *Sunday Tribune* (Dublin), 6 January 1991, and *Joe Doherty* (New York: Celtic Videos, 1989).

Black Liberation Army. He refused Britain's extradition request for Doherty.

The British government and the Reagan administration were enraged by Sprizzo's opinion. Federal attorneys took the unprecedented step of demanding a declaratory judgment to overthrow the decision. Their aim was to obtain a review to which they were not properly entitled under the rules governing extradition. On two subsequent hearings, however, the administration's strategy was denied as a way to obtain Doherty's extradition by improper means. Thus thwarted, the Reagan administration began working closely with British officials to amend the UK-US extradition treaty so that political exception would be more narrowly defined. In all of these maneuvers, it was clear that the US government took an adversarial position with respect to the IRA and was moving beyond its official duty to facilitate British extradition requests.

As in the cases of Peter McMullan and William Quinn, legal proceedings continued against Doherty while he was held in custody. Eventually the British government would succeed in two of these cases. In the early 1980s, however, the verdicts against extradition were a major victory for the republican movement. American courts were recognizing that the Provos were not merely common criminals but had coherent political objectives. These decisions enhanced IRA claims to be an army of national liberation and legitimate successors of the rebels of 1916.[17]

The Reagan administration compensated for its failure in extradition proceedings against IRA members by securing a number of important gunrunning convictions. In the most publicized arms case, however, five leading Irish-American republicans, who were caught red-handed, secured acquittal by federal court in Brooklyn. This legal victory provided yet another important morale boost to the republican movement.

The case originated in April 1976 when a British Army patrol discovered a Finnish-made Valmet rifle in the Ardoyne area of Belfast. RUC forensic experts determined it had been shipped from America. The US

17. The British and US governments were also frustrated in the case of Jim Barr, a member of the INLA who skipped bail and fled to Philadelphia after being named in evidence given by "supergrass" Harry Kirkpatrick. In 1986, Judge Clarence Newcomer rejected a British extradition warrant, claiming a lack of evidence against the defendant. In July 1993, Barr was granted political asylum after convincing immigration Judge F. Gossart that his life would be in grave danger if he returned to Northern Ireland. At the beginning of 1995, US authorities were appealing this decision. If they succeed, Barr could be subject to deportation.

Bureau of Alcohol, Tobacco and Firearms traced the weapon, via a gun shop in Wilson, North Carolina, to George De Meo—the key arms supplier in George Harrison's New York–based network.[18]

In June 1980, De Meo was tried in North Carolina and convicted of illegal arms trafficking. He received ten years imprisonment and a fine of $9,000. De Meo, dreading such a jail term, began negotiating with the FBI. He told agents he would help them smash the Harrison network in exchange for a reduced sentence. Bureau officials promised De Meo that if he participated in their undercover operation his sentence would be reduced to two years. They also promised that his jail term would be served in Allenwood minimum security prison.[19]

In early 1981, De Meo, while free on bail, visited Harrison's apartment with a FBI wire taped to his body. He told Harrison he would introduce him to a trusted gun dealer who would maintain the flow of arms while he was in prison. Agents recorded this conversation. They also began tapping Harrison's telephone.

On May 17, 1981, De Meo introduced undercover FBI agent John Winslow to Harrison and Tom Falvey, another key member of the gun-running network. Winslow posed as the arms dealer and began negotiating with the two IRA supporters. He told the men he could supply a whole range of weapons from flamethrowers to 20mm cannons.

The FBI trap, code-named "Operation Bushmills," reached its climax on June 17, 1981. Agent Winslow originally told Harrison and Falvey the cost of his first arms shipment was $15,000. Later he telephoned Harrison and said the price had to be raised to $17,000. FBI agents listening to the wire tap then heard Harrison call Michael Flannery and ask for more cash. The Noraid leader replied that the money would be supplied immediately.

On June 18, Harrison called at Flannery's house in Jackson Heights, New York. Federal agents observed him leaving with a white envelope, later found to contain $17,000. Harrison went to Tom Falvey's house and waited for Winslow to arrive with the weapons. The phony arms

18. Chris Ryder, *The R.U.C.: A Force Under Fire* (London: Methuen, 1989), 208. A number of weapons were traced back to De Meo, including an Armalite rifle used by the Balcombe Street gang in December 1975. De Meo tried to erase the serial numbers on the weapons he sold, but the RUC developed new techniques of analysis. Using infrared, magnets, and certain acids, they were able to trace even weapons with obliterated numbers.

19. Shana Alexander, "The Patriot Game," *New York Magazine*, 22 November 1982.

dealer soon drove up to the house in a van loaded with submachine guns and AK-47 assault rifles, which the men loaded into Falvey's garage. Harrison paid Winslow with the cash he had received from Flannery.

FBI agents observed and recorded the whole transaction. After Winslow's departure, they saw Harrison and Falvey leave the house with a carrier bag. The agents feared it contained one of the machine guns and decided to spring their trap prematurely. Those in charge of the operation did not want to let one weapon escape their grasp with the possibility it might be used in Northern Ireland. Harrison and Falvey were therefore apprehended by agents at gunpoint and taken into custody. Their bag contained two cans of beer.

Federal agents raided Harrison's house and confiscated records detailing his years of gunrunning to the IRA. Shortly after this, they arrested Patrick Mullin, who had stored thirteen of the weapons in his basement. It was not until October 1981 that FBI officials apprehended Michael Flannery and charged him with being the paymaster in the arms conspiracy. Daniel Gormley, the final member of the group, was arrested in April 1982, after investigations uncovered that he had also supplied cash for the operation.

The five men were brought to trial in the autumn of 1982, charged with conspiracy to ship weapons to the IRA. As usual, Paul O'Dwyer and a group of associates conducted the defense. They soon realized the amount of evidence against the men was overwhelming, so they claimed their clients believed that George De Meo was a CIA agent. As the CIA has a license to export weapons, the men argued that, not only were they acting within the law, but they had the endorsement of the US government. George Harrison testified that he suspected the CIA was involved in his operations as a means of monitoring the flow of weapons to Ireland and to remove the necessity of the IRA turning to communist countries for arms.[20]

Throughout George De Meo's long career in arms sales he had boasted to George Harrison that he was an operative for the CIA. The defense emphasized this bragging to build credibility for their case. De Meo was subpoenaed from prison and subjected to intense questioning about his CIA involvement. These questions seemed to unnerve De Meo, who

20. Robert McFadden, "Five are Acquitted in Brooklyn of Plot to Run Guns to I.R.A.," *New York Times*, 6 November 1982.

repeatedly pleaded the Fifth Amendment. He did, however, categorically deny any association with the CIA.[21]

Defense lawyers skillfully manipulated De Meo's denial to raise the jury's suspicions about his credibility. They employed former Attorney General Ramsey Clark as a key witness. He told the jury how the FBI always had a deep distrust of the CIA and never believed their denials of membership. Clark gave the impression that the CIA consistently lied to protect its operatives and were continually involved in covert operations similar to Harrison's. These statements were supported by Ralph Mc-Gehee, a retired CIA official, who further testified that it was perfectly logical for the defendants to believe the agency was involved in their gunrunning scheme.[22] Attorneys for the five men succeeded in undermining De Meo's vehement denials of CIA connections.

The accused men impressed the jury with their testimonies. They pointed out that none had criminal records and had collectively served their country in World War II, Korea, and Vietnam. As character witnesses, the men used people like Sam O'Reilly, an eighty-six-year-old IRA veteran of the Easter Rising, who told the jury of the men's great patriotism for both America and Ireland. Bernadette Devlin described the defendants as "the finest human beings I have ever known," and there were reports that her emotional statement brought two jurors to tears!

The courthouse was packed daily with Irish-American republicans giving encouragement to the defendants. George Harrison delighted them when his lawyer expressed insult that Harrison was charged with supplying weapons for only a six-month period in 1980. Harrison proudly told the judge he had been exporting guns to the IRA for more than twenty-five years.[23] Michael Flannery, with equal audacity, stated that the

21. Three CIA agents provided written evidence to the court denying all knowledge of De Meo. Perhaps significantly, the agency's deputy director of intelligence, whose office keeps files on its operatives, did not supply such a denial. See *A Turn to the Gun* (New York: Celtic Video, 1984).

22. Defense attorneys also used the testimony of Earl Redick, a former member of U.S. Army Intelligence. Redick told how he had sold arms to De Meo in the 1960s and remembered his claims to be sending weapons to the IRA on behalf of the CIA. Redick also claimed that the CIA, on the grounds of national security, pressured federal prosecutors to drop gunrunning charges against De Meo during a 1970 trial in Feyettville, North Carolina.

23. George Harrison and Tom Falvey were atypical members of the Irish-American republican network. The two men were noted for their left-wing political views and their support for antiimperialist movements throughout the world. In 1984, for example, they issued

money he gave Harrison for the weapons was not from Noraid. He claimed it came from a secret IRA fund, which donors had specifically asked be used for guns.[24]

The trial ended on November 2, 1982, with a not-guilty verdict. Several jurors said they could not believe that Harrison's arms supply network could have operated for more than twenty-five years without the knowledge of the CIA. Pandemonium in the courtroom greeted the decision. Groups of Irish-American republicans cheered and waived tricolors as Harrison and Flannery shouted "Up the IRA." The defendants were carried shoulder-high from the courtroom.

The verdict was a major embarrassment to the American government's efforts against the IRA network. Justice Department officials hoped the involvement of Michael Flannery would provide undisputed evidence Noraid was purchasing weapons. British government officials tried to respond to the defeat positively by emphasizing that the operation did smash Harrison's network and did show Flannery was handling IRA funds. They could not, however, disguise their intense disappointment at the verdict.

The British press reacted with horror at the court decision. The *Sunday Express* described the verdict as an "obscene charade" that had destroyed any confidence British intelligence officers had in the ability of their American counterparts to "plug the arms loophole."[25] The *Daily Mirror* told how one rich Irish-American businessman was so impressed by the court victory that he gave Noraid a blank check to use as they thought fit.[26]

The controversy created by the arms trial verdict caused Secretary of State James Prior to fly to the US in an attempt to counter the positive publicity Noraid was receiving. As the US government was equally alarmed at the acquittal, it made every attempt to support Prior. Internal memoranda within the State Department showed its embarrassment with the verdict and its commitment to maintain good relations with the British. On November 16, 1982, Prior met with US Deputy Secretary of State Kenneth Dam. Policy coordinators instructed Dam to assure the British

---

an open letter to "Irish Solidarity Activists" to support Socialist Workers Party candidates Mel Mason and Andrea Gonzalez in the US presidential election.

24. Michael Flannery, correspondence with author, 18 November 1992.

25. Michael Toner, "Britain Fumes at U.S. Over I.R.A. Guns," *Sunday Express*, 7 November 1982.

26. John Jackson, "Blank Check for the I.R.A.," *Daily Mirror*, 8 November 1982.

secretary that the US was committed to prosecuting IRA gunrunners and fugitives.[27]

Despite this assurance of continued US government support, Prior's visit failed to undermine the positive publicity engendered for republicans by the Flannery trial. His media appearances were canceled because of the prominence given to the death of Leonid Brezhnev; his public meetings were disrupted by Noraid demonstrations led by Owen Carron and Danny Morrison of Sinn Féin.

Militant Irish-American groups rejoiced at the controversy surrounding the arms trial. They used their victory to attack the British and American governments, publicizing the information disclosed during the trial that showed the continuous flow of information on Irish-American republicans between the FBI and RUC. Noraid alleged there was a network of British agents in America working against republican sympathizers. The *Irish Echo* called for massive demonstrations from all Irish Americans against "the illegal activities of British intelligence operatives as regarding American citizens and the cynical activities of our own intelligence agents in this whole grey area of dirty tricks."[28]

Michael Flannery and the 1983 St. Patrick's Day Parade

New York's Irish community received George Harrison and his compatriots as great heroes. The five men made guest appearances at a continuous round of banquets, socials, and fund raisers. Michael Flannery was particularly praised for his conduct during the trial. Despite being in his eighties and relying on a walking stick, Flannery delivered impassioned republican statements and won considerable admiration outside militant circles.

Republican groups began looking for ways to exploit Flannery's newfound celebrity status and win even more publicity. A movement began within New York's Irish Societies to put him forward to be grand marshal of the St. Patrick's Day Parade. Flannery's supporters claimed it would be a fitting tribute to a man who had devoted so much of his energies to charitable work within the Irish-American community.

Irish-American republicans were optimistic that their campaign for Flannery could succeed. They had considerable influence within the

27. State Department memo from Robert Blackwill to Deputy Secretary of State Kenneth Dam, dated 15 November 1982.

28. *Irish Echo* (New York), "A Remarkable Verdict," 13 November 1982.

St. Patrick's Day organizing committee. In 1982 they got Bobby Sands elected as honorary grand marshal, despite strong opposition from constitutional nationalists. The most powerful group within the committee was the Ancient Order of Hibernians. With Joseph Roche at its head, they naturally supported Michael Flannery. At a vote held in February 1983, the Noraid leader was overwhelmingly endorsed as grand marshal.

Constitutional nationalists vented their outrage at Flannery's election. Taoiseach Garret FitzGerald and Ambassador Tadhg O'Sullivan described the republican exploitation of Ireland's patron saint as "bitterly divisive and deplorable." Aer Lingus, the Irish national airline, withdrew its financial sponsorship of the parade, and the US Defense Department prohibited the participation of military bands.[29] The Friends of Ireland joined in the attacks on Flannery. Senator Daniel Moynihan and former Governor Hugh Carey, who had always been prominent guests at the parade, announced they would not participate. Flannery responded in his typically uncompromising manner and told reporters, "Everyone who comes to New York on March 17 is in favor of Irish unity. Most are IRA supporters in one way or another. It's definitely going to be a pro-IRA parade."[30]

The conflict over the St. Patrick's Day Parade became a lead item in the American media. Countless articles described various aspects of the controversy, while Flannery made frequent appearances on television explaining his republican views. Editorial comment in the mainstream American press tended to be critical of Flannery and condemn the New York Irish as "gullible" and "shameless."[31] The Irish-American press held the opposite opinion and fully endorsed Flannery for the years of work he had devoted to Irish charities in New York. John Thornton, editor of the *Irish Echo*, reported his newspaper was inundated with letters of support for Flannery.[32]

Irish-American republicans saw the parade itself as a great propaganda coup. Mayor Edward Koch, Governor Mario Cuomo, Senator Alphonse D'Amato, and Representative Geraldine Ferraro all marched despite pressure from the Irish government and Friends of Ireland to boycott. The parade attracted a record crowd and Flannery was the center of

29. James Perry, "These Irish Eyes Aren't Smiling on a Paddy's Day Parade," *Wall Street Journal*, 15 February 1983.

30. Tom Morganthau, "The Irish Connection," *Newsweek*, 21 March 1983.

31. "Shameless Hibernians," *Detroit News*, 24 February 1983.

32. Martin Gottleib, "Moynihan's Views on Parade Stir Ire of the Irish," *New York Times*, 10 March 1983.

attention. He was cheered all along Fifth Avenue by groups waiving proIRA placards and flags. When the Noraid leader approached St. Patrick's Cathedral, Cardinal Terence Cooke refused to give his traditional blessing. The cardinal appeared twenty minutes after Flannery passed and was greeted by a hostile crowd booing, hissing, and chanting "Up the Provos."[33]

The British media reaction to the parade controversy was all Noraid and the other militant groups could have hoped for. The general impression conveyed was that the whole incident showed substantial support for the IRA among Irish Americans. The *Daily Express*, for example, described the parade as "the biggest anti-British demonstration ever held in America."[34] Television news reports by the BBC relayed pictures of Flannery being cheered by the crowd and scenes of republican celebrations in Irish pubs in the Bronx.

The publicity generated in 1983 encouraged Irish-American republicans to exploit the New York's St. Patrick's Day Parade in subsequent years. In 1984, Teddy Gleason, president of the Longshoremen's Union and noted for his republican sympathies, was elected as Grand Marshal. The 1985 Grand Marshal was then–Nassau County comptroller Peter King, a strong supporter of Noraid who had recently met with Sinn Féin officials in Belfast. Although both these grand marshals did not attract as much media attention as Flannery, their election continued the controversy and was exploited for maximum publicity by republicans.[35]

The Irish-American Unity Conference

The rejuvenation of republican groups in America, and their success in achieving publicity coups, led to calls for greater cooperation and coordination of their activities. The leaders of Noraid and other militant irredentist organizations began exploring ways to maximize their efforts through joint ventures. In 1982 a movement grew to support the formation of a central coordinating group. This eventually led to the creation of the Irish American Unity Conference (IAUC) in 1983.

33. Rita Christopher, "Bitter Rain on St. Patrick's Day," *MacLeans*, 28 March 1983.
34. *Daily Express*, 18 March 1983.
35. The election of Irish-American republicans as grand marshals of St. Partick's Day parades has continued to be controversial. When Dan McCormick, a veteran Noraid activist from San Francisco, was elected in 1989, it produced a hail of criticism from British diplomats and a boycott by the Irish consul. *San Francisco Chronicle*, 12 March 1989.

One of the principal figures in the IAUC's formation was James Delaney, a millionaire real estate developer based in San Antonio, Texas. He was deeply interested in his Irish roots and rose to become a national director in the Ancient Order of Hibernians. Delaney's concern over the Ulster conflict intensified during and after the hunger strikes when the deaths of Bobby Sands and his comrades led him to adopt a more militant republican perspective.

Delaney wanted to use Irish-American influence to end the conflict in Ulster. He was frustrated, however, by the factionalism and infighting and began to plead for greater coordination and unity of purpose. At a series of AOH conventions and Irish-American conferences in 1982, Delaney built support for the formation of a new organization. Eventually the heads of the main groups decided to discuss details of Delaney's suggestion at a conference in Chicago.

From July 15 to 17, 1983, more than two hundred delegates representing 617 Irish-American groups convened at Chicago's Hyatt Regency Hotel. They began discussing ways to coordinate their activities. They achieved a remarkable degree of consensus, and they created a new coordinating group called the Irish American Unity Conference, which would work for an agreed list of objectives.

The delegates produced a thirty-five point manifesto. As Martin Galvin and Michael Flannery played an important role in these proceedings, the document was strongly republican. The manifesto called for immediate British withdrawal, US sanctions against Britain if it refused, visas for republicans, and an end to FBI harassment of Irish-American activists.[36] The conference also voted that the IAUC should produce a monthly magazine, the *Irish Newsline*, to publicize its activities and provide a republican perspective on Ulster.

After the Chicago conference, delegates began holding recruitment meetings throughout America and formed local IAUC chapters. The group established an office in Washington and began coordinating lobbying efforts with the Irish National Caucus. James Delaney also led a highly publicized visit of IAUC delegates to Belfast in the autumn of 1983. They met Sinn Féin leaders and released a subsequent report severely criticizing every aspect of British rule in Northern Ireland.[37]

36. Irish American Unity Conference. *Manifesto and Program* Political Action Resolution "C."

37. *Report on I.A.U.C. Trip to Ireland*. Produced by Professor Charles Rice of Notre Dame Law School, 16 November 1983.

The formation of the IAUC raised great enthusiasm and expectations among militant Irish-American groups. They hoped the organization would encourage unity and wield great influence in the US and in Ireland. In its first years of existence the group helped to coordinate activities and sustain the high level of activism maintained since the hunger strike. The emergence of the IAUC was also a considerable publicity victory for republicans, who presented it as a sign of the determination of Irish Americans to end British rule in Ireland once and for all.

The Irish People Tours

While formation of the IAUC and the various court victories were seen as highly successful by republicans, it was the Irish People tours of Northern Ireland, beginning in August 1983, that engendered the greatest controversy and publicity victories. Noraid organized the tours as a means of counteracting the State Department's anti-republican visa policy. It concluded that if Sinn Féin officials were denied the opportunity to present their views in the United States, then Irish Americans could hear them first hand by traveling to Ulster. Noraid also believed that such tours would inspire participants and motivate them to increased support for the republican movement in America.

The first tour group, consisting of eighty members from Noraid, the Ancient Order of Hibernians, Clan na Gael, and the IAUC, arrived in Dublin on August 2, 1983. They were welcomed by Joe Cahill and Fra McCann of Sinn Féin and then taken around republican areas in the North. The group visited Crossmaglen, Carickmore, West Belfast and Derry. They stayed each night at the houses of republican families and kept up a hectic schedule of political meetings, film shows, and rounds of drinking and Irish dancing.

A highlight of the trip occurred in Cullyhanna, South Armagh, when a group of IRA volunteers in full combat gear stopped the Noraid bus at a staged road block. One of the men, carrying an M-60 machine gun, read a statement from the Army Council praising the delegation and thanking them for their tireless fund-raising efforts. When he finished, the bus erupted into cheers of support.[38]

Some Noraid members got directly involved in the conflict and joined riots against the security forces. On August 9, Stephen Lich from Indi-

38. *Irish Times* (Dublin), 9 August 1983.

anapolis was arrested in Belfast. An RUC man observed him hurling bricks at a British Army land rover. Two days later he appeared at Belfast Magistrates Court, was fined $100, and told to leave Northern Ireland immediately. Another American, James Hennesey from Pittsburgh, received a similar sentence after his conviction for stoning a British Army patrol in Derry.[39]

Martin Galvin was the chief spokesmen for the tour. He became the most recognized figure in the republican movement in America, exploiting the media attention focused on the Noraid delegation and giving press and television interviews in which he strongly supported the IRA. State Representative Charles Doyle of Massachusetts, another member of the tour party, also issued controversial statements attacking "the centuries-old British persecution and exploitation of the Irish."[40]

The Noraid tour received wide coverage in both the Irish and British media, but most editorials and commentaries tended to be critical. Predictably, British newspapers characterized the group as "buffoons" and "ignorant, sentimental Irish Americans."[41] Yet some of the strongest condemnations came from constitutional nationalist newspapers in Ireland. They criticized Noraid for listening only to Sinn Féin and not hearing the views of the Irish government and S.D.L.P.. An editorial in the *Irish Independent* told readers, "It is a matter of record that Noraid collects money which is used to buy guns in America. These guns then pass into the hands of men and women who are nothing more than self-appointed killers."[42] The *Irish News*, Northern Ireland's largest circulating nationalist daily, commented:

> Their so-called "fact-finding" mission was an extremely curious one. Their failure to meet constitutional nationalists, who still represent most anti-unionists, reveals the type of closed mind that has bedeviled Ireland for too long. Noraid appears to have been more interested in confirming their prejudices than in finding out anything new.[43]

39. *The Times* (London), 11 August 1983.

40. William Graham, "Americans Get down to Nitty Gritty," *Irish News*, 6 August 1983. Following these statements Northern Ireland Minister of State, Nicholas Scott, withdrew an invitation to the Noraid group to discussions at Stormont.

41. *Daily Express*, 8 August 1983.

42. *Irish Independent* (Dublin), 4 August 1983.

43. "Noraid," *Irish News*, 10 August 1983. For a detailed statement of this viewpoint see Jack Holland, "Noraid Ghetto Tour Offers Skewed View of the North," *Irish Echo* (New York), 26 August 1992.

Despite these critical comments, Martin Galvin regarded the tour as a great breakthrough. He felt that by attracting large coverage in the media, Noraid had publicized the fact that the IRA had committed supporters in America. Galvin also felt that the presence of Irish Americans in Northern Ireland had given a great boost to the republican movement by showing solidarity with their struggle and ensuring continued financial assistance.[44]

Irish Northern Aid began preparations for a second tour in 1984. The group placed notices in the Irish-American press calling for people to enroll in the trip of a lifetime, to experience personally the great hospitality of northern republicans and the reality of British oppression. Noraid headquarters in the Bronx was inundated with applications. For logistical reasons, the tour had to be limited to one hundred thirty.

British Information Service officials in New York monitored preparations for the second tour and kept the Thatcher administration informed of its itinerary and objectives. News of the intended visit caused divisions within the British government. James Prior had been alarmed at the publicity Galvin attracted in 1983 and felt he should be prohibited from entering Northern Ireland.[45] Sir Oliver Wright, the British ambassador in Washington, felt that such action would be counterproductive and impossible to enforce. The ambassador won support from Foreign Secretary Geoffrey Howe who believed Galvin would exploit his exclusion for propaganda purposes. Prior and Howe tried to persuade Home Secretary Leon Brittan of the merits of their contrasting perspectives. Correspondence, later leaked to the *Guardian*, shows Brittan was more impressed by Prior's arguments. He signed an exclusion order against Galvin on July 28, 1983.[46]

In New York, Galvin casually dismissed the exclusion order and announced he would fulfil his plans to attend the internment commemoration in Belfast. He led the Noraid group to Dublin on July 31 and remained there while they traveled to Northern Ireland. The British Army and RUC increased border patrols to foil any attempt by Galvin to enter the province.

The presence of the Noraid delegation again attracted continuous media coverage and controversy. When the group visited republican graves in Coalisland, County Tyrone, Owen Carron told them that the

44. Martin Galvin, interview with author, 14 November 1992.

45. Prior was also incensed by Galvin's organization of protests against him in 1983, during which Owen Carron and Danny Morrison disrupted his speaking engagements.

46. James Prior, *A Balance of Power* (London: Hamish Hamilton, 1986), 234.

greatest need within the IRA was for modern weapons and implied they should be sent from America.[47] British and Unionist politicians were outraged when one Noraid official said it was "the moral duty of every Irish-American to get them [the IRA] US weapons to ensure democracy."[48] Another member of the delegation, when asked about Noraid funds, replied, "If they want to buy weapons with it, I say good luck to them!"[49]

In the meantime, Martin Galvin successfully breached border security and entered Derry on 9 August. He posed for press photographers beside an IRA commemorative plaque in the Bogside and gave an interview to the *Derry Journal*. Galvin boasted that it had been easy to evade the security forces and promised he would attend republican demonstrations in Belfast.[50]

The cumulative effect of the Noraid tour and Galvin's evasion of security forces was to heighten tensions during the August 12, 1984, internment march in West Belfast. The RUC, determined not to be humiliated by Galvin, waited expectantly for his appearance. Police officers screened the Noraid delegation as it marched along the Falls Road but saw no sign of their man. When the procession assembled outside Sinn Féin headquarters to hear speeches, the RUC began moving closer to the podium. They were determined to grab Galvin if he appeared.

A large crowd assembled around the podium forming a barrier between the RUC and the speakers. As they listened to Gerry Adams conclude his speech, the Sinn Féin president called Martin Galvin to the microphone. The Noraid leader emerged from republican headquarters, but before he could utter a word the RUC charged. A bloody riot developed in which police officers wielded batons and fired plastic bullets into the crowd. Ed Blanche of the *Washington Post* described to his readers how "police in jeeps fired repeated volleys into the crowd while club-wielding officers leapt from their vehicles and charged, trampling screaming protestors."[51]

During the confrontation many people were injured with plastic bullets, including members of the Noraid group. One protestor, Seán

47. "Help Us Buy Guns, Sinn Fein Man Tells Noraid Visitors," *Irish News*, 11 August 1984.

48. Statement of Richard Lawlor in *Irish Press*, 14 August 1984.

49. *New York Times*, 19 August 1984.

50. "Interview With Martin Galvin," *Derry Journal*, 10 August 1984.

51. Ed Blanche, "Man Killed as R.U.C. Seek American," *Washington Post*, 13 August 1984.

Downes, was hit in the chest by a bullet fired at point blank range. He collapsed on the roadside and died from the injury. The whole incident was captured by photographers and television camera crews. On the night of August 13, footage of the dying Seán Downes was broadcast on news reports on both sides of the Atlantic. It created international outrage and generated intense controversy that lasted for weeks.

Republicans described the death of Seán Downes as a savage act of murder. They were joined in strong condemnations of the RUC by the SDLP, while Irish government officials called for an independent investigation. Nationalist reaction was epitomized by an editorial in the *Irish News* that called the police action an "unmitigated disgrace."[52]

In America the main television networks carried footage of the Downes incident. They also ran interviews with Michael Flannery in which he castigated the RUC, described Galvin as a "brave and courageous young man," and said the incident showed why it was right to ship American weapons to the IRA.[53] In the massive editorial response to the incident some newspapers took the opportunity to condemn Noraid and blame Martin Galvin for the death and injuries. The *Tulsa World*, for example, commented:

> Galvin and others like him fuel delusions of bravery by fomenting violence from the safety of America. Galvin doesn't have to live in the mess he helps create. And his actions are all the more despicable for the fact he is an attorney, sworn to uphold the rule of law.[54]

The more typical reaction from large metropolitan newspapers was a severe attack on the actions of the RUC and a deemphasis on Galvin's role. The *Chicago Tribune* compared the incident to Bloody Sunday, while the *Richmond Times-Dispatch* said the RUC's use of plastic bullets was "abominable."[55] Many newspapers reached conclusions similar to this in the *New York Daily News*:

> The Thatcher government has a lot to answer for in this incident. It has made a bad situation worse. Those responsible must be punished with

52. "Utter Disgrace," *Irish News*, 13 August 1984.

53. Charles Rose interview with Michael Flannery, *CBS Morning News*, 16 August 1984.

54. *Tulsa World*, 23 August 1984. See also, "Americans Who Aid I.R.A. Aid Terrorists," *U.S.A. Today*, 23 August 1984.

55. *Chicago Tribune*, 25 August and *Richmond Times-Dispatch*, 17 August 1984.

the same kind of vigor that is applied to the IRA. Thatcher cannot condemn the IRA as a bunch of vicious killers with one voice and condone with another voice brutal behavior by her own policemen who ran roughshod over innocent people.[56]

In Britain, the death of Seán Downes produced a flurry of criticisms from politicians and the press. James Prior initially responded by defending the decision to place an exclusion order on Galvin. As condemnations of the policy increased, however, Prior admitted he had made a "bad mistake." He described the death of Seán Downes as "an enormous setback for me personally in my efforts to try to improve relations between the two communities."[57]

Prior's candid acknowledgement of responsibility for the Downes affair produced a heated reaction from Unionists. James Molyneaux called Prior's statement a great blow to the confidence of the security forces, while Jim Allister of the DUP said it was "gutless" and "a demeaning and vain attempt to appease the IRA's anger through groveling regret."[58] Unionists called for an emergency debate in the Northern Ireland Assembly, where they passed a vote of confidence in the RUC and overwhelmingly voted against an Alliance Party proposal calling for an official inquiry.

Noraid and Sinn Féin exploited all the controversy surrounding Downes's death for maximum benefit. Galvin held a press conference in Dublin before returning to America. Flanked by Joe Cahill and Danny Morrison, the Noraid leader appeared with his hair dyed reddish brown. He said this was a disguise to get across the border and related how during his escape in Belfast, three RUC officers had passed right by him and failed to recognize him. Galvin promised he would tell Americans about the brutality of the RUC when he returned and said that if he had had a gun at the time he would have shot the officers involved.[59]

Galvin was greeted at Kennedy Airport by a pipe band and a large crowd of supporters. Within republican circles he was given hero status, as tales circulated about his daring escapes from the RUC. Stories grew of how he was passed over people's heads to freedom during the RUC attack and used two look-alikes to fool his pursuers.[60] British press reports

56. *New York Daily News*, 14 August 1984.
57. "Mistake Admitted in Ulster Shooting," *Baltimore Sun*, 15 August 1984.
58. *New York Times*, 16 August 1984.
59. "Galvanized Reaction," *An Phoblacht/Republican News* (Belfast), 23 August 1984.
60. *U.S.A. Today*, 14 August 1984.

lamented that the American reaction to the Downes killing greatly benefited republican groups. The *London Times* said it had "provided Noraid
with a stunning propaganda victory which would be successfully used to
loosen Irish-American purses from Los Angeles to Long Island."[61]

The political controversy caused in Northern Ireland by Irish Americans did not end with Galvin's departure. On September 1, 1984, twenty-
four members of the New York City Police Department pipe band led a
hunger strike commemoration parade in Bundoran, County Donegal. The
officers belonged to the Police Department Emerald Society and had
been in Ireland for the Rose of Tralee festival and Gaelic Athletic Association (GAA) centenary celebrations. They marched in the hunger strike
parade in response to invitations from Sinn Féin and Noraid.

The action of the New York policemen caused more controversy.
Garret FitzGerald attacked their participation in the parade as "grossly insensitive," while the lord mayor of Dublin canceled a planned reception
for the officers at his residence. Ulster Unionists issued outraged condemnations of the policemen for endorsing terrorism. Harold McCusker said
their action was as insulting to unionists as the RUC attending a function
of the Ku Klux Klan would be to Americans.[62] Robert Kane, the US ambassador in Dublin, wrote to New York Police Commissioner Benjamin
Ward and Mayor Koch strongly condemning the band members.[63]

British officials decided to continue their exclusion order on Martin
Galvin. Recently appointed Northern Ireland Secretary Douglas Hurd
maintained the ban after intense pressure from Unionists and right-wing
Conservative MPs. The decision gave the Noraid leader yet another opportunity to embarrass the government and win further publicity. He led
a Noraid delegation of one hundred twenty-five members to Ireland in
1985. On August 9, he appeared in Derry to act as pallbearer at the funeral of Charles English, an IRA volunteer who died in a premature gre-
nade explosion. Galvin was only one hundred yards away from RUC
constables observing the funeral; his photograph appeared on the front
pages of most British and Irish newspapers the following day.

Galvin said that he would not appear at the internment rally in Belfast
because he didn't want to give the RUC an excuse to kill more innocent
civilians. His mere presence again attracted continued controversy. In the

61. *The Times* (London), 14 August 1984.

62. *Belfast News Letter*, 3 September 1984.

63. Mentioned in memo from State Department to consul general in Belfast, September 1984.

Republic of Ireland, Radio Telefís Éireann journalists held a one-day work stoppage because the network refused to broadcast interviews with the Noraid leader. Those involved in the protest accused RTE of flagrant censorship and yielding to government pressure.[64]

Following the 1985 Noraid tour, the Emerald Society pipe band again marched in the hunger strike commemoration in Bundoran, despite renewed pressure from both the Irish government and US State Department not to participate. Martin Galvin and Joseph Roche praised the police officers for their solidarity with the republican movement during speeches after the parade. Officer Daniel Danaher characterized the attitude of his comrades:

> We're playing for the ten young men who died on hunger strike. I've been told that they were terrorists, that they were murderers, but so were the leaders of 1916 until they were shot. I've been dealing with murderers all my life. I've never seen one of them who would put himself through that agony, through that kind of death, for what he believed in.[65]

The Noraid tours between 1983 and 1985 achieved their desired objectives and benefited the republican movement. They attracted widespread media coverage in Britain and Ireland, which tended to elevate the significance of Irish-American power and influence in aiding the IRA. Noraid capitalized on the American media attacks against the RUC after the Downes affair and used the incident to bolster its fund-raising appeals. The group brought Downes's widow to the United States for even more publicity and to give her personal account of police brutality against the demonstrators.

Republicans delighted in the embarrassment the Downes incident caused James Prior. They relished the severe criticisms leveled against the secretary of state and contended the affair hastened his replacement by Douglas Hurd. Noraid and Sinn Féin also welcomed the damage caused to the RUC's image. For some years the Northern Ireland Office had proudly claimed that there was a growing respect for the police in the nationalist community. British officials acknowledged that the events of August 11, 1984, had seriously affected community relations and that confidence in the force had been shattered.

64. *Irish Press*, 12 August 1985.

65. "Are the Pipers Coming?" Interview with Officer Dan Danaher, reported in *The Irish Nation*, June 1985.

Noraid claimed that its visits gave a great morale boost to the IRA and Sinn Féin. Most republicans in the North welcomed Noraid and acknowledged the positive results of its efforts. Members of the delegation always got loud cheers of support when they marched in the annual internment rally and were usually well received at the social functions held for their benefit in republican areas.

There were some republicans, however, who remained ambivalent about the annual Irish-American visitors. They claimed that Noraid's presence forced the IRA into ill-prepared attacks on the security forces. There was a feeling that the lives of Provo volunteers were jeopardized by military actions designed to impress the Americans. In one such instance, volunteer Kevin Watters died when a nail bomb exploded prematurely during the 1983 Noraid tour. Charles English died in a similarly botched attack during the 1985 visit.

Some residents of West Belfast condemned Martin Galvin's actions in 1984. They felt that if he had kept away from the internment rally, Seán Downes would still be alive. Others resented members of the Noraid group spouting support for the armed struggle yet not having to live with its consequences. Some also lampooned the political naïveté of Irish Americans after incidents in which they wandered into Belfast city center clad in T-shirts and baseball caps with pro-republican slogans on the front.

These resentments were not extensive, and participants in the Noraid tours universally praised the way they were received in republican areas. Irish Northern Aid claims that the experiences of their group strengthened commitment to the republican movement in America. Sinn Féin organized the itinerary of the tours to ensure participants would be presented with the republican political perspective. The results were predictable. Lillian Roche from Baltimore, who went on the 1985 tour, told the *Washington Post* on her return, "The things I've read didn't tell nearly the whole story. I've seen how the Catholic community is totally oppressed and suffers constant harassment from the British."[66] Another member of the tour, Jeanne Clarizio from Connecticut, told the *Hartford Courant*, "Before I went I almost had to apologize for the IRA. After this I'm not going to do that anymore."[67]

66. *Washington Post*, 12 August 1985.

67. James Eisner, "Noraid Tour Converts Americans to I.R.A. Cause," *Hartford Courant*, 11 August 1985. For an excellent presentation of the 1983 Noraid tour and its effects on participants, see *The Old Man and the Gun* (WGBH Boston: *Frontline*, 1984).

Many who went on the Noraid tours redoubled their republican activities when they returned to America. They spoke before Irish-American audiences to describe their experiences, wrote anti-British articles in the press, organized new fund-raising ventures for Noraid, and pressured their political representatives to support Irish republican issues in Washington. The feelings expressed by Dr. Séamus Metress seem typical of tour participants:

> After staying in the six counties, my colleagues have a greater sense of the social and political obscenity that is British-occupied Ireland. Many, including myself, have drawn a new sense of strength and dedication from the nationalist people they have come to know. Further, they have come away resolved to continue to work for the movement they now know more intimately. The revolution that continues daily in the six counties will not be forgotten by those who experienced it.[68]

The Irish People tours brought many benefits to the republican network in America and provided Sinn Féin with positive international attention for its political campaigns. These achievements were matched by a number of important publicity coups. Extradition victories, the Harrison/Flannery trial and the subsequent St. Patrick's Day Parade controversy sustained a republican revival that was inspired by the success of the hunger strike campaign. This new vitality in militant Irish-American nationalism was continued despite constant harassment from federal authorities and pressure from constitutional nationalists.[69]

68. Séamus Metress, "Witness to Oppression," *An Phoblacht/Republican News* (Belfast), 22 August 1985.

69. Martin Galvin continued to lead the Noraid tours to Belfast from 1985 onward. In 1989 he was arrested in Derry and deported back to the United States. British authorities could have held him in prison but felt this would only have provided Irish-American republicans with a martyr. In this no-win situation, the exclusion order against Galvin was quietly lifted in 1990. Since then, Galvin has entered Northern Ireland legally, but he still creates controversy. On 7 December 1990, he caused outrage among unionists when he was photographed sitting in the Lord Mayor's chair in Belfast City Hall. When asked by reporters to comment on the building he said, "The place would look much better if they removed the foreign flags [Union Jacks] and replaced them with tricolors." *Irish Echo* (New York), 19 December 1990.

◆

CHAPTER 9

THE CONGRESSIONAL FRIENDS

OF IRELAND AND THE ANGLO-IRISH

AGREEMENT, 1981–1985

◆

The rejuvenation of Irish-American republicanism in the early 1980s greatly alarmed both the US government and constitutional nationalists. Yet despite the series of legal and publicity defeats, the forces working against the IRA network did achieve their own successes. American law-enforcement agencies persistently hounded Noraid and secured convictions in a number of important gunrunning conspiracies. The Friends of Ireland continued to play an influential role in Ulster politics and made a significant contribution to the Anglo-Irish Agreement in 1985.

From 1981, the Reagan administration intensified the FARA court case against Noraid. Federal attorneys worked relentlessly to force the group to acknowledge the Provisional IRA as its foreign principal. This legal action also had the objective of making Noraid provide greater details about its fund-raising activities. The Justice Department hoped that victory in the case would bolster its contention that Noraid was bank-rolling IRA violence in Northern Ireland.

Noraid fought a prolonged legal battle against the Justice Department but in May 1981, Judge Charles Haight, Jr., finally ruled that the group must register as an agent of the Provos. A Federal Court of Appeals upheld the Haight verdict in January 1982.

Noraid continued the legal controversy by refusing to file its returns under the FARA. In early 1984, the Justice Department successfully charged the group with contempt of court. It was given ninety days to comply with the Haight ruling or risk a hefty fine. In this situation, Noraid agreed to register the IRA as its foreign principal but insisted on including a written disclaimer against the court ruling. Federal attorneys agreed to this, and Noraid resumed filing its financial returns in July 1984.

With enforcement of the Haight ruling, the Justice Department could show that Noraid was officially registered as an agent of the IRA. This bolstered US government claims that the group supported violence. As noted earlier, however, there is little evidence to show that this formal legal connection had any detrimental effects on membership or financial support.

In conjunction with the FARA case, the State Department also tried to weaken the republican network by tightening its visa denial policy. The most noted example was the continued refusal to permit Gerry Adams entry to the United States, despite his election to the British Parliament in 1983. Adams received numerous invitations to speak in America but each visa application was refused on the basis of his support of violence. His case became a cause célèbre for Irish-American republicans. A Committee for Free Speech in Northern Ireland formed specifically to win a visa for Adams, while members of the Ad Hoc Committee repeatedly appealed to the State Department to lift their ban.

Prominent republicans admitted that the visa denial policy seriously impeded their activities and effectively undermined the presentation of Sinn Féin's position in America.[1] Yet militant nationalists did reap some benefits from the fact that many leading newspapers, especially *The New York Times*, strongly attacked the visa denials for "damaging America's reputation as an open society of intelligent, free citizens, capable of deciding for themselves whether to hear or ignore a speaker."[2]

---

1. Ted Howell, director of Sinn Féin Foreign Affairs Bureau, interview with author, 2 June 1992.

2. "Nanny at the Gates," *New York Times*, 9 June 1983.

A number of republicans were able to enter the US illegally. Canadian sympathizers organized an "underground railway" through which members of Sinn Féin and the IRA would be provided with forged documents and escorted across the American border. Some participated in clandestine fund raising and weapons procurement ventures while others simply tried to blend into society and avoid federal agents.

In the early 1980s, US immigration officers began investigating this Canadian pipeline and conducted surveillance of republican suspects under "Operation Shamrock." Information from this investigation led to the apprehension of Owen Carron and Danny Morrison in January 1982. Shortly afterward, agents captured Edward Howell and Desmond Ellis as they were trying to enter the United States illegally at the Whirlpool Bridge near Niagara Falls. The authorities described both men as key IRA explosives experts.[3]

Fear of arrest temporarily blocked the Canadian route for illegal entry but did not stop republicans from getting to America. Joe Cahill and Jimmy Drumm, for example, were caught in New York City in May 1984 after using false immigration documents. The two men were suspected of organizing an arms shipment for the IRA. Although they were not formally charged with this conspiracy, they were deported to Ireland.[4]

Gunrunning Convictions

The most effective measures taken by US law enforcement agencies, however, were against IRA gunrunning. Despite the failure of and embarrassment from the Harrison/Flannery case, FBI agents continued their undercover operations. One of the first successful convictions in the period was the case of Barney McKeon.

In 1979 George Harrison acquired a large consignment of arms stolen from Camp Lejeune, North Carolina. Before shipment to Ireland, the weapons were stored in a garage belonging to Barney McKeon, an American citizen originally from Northern Ireland who was very active in Noraid. Before the arms shipment left New York, one of the conspirators

3. Howell and Ellis were caught along with three Canadians. They had a shopping list for weapons and $10,000 in British currency. Among the items on the list were detonators for remote-control bombs and small model aircraft capable of carrying twenty pounds of explosives.

4. J. L. Stone, "Irish Terrorism Investigations," *F.B.I. Law Enforcement Bulletin* 56 (October 1987): 21.

telephoned IRA contacts in Dublin and gave details of its arrival. Irish detectives recorded the call from a wire tap and immediately informed their counterparts in America of the gunrunning scheme.[5]

When the weapons arrived in Dublin in late October 1979, Irish authorities laid a trap for the IRA. The Provos learned of it, and no one appeared to collect them. The Gárdaí were forced to seize the arms on November 2, 1979. Some of the rifles had intact serial numbers and could be traced to George De Meo. Police also found a shipping document that linked the weapons to Barney McKeon. From this mistake, McKeon was convicted on June 24, 1983, of conspiracy to export weapons to the IRA. He received three years' imprisonment and a fine of $10,000.

Although McKeown was jailed and the arms-supply line broken, the court case produced a major controversy which greatly embarrassed American law enforcement agencies. During the first trial, in December 1982 (which ended in a hung jury), Stephen Rogers, a senior US Customs official who had supervised gunrunning investigations in New York, testified on behalf of McKeon. Rogers said he did this because of "serious wrong-doing" by the prosecution. He alleged that Joseph King, a US Customs agent, had perjured himself by telling the court he did not know of the Gárda telephone tap in Dublin. Rogers claimed that King knew of the covert surveillance from its inception.[6]

After McKeon's conviction, the controversy over Rogers's testimony continued. British and Irish officials were infuriated by his revelations. They were particularly incensed because Rogers disclosed details of a secret meeting between British intelligence and US law-enforcement agents. Further, he named British intelligence officers in open court. Reports circulated that both the British and Irish authorities began withholding information because of their lack of confidence in the US Customs Service. In response an internal investigation of New York customs agents was launched to uncover alleged IRA sympathizers. Later William von Raab, the commissioner for customs, traveled to London and Dublin to reassure both governments that there were no republican informers within his service.[7]

5. David Blundy, "U.S. Lawmen Uncover Provo Arms Pipeline," *Sunday Times*, 18 May 1980.

6. Mark Hosenball, "Fear of I.R.A. Men in U.S. Intelligence," *Sunday Times*, 2 September 1984.

7. The confidence of British security forces in US Customs was largely reestablished in 1985. Customs agents in New York played an important role in tracing Provo funds

On November 1984, Stephen Rogers was fired from the Customs Service because of his conduct at the McKeown trial. He brought unfair dismissal proceedings before the Federal Merit Systems Protection Board in May 1985. Rogers demanded that secret documents outlining the role of British and Irish agents in the McKeon case be made available for his defense. Reports allege that British intelligence made it clear to the US authorities it did not want any more confidential information disclosed to the public. Without this information, which Rogers claimed was essential, the Board reinstated him with back pay. It also concluded that Rogers's naming of the British agent was "inadvertent rather than a result of IRA sympathy."[8]

Government agents were investigating other gunrunning operations, one of which was an arms conspiracy led by Gabriel Megahey and involving perhaps eleven other republican sympathizers. Megahey was born in Belfast and had a long connection with the republican movement. He worked in England for many years at the Southampton docks. In the mid-seventies he was expelled from the country because of his involvement in a scheme to import explosives and weapons from New York. Megahey then went to America and worked as a bartender in Queens. He maintained his republican connections and was alleged to be leader of the IRA in the United States. Megahey was also involved in gunrunning and soon became the focus of FBI surveillance.[9]

When Desmond Ellis and Edward Howell were arrested crossing the Canadian border in February 1982, Gabriel Megahey's name was found on their shopping list for weapons. The FBI put a tap on Megahey's phone. They recorded his alarm at the arrest of the two men but were unable to get hard evidence linking him to IRA gunrunning.

The FBI investigation of Megahey took an unexpected turn when Michael Hanratty approached government agents and offered to help smash the arms conspiracy. Hanratty, an electronics surveillance expert, was contacted by Andrew Duggan in June 1981 for help in purchasing sophisticated technical devices for remote-control bombs. Duggan, an Irish

---

that had been extorted during the kidnap of Donald Tidey. See *Boston Globe*, 22 February 1985.

8. Mark Hosenball, "U.S. Leak Blows British Secrets," *The Times* (London), 26 January 1985.

9. James Adams, *The Financing of Terror* (New York: Simon and Schuster, 1986), 149.

American active in Noraid, was a main figure in the Megahey network. He told Hanratty they wanted to send a large consignment of military material to the IRA.

Hanratty claimed he turned informer for "patriotic reasons." He began cooperating in an FBI sting operation. He and agent Enrique Ghimenti, who posed as an arms dealer, arranged a meeting with Duggan in New York. The FBI had the room bugged and also installed a video camera. The operation was only partly successful because Duggan sat down in the wrong place and only his voice was recorded.

Duggan was interested in the arms sale Ghimenti proposed. At a second meeting, this time in New Orleans, agents filmed Duggan and two IRA fugitives agreeing to buy five Redeye missiles at $10,000 each. The IRA men also asked for a whole range of automatic rifles, machine guns, and even a mini-submarine.

At a third meeting, Megahey appeared and was filmed affirming the order for Redeyes. He also proposed that a hostage from each side should be held until the arms deal was complete.[10]

The FBI operation reached a climax in June 1982 when Megahey and his co-conspirators tried to send a consignment of fifty-one rifles and remote-control devices to Ireland. The weapons were packed into a container labeled "roller skates and comforters." United States agents working in close cooperation with their British and Irish counterparts seized the arms at Port Newark but allowed a small consignment to travel on to Limerick on board a cargo ship. When the weapons arrived in Ireland, Gárdaí apprehended two IRA men sent to pick up the container. The men, Patrick McVeigh and John Moloney, were later jailed for seven and three years respectively for possession of an Armalite rifle and IRA membership.[11]

On June 21, 1982, the FBI arrested Megahey and Duggan at a construction site in Manhattan. They also apprehended two brothers from Northern Ireland, Colm and Eamonn Meehan, who were involved in the conspiracy. The four immediately received legal aid from Irish-American

10. Chris Thomas, "Irish Arms Buyers Shadowed by F.B.I.," *The Times* (London), 31 March 1983.

11. *Irish Times* (Dublin), 28 January 1983. The Gárdaí also arrested Father Pat Moloney, brother of John, a Melikite priest working with homeless teenagers in New York. He was released soon afterward without being charged. In 1993 Father Moloney was again arrested in connection with the robbery of a Brinks security van in Rochester, which netted $7.4 million. Also charged in the case were Tom O'Connor, a security guard who was active

republicans, and a panel of lawyers began investigating ways to thwart the prosecution.[12]

Attorneys for the Meehans based their defense on the fact the brothers had been held as internees in Long Kesh. They claimed that the two suffered from post-trauma distress disorder, because of their experience in prison, and entered a plea of not guilty because of insanity. The Meehans were examined by a psychiatrist who concluded their claim to insanity was "only a diagnostic possibility." Judge Charles Sifton denied their defense.

When this line of defense collapsed, lawyers for the four men copied the tactic used in the Flannery trial. They claimed the defendants thought Michael Hanratty was a CIA agent and therefore that their gunrunning scheme had US government approval. Assistant US Attorney Carol Amon produced CIA affidavits stating that Hanratty was not one of their operatives. Defense lawyers focussed on the involvement of British intelligence in the case and unsuccessfully tried to force FBI witnesses to divulge classified information.

The trial lasted for nine weeks. On May 13, 1983, after five days of deliberation, the jury found the men guilty on most charges. As Gabriel Megahey was the leader of the arms conspiracy, he received seven years' imprisonment.[13] Andrew Duggan and Eamonn Meehan each got three. Colm Meehan received two, following his acquittal on some of the conspiracy charges.[14]

---

in Noraid, Sam Miller, an illegal immigrant who had served time in the Maze Prison for republican activities, and Charles McCormick, a New York City teacher and social worker. Only $2.2 million of the stolen money was recovered and the FBI has hinted that at least some of this cash went to the IRA. On 8 November 1994, McCormick and O'Connor were acquitted of all charges, while Miller and Moloney were found guilty of conspiracy to receive and possess stolen money. Moloney and Miller later received four-year and five-year prison sentences respectively.

12. A number of militant groups came together in response to the arrests and formed an Irish-American Defense Fund. It held collections to defray the legal expenses of IRA gunrunners and fugitives. Within three years it claimed to have raised a total of $422,117. *Irish-American Defense Fund Program*, Annual Testimonial, 10 May 1985.

13. The INS began deportation proceedings against Megahey following his release from prison. Megahey is currently fighting to remain in the United States.

14. Just two weeks after the Megahey conviction, the FBI won a second victory when a federal court in Brooklyn found Vincent Toner and Colm Murphy guilty of gunrunning. The two men were both from South Armagh and were involved in a scheme to send Armalite rifles to the INLA. Federal agents infiltrated the operation by posing as mafia arms dealers. Murphy received five years in prison and a fine of $10,000; Toner got eighteen months and a $7,500 fine.

Following this victory, federal agents continued to investigate others who were suspected of involvement in the Megahey conspiracy. Their attempts to secure further convictions had mixed results. Patrick McParland, an associate of Megahey, fled to Ireland when he heard of the FBI sting. After months on the run he decided to surrender and voluntarily return for trial. McParland's lawyers successfully argued that although he had transported boxes of weapons for the Meehan brothers, he did not know their contents. In November 1983, he was acquitted on all charges.[15]

In April 1985, the FBI arrested Liam Ryan and charged him with using false documents to purchase three Armalite rifles that were part of the Megahey consignment. Ryan, a naturalized American citizen, originally from County Tyrone, was alleged to be the IRA's officer-in-command in New York. He had close associations with Irish-American republican groups and was a personal friend of Martin Galvin. Agents matched Ryan's fingerprints with those found on the armalites and on the falsified purchase certificates. In September 1985 he pleaded guilty to making fraudulent statements in buying the weapons and received a suspended sentence.[16]

The largest and most intriguing gunrunning operation to be uncovered in this period involved John Crawley. Born in New York in 1957, Crawley moved to Dublin with his family as a teenager. In 1975 he returned to the United States to join the military. After four years' service, Crawley went back to Dublin and became involved with the IRA. In 1984 he was sent to Boston to help assemble a $1.2 million arms cache for the Provos,

15. "McParland's Victory," *Irish People* (New York), 26 November 1983. Gerry McGeough, an IRA volunteer from Tyrone, was also named as a participant in the gunrunning scheme. In May 1992, after a German court failed to convict him of alleged offenses against British forces stationed in Europe, McGeough was extradited to the US to face the outstanding charges against him. He subsequently reached a plea bargain with prosecutors under which a number of minor charges were dropped and he received a three-year prison sentence in June 1993. After a series of unsuccessful appeals against his sentence, McGeough began his prison term in the spring of 1994.

16. During the trial Martin Galvin posted $750,000 bail for Ryan, which was partly secured by Michael Flannery's house in New York. Liam Ryan later returned to Ireland to manage his family pub in Ardboe, County Tyrone. In December 1989 he was killed when the UVF sprayed the bar with gunfire. Ironically, Ryan's death, combined with evidence of information leaks between the security forces and loyalist paramilitaries, enhanced the ability of some republicans to resist deportation from America. Seán Mackin, Seán McGowan, and Francis Gildernew, republicans who had served time in prison and later entered the US, successfully fought deportation proceedings by convincing INS judges that their lives would be in danger if they were returned to Northern Ireland.

which included machine guns, missile warheads, grenades, night sights, and flack jackets.

In mid-September 1984, Crawley loaded the arsenal on board a fishing vessel called the *Valhalla* and sailed out of Boston bound for Ireland. Unknown to him and his associates, an informer had alerted the authorities about the conspiracy. This initiated a joint surveillance operation involving American, British, and Irish authorities. Reports surfaced that as the *Valhalla* sailed across the Atlantic, it was tracked by an American satellite which closely monitored the ship's progress. A crack force of Gárda detectives joined to monitor the Irish end of the operation. Two Irish navy corvettes, the *Emer* and *Aisling*, followed a rendezvous ship, the *Marita Ann*, as it left port in Kerry. While the arms were transferred between the two trawlers in mid-Atlantic, a Royal Navy Nimrod aircraft photographed the operation with special magnifying cameras.[17]

Irish authorities intercepted the *Marita Ann* as it sailed back to its home port laden with weapons. On board, they found five crew members including Crawley and Martin Ferris, a prominent Kerry republican and suspected member of the IRA Army Council. The men were tried and convicted in the Special Criminal Court on December 11, 1984. Crawley, Ferris, and Nick Browne, the ship's captain, were each given ten years' imprisonment. Two crew members who claimed they did not know about the *Marita Ann's* mission, received five-year suspended sentences.

Despite international security cooperation, the *Valhalla* slipped past US authorities on its homeward voyage with two IRA fugitives on board. The trawler was in port for three days before its discovery by customs officers on October 16, 1984. Federal agents began an investigation that eventually linked the gunrunning operation to organized crime in Boston and to drug trafficking. It was not until April 1986, however, that a grand jury indicted a group of men accused of involvement in the conspiracy.

The leading figure in the indictment was Joseph Murray, an Irish-American from Charlestown, Massachusetts. Murray was a principal figure in the Boston underworld and had connections with the IRA and drug trafficking. When police raided Murray's home they found a consignment of weapons and over more than ten thousand rounds of ammunition. He was charged with conspiracy to supply guns to the IRA and

17. William Doherty, "Five Charged in Hub with Exporting Weapons to Ireland," *Boston Globe*, 17 April 1986.

American weapons seized from the trawler *Marita Ann* in 1984, on display at Gárda headquarters in Dublin. UPI/BETTMANN

with smuggling thirty-six tons of marijuana into Boston to pay for them.[18]

Among others indicted were Patrick Nee, who was accused of playing a major role in acquiring the weapons. Nee was born in Ireland and, like Murray, was involved in Boston's organized crime network.[19] Robert Anderson, captain of the *Valhalla*, was also charged with gunrunning and was allegedly paid $10,000 by Murray for undertaking the voyage. Anderson was noted for his swashbuckling lifestyle and had used the *Valhalla* for a number of drug-running ventures.

18. In 1984, Murray had pleaded guilty to importing the marijuana onboard the British registered cargo ship *Ramsland*.

19. In December 1990, Nee was arrested for his part in a bank robbery in Boston. One of his accomplices was Michael McNaught, a former member of the IRA who fled to America after discovering his name was on a loyalist assassination list. They each received fourteen-year prison sentences. *Boston Globe*, 12 January 1991.

As part of a bargain with the government, in May 1987 the three men pleaded guilty to gunrunning. Prosecutors dropped the drug charges and recommended sentences for less than the twenty-two-year maximum. Murray was sentenced to ten years, while Patrick Nee and Robert Anderson got four years each.

The trial was a major news item on both sides of the Atlantic because of its exposure of links between IRA gunrunning and organized crime in Boston. It also uncovered connections between Murray and Dr. William Herbert, an ambassador to the United Nations for the Caribbean islands of St. Kitts and Nevis. The trial revealed that Murray used Herbert to launder money he made from drug deals. The ambassador resigned in April 1987 when the FBI produced documents showing his connections with Murray.[20]

A controversy also developed over the case of John McIntyre, one of the crewmen on the *Valhalla*. He was questioned by customs agents after the ship's seizure in Boston. McIntyre had been cooperating in a federal sting operation against Joe Murray, but he disappeared soon afterward and has never been found. John Loftus, the McIntyre family lawyer, later co-authored a book entitled, *Valhalla's Wake*. He claims that John McIntyre was murdered in the US by two British agents in order to protect the IRA mole who had supplied information on the *Marita Ann* operation. In *The IRA: A History*, Tim Pat Coogan maintains that this smoke screen did not fool the Provos, and they subsequently executed the informer in Ireland. British and American authorities deny all these allegations but many unresolved issues remain in the case.[21]

A final controversy emerged over the involvement of police officers in the *Marita Ann* affair. When the ship was seized, Irish detectives discovered eleven bullet-proof vests. Ten of these were subsequently traced to Charles Tourkantonis and Michael Hanley, both officers with the Boston Police Department. An internal investigation revealed that the two officers had bought the vests for John Crawley. No disciplinary proceedings

20. In September 1992, Murray was murdered by his estranged wife, Susan. She successfully avoided charges by claiming self-defense. *Boston Globe*, 17 September 1992.

21. John Loftus and Emily McIntyre, *Valhalla's Wake: The I.R.A., MI6 and the Assassination of a Young American* (New York: Atlantic Monthly Press, 1989) and Tim Pat Coogan, *The I.R.A.: A History* (Colorado: Roberts Rinehart, 1993), 399.

were taken, however, because the officers claimed they did not know the flack jackets were to be used illegally.[22]

The convictions secured by US law enforcement agencies against the gunrunning network in the mid-1980s caused serious problems for the IRA. After the seizure of the *Marita Ann*, the Provos began to concentrate their arms procurement ventures in Europe and the Middle East. Although the IRA continued to ship some weapons from America, US authorities successfully undermined the transatlantic arms network.[23]

In addition to these problems, Irish-American republicanism continued to suffer from the adverse publicity generated by IRA bombings. Attacks such as the Hyde Park bombs of 1982 and the explosion at the 1984 Conservative Party Conference in Brighton were given prominent coverage in the United States. Each initiated further criticism of the IRA. The strongest reaction against the Provos came after the bombing of Harrods department store in London on December 19, 1983. An IRA unit drove two cars packed with explosives and parked them outside the building. They phoned a warning that was hopelessly late for police to clear the streets. The bombs ripped through Christmas shoppers, killing eight and severely injuring many others. Kenneth Salvesen, a businessman from Chicago, was among the dead and three other Americans were injured.

The bombing caused outraged reactions in Britain and Ireland, while the death of Salvesen brought some of the strongest attacks on Noraid ever launched in the American press. Numerous editorials alleged Noraid money had directly financed the bombs, and, therefore, brought death and injury to US citizens. Martin Galvin, recognizing the disastrous effect of the bomb in America, claimed that the action was taken without the Army Council's authority and that a warning beforehand "showed a principled morality that divides the freedom fighter from the terrorist."[24]

Galvin's defense of the IRA led only to greater condemnations of Noraid in the American press. The inaccuracy of his statement was

22. One vest was also traced to officer Michael Flemmi. He was cleared of misconduct when he reported that the vest had been stolen from his car. The whole affair tended to reinforce the belief of British security agencies that there was significant republican sympathy among metropolitain police forces on the East Coast.

23. Patrick Bishop and Eamonn Mallie, *The Provisional I.R.A.* (London: Heinemann, 1987), 130–31.

24. *Irish People* (New York), 24 December 1983.

exposed later when evidence showed that the IRA team was on an official mission that had indeed been approved by the Army Council.[25] The American ambassador in London attacked the IRA's "savage bestiality"; the Friends of Ireland called the attack "despicable and deranged." The *Chicago Tribune's* reaction to the Hyde Park attack was representative of most American editorial opinion on IRA bombings:

> IRA front groups . . . claim that they are raising funds for the families of slain or imprisoned IRA men. They lie. The money goes for arms, ammunition, and bombs. It buys the high explosives and the remote control detonators that blew up in London. The money bank rolls the sort of sub-humans who can pack six inch nails around a bomb and put it in a place where women and children and tourists will gather.[26]

America and the Anglo-Irish Agreement

The Friends of Ireland used every IRA atrocity to convince Irish Americans of the futility of violence. In addition, they continued to exert their influence on Capitol Hill to encourage new political initiatives in Ulster. Eventually, through close cooperation with the SDLP and Irish government, the Friends played an important role in the Anglo-Irish Agreement of 1985. Pressure and influence from these Irish-American political leaders was, at certain stages, an integral factor in bringing the Agreement to fruition.

The Anglo-Irish Agreement was very much a consequence of the political changes in Ulster after the hunger strike. Sinn Féin electoral victories, during and after the prison dispute, created intense pressure on the SDLP. John Hume realized that his party needed a major political achievement if it was to resist the challenge from republicanism. He hoped to secure concessions from the British government through direct Anglo-Irish negotiations. Yet the likelihood of securing this objective seemed remote. In 1982 the British were intent on pursuing an internal solution by devolved government through the establishment of James

25. Bishop and Mallie, *The Provisional I.R.A.*, 307. See also Trevor Fishlock, "How the I.R.A. Bombs Backfire in America," *The Times* (London), 22 December 1983.

26. "Where Aid to the I.R.A. Goes," *Chicago Tribune*, 22 July 1982. Similar outraged reactions were leveled at the IRA following every major bomb attack in the eighties. They reached an unprecedented groundswell of outrage after the Enniskillen Remembrance Day explosion in November 1987.

Prior's Assembly. They were consequently unresponsive to the Anglo-Irish dimension.

Hume's hope of achieving a political breakthrough was further eroded by the chill in Anglo-Irish relations that began after Charles Haughey's electoral victory in March 1982. The new Taoiseach antagonized Margaret Thatcher with his nationalistic rhetoric and strong attacks against the Prior Assembly.

Anglo-Irish relations reached their lowest ebb during the Falklands War. Haughey gave the Thatcher government only limited and grudging support to economic sanctions enforced by the EEC on Argentina and made a forceful condemnation of the sinking of the battleship *Belgrano*. In *Maggie: An Intimate Portrait of a Woman in Power*, Chris Ogden claims that the British prime minister considered Irish actions as an "unforgivable betrayal." He says it reinforced her "natural antipathy toward the Irish, whom she considered, in large part, shiftless, sniveling, and spineless."[27]

These Anglo-Irish antagonisms greatly concerned the Friends of Ireland. The group was alarmed at positive republican publicity over the Flannery trial and the St. Patrick's Day Parade controversy. Senator Edward Kennedy and Tip O'Neill were frustrated that they could not counteract Irish-American republicanism by pointing to some political advances by constitutional nationalists in Ireland. Their frustration was compounded by the deterioration in relations between London and Dublin which seemed to block fresh political initiatives in Ulster.[28]

In this unpromising situation, the Friends of Ireland worked for a political breakthrough. In their 1982 St. Patrick's Day statement they appealed for greater dialogue between the Haughey and Thatcher administrations. In May the Friends sent a delegation to Ireland led by Congressman Tom Foley and Senator Chris Dodd. They helped form a counterpart to the Friends of Ireland in the Dáil called the Irish–US Parliamentary Group. This new organization aimed at strengthening transatlantic communications between constitutional nationalists in order to coordinate political action on Capitol Hill.

The Friends of Ireland delegation also traveled to Belfast and met Lord Gowrie of the Northern Ireland Office. Congressman Foley and

27. Chris Ogden, *Maggie: The Portrait of a Woman in Power* (New York: Simon and Schuster, 1990), 189.

28. Senator Edward Kennedy, correspondence with author, 16 April 1989.

Senator Dodd told him they were concerned about the lack of political progress in Ulster and endorsed the Anglo-Irish approach as the best way forward. In order to show the British their commitment, key members of the Friends tabled joint-congressional resolutions calling for a ban on the use of plastic bullets and the outlawing of the Ulster Defense Association.

Sinn Féin's success in the October 1982 Assembly elections was a major blow to constitutional nationalism. The results confirmed John Hume's view that a new initiative was imperative to consolidate the SDLP's position and counteract the rising republican threat. He began to press Garret FitzGerald, elected Taoiseach in December 1982, to embark on a new political drive aimed at defining the objectives of constitutional nationalists. FitzGerald was intensely aware of the threat posed by Sinn Féin and announced the formation of a New Ireland Forum.

The New Ireland Forum began discussions in late May 1983. All constitutional nationalist parties submitted proposals on how to unify Ireland while still protecting the Protestant/unionist identity. Sinn Féin was not asked to participate, because of its support of violence; all Unionist political parties rejected the exercise as "obviously biased" against their interests. Despite frequent disagreements between the parties involved, the Forum continued to take testimony and discuss political alternatives throughout the year.

John Hume and the FitzGerald administration were committed to getting support for the Forum from the Friends of Ireland. Before the discussions began, Hume contacted all his associates in Washington and asked for a firm endorsement of the new initiative. Together they formulated a "United Ireland" resolution, which was sponsored by twenty-eight senators and fifty-three congressmen. The resolution was issued on St. Patrick's Day 1983 and gave strong support to the New Ireland Forum, describing it as a great sign of hope for the peaceful unification of Ireland. The Friends repeated their attack on James Prior's "unworkable" Assembly and maintained that a real solution would require, "the bold cooperation of both the British and Irish governments jointly pursuing, at the highest levels, a new strategy of reconciliation."[29]

The *Irish Times* described the resolution as "the most important Irish initiative to be put to Congress since 1920."[30] John Hume and Irish For-

---

29. "Statement of the Friends of Ireland," 98th. Cong., 1st. sess., *Congressional Record*, no. 34 (17 March 1983): 129.

30. *Irish Times* (Dublin), 18 March 1983.

eign Minister Peter Barry traveled to Washington to support the resolution. Barry also held extensive discussions with Ronald Reagan and
asked for support for the New Ireland Forum. The president was
impressed by the new initiative. Although he maintained the traditional
position that the United States would not chart a course for Ulster, he acknowledged that "we do have an obligation to urge our long-time friends
in that part of the world to seek reconciliation."[31]

As the New Ireland Forum discussions progressed, the Friends of Ireland were kept informed of the latest developments. On July 27, 1983, a
delegation from Dáil Éireann traveled to Washington and met with their
American counterparts. Members of the Friends considered the visit so
important they suspended confirmation hearings for Paul Volcker as Federal Reserve chairman in order to meet the Irish politicians.

The discussions concentrated on a growing conflict within the Forum
between Charles Haughey and Garret FitzGerald. Press reports in Ireland and America suggested Haughey was using the Forum as a means
to embarrass the Taoiseach. This political maneuvering alarmed the
Friends. Journalist Michael Kilian of the *Chicago Tribune*, contends
that they asked the Dáil delegation to advise Haughey not to disrupt
the discussions. Tip O'Neill stressed that the Forum needed to present a united front in order to win the support of the United States government and to enhance constitutional nationalist efforts on Capitol
Hill.[32]

The Friends of Ireland tried to aid the Forum by continuing to encourage meaningful dialogue between the Irish and British governments. In
October 1983 they sponsored a resolution calling on President Reagan to
appoint a special US envoy to Northern Ireland. In an accompanying statement, Senator Edward Kennedy said an American envoy could play an
important role in encouraging Anglo-Irish talks. Although the proposal
was rejected by the Reagan administration, it did give the British yet another indication of the Irish-American concern to see a new political move
in Ulster.[33]

---

31. *Statement of the Presidents: The Reagan Administration*, 17 March 1983.

32. Michael Kilian, "Look Who's Interested In Ulster," *Chicago Tribune*, 23 August
1983.

33. *Statement by Senator Kennedy Urging Reagan to Appoint a Special Envoy for
Northern Ireland*, 5 October 1983. The special envoy idea had first been forwarded in
August 1983 by New York Assemblyman John Dearie. It won widespread support from
major Irish-American groups, including Noraid.

The Forum Report was finally released in May 1984 and offered three political options as possible solutions to the Ulster conflict. After strong pressure from Charles Haughey, it proposed that "the most favored solution" was a united Ireland, safeguarding unionist rights. The report also suggested a highly complicated federal-confederal system. Under this formula, both parts of Ireland would have their own assembly, presided over by a national government. The final option proposed that Northern Ireland could be ruled jointly by both the Dublin and Westminster governments.

The Friends of Ireland immediately supported the Forum Report and began working for the endorsement of the Reagan administration. To enhance this effort, Peter Barry flew to Washington on May 4, 1984, and held high-level discussions with State Department officials. The talks proved successful and the US government later praised "the Irish statesmen for their courageous and forthright efforts embodied in the New Ireland Forum."[34]

The British Parliament debated the Forum Report on July 2, 1984. There was considerable praise for its attempt to accommodate unionist aspirations and its strong condemnation of terrorism. The Thatcher government refused to give an official reaction until the next scheduled Anglo-Irish summit in November. There was widespread anticipation on both sides of the Atlantic that the British prime minister would make a magnanimous gesture toward constitutional nationalism.

The Anglo-Irish summit was held at Thatcher's retreat, Chequers, on November 15, 1984. Since the release of the Forum Report, both governments had been conducting private discussions which would lay the basis for the Anglo-Irish Agreement. At Chequers, Garret FitzGerald tried to move these talks to a higher level. He suggested a political formula under which his government would amend articles two and three of the Irish constitution, which claim sovereignty over Northern Ireland. The Taoiseach hoped that in exchange, Britain would agree to a formal political role for Dublin in Ulster's affairs.

Secretary of State Douglas Hurd opposed FitzGerald's offer. He felt the constitutional amendment was too great a gamble and would be extremely counterproductive if it failed. Consequently, the British delegation tried to retard the pace of discussions. Although both governments continued to work toward an Anglo-Irish agreement, FitzGerald recalled,

34. Seán Cronin, *Washington's Irish Policy* (Dublin: Anvil Books, 1987).

"The British were tending to pull back from what had been discussed already. It was a somewhat disappointing meeting because the negotiations were moved to a lower and subtractive level."[35]

Following the meeting at Chequers, Margaret Thatcher held a press conference. For the first forty-five minutes she gave a very positive appraisal of Anglo-Irish negotiations. When she was asked about the three political options advanced in the Forum Report, however, she dismissed them all in her now-infamous "Out, Out, Out" remarks.

Thatcher's seemingly insensitive reaction to the efforts of constitutional nationalists caused an immediate political backlash in Ireland. The normally restrained *Irish Times* said the prime minister was "as offhand and patronizing as she is callous and imperious." The *Irish Press* said Thatcher's vehement delivery had an element of rudeness usually reserved for bitter enemies and that she made "Out" sound like a four-letter word. The newspaper concluded her statement was a devastating rejection of all the hopes and efforts that went into the Forum.

Relations between the London and Dublin governments entered a period of confusion and misunderstanding after Thatcher's press conference. Many Irish politicians believed the British prime minister was deliberately trying to humiliate Garret FitzGerald and scuttle Anglo-Irish talks. The Taoiseach had to resist pressure from within his own administration to attack Thatcher. He did reportedly describe her reaction as "gratuitously offensive."

Constitutional nationalists were greatly concerned that the confusion in Anglo-Irish relations would destroy the prospects for a new political move in Ulster. The SDLP was particularly alarmed at this development, because they would have no political breakthrough with which to counteract Sinn Féin. Faced with this situation, John Hume and Irish government officials began to enlist the services of their Irish-American supporters. They contacted the Friends of Ireland and urged them to get Ronald Reagan's assistance. Constitutional nationalists hoped they could persuade the president to use his influence with Thatcher and register his concern for Anglo-Irish dialogue.[36]

Among the key figures in this attempt to get Reagan's support was William Clark, former national security advisor. Clark was a long-time friend and confidant of the president. He also had a close relationship

35. Garret FitzGerald, interview with author, 19 December 1990.
36. John Hume, interview with author, 3 January 1989.

with the Irish diplomatic corps in Washington, especially Seán Donlon. Clark became very supportive of the constitutional nationalist position. While he was deputy secretary of state in 1981, Clark conducted a tour of Ireland. He greatly angered unionists when he admitted his membership of the Ancient Order of Hibernians and told a reporter, "It is the hope and prayer of all Americans that Ireland will be united."[37]

Seán Donlon contacted Clark following Thatcher's "Out, Out, Out" remarks. He agreed to use his influence with Reagan to assist the constitutional nationalist cause. The president was scheduled to meet the British prime minister at Camp David on December 22, 1984. Before the meeting, Clark asked Reagan to discuss Anglo-Irish relations with the Prime Minister and to express his desire for political progress. The Friends of Ireland backed Clark in a telegram to the president on December 21. They also told Reagan of their "disappointment at Mrs. Thatcher's public peremptory dismissal of the reasonable alternatives put forward in the Forum Report."[38]

American press reports that appeared after the Camp David meeting said the two leaders discussed only Western European reaction to the "Star Wars" defense initiative. Not until January 17, 1985, did the Reagan administration officially acknowledge that Anglo-Irish affairs had been on the agenda. In a letter to Mario Biaggi, the White House stated the president and Mrs. Thatcher "exchanged views on Northern Ireland" and that the president "stressed the need for progress and the need for all parties concerned to take steps which will contribute to a peaceful resolution."[39]

Garret FitzGerald believes William Clark's intervention was the crucial factor in persuading Reagan to discuss Irish affairs. Against specific advice from the State Department, the president raised the issue. During the meeting, it seems that Reagan expressed a desire to see progress in the Anglo-Irish talks. He also said he would like to discuss the issue further with Thatcher when she returned to the US in February 1985.

Reagan's concern with Anglo-Irish relations, and his desire for further discussions, put Thatcher under a certain amount of pressure. She was encouraged to make some new proposals to the Irish government before her return to Washington in February. Garret FitzGerald and Seán Donlon

37. From interview of William Clark on RTE's *Today Tonight* program, 7 December 1981.

38. Seán Cronin, "Reagan Urged to Raise Northern Ireland With Thatcher," *Irish Times* (Dublin), 22 December 1984.

39. Letter from State Department to Mario Biaggi, 17 January 1985.

believe that American pressure played a, "decisive role in persuading Thatcher to modify her position."[40] The British thus offered a new Anglo-Irish package on January 21, 1985. This new deal was a significant advance on what had been discussed at Chequers. It offered an institutionalized role for the Irish government in the administration of Northern Ireland.[41]

Although American pressure was a factor in Thatcher's more positive proposal of January 21, she was also influenced by her political colleagues in Britain. Members of her cabinet and staff emphasized that her "Out, Out, Out" remarks had damaged Garret FitzGerald's political position in Ireland and would give encouragement to Sinn Féin. They advised Thatcher to compromise and offer more significant concessions to the Irish.

Despite Thatcher's new proposal, the FitzGerald administration continued to "play the American card." Seán Donlon and John Hume contacted Tip O'Neill before the British prime minister was due to address a joint session of Congress on February 20, 1985. They asked the house speaker to ensure that Thatcher discuss the Northern Ireland problem in her speech. O'Neill conveyed this request to Sir Oliver Wright, the British ambassador. To emphasize his concern, O'Neill met Thatcher on her arrival in Washington he again asked her to include the Ulster conflict in her address.

O'Neill's pressure produced results. When Thatcher addressed Congress, she not only discussed Northern Ireland but was also extremely conciliatory toward the Irish government. She said that relations between her and Garret FitzGerald were "excellent" and that she would cooperate with his administration to find a political solution in Ulster. She also

40. Garret FitzGerald, interview with author, 19 December 1990. Seán Donlon, "Bringing Irish Diplomatic and Political Pressure to Bear on Washington," *Irish Times* (Dublin), 25 January 1993.

41. Between 6–9 January 1985, a major conference on the Ulster conflict was held at Airlie House in Virginia. It was attended by academics, journalists, representatives from Northern Ireland's political parties, and officials from the Irish and British government. The conference was designed as an exercise in "Track Two" diplomacy, getting adversary groups together in an informal environment in the hope of encouraging mutual understanding. While there were no major breakthroughs in relations between Unionist and nationalist politicians, the Airlie House meeting did produce the opportunity for further contacts between British and Irish officials and was one of a number of activities helping to build up trust. Information from Professor Paul Arthur, correspondence with author, 8 February 1994.

expressed hope that joint efforts to launch new political dialogue would receive full support from America.[42]

As a complement to using its influence with Tip O'Neill, the Irish government also tried to get support from the State Department. On February 15, 1985, Peter Barry and Seán Donlon met with Rick Burt, assistant secretary of state for European affairs. They asked the State Department to include the Ulster problem in talks with Thatcher following her congressional address.

Burt, because of Reagan's interest in the issue, agreed to the Irish request and succeeded in reversing the State Department's traditional avoidance of the Northern Ireland conflict. He convinced Secretary of State George Shultz to raise the question with Thatcher. At a meeting in California, Shultz and Reagan told the prime minister of their desire to see progress in Anglo-Irish discussions and offered American financial support in the event of an agreed political initiative.[43]

There was considerable speculation over the nature of American governmental involvement in the Anglo-Irish process. Some unionists alleged it was all part of a sinister conspiracy under which the British would withdraw from Northern Ireland. Enoch Powell, MP, believed the US was encouraging an Anglo-Irish agreement in order to establish a united Ireland. This new state would end its neutrality, enter the NATO alliance, and permit the establishment of American military bases. Powell claimed this would greatly enhance the strategic defense of Western Europe.[44]

Perhaps a more plausible explanation of US involvement was Ronald Reagan's personal interest in Irish affairs. The president was proud of his Irish roots and was informed of the latest political developments by William Clark and other Irish Americans in his administration. These included Robert McFarlane in the National Security Council, Secretary of the Treasury Donald Regan, Secretary of Labor Donovan, and CIA Director William Casey.

Irish government ministers took every opportunity to convince the Reagan administration of the threat posed by the rise of Sinn Féin. When

42. "Margaret Thatcher Addresses Congress," British Information Service, 21 February 1985.

43. Garret FitzGerald, interview with author, 19 December 1990. Tip O'Neill met Reagan before this conference with Thatcher and also pushed the idea of American financial support for an agreement.

44. Paul Arthur, *Northern Ireland Since 1968* (Belfast: Blackstaff, 1988), 87.

Vice-President George Bush stopped in Dublin for talks with Garret FitzGerald in July 1983, the Taoiseach warned him that Sinn Féin political success could destroy democracy in Ireland. Irish officials reinforced this point when Reagan himself visited Ireland in June 1984. They tried to convince the president that the only way to stop Sinn Féin was through a new political agreement achieved through Anglo-Irish discussions.

Reagan, as a self-proclaimed champion against world terrorism, sympathized with the Irish government and strongly opposed the IRA. Each St. Patrick's Day he issued vehement attacks against the organization and urged Irish Americans not to fund violence in Ulster. He therefore had a concrete reason for supporting an agreement that offered the prospect of stifling the republican movement.

From these various influences, Reagan encouraged Anglo-Irish talks. Following the February 20 meeting with Thatcher, the British government intensified negotiations with the FitzGerald administration. Chris Ogden implies that Reagan offered to increase activities against the Irish-American republican network if the British were more conciliatory toward the Irish. He says that Thatcher partly accepted the Anglo-Irish Agreement because "If she did not, she knew she would get precious little help stopping the flow of guns and money from America to the IRA or in getting IRA suspects extradited from the US."[45]

Throughout the final stages of the Anglo-Irish Agreement, the Irish continued to enlist the assistance of their American supporters. In early March 1985, Tip O'Neill led a delegation of the Friends to Dublin. They held discussions with Garret FitzGerald and Peter Barry on the progress of Anglo-Irish talks. O'Neill also went to London and assured British officials he would use all his influence to secure American financial support for a political agreement. He convinced them that, as speaker of the house, he was in a unique position to guide a financial assistance bill through Congress.

In early May 1985, Garret FitzGerald traveled to Washington for further talks about the United States aid to Ireland. With Tip O'Neill and Edward Kennedy he discussed the practicalities of getting the bill through Congress. FitzGerald also went to Ottawa for a meeting with Prime Minister Brian Mulroney. The Taoiseach told him the Anglo-Irish

45. Chris Ogden, *Maggie: The Portrait of a Woman in Power*, 223.

Agreement was near completion. Mulroney was so delighted he promised Canadian financial assistance.[46]

The final hurdle to the Agreement came in late October 1985. Charles Haughey, then leader of the Fianna Fáil opposition, was dissatisfied with the Anglo-Irish discussions, believing that they were a "sell-out" to British interests. He dispatched Brian Lenihan to Washington in an attempt to convince the Friends to oppose the accord. Tip O'Neill and Edward Kennedy rejected Haughey's contentions, muted Haughey's opposition, and thereby saved the Agreement from a potentially serious challenge.[47]

The months of prolonged negotiations ended on November 15, 1985, when Margaret Thatcher and Garret FitzGerald met in Hillsborough Castle and signed the Anglo-Irish Agreement. The key element of the new accord was the establishment of an Intergovernmental Conference, at which British and Irish officials would meet regularly to discuss matters relating to the government of Northern Ireland. An Anglo-Irish secretariat was also established in Belfast, to support the work of the Intergovernmental Conference. These provisions meant that the Republic of Ireland was given a formal role in Ulster for the first time since the formation of the state in 1921.

Under the Agreement, Dublin formally acknowledged the right of the unionist community to remain within the United Kingdom. This was affirmed under Article One, which stated that any change in the status of Northern Ireland would come about only with the consent of a majority of the people of Northern Ireland. Other provisions expressed a desire "to protect human rights and to prevent discrimination." The accord also promised much greater levels of cross-border security cooperation, to be coordinated by the chief constable of the RUC and the commissioner of the Gárda Siochána.

The unionist reaction to the Anglo-Irish Agreement was immediate and hostile. None of their political representatives had been consulted during the negotiations and they saw it as a sell out by the British. Leaders of the Ulster Unionist Party and Democratic Unionist Party embarked on a series of mass rallies and days of protest. All Unionist MPs withdrew from their seats at Westminster and eventually forced an election over the Hillsborough accord.

46. Garret FitzGerald, interview with author, 19 December 1990.
47. "Brian Lenihan: The Party Linesman," *Sunday Tribune*, 21 October 1990.

The American reaction, in contrast, was extremely positive. The Agreement received enormous political and editorial support. All the major newspapers characterized it as a major step toward reconciliation in Ulster and praised Thatcher and FitzGerald for their political courage. The *New York Times* described the accord as "creative and ingenious" and warned unionists that the only group that would benefit from their opposition was the IRA.[48] The *Washington Post* suggested that the strong American backing for the Agreement would lead to a significant erosion of Irish-American support for the Provisionals.[49]

The major Irish-American newspapers were more reserved in their reaction. All welcomed the fact that Dublin was given a formal role in Northern Ireland but questioned the unionist right to remain in the United Kingdom.[50] Mario Biaggi and the Ad Hoc Committee were also ambivalent. Though their statements seemed to support the Agreement, their phrasing left open the possibility of an attack in the future.[51] There was no such indecision in Noraid's reaction. The group followed Sinn Féin's lead in describing the Agreement as a sham and a betrayal of Irish national sovereignty. Martin Galvin reasserted that the only way peace would be achieved was through British withdrawal.[52]

On the day the Anglo-Irish Agreement was signed, Ronald Reagan and Tip O'Neill held a press reception in the Oval Office. They praised the new initiative and gave concrete assurance that the United States would provide financial aid to the embryonic International Fund for Ireland. Reagan also condemned IRA supporters in America.[53] On December 9, the House of Representatives passed a resolution supporting the Agreement by a vote of 380 to 1. The resolution received a similar endorsement in the Senate one day later.

The signing of the Anglo-Irish Agreement brought great hope to constitutional nationalists. The political benefits promised by Dublin's role in Ulster affairs seemed to suggest a new era, in which Sinn Féin's influence would be minimized. The Agreement could be used by the SDLP to win support and reestablish its leadership of the nationalist community.

48. "A Brave Bid For Ulster Peace," *New York Times*, 16 November 1985.

49. "Towards Peace in Ulster," *Washington Post*, 17 November 1985.

50. For example, see "Who Can Complain?" *Advocate* (New York), 9 November 1985.

51. Letter from Mario Biaggi to *New York Times*, 1 December 1985.

52. "Anglo-Irish Sellout," *Irish People* (New York), 29 November 1985.

53. "Presidential Statement on U.K.-Ireland Agreement Concerning Northern Ireland," *Department of State Bulletin* (January 1986), 56.

Furthermore, the provisions for extensive cross-border security cooperation seemed to imply a new commitment that would severely hamper IRA operations.

In America, the Friends of Ireland considered the Agreement as one of their most significant interventions in Irish politics. Tip O'Neill and Edward Kennedy firmly believed their efforts played a very important role in securing the accord. Without their sustained pressure and influence the British government would have been much less inclined to engage in serious discussions.

Most significantly, the Friends and the Irish government persuaded Ronald Reagan to add his support to the Agreement. The president used his "special relationship" with Margaret Thatcher to further the process of Anglo-Irish discussions. The US contribution to the International Fund marked the first time the American government became officially involved in the Ulster conflict. Journalist Alex Brummer correctly observed:

> Without the encouragement and prodding of the Reagan administration and the sustained pressure for political reform from the United States Congress, Mrs. Thatcher and Garret FitzGerald may never have made it to Hillsborough.[54]

The Friends of Ireland stressed that all the breakthroughs of the Agreement were achieved through political discussion. They hoped that this example would persuade Irish Americans of the futility of supporting violence and that constitutional action was the only way to bring about change in Ireland. The Friends were filled with optimism that, as the benefits of the Anglo-Irish Agreement became increasingly apparent, the republican network in America would decline to insignificance.

54. Alex Brummer, "The Greening of the White House," *Guardian* (Manchester), 26 November 1985.

CHAPTER 10

◆

FROM THE ANGLO-IRISH AGREEMENT

TO THE NORAID SPLIT, 1985–1993

◆

Constitutional nationalist euphoria over the Anglo-Irish Agreement gradually diminished. Despite the establishment of an Intergovernmental Conference, serious grievances within the Catholic community still persisted. There were continued disputes between the British and Irish governments. Yet, while a range of problems remained, there were significant benefits for constitutional nationalism. In successive Northern Ireland elections after 1985, Sinn Féin's vote leveled off at around 11.5 percent; in the Republic of Ireland it secured less than 2 percent of the vote. The SDLP, on the other hand, regained its position as the majority electoral voice of northern nationalists. The Anglo-Irish Agreement, therefore, achieved one of its principal objectives and contributed to the stemming of republican support.

The SDLP's association with the Anglo-Irish Agreement also brought a number of benefits in the United States. John Hume, in particular, was singled out for lavish praise and multiple honorary awards. Newspaper articles and commentaries compared him to Martin Luther King and

Ghandi, while editorials contrasted his "heroic devotion" to reconciliation with "patriotic sympathizers cheering on bloodshed from the air-conditioned comfort of America."[1]

John Hume capitalized on this positive publicity and began appealing for financial contributions to the SDLP. He used his connections on Capitol Hill to establish contacts with the National Democratic Institute, a private organization that supplied funds throughout the world for the promotion of "democratic government." The NDI was sufficiently impressed with the SDLP's work that it donated thirty thousand dollars. An affiliated organization, American Trade Union, also made a contribution of $50,000.[2] Both Unionist and Sinn Féin politicians strongly condemned this US financial support, claiming it provided an important boost to the SDLP's electoral campaigns.[3]

John Hume's American connections also brought dividends through the creation of Boston-Derry Ventures in October 1987. This scheme was given impetus by the network of individuals, committed to constitutionalism, who helped organize the Kennedy Library Symposiums in the early 1980s. It aimed at encouraging economic development in Derry through commercial links with Boston. The scheme was eventually endorsed by Mayor Raymond Flynn, following his break with Noraid and subsequent association with constitutional nationalism.[4]

In May 1988, Mayor Flynn and John Hume helped organize the first of a series of Boston Irish Trade Festivals at which Derry firms could display their products. These annual fairs have become an important source of attracting investment and establishing overseas markets. One of the scheme's biggest successes came in 1989 when O'Connell Development

1. *Chicago Tribune*, 18 November 1986. This extremely positive portrayal of Hume has continued into the 1990s and can be seen in articles such as James Clarity, "No Friend to Protestants and Nemesis of I.R.A.," *New York Times*, 4 November 1993, and Jack Holland, "John Hume: A Man for all Reasons," *Irish Echo* (New York), 17 March 1994.

2. David Shipler, "Missionaries for Democracy: U.S. Funding of Global Pluralism," *New York Times*, 1 June 1986.

3. Mervyn Pauley, "Money From America Rumpus," *Belfast News Letter*, 24 June 1993.

4. In the late 1970s, Ray Flynn consistently courted Irish-American republicanism, attending Noraid dinners and political rallies. After his election as mayor, however, Flynn was lobbied by John Hume and various Irish Americans who were working for the constitutional approach. He subsequently cut his connections to Noraid and became an enthusiastic supporter of the Boston-Derry Ventures proclaiming, "I'd rather build up Ireland than blow it up!"

Company of Massachusetts decided to invest $65 million in a new Foyle-side retail and office complex.[5]

Another investment organization which formed at this time was the Irish American Partnership (IAP). With national headquarters in Boston, the IAP received annual contributions of over $500,000 through solicitation of Irish-American businessmen and professionals. The "Partnership" sought to encourage peace in Ulster through support for economic development and education. It has thus provided funding for cross-community business ventures such as the Townsend Enterprise Park in Belfast and established education grants in "disadvantaged" areas of Derry. As with the Boston-Derry Ventures, the Irish-American Partnership has offered Irish Americans the opportunity to support economic investment as a means of reconciliation in Northern Ireland.[6]

The International Fund for Ireland

The most publicized and controversial source of US financial assistance to Ulster has been the International Fund for Ireland (IFI), established as part of the Anglo-Irish Agreement. The British and Irish governments, SDLP, and Friends of Ireland have devoted considerable energies to ensure this aid is maintained. Supporters claim it has become one of the most positive aspects of the Agreement and has gained increasing acceptance.

The concept of US financial aid to support the Anglo-Irish Agreement was discussed from early 1985, but the details were formulated during the last four months of negotiations. The International Fund was strongly endorsed by constitutional nationalists and their allies in Congress, but there was considerable apprehension on the British side. Margaret Thatcher initially believed that financial aid should be based on voluntary donations and not become an official government aid program. Some officials in the Northern Ireland Office were unenthusiastic about asking for international aid, because they saw it as a bad reflection on their handling of the province. Others rightly predicted that unionists would view the cash as a bribe to sweeten the Anglo-Irish Agreement.[7]

5. Boston-Derry Ventures was part of a wider economic development scheme, which included the city of Galway. Since 1989 Derry has attracted over $40 million in business from the United States. See "Humeland," *The Economist*, 27 November 1993.

6. *Irish-American Partnership Newsletter*, Winter/Spring 1995.

7. Garret FitzGerald, interview with author, 19 December 1990.

In July 1985, Seán Donlon traveled to Washington and received assurances from the White House and Capitol Hill that financial support for a political breakthrough would be forthcoming. Following this assurance, British negotiators became more receptive to the scheme. Diplomats from both countries traveled to the US in the weeks before the Agreement was signed. Their efforts culminated in the Oval Office press conference at which Reagan and O'Neill made their first public pledge of US cash, maintaining it was the realization of Jimmy Carter's promise in 1977.

Legislation providing for financial aid through the IFI became politically entangled in Congress. The Reagan administration began working on a bill to provide $250 million over five years. This aid was to be given mostly in the form of loans, guarantees, and business incentives. Senator Edward Kennedy and other members of the Friends opposed this measure. They supported a bill providing $250 million in cash. Then, as the two sides tried to reach a compromise, the aid package became entangled in a new extradition treaty between Britain and the United States.[8]

In response to the series of court decisions favorable toward IRA fugitives in the early 1980s, the Reagan and Thatcher administrations began formulating revisions of the 1972 Anglo-American extradition treaty. In March 1985 representatives from both governments met in Washington and drafted new guidelines to restrict the political exception clause. Under a Supplementary Treaty, crimes such as aircraft hijacking, murder, hostage-taking, and offenses involving firearms, explosives, and damage to property were separated from genuine political actions. The revised legislation allowed extradition for crimes committed before the new treaty was ratified.[9]

President Reagan claimed the Supplementary Treaty was essential in the battle against world terrorism and presented it to the Senate in July 1985. During debates in the Committee on Foreign Relations, however, significant opposition developed. Senator Joe Biden (D, Del.) was particularly vocal in his criticisms and continually raised awkward questions about legal abuses in Northern Ireland. At public hearings between September and November, Irish-American activists gave impassioned testimony against the treaty as a betrayal of the US's historic role of pro-

8. The financial contribution to the IFI also encountered problems due to concern for the mounting US deficit and provisions imposed by the Gramm-Rudman-Hollings Act.

9. The Supplementary Treaty also eliminated a fugitive's ability to appeal to the statute of limitations and extended the period in which a requesting party could prepare its extradition case.

viding sanctuary to the politically oppressed. Following these debates a
majority on the Senate committee opposed the treaty in its original form.
It appeared that the new legislation would have to be diluted or perhaps
quietly forgotten.[10]

In March 1986, however, the Supplementary Treaty was unexpectedly
revived by a series of favorable developments. Senator Richard Lugar
(R, Ind.), chairman of the Foreign Relations Committee, linked the political battle over the International Fund to extradition. In a time-honored
practice of holding one measure hostage for another, he introduced a
package under which the financial aid could not be released until the
Supplementary Treaty was passed. Lugar hoped thereby to persuade the
Democratic senators opposing the treaty, a number of whom were members of the Friends of Ireland, to moderate their position.

On April 15, 1986, US jets bombed Tripoli in retaliation for Libyan-
engineered attacks on American targets in Europe. As the planes were allowed to take off from Britain, there was enthusiastic support for Margaret
Thatcher in Washington. The prime minister made it known that passage
of the Supplementary Treaty would be appreciated as reward for British
assistance. Leading US newspapers acknowledged this debt and generally
supported an editorial line in the *Wall Street Journal*, which argued, "It
would be unthinkably squalid if the Senate Foreign Relations Committee
repaid Thatcher's courage by refusing to help with her own terrorist
problems."[11]

Encouraged by these changed circumstances, the Reagan administration launched a second initiative to secure passage of the new extradition
treaty. Northern Ireland secretaries Douglas Hurd and Tom King flew to
Washington to assist the lobbying effort. They joined with Reagan aides
in drawing attention to the IRA's weapons links with Libya. On May 31
the president himself made a direct radio appeal to the Senate commit-

10. In Boston, a small group of activists who were dedicated to constitutional nationalism formed the Committee for a New Ireland. The organization subsequently based its operations in Washington and provided organizational support for congressional staffers who
needed to get information on Northern Ireland. When the vote on the International Fund
was pending in March 1986, the CNI arranged for a fact-finding trip to Ulster for aides to
Senators Lugar, Pell, and Kennedy.

11. "In Aid of Terrorism," *Wall Street Journal*, 29 April 1986. Some analysts allege
British bases were used specifically because Reagan and Thatcher knew this would help
passage of the Supplementary Treaty. See William Kennedy, "Why Were F-111's Misused
in the Raid on Libya?" *Chicago Tribune*, 19 August 1986.

tee, emphasizing Margaret Thatcher's vital support against "Qaddafi's terrorism."

Intense negotiations continued but the recalcitrant senators remained sceptical about the Supplementary Treaty. Consequently, on June 3, Richard Lugar offered a compromise to eliminate "possession of firearms" and "conspiracy" from the list of offenses to which political exception could no longer be claimed. He also included provisions that "race, religion, nationality or political opinions" should not be used as grounds for extradition, and that judges could consider the fairness of the British court system in making their decisions. Despite continued debate, these changes were sufficient to make the Supplementary Treaty acceptable to most Democrats, and on June 12 they voted 15–2 in its favor. The treaty was then ratified 87–10 by Congress on July 17, 1986.

Democrats on the Senate committee claimed they had won significant concessions. Many legal analysts, however, saw the treaty as an important victory for the Reagan and Thatcher governments. They argued convincingly that the new provisions had severely undermined the political offense exception. Irish-American republicans immediately saw the potential threat the treaty posed to their cause and characterized it as "an expeditious means for the United States to deliver Irish nationalists to the tyranny of the British legal system."[12]

Moments after ratification of the Supplementary Treaty, the US financial contribution to the International Fund was passed without further opposition. The aid bill finally adopted provided $120 million in cash over a three-year period. It granted $50 million in 1986 and two payments of $35 million for each subsequent year. The Canadian government joined America and promised installments amounting to $10 million, while New Zealand provided a fixed figure of $300,000. Cash would later be provided by the European Community.

The Irish and British governments appointed a seven-member independent board of managers to administer this aid. Its first chairman was Charles Brett, former head of the Northern Ireland Housing Executive. Donor countries were represented by observers nominated by their respective governments and every attempt was taken to ensure the appearance of impartiality.

12. Robert E. Connolly, *The Connolly Report* (Fort Wayne, Ind.: Cuchullain Publications, 1988), 114.

The International Fund Board began meeting regularly in late 1986 and soon received its first $50 million from the United States. In accordance with the wishes of donor countries, the IFI earmarked three-quarters of its cash for Northern Ireland and the remainder for border areas of the Irish Republic. Two venture capital companies, with budgets of $5 million, were established in Belfast and Dundalk to stimulate business. By the end of its first three years the Fund announced it had supported over 1,300 projects with a "potential" of six to eight thousand new jobs.[13]

Although the IFI's annual reports emphasized its achievements, serious problems surfaced beginning in 1988. After the US had fulfilled its initial financial obligations an intense debate grew in Congress over successive donations. This discussion was sharpened by concern for the growing national deficit and by reports the IFI was funding inappropriate projects. The *Washington Post* and the *Wall Street Journal* were particularly critical of the large sums of money being given to hoteliers to develop their already elaborate facilities. Controversy also raged over the allocation of $1.9 million for a British government marine research vessel. Irish-American groups were incensed that these grants should have been awarded while economically deprived nationalist areas in Belfast and Derry received only meager funds.[14]

For 1989 Congress reduced support for the International Fund to $10 million. Before debates on the 1990 allocation, a number of congressmen traveled to Belfast and sharply criticized the IFI's distribution of grants. The most prominent critic, Brian Donnelly (D, Mass.), chairman of the Friends of Ireland, met with Charles Brett and Tom King in January 1989. He made clear that his continued backing for the Fund was conditional upon cash being targeted to "disadvantaged areas."

The IFI board was particularly sensitive to this criticism especially since a congressional hearing on its performance was due in April 1989. Partly from this pressure, the board granted $6.9 million to two projects in West Belfast on 17 February. This was its largest allocation to date and promised the creation of five hundred jobs.

At the hearing before the House Subcommittee on Europe on April 26, Brian Donnelly acknowledged the IFI had made some mistakes but

---

13. In its 1994 annual report, the IFI claimed that it had funded thousands of projects since its inception which had helped create over 20,000 jobs.

14. John Cussack, "Fund a Target for Controversy and Criticism from its Birth," *Irish Times* (Dublin), 28 February 1994.

asserted that these were being corrected. He highlighted the recent grants to West Belfast and said he had been assured that future awards would be channeled to areas of high unemployment. Donnelly also mentioned that special consideration would be given to nationalist areas so that future grant proposals would be better packaged.

Militant Irish-American groups organized testimony against the IFI. Father Seán McManus complained that 87 percent of its grants in Fermanagh were going to Protestants and thus supporting anti-Catholic discrimination. Others singled out specific abuses of grant money and condemned the continued refusal to finance the Conway Mill Project in West Belfast.[15] House Speaker Tom Foley (D, Wash.), a leading member of the Friends, strongly opposed these groups. After consultations with British and Irish diplomats, he accused them of being IRA supporters aiming to destroy the Anglo-Irish Agreement. Foley and other Friends successfully undermined opposition to the Fund and ensured the US contribution was raised to $20 million for the following year.

In 1989 John McGuckian, deputy head of Ulster Television, became the new IFI chairman. He revised methods of screening applicants in order to respond to areas of economic need. Grants were directed toward five enterprise centers in Belfast, local employment training schemes, and several cross-border cooperative ventures. By the end of 1992, 70 percent of all IFI grants were going to "disadvantaged areas" through community-led regeneration projects. Congress approved another $19.6 million donation, bringing the total US contribution to $190 million.

With this new focus the IFI disarmed many of its former critics. In the early 1990s, allocations included $400,000 to Father Des Wilson's Springhill Community Center in West Belfast and a $1.9 million development grant for the nationalist village of Coalisland, County Tyrone. Supporters of the IFI characterize it as an important catalyst for economic development. They say makes a valuable contribution to reconciliation in Ulster.

The Friends of Ireland remain the Fund's most vocal adherents on Capitol Hill. Senator Edward Kennedy expressed the opinion of most of its members when he stated:

15. Conway Mill is a former linen factory converted into a center for community projects, cultural events, and business development. The IFI board and the British government both refused financial aid for the scheme because of alleged links with the IRA. Supporters of the project subsequently established the Doors of Hope charity in New Jersey to solicit donations.

For the vast majority of people on both sides of the conflict in Northern Ireland, the Fund has become a symbol of hope for a better future. It is helping to reduce the violence, mistrust, and discrimination that have plagued Northern Ireland for too long.[16]

While the most visible role of the Friends of Ireland in this period was supporting the International Fund, they have continued working with the Irish government and SDLP against Irish-American republicanism. Despite the fact that their St. Patrick's Day statements strongly criticized British policy in the late 1980s, they constantly condemned those who supported the IRA. The Friends also maintained their efforts against the Ad Hoc Committee in Washington, a task made significantly easier by the resignation in 1988 of Mario Biaggi after his conviction on corruption charges.[17]

Extradition, Deportation, and Gunrunning

While Irish-American republicans were continuously challenged by constitutional nationalists, they also faced renewed extradition and deportation proceedings against IRA fugitives. The British government, buoyed by ratification of the Supplementary Treaty and with full cooperation from the Reagan administration, reopened its legal battles. There were eventually important reversals of earlier court decisions.

Following Judge Robert Aguilar's 1983 decision against the extradition of William Quinn, the case was sent to the Ninth Circuit Court of Appeals. In February 1986 this court reached a majority decision. While Judge Betty Fletcher accepted that Quinn's activities in England were part of the Ulster conflict, Judges Stephen Reinhardt and Ben Duniway disagreed and supported Britain's extradition request.

16. Michael Scanlon, "Ted Kennedy: Staying the Course," *Irish-America* (May 1991), 25–31. Despite the views of Kennedy and company, the Fund still has prominent critics. In May 1994 Congressman Scott Klung (R, Wis.) released a statement entitled "The Leprechauns are Looting Our Gold." Klung alleged the IFI was wasting US tax dollars supporting projects such as a model railway and a golf video made by Jack Nicklaus. A number of prominent critics in Ireland, including Bernadette Devlin/McAliskey, claim US money does not promote reconciliation and only helps rich businessmen get richer. *Inside Edition: ABC*, 3 November 1884.

17. On 4 August 1988, Biaggi was convicted of tax evasion and receiving bribes as part of the Wedtech scandal. He resigned his congressional seat rather than face expulsion by the House Ethics Committee.

Quinn's case was ordered back to District Court where, in light of the new restrictions on political exception, the earlier Aguilar decision was reversed. Defense lawyers bitterly contested this verdict and tried to have a hearing before the Supreme Court. When this strategy failed, Quinn became the first republican extradited from the United States. On October 20, 1986, he was handed over to British agents in San Francisco and returned to England on a Royal Air Force transport plane. After trial at London's Central Criminal Court, Quinn was convicted of the murder of Police Constable Stephen Tibble and given a life sentence.

Greatly encouraged by success in the Quinn case, federal prosecutors and British officials intensified their efforts against Joe Doherty. Though armed with the Supplementary Treaty, they felt their best strategy was to continue deportation proceedings that had already been initiated. On September 19, 1986, an immigration court ruled that Doherty had entered the US illegally and should be deported to the Irish Republic. Doherty was willing to accept this decision, but federal attorneys acting on Britain's behalf claimed such action was "prejudicial to the interests of the United States." The Immigration Service then began unprecedented maneuvers designed to secure Doherty's deportation to Britain.

Doherty fought this move and in March 1987 convinced the Board of Immigration Appeals (BIA) to support his original deportation to the Irish Republic. This victory was short lived, however, as Britain and Ireland signed a new extradition treaty on December 1, 1987. This increased the likelihood that if Doherty was deported to Dublin he could then be extradited to the North. He immediately withdrew his deportation request and renewed an earlier application for political asylum.

The Immigration Service meanwhile referred the earlier favorable decision of the BIA to Attorney General Edwin Meese for review. He reversed the board's decision, claiming that deportation to the UK was in "the best interest of the United States." While the attorney general acted within his powers, it was the first time such an action had been used in a deportation case. Meese's decision clearly showed the determination of the Reagan administration to deliver Doherty to Britain.

On November 14, 1988, the BIA heard Doherty's renewed motion for political asylum and ruled he had a right to proceed with his application. This verdict was again challenged by the Immigration Service and referred to new Attorney General Richard Thornburgh. On June 30, 1989, following Ed Meese's earlier example, he rejected the BIA decision, denied Doherty's right to a political asylum hearing, and supported his deportation to Britain.

Doherty's lawyers then brought the case to the Second Circuit Court of Appeals. On June 19, 1990, the court allowed the request for an asylum hearing. The court also criticized Richard Thornburgh for allowing political and foreign policy considerations to influence his decision against Doherty.[18]

In December 1990 the attorney general petitioned the Supreme Court for a review of the Appeals Court decision allowing Doherty a political asylum hearing. Thornburgh also asked for a judgment on his right to employ foreign policy considerations in such cases.

As the Supreme Court prepared for deliberation, Doherty's judicial ordeal became the focus of numerous investigative reports on network television and the press. He received support from Cardinals Tomás O Fiaich and John O'Connor of New York, the UN high commissioner for refugees, and politicians ranging from Jesse Jackson to the conservative Orrin Hatch (R, Utah). Before the Supreme Court decision, 132 congressmen signed a resolution endorsing Doherty's right to an asylum hearing and bail. Gary Ackerman (D, N.Y.) even offered $100,000 of his personal assets as security. Resolutions supporting Doherty were passed in many state assemblies while New York City Council renamed the street intersection outside his cell in the Metropolitan Correctional Center "Joe Doherty Corner."[19]

During presentation of evidence before the Supreme Court, federal attorneys stressed that legal action against Doherty was part of a long-

18. While waiting for the asylum decision, Doherty unsuccessfully applied for bail. Despite claiming he was no longer in the IRA, Judge Miriam Cedarbaum ruled there was a risk Doherty would flee if released.

19. Martin Dillon, *Killer in Clowntown: Joe Doherty, the IRA, and the Special Relationship* (London: Hutchinson, 1992), 214–17. Doherty was temporarily encouraged by developments in the Peter McMullan case. On December 23, 1986, the day the Supplementary Treaty took effect, British officials blocked McMullan's deportation to the Irish Republic by submitting a new extradition request. In July 1991, a federal court in Manhattan ruled that the treaty was an illegal bill of attainder which determined guilt without the protection of a judicial trial. The effectiveness of the Supplementary Treaty seemed significantly reduced and Doherty hoped that this might eventually have a beneficial effect on his case.

Later, however, the US Court of Appeals, Second Circuit, overturned the ruling that the Supplementary Treaty contravened American law. McMullan then launched an unsuccessful appeal against this decision before the US Supreme Court. At the beginning of 1995, McMullan was continuing his legal battle from the Metropolitan Correctional Center in New York.

standing policy of cooperation with Britain to prevent the US becoming a sanctuary for IRA terrorists. Defense lawyers claimed that the government was exceeding its bounds in trying to interfere with the judiciary and the nine lower court decisions in Doherty's favor.

In a shattering blow to Doherty and his supporters, the Supreme Court, on July 15, 1992, ruled in favor (5–3) of the government. The decision denied a political asylum hearing and concluded Attorney General Thornburgh was acting within his authority in overturning the decision of the Board of Immigration Appeals. On 19 February Doherty was deported to Britain and returned to Crumlin Road Jail from which he had escaped eleven years earlier.[20]

The Doherty case showed the determination and lengths to which the British and US governments were prepared to go against IRA fugitives. Despite a sustained Irish-American publicity campaign, successive US administrations were unremitting in their pursuit of Doherty. Many analysts suggest this was a further reward for British support during the 1986 raid on Tripoli.[21]

The US government's commitment to combating the IRA was also manifested through the deployment of greater resources to FBI units working against Irish-American republicanism. Special agent Frank Schulte in New York, the central figure in this group, was joined by other key FBI personnel such as Brendan Cleary in Boston and Ed Buckley in Chicago. The unit they forged expanded surveillance operations and nurtured informers within the Irish-American community, allegedly through the inducement of instant green cards to illegal immigrants.[22] Frequent liaison with British and Irish security forces produced detailed knowledge of IRA financial and military requirements.[23] With information from these

20. Doherty was later transferred to the Maze prison. He is currently fighting the British government's decision not to reduce his sentence for time served in the United States. As of March 1995 Doherty has been unsuccessful in his appeals against this decision.

21. Martin Dillon, *Killer in Clowntown*, 341–47.

22. Pat Farrelly, "Blackmail," *Irish Voice* (New York), 1 September 1990 and Terry Golway, "Irish-American Community Gets Close F.B.I. Surveillance," *New York Observer*, 17 August 1992. There were even reports that the FBI was using routine murder investigations to collect information on Irish-American activists. See John Conroy, "The Irish Connection," *The Reader* (Chicago), 10 April 1992.

23. Members of the FBI team made trips to Ireland during which they met with leading British and Irish security personnel. British intelligence also established a liaison office with the FBI at their embassy in Washington. See Mark Urban, *Big Boys' Rules: The S.A.S. and the Secret War Against the I.R.A.* (London: Faber, 1992), 126.

sources, Schulte's team were responsible for the arrest of prominent IRA fugitives, including Joe Doherty, and the infiltration of extremely important gunrunning conspiracies.

In the mid-eighties, partly because of the success of this FBI team, the IRA increasingly used Eastern Europe and the Middle East, especially Libya, as sources for weapons. Yet America remained important to Provo gunrunners, primarily for sophisticated bomb components and missiles.

Throughout the 1980s one of the IRA's principal objectives was to acquire the means to bring down British helicopters. These aircraft were a major strategic advantage against the Provos, particularly in South Armagh, where they were used for surveillance, troop deployment, and supply. Helicopters were much less vulnerable to attack than motorized convoys. The IRA was thus determined to overcome British air power, and it was to the US they turned for the required technology and supplies. Provo arms buyers, always willing to acquire Armalites and pistols, were from the mid-eighties onward increasingly looking to obtain missiles. One of the first conspiracies broken in this period involved a network of eight IRA volunteers and sympathizers in Massachusetts. In early 1985, acting on information supplied by informants, an undercover FBI agent began frequenting known republican bars in the Boston area and offering to supply weapons. Jackie McDonald, an Irish American with links to organized crime, told the agent he had connections with the IRA. McDonald arranged a meeting between the FBI man and Noel Murphy, an Irish citizen living in Boston. After a number of contacts, Murphy placed an order for one hundred M-16s, 2 submachine guns, and a Redeye surface-to-air missile, for a total cost of $73,000.[24]

In spring 1986, the IRA sent Cairan Hughes to Boston to arrange shipment of these weapons back to Ireland. On May 20 the undercover agent met with Hughes and Murphy at a hotel outside Boston. Also present were five Irish citizens and Irish Americans who were to help load the weapons. They were later identified as John FitzGerald, Roy Paul Willey, James Boyle, Stephen McDonald, and Michael McLoughlin.

The FBI agent told Cairan Hughes that the weapons would be delivered by private jet and they left with Noel Murphy to Hanscom airfield. The rest remained in the hotel along with two other federal

---

24. J. L. Stone, "Irish Terrorism Investigations," *F.B.I. Law Enforcement Bulletin* 56 (October 1987), 23.

agents. At an appointed time, all the conspirators were simultaneously arrested.[25]

A federal grand jury indicted the men on violation of the Arms Export Control Act. Murphy and Hughes were further charged with illicit weapons dealing. During their trial in October 1986, both men unsuccessfully contested government charges. They received jail sentences of nine and eight years respectively. The others entered guilty pleas and were sentenced to terms ranging from six to eighteen months.[26]

The most important and sophisticated scheme to obtain missiles, centered around a group who would later be known as the Boston Three. One of the central figures in the conspiracy was Richard Clark Johnson, an electronics expert employed by the Mitre Corporation in Massachusetts. Johnson had top secret clearance to handle classified government information. He used his expertise to help the IRA with remote-control bombs and eventually began developing advanced rocket systems for use against British helicopters.

Johnson established contacts with the IRA during trips to Ireland in the mid-seventies. While working for the Northrop Corporation in California, he began to send FX-401 tone frequency switches to the Provos. The switch has a microchip decoder that responds only to an encoded radio signal. When the decoder is attached to a bomb, the operator can activate the detonator with a digitally encoded tone. These remote-controlled devices were treasured by the IRA, as they gave much more flexibility than traditional bombs with command wires or timers.

25. Following his conviction, Noel Murphy fought a protracted legal battle in which he claimed his trial was unfair because prosecuting attorneys removed all Irish Americans from the jury in Boston. An appeal based on this contention was rejected by the US Supreme Court in 1989. Federal prosecutors alleged he was a threat to US national security and thus could not be released on bail. Therefore, when in the spring of 1994 he was deported to Ireland, he had already served more than two years beyond his original sentence.

26. Shortly after the "Boston Eight" case, FBI agents broke a gunrunning scheme to the INLA. The plot centered around Bill Norton, a prominent Hollywood screenwriter, who tried to ship a consignment of assault rifles and machine pistols to Ireland via France. He was apprehended in Le Havre and subsequently sentenced, along with three INLA volunteers, to four years' imprisonment (Jack Holland and Henry McDonald, *INLA Deadly Divisions: The Story of One of Ireland's Most Ruthless Terrorist Organisations,* (Dublin: Torc, 1994), 147–48. In February 1989, federal agents arrested IRA man Donal Moyna in New York. He was carrying $13,500 in counterfeit $50 bills. They were believed to be part of a batch of fake notes seized in Dublin in 1988 which were being used to finance IRA arms supplies. Moyna was subsequently given a four month sentence and deported to the Irish Republic.

In 1984 the security forces in Northern Ireland defused a number of bombs with FX-401 switches. They sent code numbers on the devices to the FBI, which traced them to Johnson. Johnson initially denied any knowledge of the switches, but in 1986, after further inquiry, he said they were for a security system to be installed in the house of a wealthy Irish businessman. Though federal agents were sceptical of this explanation, they suspended their investigation of Johnson.[27]

Following these interrogations, Johnson, wary of FBI surveillance, temporarily ended his contacts with the IRA. In the mid-1980s, however, the Provos obtained a number of SAM-7 missiles from Libya. They remained ineffective because British helicopters were equipped with electronic jamming devices and practiced low-flying at speed. To counteract these defenses the IRA reestablished contact with Johnson and persuaded him to work on a missile incorporating a proximity fuse. With such a feature the rocket did not have to hit its target directly to explode. This would greatly increase the potential of bringing down aircraft.

Johnson received assistance in this scheme from Gerald Hoy, a computer instructor at Penn State University who sympathized with the republican cause. They were also joined by Christina Reid, an engineering student at San Francisco University, who acted as a courier for the group.[28]

While Johnson worked on this scheme, a series of developments again brought him to the attention of federal agents. In November 1987 Irish detectives raided the Dublin home of Peter Maguire, suspected of being a leading IRA explosives experts. They discovered cryptic letters describing electronic components for use in bombs. When these letters were sent to the FBI for analysis, agent Brendan Cleary, who had worked on the earlier FX-401 switches case, recognized the handwriting as that of Johnson.[29]

In the summer of 1988, after obtaining approval from the Foreign Intelligence Surveillance Court, the FBI tapped Johnson's phone, intercepted his mail, and installed a bug in his car. They recorded a meeting between Johnson and Peter Maguire on February 15, 1989, during which the two men discussed anti-helicopter devices, proximity fuses, and

27. Ronald Kessler, *The F.B.I.* (New York: Pocket Books, 1993), 311–18.

28. John Barron, "Breaking the I.R.A.'s American Connection," *Reader's Digest* 138 (April 1991).

29. Irish authorities also revealed that Johnson had been stopped and questioned by Gárdaí while traveling in a car driven by Art Sherwin, an alleged IRA recruitment officer.

remote controlled bombs. When Maguire returned to Ireland, federal agents secretly searched his luggage and found electronic diagrams and plans for a radar gun modified to signal a detonator.[30]

The FBI also recorded meetings between Johnson and Peter Quigley, an IRA technical expert temporarily based in the United States. Both men spent the weekend of April 28, 1989, at Johnson's parents' home on Cape Cod, working on details of the rocket system.[31] Before one of the meetings with Quigley the FBI tried to break into Johnson's car and replace the recording bug. An agent was in the process of doing this in the parking lot of the Mitre Corporation when Johnson inadvertently spotted him. The agent was unable to explain his actions so the FBI decided to arrest Johnson and all the other conspirators. Only Peter Maguire escaped and eventually fled to Africa.[32]

Evidence given during the trial in May 1990 revealed the depth of FBI surveillance in the case and the high-level of cooperation between US, British, and Irish authorities. All four defendants pleaded innocent, claiming they were merely amateur radio enthusiasts and rocket hobbyists.

The government produced a massive body of evidence to prove their case, including a prototype rocket launcher. Gerald Hoy changed his plea to guilty in the hope of a reduced sentence, thus shattering the case for the defense. On June 18, 1990, all four were found guilty. At a sentencing hearing on August 20 Johnson received ten years, Quigley eight years, Christina Reid three. Following his guilty plea, Hoy's sentence was reduced from eight to two years.[33]

30. Kevin Cullen, "Piercing the Perfect Cover," *Boston Sunday Globe*, 16 July 1989.

31. Quigley also wanted powerful Kevlar cable for a barrage balloon and a .50–caliber rifle, both to be used against helicopters.

32. Maguire worked for Nigerian Airlines for three years. When he went on a business trip to South Africa in December 1992, he was arrested but successfully fought a US extradition request. When he returned to Ireland in February 1993, he was taken into custody by officers of the Gárda Special Branch. In April a District Court in Dublin ruled that Maguire could be extradited to the United States; he was delivered to federal authorities in Boston in February 1994. In April he pleaded guilty to gunrunning, largely to preclude a new trial in which Johnson and his associates would be obliged to testify. Maguire later received a six-year prison sentence for violating the US Arms Export Control Act.

33. Marie Crowe, "Conviction of I.R.A. Conspirators a Blow to Provos," *Sunday Tribune*, 24 June 1990. With the service of noted attorney Alan Dershowitz, Johnson appealed his conviction all the way to the Supreme Court. Despite fervent advocacy, the court upheld the original sentence. In 1994 supporters of Johnson began a letter-writing campaign to petition President Clinton to commute his prison term. At the beginning of 1995 Johnson was still waiting for a response.

The conviction of those involved in the Johnson case was one of the most important victories in the FBI's activities against the republican network in America. It eliminated an IRA scheme to develop its own weapons technology rather than relying on black-market arms dealers— a scheme that would have given the Provos a spectacular propaganda coup and an important strategic advantage over British helicopters.

Shortly after the arrest of Johnson and his group, the FBI uncovered another major conspiracy to deliver guns and missiles to the IRA. The scheme involved a group of republicans based in Ft. Lauderdale, Florida. On November 13, 1989, Alan Budoff, an FBI informer, told federal agents he had been approached by the IRA about the possibility of acquiring weapons.

The FBI persuaded Budoff to arrange a meeting with the men at which an undercover agent would pose as an international arms dealer. On November 20 Budoff and the FBI agent met Kevin McKinley and Séamus Moley, both IRA volunteers from Crossmaglen. They negotiated to buy explosives, detonators, and .50-caliber sniper rifles. The conspirators also wanted a Stinger missile, highly prized because it was capable of breaching the electronic defenses on British helicopters. On January 12, 1990, after satisfactory terms had been agreed, Moley placed $47,000 in a safety deposit box, which was to be transferred to the federal agents after the weapons were delivered.

Joe McColgan, an IRA weapons specialist, flew in from Belfast to check the quality of the merchandise. The FBI's plan was to switch a fake Stinger missile, let it be shipped to Ireland, and allow authorities on the other side of the Atlantic to apprehend those involved. Unexpectedly, however, McColgan placed the real missile in his car. The switch could not be made, so all the conspirators were arrested on January 12, 1990.

The three defendants were held without bail until their trial in November 1990. Defense attorneys claimed entrapment and attempted to destroy the credibility of informer Alan Budoff by revealing his history of psychiatric problems and drug abuse. The three men were nevertheless found guilty of the main charges. In June 1991 Judge Norman Roettger imposed sentences of more than four years on all of the defendants, the longest possible term under sentencing laws.[34]

34. In November 1992 Séamus Moley, Kevin McKinley, and twelve others were indicted in a related arms case. The men were linked to a conspiracy to supply the IRA with bomb detonators, a stinger misslie, and .50-caliber rifles. In April 1994, six of the defendants were acquitted by a jury in Tucson; charges against a number of others were

These FBI gunrunning convictions and the extradition of IRA fugitives severely challenged the Irish-American republican network. Despite these pressures, militant nationalist groups carried on their activities with unremitting determination. The Irish American Unity Conference and American Irish Political Education Committee, in particular, played an important role in publicizing human rights issues in Northern Ireland. They highlighted allegations that the security forces were implementing a shoot-to-kill policy and focused public attention on controversial incidents. They also played a prominent role in the Guildford Four and Birmingham Six campaigns against the wrongful imprisonment of Irishmen convicted of IRA bomb attacks in England. Both organizations established offices in Washington, hired professional lobbyists to work for their agenda, and paid for a number of congressmen to participate in fact-finding tours of Northern Ireland.[35]

An active new group formed to publicize these human rights issues had the unlikely name of American Protestants for Truth About Ireland (APTI). It was formed in 1986 by Rachel Hoffman, a German-American Protestant with no family ties to Ireland. She and others who were concerned with human rights violations made several investigative trips to Belfast. Through its monthly *Advocacy Letter*, the APTI produced detailed information on shoot-to-kill cases, leaks by the security forces to loyalists, and on judicial abuse.[36]

The MacBride Principles

The most successful of these human rights campaigns is for the MacBride Principles. The campaign was primarily a response to successive independent studies that showed significant levels of Catholic economic disadvantage, despite enactment of a Fair Employment Act in

---

dropped. (For details see Brian Rohan, "High Noon in Tucson," *Irish Voice*, 13 April 1994.) In the spring of 1995, however, Moley and McKinley, as part of a bargain with government prosecutors, pleaded guilty to possessing bomb detonators and transporting them from Tucson, via New York, to the IRA. In return, three other charges against both men were dropped and they will not be forced to testify against others indicted in the case. A sentencing hearing is scheduled for June 1995.

35. James Brady, "The Greening of America," *Irish Echo* (New York), 15 December 1993.

36. Rachel Hoffman, correspondence with author, 30 November 1989. See also Pam Henaghen, "Philly Group Counters Old Religious Divisions," *Irish Echo* (New York), 11 November 1989.

1976. The MacBride Principles were aimed at helping correct this problem by pressuring the British government and also ensuring that US companies with operations in Ulster practiced fair employment.

In the late 1960s, the American Congress for Irish Freedom was the first group to express concern about reports that US firms in Northern Ireland were perpetuating discrimination. ACIF attempts to highlight this issue received little response so it remained dormant for several years. By the early 1980s, however, America was the largest foreign investor in Northern Ireland, with more than thirty companies providing 11 percent of its manufacturing jobs. The Irish National Caucus became particularly concerned about continued allegations of discrimination in these firms. During a visit to Northern Ireland in the summer of 1979, Father Seán McManus announced the Caucus would be working along with Father Brian Brady to investigate the problem.

On July 22, 1981, the INC organized a hearing before the Ad Hoc Committee, at which Father Brady testified about substantial anti-Catholic discrimination at American plants. The Caucus persuaded Congressman Richard Ottinger (D, N.Y.) to introduce a bill requiring US companies in Ulster to comply with a set of fair employment guidelines. They were modeled after the Sullivan Principles, formulated in 1977 to ensure that US corporations with holdings in South Africa practiced equal employment opportunities there.[37]

Despite substantial media coverage in Ireland, the Ottinger initiative received little support on Capitol Hill. Father McManus claims, however, that this was the birth of the MacBride Principles as it produced a blueprint to achieve fair employment in US firms.[38] In 1983 New York City Comptroller Harrison Goldin appointed Pat Doherty, a member of his staff, to help formulate guidelines for discrimination in Northern Ireland. Doherty collaborated with the Irish National Caucus and officially launched the nine fair-employment guidelines in November 1984. They were named after Seán MacBride, the respected Irish statesman who had established a close friendship with McManus.

While the MacBride Principles campaign aimed at securing federal legislation and targeted individual companies through shareholders' resolutions, the primary focus was at the state and municipal levels. City and

37. Father Seán McManus, *The MacBride Principles: Genesis and History* (Washington: INC Publications, 1993).

38. Father Seán McManus, interview with author, 11 July 1991.

state governments control large retirement funds for their employees, some of which are invested in companies with operations in Ulster. MacBride activists organized political campaigns to encourage companies in the retirement systems' portfolios to adopt the fair-employment guidelines.[39]

The MacBride campaign generated immediate controversy and attracted strong criticism from a variety of sources. The British government immediately opposed the principles and was initially joined by the FitzGerald administration in Ireland. John Hume, Senator Edward Kennedy, and other members of the Friends also expressed reservations. Hume explained that he did not object to the principles in themselves but felt that energy should be directed instead toward job creation and securing investment. He believed they offered a disincentive to American firms, which would make them less inclined to locate or invest in Northern Ireland. Speaking of US companies, Hume asserted:

> In ordinary human and common sense terms, and I have evidence of this, the likelihood is that they will wish to avoid what they see as extra hassle and go elsewhere. I wish all the effort put into the MacBride campaign would be put into encouraging investment. What is the use of fair employment principles if there are no jobs.[40]

British government officials attacked the second MacBride principle, which asked employers to provide security for the employee both at the workplace and while traveling there. They asserted that no employer could give such security guarantees. The Thatcher administration also suggested that principles 1, 7, and 8, dealing with policies designed to increase the Catholic work force, were extremely ambiguous and might be illegal under the existing Fair Employment Act. In addition, the British disliked the MacBride effort because of what they saw as its simplistic linking of conditions in South Africa with Northern Ireland.

MacBride activists strongly disputed John Hume's argument about the "hassle factor." They argued that fair employment requirements had become normal for US companies since the civil rights legislation of the sixties and would provide no additional problems. MacBride campaign-

39. Helen Booth, *U.S. Companies and Fair Employment practices in Northern Ireland* (Washington: Investor Responsibility Research Center, 1988).

40. John Hume, interview with author, 3 January 1989.

ers claimed that political instability was the principal disincentive to investment in Ulster. As discrimination and inequality in employment contributed to this instability, their elimination, through MacBride legislation, would actually encourage investment in the long term.

In response to legal objections, MacBride activists amplified the original principles in 1986. They also brought litigation against American Brands, a company with holdings in Northern Ireland which refused to introduce a MacBride resolution at its annual general meeting. On May 12, a District Court in New York ruled that the company was at fault and that the MacBride Principles did not violate British law.

The Thatcher administration ignored these changes and launched a concerted effort to destroy the MacBride campaign. The British Information Service in New York and consuls nationwide worked against proposed state and municipal legislation. By the end of 1988, press reports claimed that over $30 million had been spent on this initiative.[41]

As part of this anti-MacBride effort, British ministers made frequent visits to the US to lobby politicians and present arguments against the principles. They financed "experts" from Northern Ireland to testify before state assemblies.[42] The British also hired professional lobbying firms and even persuaded State Department officials to pressure governors not to sign MacBride legislation into law.

One of the most consistent British arguments against the MacBride campaign was that Irish-American republicans were using it, not as a way of improving economic conditions, but to increase instability. BIS officials pointed out that Sinn Féin was the only party in Ulster to give full support to MacBride and claimed the initiative was "a thinly veiled attempt by the IRA to use misguided people in the US for their own interests."[43]

There were some Irish-American republicans, as the British maintained, who worked for MacBride legislation in the belief it would increase instability in Northern Ireland. Their strategy was based on the assumption that if discrimination was eliminated, then Britain could not

---

41. *Sunday News*, 13 November 1988.

42. Among those who participated were Bob Cooper of the Fair Employment Agency, John Cushnahan and Seán Neeson of the Alliance Party, and Paddy Devlin, one of the leading figures in the NICRA.

43. Graham Burton, British Consul-General Los Angeles, quoted in the *Los Angeles Times*, 13 May 1987. A similar argument is presented by John McCarthy, *Dissent from Irish America* (New York: University Press of America, 1993), 130.

use this device as a material incentive to Protestants to preserve the union. Republicans argued that the basis for loyalism would be eroded and the way opened for a united Ireland.[44]

Yet the MacBride campaign also attracted many individuals and groups who were solely concerned about discrimination. The British government's attempt to characterize MacBride activists as militant republicans infuriated these moderates and increased their determination to pass legislation. Furthermore, the persistent British publicity efforts conveyed the impression they were not totally committed to fair employment in Ulster. This perception actually enhanced the MacBride effort and contributed to its achievements.

The MacBride Principles campaign, as expected by its supporters, was least effective at the federal level. On June 20, 1987, Hamilton Fish (R, N.Y.) and Al D'Amato (R, N.Y.) introduced joint bills to prevent US firms in Northern Ireland from exporting their products back to America unless they were in compliance with MacBride. Although the measure received support from members of the Ad Hoc Committee, it languished in face of strong opposition from both the Reagan and Bush administrations. MacBride activists did persuade leading Democratic politicians to endorse the principles. During the 1988 primaries, Senator Al Gore and Jesse Jackson both backed the campaign. Michael Dukakis, in his bid for the presidency, took pride in the fact that as governor of Massachusetts he had signed MacBride legislation into law and promised he would do the same if elected to the White House.[45]

The primary focus of the shareholder campaign was to bring discrimination to the attention of US companies and persuade them to adopt the MacBride Principles. Irish-American activists worked alongside church groups affiliated with the Interfaith Center for Corporate Responsibility and have submitted resolutions at company annual general meetings since 1985. While investor support for fair employment proposals has been mixed, the campaign has had considerable influence.[46]

In response to a proposed MacBride resolution from investors, the Ford Motor Company agreed to conduct a review of its work force in

44. *Irish People* (New York), 4 June 1988.

45. Laura Flanders, "Principles at Stake in Duke's Bush War," *Fortnight* (Belfast), August 1988.

46. The Interfaith Center for Corporate Responsibility is an ecumenical group which has been active on a number of social issues. It is composed of over 200 Catholic and 24 Protestant organizations which hold more than $500 billion worth of stock.

Northern Ireland. The report was released on September 15, 1987. It defended Ford's recruitment practices but did acknowledge that Catholics were under-represented in senior management and clerical positions. The report prompted the company to devise its own fair employment guidelines to help correct this imbalance.

Despite Ford's efforts, Father Seán McManus demanded more action to improve the status of Catholic employees. He launched a boycott campaign and continued to exert pressure through shareholder resolutions. By 1989 this contributed to important changes. An independent survey of Ford operations in Northern Ireland found that the top two staff positions were held by Catholics, and Catholics were better represented at the managerial level.

Father McManus did acknowledge an improvement at Ford but continued to pressure its board of directors to make even more changes. The Caucus extended boycott campaigns to other firms it claimed were perpetuating discrimination in Ulster. The publicity surrounding these efforts partly contributed to the pledges of several companies, ranging from Proctor and Gamble to Fruit of the Loom, to make "all lawful efforts to implement the fair employment standards embodied in the MacBride Principles."

The MacBride campaign has also contributed to changes within Northern Ireland–based companies. In the early 1980s, Short Brothers engineering works, with a 5 percent Catholic work force, won a lucrative contract with the US Air Force to build Sherpa transport planes. MacBride activists attacked the company's record on Catholic employment and were strongly supported in Congress by Joe Kennedy (D, Mass.).[47] Partly because of this pressure, Shorts developed an affirmative action program which set aside work for minority sub-contractors and established specific goals and deadlines for hiring Catholics. By 1992 the Catholic work force in Shorts had risen to 12.4 percent. The company also led the way in placing restrictions on the display of provocative religious and political emblems in the workplace.[48]

The most noted victories of the MacBride campaign have been at the state and municipal levels. The first bill was introduced in New York City

47. After a controversial visit to Northern Ireland in 1988, Kennedy tabled amendments to the US defense bill requiring Shorts to report on its employment practices.

48. Barry White, "Shorts: How They Have Become One of the Biggest Employers of Catholics in the Province," *Belfast Telegraph*, 19 August 1988. MacBride activists have continued to target Shorts despite its take-over by the Canadian corporation Bombardier.

on December 19, 1984, by Councilman Sal Albanese and became the
model for legislation in other areas. These bills were generally moderate,
calling on companies to monitor employment practices in Northern Ireland and adhere to the essence of the MacBride Principles. Though the
progress of legislation was far from unremitting, by 1994 fifteen states
and more than thirty cities, mostly in the East and Midwest, had passed
MacBride bills.

A number of factors combined to enhance the MacBride campaign.
Perhaps the most significant was the unusually high degree of cooperation between Irish-American organizations. It provided them with a
direct, realizable, and meaningful way of addressing injustice in Northern Ireland which did not necessarily require support for the IRA. A typical example of this concerted action occurred during the 1987 Illinois
state hearings in Chicago. Previous animosities and differences in philosophy were subordinated to a joint commitment to pass legislation. One
journalist observed:

> The MacBride campaign has galvanized the entire Irish-American
> community and focused its attention on Northern Ireland like no other
> issue over the past eighteen years. The emotional strength of an issue
> which seeks basic human rights for Catholics has proved irresistible![49]

The MacBride campaign also benefited from the fact that there was no
monolithic block of forces against it. Constitutional nationalists, in particular, were divided in their reaction. While John Hume remains extremely sceptical of the whole initiative, the Irish government now views
the principles as totally acceptable and a positive contribution to fair employment. Among the Friends of Ireland, Senator Edward Kennedy has
endorsed John Hume's position, but others have praised the campaign
and helped work for legislation.[50]

The MacBride campaign also received momentum from the Sullivan
Principles. Many of the organizations that worked for change in South

49. Seán O Murchu, "Illinois Weighs Up the MacBride Principles," *Irish-America*, December 1987.

50. Even in Britain there was no unified opposition. While the Thatcher administration
campaigned extensively against the principles, the Labour Party has given them conditional
support. In 1986, for example, Peter Archer, shadow secretary of state for Northern Ireland,
submitted an affidavit in the American Brands case supporting the legality of the principles
under British law. Kevin McNamara, Labour spokesman for Northern Ireland, also welcomed aspects of the MacBride initiative.

Africa—liberal groups, church organizations, and African-American coalitions—were naturally supportive of fair employment in Northern Ireland. They saw the MacBride Principles as reasonable and in line with affirmative action policies in the United States.[51] Local politicians, susceptible to organized Irish-American lobbying, have been quick to endorse this view.[52]

Perhaps the most impressive achievement of the MacBride campaign has been its role in hastening reform in Northern Ireland. From 1985 onward, investigations by the Fair Employment Agency revealed significant levels of disadvantage in Catholic employment. In 1987 the Standing Advisory Commission on Human Rights issued sweeping criticisms of existing fair employment legislation and recommended new measures. The Irish government responded to these reports by encouraging reform through the Intergovernmental Conference. While all these domestic pressures influenced the Thatcher government, the MacBride initiative played a crucial role in transforming heightened awareness of discrimination into legislation for change.[53]

The process of reform culminated in the passage of a new Fair Employment Act in 1989. It established compulsory monitoring of all public and private sector employees and the creation of a new Fair Employment Commission with power to investigate and include goals and timetables in affirmative action. It also created a Fair Employment Tribunal to review individual complaints and promised that employers failing to meet obligations under the law would be denied government contracts.

British officials publicly denied the importance of Irish-American pressure, but privately they admitted its pervasive influence. The Thatcher administration launched a publicity drive in the US that showed that the new Fair Employment Act was more comprehensive and effective

51. Minority legislators also supported MacBride because the arguments used by the British to explain continued Catholic disadvantage in Ulster are similar to the reasons given to account for the failure of affirmative action programs in the United States. See *Unfinished Business: The Fight for the MacBride Principles* (New York: Celtic Video, 1993).

52. Jesse Jackson, former mayor of New York David Dinkins, and members of the Congressional Black Caucus have all endorsed the MacBride Principles. In order to nurture African-American support, Father Seán McManus continually tried to link apartheid in South Africa with discrimination in Ulster. He was arrested in a protest outside the South African embassy in December 1984.

53. R. J. Cormack and R. D. Osborne, "Fair Employment: Towards Reform in Northern Ireland," *Policy and Politics* 17, no. 4 (October 1989): 287–94.

than the MacBride Principles. British diplomats stressed that the new act had comprehensive monitoring, goals, timetables, and applied to all companies in Northern Ireland. It also carried penalties, such as the loss of government contracts, which were not part of MacBride. The British hoped that these reforms would effectively cripple the fair employment issue in America.

Although MacBride activists were greatly encouraged by the influence of their efforts, they believed the new Fair Employment Act was inherently flawed and the British could not be trusted to combat discrimination effectively. Problems which developed in the tribunal system and reports that the new law was ineffective encouraged this view. MacBride supporters therefore determined to increase their efforts by launching a "second wave" of legislation aimed at enforcement of the principles.[54]

In December 1990, Mayor Ray Flynn signed legislation that enabled Boston to withdraw public funds invested in companies with operations in Northern Ireland that did not adhere to the MacBride Principles. This money could then be reinvested in firms that were in compliance. In June 1991 New York City adopted a bill requiring city contracts with US companies doing business in Northern Ireland to be based on compliance with MacBride. A similar contract compliance bill was enacted by New York State in October 1992.[55]

The "second wave" of the MacBride campaign also suffered some serious defeats. Activists devoted extensive resources and energy in sponsoring legislation in California, viewed as extremely important because of its large economy. All the bills that passed the state assembly were vetoed by the governor. There were other noted failures in Ohio, New Mexico, and Virginia.[56]

Frustration caused by these defeats contributed to antagonism within the MacBride coalition. Conflicts flared between republican groups strongly endorsing bills with disinvestment provisions and moderates who favored less-stringent penalties. In December 1994, despite these tensions, MacBride supporters held a major conference in New York City

54. See Father Seán McManus, *The Failure of British Fair Employment Laws and the Need for the MacBride Principles* (Washington: INC Publications, 1992).

55. *Unfinished Business: The Fight for the MacBride Principles* (New York: Celtic Video, 1993).

56. At the end of 1994, Governor William Weld refused to consider a cotract-compliance bill for Massachusetts and forced MacBride activists to accept a much weaker piece of legislation.

to celebrate the tenth anniversary of their campaign. Delegates renewed their commitment to work together and pledged to continue their efforts to achieve fair employment in Northern Ireland.

Noraid and the Friends of Irish Freedom

Noraid was one of the most prominent groups working for the MacBride Principles. Its greater involvement in publicity and political activities in the 1980s was a direct consequence of the breakthroughs achieved during the hunger strikes. Martin Galvin led a group who wished to develop a political agenda for Irish-American republicans based on campaigns against Britain's human rights record in Ulster. They hoped successful political activities in the United States would benefit Sinn Féin by highlighting international support for its policies.[57]

The adherents of an increased political role for Noraid were mostly, though not exclusively, second and third-generation Irish Americans. Their leaders tended to be college-educated professionals, familiar with the American political system and convinced they could act as a pressure group to win support for republican issues. They were opposed by an older faction of traditionalists, mostly Irish-born and with little experience of using the American political system. This group believed that involvement in politics would detract from the primary function of raising cash and would force Noraid to compromise its support for the "armed struggle." As antagonism rose between these two Noraid factions in the mid-eighties, a fundamental conflict developed over the group's primary function and future role.

Partly in response to this growing tension, Noraid delegates held a two-day meeting to discuss strategy with Sinn Féin leaders in Dublin during Easter Week 1986. At this conference Gerry Adams fully endorsed politicization, emphasizing the necessity of adding publicity and political lobbying to the original, single objective of fund raising. He stressed how important and successful this work had been during the hunger strikes and that it would be an invaluable support for the political efforts of Sinn Féin in Ireland.

Adams encouraged Noraid leaders to pursue "solidarity politics." This involved forming links with politicians, minority groups, and humanitar-

---

57. Kevin Cullen, "Noraid Seeks Broader Support for I.R.A.," *Boston Globe*, 20 June 1989.

ian organizations, regardless of their views on the IRA's campaign of violence.[58] To calm the fears of Noraid traditionalists, Adams claimed that
this new direction would enhance fund raising. He tried to show that republican supporters, given a greater awareness by publicity and political
campaigns, would actually contribute more to the cause.[59]

In May 1986, Joe Cahill wrote a circular letter to all Irish-American
republicans explaining the necessity for this new emphasis in policy. He
said there would be a restructuring of the Noraid National Executive to
assign responsibility for publicity and political action. Cahill emphasized
that the policy had the full support of the republican movement in Ireland
and all leading Noraid officials.

Despite Cahill's claim of unity, a group of Noraid traditionalists led
by Michael Flannery had strong reservations about the new policy direction. Their reluctance to embrace politicization was further compounded
by developments within the republican movement in Ireland.[60] During the
1986 Sinn Féin Ard Fheis in Dublin, a resolution was proposed to end the
traditional policy of abstention from the Irish parliament. Following an
impassioned debate, the party voted for the proposal and henceforth allowed their elected officials to take seats in the Dáil. This decision was
strongly attacked by Dáithí O Conaill and Ruairí O Brádaigh. They led a
minority of delegates in a walk-out, broke with Gerry Adams, and later
formed a new group called Republican Sinn Féin.

The dropping of abstention had an immediate effect on Noraid. On
November 2, 1986, Martin Galvin reaffirmed the group's "unequivo-
cal moral and political support for Sinn Féin" and claimed, "This tacti-
cal change in policy will ultimately help shorten the war." Soon afterward, however, press reports in Ireland and the US alleged there was a
major divergence of opinion within Irish-American republicanism.[61]
Michael Flannery denied these "rumors" but privately could not reconcile his republicanism with the abstention decision. He tried to resolve
the dispute within Noraid but was opposed by a majority of the National
Executive. Flannery consequently resigned from the organization he had
founded.

58. Adams believed there was considerable potential for developing links with Americans who were active in supporting rebels in South Africa, El Salvador, and Nicaragua.

59. Ted Howell, director of Sinn Féin Foreign Affairs Bureau, interview with author,
2 June 1992.

60. Michael Flannery, correspondence with author, 18 September 1992.

61. *Sunday Press*, 11 January 1987.

Later, along with veteran republicans George Harrison and Joe Stynes, Flannery founded a new organization called Cumann na Saoirse. It was committed to abstention and collecting funds for Republican Sinn Féin. Cumann na Saoirse had only a few activists in New York and New Jersey. Most Noraid members who disagreed with the abstention decision retained their membership, believing they could better resist politicization from inside the group.[62]

Noraid became deeply involved in the MacBride Principles campaign as part of the shift toward publicity and political lobbying. Some traditionalists within Noraid were impressed by the progress of this effort and were partly convinced of the benefits of political activity, while others were hostile and fought against what they saw as the creeping erosion of sacred republican ideals. The politically conservative among these dissidents were further alienated by Noraid's pursuit of "solidarity politics" involving cooperation with liberal and minority groups.[63]

In light of the continued resistance to Noraid's new policies, another high-level conference took place between the National Executive and Sinn Féin in December 1988. Gerry Adams again praised the benefits of publicity and political lobbying, and refused to compromise his support for the new policy direction.[64] When news of this second meeting filtered back to America, the traditionalists were frustrated that no attempt was made to accommodate their views. Some suggested that Noraid establish two separate funds, one for political activity and the other to be used entirely to help prisoners' dependents. In this way the dissidents could continue contributing and know all their cash was being channeled where they wanted it.[65]

At a conference later held in Toledo, Noraid's National Executive refused to endorse the creation of separate funds. They felt that it would weaken their organization and institutionalize division and disunity. The

62. Flannery maintained his uncompromising adherence to militant republicanism. Just before his death on 30 September 1994, he strongly condemned the newly announced IRA cease-fire.

63. John McCarthy, "Irish-American Conservatives and the I.R.A.," *Four Quarters* 3 (Autumn 1989): 6–8. See also Kevin Cullen, "Noraid Splits as Old Guard Shuns Politics," *Boston Globe*, 30 October 1989.

64. *Irish People* (New York), 9 September 1989. Adams's views were reinforced by Sinn Féin representatives who traveled to the US throughout 1988 to assess Noraid operations.

65. Chris Fogarty, vice-chairman of the Friends of Irish Freedom, interview with author, 25 July 1992.

traditionalists subsequently accused Martin Galvin and his supporters of squandering Noraid cash on business trips to Ireland, implying he had accumulated huge bills while staying in Dublin's exclusive Gresham Hotel. Galvin strongly refuted these claims, but the divisions within his organization could no longer be contained.[66]

The conflict finally reached a head in July 1989. Pat O'Connell, one of the most prominent dissidents and critics of Galvin, left Noraid and established an independent office in the Bronx. He condemned the growing emphasis on politics and appealed for support from disgruntled Irish-American republicans. O'Connell's action was also partly determined by his belief that Galvin was about to expel him from the National Executive.[67]

In response, Noraid officials met on August 27 and discussed ways in which the conflict could be resolved internally. While the *Irish People* assured its readers there was "No Split in Noraid," Galvin desperately organized a meeting with O'Connell and the dissidents in New York. Instead of settling the dispute, however, this meeting actually exacerbated divisions. O'Connell vehemently denounced Galvin and won support from such prominent figures in the Irish-American network as Jim Maunsell, a leader of Noraid's organization in Boston, and Frank O'Neill, an influential republican activist in Chicago.

The National Executive tried to hold a second meeting on October 7. But before this could happen, the dissidents published a full-page notice in the *Irish Echo* and the *Irish Voice* attacking Noraid's leaders for betraying the organization's original objectives. It was signed by four former members of the National Executive, two former national presidents, and seven chapter heads. Michael Flannery added his name to the long list of critics.[68]

Martin Galvin reported all these developments to the republican movement in Belfast. On October 7, Sinn Féin issued a statement calling for unity and stressing that such open displays of division served only British propaganda. Despite this plea, the split in Noraid intensified. In mid-October O'Connell and his supporters announced they were forming a new organization called the Friends of Irish Freedom (FOIF), "devoted exclusively to raising funds for the families of republican prisoners." Jim Maunsell was named national president, Pat O'Connell as vice-president,

66. Martin Galvin, interview with author, 14 November 1992.
67. Chris Fogarty, interview with author, 25 July 1992.
68. "Attention All I.N.A. Supporters," *Irish Voice* (New York), 1 October 1989.

and veteran republican John Hurley was national coordinator. The new group pulled its main strength from the Boston area, centered on the Irish-American club in Malden, but chapters were soon established in New York and Chicago. It formulated a constitution and began recruiting members. In November, Pat O'Connell announced that the group's initial fund-raising ventures would support Father Raymond Murray's Christmas collection for women prisoners in Armagh Jail.[69]

Republican leaders in Belfast were deeply irritated by formation of the FOIF. They sent Brendan Hughes, highly influential leader of the Maze hunger strike in 1980, to the United States. His primary mission was to support the Noraid National Executive and convince republicans not to go over to the FOIF. In November, he was joined by Seán Adams, cousin of Gerry, and Siobhan O'Hanlon, niece of Joe Cahill. This initiative was cut short, however, when Adams and O'Hanlon were arrested by the FBI and subsequently deported back to Ireland.[70]

Leaders of the Friends refused to listen to emissaries from Belfast and continued their own independent activities. In response, Sinn Féin sent Bob Smith, national secretary of An Cumann Cabhrach, to America in February 1990. He spoke at republican meetings on the East Coast and announced his organization would not accept donations from the FOIF. Smith stressed that Noraid was the only group recognized as a fundraising organization by the republican movement in Ireland. These points were later endorsed in a statement from republican prisoners smuggled out of Long Kesh and printed in the *Irish People*.[71]

Sinn Féin assumed that these major statements, from An Cumann Cabhrach and the republican prisoners themselves, would make the FOIF's position untenable. The Friends continued to resist, however, and began sending cash to a number of other groups. In August 1990 they contributed $1,500 to the Birmingham Six Campaign and later donated $13,000 to the Felons Club in Andersonstown, to assist in the purchase

69. The FOIF later announced it sent $8,500 to Father Murray. Part of this money was also donated to Sister Sarah Clarke to assist her work for Irish prisoners in Britain. O'Connell and his associates have maintained this financial support to the present. One of the principal figures in this fund raising is Edward "Big Red" Murphy, secretary of the Bobby Sands Unit FOIF in Boston. During the trial of Richard Johnson, Murphy used his home and longshoreman's pension as a guarantee to get Martin Quigley out on bail.

70. Richard May of Sinn Féin was also deported after his arrest by federal agents in Albany, New York.

71. *Irish People* (New York), 3 February 1990.

of a van to transport families to Long Kesh. The FOIF also announced they were sending cash to the Tyrone Prisoner Dependents Fund and to Cabhair, Republican Sinn Féin's dependents branch.

In March 1991 Gerry Adams intervened directly in the split, announcing that the FOIF had "no mandate from anyone involved in the struggle in Ireland" and that "every dollar contributed to them is a dollar lost to the dependents of Irish prisoners of war."[72] Relations between Noraid and the Friends subsequently deteriorated into wild accusations and rabid personal attacks. Noraid supporters accused prominent figures in the FOIF of cooperating with federal authorities in order to divert funds from the "liberation struggle."[73] The "Friends" responded with their own claims that a number of Noraid activists were working as FBI informants.

Noraid continued to proclaim the increasing success of its publicity and political campaigns. As an example, Martin Galvin publicized his participation in the 1992 Irish-American Presidential Forum, during which he questioned Bill Clinton about his position on Ulster. Yet despite such exposure, the split within Noraid had adverse consequences. The National Executive, under the chairmanship of Paul Murray, was forced to divert time, energy, and resources to counteracting the FOIF, which at the very least detracted from Noraid's full pursuit of its political agenda.

Noraid supporters also had to deal with continued divisions within their ranks. In January 1992, John McDonagh, editor of the *Irish People*, was forced to take an "extended vacation" from his duties. McDonagh and a group of his associates had made a number of controversial editorial decisions. Noraid activists were particularly enraged by the suspension of Joe Doherty's weekly column after he criticized an IRA bomb attack on Musgrave Park Hospital in November 1991. An order of protection was later issued against two former associates of McDonagh after they telephoned threats against his life. The whole affair generated extremely negative publicity for Noraid both within and outside the Irish-American community.[74]

72. *Irish Echo* (New York), 5 March 1991.

73. "The Conspiracy That Won't Go Away," *Lumpen Times* (Chicago), June 1993. Some FOIF leaders claim that these accusations are a cover for the FBI to assassinate them and pin the blame for their murders on the IRA.

74. In the spring of 1994, the Irish American Unity Conference also suffered an internal split. Helen McClafferty, a prominent IAUC activist from New Jersey, and Owen Rodgers, president of the IAUC's Manhattan chapter, left the organization following a bitter

Sinn Féin and Noraid both claimed that the Friends of Irish Freedom had only a handful of followers and that their activities were a "minor irritation," but Chris Fogarty, vice-chairman of the FOIF, maintained that support for his organization was growing rapidly and its financial ventures were highly successful. It ran benefit concerts by Irish traditional musicians, solicited mail contributions from Irish-American activists, and held regular fund-raising dinners in New York, Philadelphia, Boston, and Chicago.[75]

There is much greater controversy over the FOIF's alleged involvement in weapons procurement for the IRA. Federal agents conducted a number of covert surveillance operations against the group. At a Friends meeting in Chicago in 1991, an FBI informant was discovered trying to record discussions about the purchase of automatic rifles and Stinger missiles. Federal prosecutors aggressively pursued a case against four FOIF activists but were forced to drop charges because of lack of information and the unreliability of the informer as a witness. Despite the collapse of the "Friends Four" case, FBI agents continued to allege the group was involved in gunrunning and in providing financial support for the IRA in South Armagh.[76]

The announcement of the IRA cease-fire on August 31, 1994, seems to have accentuated the tensions within Irish-American republicanism. The FOIF has generally adopted the position of Republican Sinn Féin in Ireland. They remain extremely sceptical of the whole peace process, maintaining that the British cannot be trusted and that Sinn Féin is betraying republican principles. In September 1994 the FOIF brought Mary Ward, vice president of RSF, to the United States. Her attacks against the cease-fire were strongly endorsed by Michael Flannery and George Harrison. The Friends have also invited Ruairí O Brádaigh, but as of March 1995 the Clinton administration were refusing him a visa. Many FOIF activists remain convinced the cease-fire will soon collapse and they will assume a leading role in supporting the renewed "armed struggle."

---

dispute with IAUC National President Bob Linnen. McClafferty and Rodgers later formed the Irish Action Coalition, which, among other activities, works to "counter British and Anglophile dogma in the U.S."

75. The Friends of Irish Freedom are not listed under the Foreign Agents Registration Act and they do not issue official membership figures or financial statements. Consequently, conflicting claims about the group's support and fund raising are very difficult to verify.

76. Kevin Cullen, "When Irish Eyes Aren't Smiling: The Conflict in Northern Ireland Comes to Chicago," *Chicago Tribune Magazine*, 4 July 1993.

The Noraid National Executive has encorsed the cease-fire, but there have been growing signs of internal division. In March 1995, Sinn Féin established an office in Washington and announced the formation of a new fund-raising organization, Chairde Sinn Féin. Some Noraid activists see these developments as undercutting their organization. Others resent what they perceive as interference from Sinn Féin in Belfast. The uncertainty over the future role of Noraid has fueled speculation about a split and possible defections to the FOIF. As one INA activist recently asserted:

> Noraid is an organization developed and supported by Irish Americans, not as an appendage of any all-Irish organization. Most Americans want to know that their money goes to the prisoners and their families, not political organizations whose philosophy, aside from Irish unification, most Americans do not support. The Americans of Irish background, while hostile to the English occupation of the north, are solid and conservative in nature, not frustrated socialists![77]

In the ever-changing political situation that has been created by the cease-fire, it is difficult to assess what the future of Irish-American republicanism will be. Some analysts suggest that further fragmentation may render militant nationalist groups ineffective. Yet Irish-American republicans have endured internal feuds in the past. Despite seemingly irreconcilable differences in the US, they have managed to maintain their activities and continue support for the movement in Ireland. Despite the major transitions created by the cease-fire, it may yet be true that, as Michael Flannery once prophetically remarked, "As long as the Brits are in Belfast, there will be someone like me in America!"[78]

77. Letter from G. J. Devery to the *Irish Echo*, 22 February 1995.
78. Michael Flannery, quoted in Jimmy Breslin, "The Fighting Irish," *Los Angeles Times*, 13 February 1983.

CONCLUSION

In the nineteenth century, Irish Americans played a key role in providing political and material support for both constitutional and physical force nationalism. Later, they also made a significant contribution to the 1916 Easter Rising and to the War of Independence, 1919–21. Despite its long history and importance, Irish-American nationalism diminished after the establishment of the Irish Free State. The degree of independence achieved by the twenty-six counties satisfied most of the diaspora. Others were sickened by the bloodletting and fratricide during the Irish Civil War.

Irish-American nationalism declined further after World War II. Increasing socioeconomic success produced a flight to the suburbs and emptied most of the old Irish-American ghettos. Powerful trends toward assimilation led to an erosion of ethnic solidarity. Irish Americans became more concerned with their position in the United States than with political events in Ireland. The election of President John F. Kennedy in 1960 symbolized their incorporation into mainstream American society. Consequently, when the Ulster Troubles erupted in 1968, the majority of Irish Americans remained largely uninvolved.

Despite these profound changes within the Irish-American community, some groups and individuals tried to preserve an interest in their ancestral homeland. They contributed to the growing popularity of university courses in Irish literature and history in the 1970s. A number of cultural societies also encouraged a revival of interest in traditional music and the Gaelic language.

For some of these Irish Americans, concern with their ethnic roots stimulated an interest in the Ulster conflict. Most supported Irish unification but disagreed with the violent tactics of the IRA. From the mid-seventies their views were represented by Senators Edward Kennedy and Daniel Moynihan, Speaker of the House Thomas "Tip" O'Neill, and Governor Hugh Carey of New York—the "Four Horsemen" of Irish-American politics.

During the initial stages of the Ulster crisis, these leading politicians inclined toward the militant nationalist perspective. In 1971, for example, Senator Kennedy caused considerable political controversy by demanding the immediate withdrawal of British troops. Such statements alarmed not only the British government but also constitutional nationalists in Ireland, who felt Irish-American political leaders were giving encouragement to the IRA. John Hume of the SDLP and high-ranking Irish government officials established contacts with Kennedy and influenced him to adopt a more moderate approach. Eventually the Four Horsemen became an important source of support for constitutional nationalism on Capitol Hill.

On St. Patrick's Day 1977, the Four Horsemen issued their first joint annual statement. They endorsed political dialogue as the only way to achieve a solution to the Northern Ireland problem and strongly condemned Americans who supported the IRA. While militant groups denounced this statement as a betrayal of the oppressed nationalist community in Ulster by the "lace curtain Irish," it did contribute to a general decline in Irish-American republicanism during the late seventies. This process was accelerated by the emergence of grassroots organizations that promoted reconciliation, constitutional approaches, and economic investment as the best way to bring peace to Ulster.

In subsequent St. Patrick's Day statements, the Four Horsemen combined their denunciations of IRA violence with strong attacks on British government policy. They used their influence in Washington to work for a new political initiative in Ulster. Edward Kennedy and Tip O'Neill specifically backed a power-sharing arrangement in which the SDLP would have considerable leverage. This American political pressure was a main factor in the British government's launching of the 1980 Atkins Conference. Although this initiative produced no agreement between the SDLP and Unionist parties, it was the first major example of Irish-American political pressure affecting British policy in Northern Ireland.

In March 1981 the Four Horsemen consolidated their position on Capitol Hill by forming the congressional Friends of Ireland. This group contained some of the most powerful politicians in America. They effectively marginalized the influence of the Ad Hoc Committee on Irish Affairs and its more militant agenda.[1]

In July 1981, following a request from Garret FitzGerald, the Friends failed to secure Ronald Reagan's intervention in the hunger strike. Despite this setback, they continued to support the initiatives of constitutional nationalism in Ireland. The Friends gave strong encouragement to the New Ireland Forum and appealed to the British government to make a positive response. Their greatest achievement in this period came with the signing of the Anglo-Irish Agreement.

The contribution of the Friends of Ireland to the Agreement was most influential following the summit between Margaret Thatcher and Garret FitzGerald in November 1984. The British prime minister's blunt rejection of the Forum Report seemed to signal a deterioration in Anglo-Irish relations. Faced with this possibility, the FitzGerald government appealed to Irish-American political leaders for assistance. On this occasion the Friends obtained Ronald Reagan's intervention, despite his close friendship with Thatcher.

During a December 1984 meeting at Camp David, Reagan discussed Anglo-Irish relations with the British prime minister. He took this initiative on the advice of Secretary of the Interior William Clark, against the wishes of the State Department. Clark, in turn, had been influenced by the Friends of Ireland and the Irish government.

This American pressure, combined with domestic influences, encouraged Margaret Thatcher to be more conciliatory. She presented the Irish

1. Despite traditional differences, the Friends and the Ad Hoc Committee have recently cooperated on issues of mutual concern. In the late 1980s, both groups campaigned for the release of the Birmingham Six and others wrongfully convicted of IRA-related offenses in England. During the current Ulster peace process they have pursued almost identical agendas, working to secure a visa and the right to raise funds for Gerry Adams. In addition, politicians are increasingly joining both groups. James Walsh (R, N.Y.), the new chairman of the Friends, is also a member of the Ad Hoc Committee. Peter King (R, N.Y.) and Ben Gilman (R, N.Y.), outspoken co-chairmen of the Ad Hoc Committee, recently joined the Friends. In February 1995, partly as a consequence of these developments, the two groups held their first joint reception to honor Tanaiste Dick Spring in Washington. There is mounting speculation that the Friends and the Ad Hoc Committee will soon amalgamate, perhaps reflecting the "pan-nationalist front" that seems to be emerging in Ireland due to the peace process.

government with a comprehensive political proposal in January 1985. When Thatcher came to the United States in February to address a joint session of Congress, Tip O'Neill insisted that she discuss Northern Ireland. In her speech the British prime minister described her relationship with Garret FitzGerald as excellent and implied there would be renewed Anglo-Irish efforts aimed at solving the Ulster conflict.

After January 1985 the pace of Anglo-Irish discussions greatly intensified. During these talks, leaders of the Friends traveled to Dublin and gave assurances of US financial support for a political settlement. They also helped block a potentially serious challenge to the Agreement from Fianna Fáil leader Charles Haughey. When the accord was finally signed on November 15, 1985, it represented not only a major achievement for Garret FitzGerald and the SDLP but also the most significant intervention of the Friends of Ireland in the Ulster conflict to that date.

Following the Anglo-Irish Agreement, the Friends used their power in Washington to ensure continuation of the US financial contribution to the International Fund for Ireland. House Speaker Thomas Foley (D, Wash.) gave vital assistance in the first few years, when the Fund's survival seemed in jeopardy after severe criticism of its allocation of grant money. Leading members of the Friends also played an important role in the IRA cease-fire announcement on August 31, 1995, and continue to exert considerable influence on the development of peace negotiations.

While most concerned Irish Americans tended to support the Friends of Ireland, a number of activist organizations adopted militant nationalism. Groups such as the Irish National Caucus, the Irish American Unity Conference, and the American Irish Political Education Committee, though not officially endorsing the IRA's campaign of violence, did recognize their right to "resist oppression." They concentrated their resources on publicizing human rights violations by the security forces in Ulster and working for a British withdrawal.

Despite formation of the Ad Hoc Committee in 1977, these militant nationalist groups had only limited influence in Washington. Their activities were more effective at the state and municipal levels, where local politicians are susceptible to organized Irish-American lobbying. The MacBride Principles campaign stands as their greatest achievement. It won support from a wide spectrum of political organizations and played a key role in pushing the British government toward reform of its fair employment legislation in 1989.

Since its formation in 1970, the Irish Northern Aid Committee (Noraid) has been the most prominent and controversial militant nationalist group in America. It has given firm support to the IRA's "armed struggle," provided important financial aid to the republican movement, and orchestrated continuous anti-British publicity campaigns.

Noraid reports to the Justice Department show it sent nearly $3 million to republican agencies in Ireland from 1971 to 1990. This figure does not include disbursements between July 1981 and 1984, when the group refused to file financial records because of a legal dispute over its relationship to the IRA. Noraid continually asserted that its funds went to the families of imprisoned republicans for welfare purposes. Martin Galvin claimed:

No Irish Northern Aid money has ever gone for the purchase of weapons. There are people within the Irish-American community who recognize, or who believe, that the fastest way to bring peace to Ireland is to help bring the means of defense to the soldiers of the IRA. Now I understand these people, I understand their motivations, I understand what they are trying to do, and I sympathize with them. But Irish Northern Aid is not a part of that effort. Irish Northern Aid does not contribute to it.[2]

British, Irish, and American authorities dismissed Noraid's "charitable façade" and alleged most donations went to the IRA for weapons. The Justice Department further claimed that the group's financial reports to the government were significantly understated and that large amounts of cash were secretly sent to the Provos. Although there was a substantial body of circumstantial evidence supporting these claims, law-enforcement agents never uncovered a direct link between Noraid funds and the purchase of weapons.[3]

In *The American Connection*, Jack Holland correctly points out that the dispute over the use of funds is mostly academic. Noraid money helped the IRA because it freed other cash, which could be used to buy arms. It is also true that, even if all Noraid funds went to republican fami-

2. Martin Galvin, quoted in *A Turn to the Gun* (New York: Celtic Videos, 1984).

3. When Michael Flannery was caught gunrunning in 1982, he claimed the money he used was not from Noraid but from a secret IRA fund specifically used to buy weapons. There are obviously no official records of this fund or how much has been sent to the Provos. Irish-American republicans remain evasive about this money but imply it has amounted to millions of dollars during the course of the Troubles.

lies, it still performed an important role in sustaining morale. The well-being of dependents was a major priority to the Army Council, for, as Michael Flannery once bluntly commented, "An IRA soldier freed from financial worries for his family is a much better fighter!"[4] Although the IRA's reliance on the Irish-American donation steadily decreased in the 1980s, that donation continued to make a significant contribution to the "armed struggle" right up to the cease-fire of September 1994.[5]

Irish-American republicans helped the IRA most directly through transatlantic gunrunning. In the early 1970s, George Harrison was one of the principal arms suppliers. He sent the first consignment of American rifles to Ireland in 1968. They arrived in Belfast in the summer of 1969 and were used by the IRA to defend nationalist areas during the bloody sectarian riots of that year.

In 1969 the Provisionals sent Seán Keenan to America to coordinate the gunrunning network. He contacted a group of Irish Americans in Philadelphia, who supplied the first batch of Armalite rifles. This weapon, which was easy to use and conceal, was ideal for the IRA's guerrilla campaign. Continuing supplies of the Armalite modernized the Provos' firepower and enabled the continuation of their military operations throughout the seventies.

By 1977, the British government claimed that 80 percent of the IRA's weapons came from the United States. The Royal Ulster Constabulary released figures showing that American guns were used in 70 percent of Provo killings. American authorities also acknowledged the importance of transatlantic gunrunning but denied it was as extensive as British estimates.[6]

4. Michael Flannery quoted in Linda Charlton, "Fund-Raising by a Group in US Called Vital to IRA Operations," *New York Times*, 23 September 1979.

5. James Adams, *The Financing of Terror* (New York: Simon and Schuster, 1986), claims that in the early 1970s Noraid supplied about 50 percent of the cash needed by the IRA. This fell significantly as the Provos developed a variety of operations, ranging from black taxis to drinking clubs, which made it financially independent. See also Scott Anderson, "Making a Killing," *Harper's* 288 no.1725 (February 1994), 45–56, and Liam Clarke and John Burns, "IRA Godfathers Strive to Build up New Mafia," *The Sunday Times* (London), 12 March 1995.

6. There have been suggestions that the British purposely inflated this figure to ensure that US authorities continued their activities against the republican network. It is also important to note that US weapons arrived in Ulster from a variety of countries, to which they may have originally been shipped legally.

From the late seventies, IRA weapons procurement focused less on the United States and increasingly turned to Eastern Europe and the Middle East. Despite this trend, Irish-American gunrunners continued to make an important contribution to the Provo arsenal. They tried to maintain supplies of weapons such as the M-60 machine gun and the Barrett .50-calibre sniper rifle, which were more difficult to acquire from other sources. A number of individuals also gave technological advice to help the Provos in their "electronic war" and provided sophisticated components for remote-control bombs.

One of the IRA's primary objectives in the late 1980s was to obtain weapons to shoot down British helicopters. The Irish-American republican network again played a key role in this strategy. Richard Clark Johnson and his associates tried to develop more effective rockets through the incorporation of proximity fuses. There were other conspiracies to acquire the Stinger surface-to-air missile, desirable for its capacity to penetrate the electronic defenses on British helicopters.

The IRA also used America as an escape route for some of its members on the run or lying low after military operations. Irish-American republicans provided cover for a succession of Provos. Supplying forged identities, employment, and housing, they helped these fugitives blend into society. The most recent example of this involved Jimmy Smyth, Pol Brennan, Kevin Barry Artt, and Terence Kirby. All four were IRA inmates who escaped from the Maze Prison in 1983. With the assistance of Provo sympathizers, they were able to establish "normal" lives in California until 1992, when they were discovered by the FBI.[7]

Irish-American republican groups launched anti-British publicity campaigns throughout the Troubles. Although these efforts always suffered from the negative public reaction to IRA atrocities, there were a number of important breakthroughs. In 1972 militant nationalists effectively capitalized on the popular revulsion generated by the killing of thirteen Catholics during Bloody Sunday. During the hunger strikes of 1980–81, Noraid orchestrated a campaign of major public demonstrations and helped convince many politicians and newspapers that Margaret Thatcher

7. The H-Block Four, as they have become known, are all facing extradition to Britain. In September 1994, Jimmy Smyth won a hearing against extradition, arguing his life would be in danger if he were returned to Northern Ireland. As of April 1995, he is free on bail awaiting the outcome of a British appeal of the ruling. Brennan, Artt, and Kirby were denied bail and have been imprisoned since their arrests. See Michelle Quinn, "In a Court, a Seminar on Conflict in Ulster," *New York Times*, 5 November 1993.

was largely responsible for the prison crisis. The group's fund raising reached unprecedented heights and its membership increased nationwide.

Noraid's rejuvenation during the hunger strikes convinced its leaders to organize annual tours of Northern Ireland. Beginning in 1983, militant activists traveled to the province to experience life directly under "British oppression." They stayed with republican families, participated in pro-IRA demonstrations, and attended Sinn Féin political seminars.

These annual Noraid tours became valuable publicity events for the republican movement in Ireland. They helped create the impression that there was substantial Irish-American support for the IRA and thus enhanced its claims to legitimacy. Martin Galvin's repeated evasion of the exclusion order against him also caused considerable embarrassment to the British government. In addition, those who participated in the tours returned to America with a renewed dedication to working for the republican cause.

From the beginning of the Troubles, the US government was generally responsive to British requests for action against the Irish-American republican network. This was particularly true under the Reagan and Bush administrations, when Justice Department officials tried to undermine Noraid fund raising and the FBI broke major gunrunning conspiracies. A highly restrictive visa policy was enforced on Sinn Féin, and the Immigration Service launched deportation and extradition proceedings against numerous IRA fugitives.

The pressure exerted on Irish-American republicanism by federal authorities was compounded by the activities of constitutional nationalists and the British government. Militant irredentist organizations were also plagued by internal divisions and by hostility from the US media. Yet, despite all these forces working against them, Irish-American republicans made an extremely important contribution to the IRA for more than twenty-five years. Although the September 1994 cease-fire may necessitate a reassessment of traditional activities, they remain determined to influence future developments in Northern Ireland.

POSTSCRIPT

In April 1992, during the campaign for the Democratic presidential nomination, Bill Clinton appeared before an Irish-American political forum in New York. He pledged that, if elected to the White House, he would appoint a special envoy for Northern Ireland and grant a US visa to Gerry Adams. Critics accused the then-governor of Arkansas of cynically playing for Irish-American votes. Clinton denied this and later claimed his interest in the Ulster conflict began while he was a Rhodes scholar at Oxford University in the late sixties.

During the first months of his presidency, Clinton—bowing to strong opposition from Unionist leaders and the British government—shelved plans for a special envoy. He also maintained the restrictive visa policy against Sinn Féin, refusing Gerry Adams's application to conduct a US book promotion tour. Many Irish-American activists condemned the new administration, fearing that promises made during the election campaign would quickly be forgotten. In Ireland, however, the momentous political developments taking place opened the way for Clinton to play a pivotal role.

In the late 1980s, influential figures in the republican movement concluded that the Ulster conflict had reached a stalemate. They realized that, though the IRA could continue the "armed struggle" indefinitely, it was increasingly unlikely that the British could be forced to withdraw. Sinn Féin activists also developed a greater appreciation of the negative impact the IRA's military operations had on electoral support. From these considerations, republican leaders believed they might secure more of their objectives through negotiations than with continued violence.

In April 1993, Gerry Adams entered into exploratory talks with John Hume. The principal objective was to outline conditions under which the IRA could end hostilities. The two leaders eventually produced a blueprint, which was sent to both the British and Irish governments. As the Hume-Adams initiative continued, secret contacts were made between Sinn Féin and British officials.

All of these developments provided impetus to the Downing Street Declaration announced by Prime Minister John Major and Taoiseach Albert Reynolds on December 15, 1993. In essence, the Declaration offered Sinn Féin a place at future discussions on the future of Northern Ireland if the IRA abandoned its campaign of violence. The British also stated they were not opposed to Irish self-determination by consent and that they had no selfish or strategic interest in Ulster.

The Downing Street Declaration intensified debate within the republican movement. Gerry Adams and his supporters were willing to test what could be achieved by continued discussion. They demanded a resumption of contacts with the British and clarification of the terms of the Declaration. Militants argued that politicians could never be trusted and that a prolonged period of inaction would sap the IRA's strength. In March 1994, as an example of their military capability, the Provos launched three mortar attacks within a week on London's Heathrow Airport.

The US government was briefed on all of the negotiations leading to the Downing Street Declaration. President Clinton welcomed the new initiative and encouraged John Major and Albert Reynolds to "go the extra mile" in working for peace. White House staff also began considering options that might encourage the IRA to embrace political dialogue. Some concluded that progress could be made by granting a US visa to Gerry Adams.

Support for the Adams visa came from a number of highly influential sources. John Hume contacted his friends on Capitol Hill and lobbied for a major US concession to Sinn Féin. Senators Ted Kennedy and Daniel Moynihan were among the most prominent adherents of this proposal. As chairmen of key Senate committees, their cooperation was vital to the passage of Clinton's welfare and health care reform plans. Anthony Lake, National Security Advisor, and Nancy Soderberg, who was responsible for Irish affairs at the National Security Council, also played leading roles in working for the visa. Their efforts were reinforced by US Ambassador to Ireland Jean Kennedy-Smith and former congressman Bruce Morrison, chairman of the lobbying group Americans for a New Irish Agenda.[1]

Those lobbying for Adams argued that granting a visa would strengthen moderates within the republican movement. They also claimed it would show the IRA that British concerns no longer dominated American policy and that further gains could be achieved if violence was ended.

Attorney General Janet Reno and Secretary of State Warren Christopher, reflecting the views of the Justice Department, State Department, FBI, and CIA, strongly opposed the visa. They claimed it would undermine US credibility in fighting international terrorism. House Speaker Thomas Foley endorsed this position, emphasizing that Adams would turn a US visit into a major publicity victory for the IRA.[2]

On January 28, 1994, just before a final decision was made on the visa, US Consul-General Valentino Martinez met with Gerry Adams in Belfast. Martinez later reported back to Washington that, although the Sinn Féin president had made constructive comments, he had not significantly changed his views on IRA violence.[3]

Despite considerable opposition to the visa, Clinton decided to gamble on the potential of a breakthrough in the peace process. Adams was thus allowed into New York for forty-eight hours to address the National Committee on American Foreign Policy. While there, the Sinn Féin president received unprecedented media attention. In numerous interviews he adeptly presented himself as a man of peace who was being frustrated by the British government's unwillingness to offer simple clarifications of the Downing Street Declaration. Adams's articulate expression of his case won a dazzling publicity victory, with some newspapers describing him as the Irish Nelson Mandela.

The Adams visa was a significant achievement for all those who had worked to convince the president of the need for a bold policy move. Clinton's decision also reflected a decline in the importance of the "spe-

1. Ambrose Evans-Prichard, "The Clinton Clique Takes Charge of Irish Policy," *Sunday Telegraph* 12 March 1995.

2. The House Speaker's opinion changed after the IRA cease-fire announcement. In October 1994, during his second US trip, Gerry Adams was formally greeted by Foley on Capitol Hill.

3. Martin Fletcher, "Adams Visa Charade," *The Times* (London) 5 February 1994. Newspaper publisher Niall O'Dowd played an important role as an emissary in this period. He made a number of trips to Ireland, relaying messages between the Clinton administration and Sinn Féin. See John Farrell, "Bridge to Irish," *Boston Globe* 10 February 1995.

cial relationship" with Britain, brought on by the changed circumstances of the post–Cold War era. This was further compounded by resentment within the Clinton administration over the assistance given by senior Conservative Party strategists to the re-election campaign of George Bush in 1992.[4]

It now seems that Adams's treatment as an international statesman in New York reinforced his position within the republican movement and helped generate greater momentum for peace. President Clinton had made a very difficult decision in granting the visa. In addition to opposing his own government agencies and antagonizing the British, he also ran the risk of the IRA greatly embarrassing him by committing a major act of violence. Many leading Irish-American politicians had similarly gone out on a limb for Adams. This put considerable pressure on the Sinn Féin president to reward the confidence shown in him, by helping to deliver an end to IRA violence. Adams later acknowledged that, "By granting me a visa to come to the U.S., Mr. Clinton helped create the conditions for the cease-fire."[5]

The debate within the republican movement over strategy continued throughout the spring and early summer of 1994. In July, at a special conference in Letterkenny, Sinn Féin rejected important aspects of the Downing Street Declaration. While this seemed to indicate a resurgence of militancy, the support for ending hostilities was overwhelming. The only issue still to be settled was whether the cease-fire would be open ended or limited to a fixed period.

On August 26, 1994, Bruce Morrison and a group of influential Irish-Americans met with Gerry Adams in Belfast. Morrison, who had remained in close contact with officials at the NSC, suggested US restric-

4. John Darnton, "Rift on Ulster and Bosnia Takes Bloom Off U.S.-British Ties," *New York Times* 24 October 1994.

5. Gerry Adams, "Ireland's Moment," *New York Times* 4 October 1994. The Clinton administration also tried to encourage Unionists to engage in dialogue. In April 1994 both the DUP and UUP sent delegations to Washington to present their views. The most publicized of these initiatives came when Ulster Unionist MP Ken Maginnis debated with Gerry Adams on the *Larry King Live Show* in September 1994.

Elements representing paramilitary thinking have also taken the opportunity to express their position. A delegation, which included Gusty Spence, David Ervine, and Gary McMichael, traveled to New York to speak before the National Committee on American Foreign Policy in October 1994. Gary McMichael, son of UDA leader John McMichael who was killed by the IRA, later accepted an invitation to join Gerry Adams at the White House St. Patrick's Day gala in 1995.

tions against republicans could be gradually lifted if the "armed struggle" was ended. The Irish-American delegation also expressed their desire for a cease-fire without conditions. This appeal seems to have had some influence. On August 31, the IRA announced a complete cessation of violence, even waiving the right to respond to loyalist attacks.[6]

Sinn Féin leaders believed it was essential to explain details of the cease-fire to Irish-American republicans. When they requested that Joe Cahill be allowed into the US for this purpose, the State and Justice Departments resisted. Cahill had twice been deported from the US on suspicion of involvement in arms procurement. Despite this, Clinton again decided to issue a visa. Those involved in the cease-fire negotiations claim that the president's action was crucial. Taoiseach Albert Reynolds, among others, later stated, "I don't think the IRA would have gone through with the decision if he [Cahill] hadn't been out there to put his weight behind the new direction."[7]

Cahill was prohibited from giving media interviews and instead spoke to private gatherings of Noraid supporters. His principal message was that the cease-fire had total support within the republican movement. Cahill also implied that, as the peace process developed, FBI operations against the Irish-American republican network would be reduced. In addition, he suggested that members of the IRA serving sentences in America would be included in a future amnesty for republican prisoners in Britain and Ireland.[8]

On October 13, 1994, as the IRA cease-fire continued to hold, the Combined Loyalist Military Command, representing the UVF and UDA, announced their own cessation of violence. Despite these developments, the British government refused to enter into negotiations until it was convinced the ending of hostilities was permanent. The Clinton administration, on the other hand, responded with increased concessions. In September 1994, Gerry Adams was given an unrestricted visa and allowed to travel throughout America. On October 3, he was contacted by Vice-President Al Gore, who arranged a conference with US government representatives in Washington. The following day Adams met with Nancy

6. Chuck Feeney, a member of the Morrison delegation and chairman of General Atlantic Corporation, later gave $15,000 to help establish the first Sinn Féin office in Washington.

7. *Irish Echo* 21 September 1994.

8. Joe Cahill, speech at the Irish-American Heritage Center Chicago, 11 September 1994.

Soderberg and officials from the State Department. This formal opening of contacts between Irish republicans and the US government marked a major step in the elevation of Sinn Féin to political respectability.[9]

In December 1994 the British finally acknowledged that the cease-fire was genuine and announced that civil servants would begin exploratory talks with Sinn Féin. Just prior to the first of these sessions, Gerry Adams made another visit to Washington. On December 6, in an upgrade of the level of contacts, he conferred with Anthony Lake and Commerce Secretary Ron Brown at the White House. Adams expressed concern for republican prisoners in America and for those facing deportation and extradition proceedings. He also discussed the possibility of being allowed to raise funds in the United States. Later, the Sinn Féin leader appealed for a lobbying effort to support this request.

At the beginning of 1995, Irish Americans once again exerted their influence in Washington. Senator Edward Kennedy persuaded a group of his congressional colleagues to endorse Adams's appeal to raise funds. Many of these politicians were central figures in the Democratic Party; their support would be vital to President Clinton's re-election hopes in 1996. Anthony Lake, Nancy Soderberg, and Jean Kennedy-Smith were again aligned with the pro-Adams faction. They argued that permitting fund raising was essential to Sinn Féin's full participation in constitutional politics. This view was enhanced by the fact that Adams was already permitted to raise money in Ireland and Britain.[10]

President Clinton, before deciding on fund raising, wanted to extract a positive response from Sinn Féin on the issue of IRA weapons. Intense negotiations ensued between White House officials and republican leaders. On March 10, 1995, Gerry Adams agreed that the decommissioning of arms could be discussed at ministerial-level meetings between the British and Sinn Féin. Clinton, despite British objections, accepted this

9. Media reports claim that the Clinton administration originally tried to placate Britain by offering Adams only a meeting with a desk officer at the State Department. When the Sinn Féin leader threatened to cancel his visit to Washington, the meeting was upgraded to include Soderberg and higher-ranking State Department officials. This concession was granted despite its being an inevitable snub to the British. See John Darnton, "Rift on Ulster and Bosnia Takes Bloom Off U.S.-British Ties," *New York Times* 24 October 1994.

10. In February 1995, Tanaiste Dick Spring subscribed to these points during a visit to Washington. In meetings with US government officials he stressed the IRA had permanently forsaken the gun and that permitting Adams to raise funds would strengthen the peace process.

statement as a genuine attempt at progress. Not only did he agree to lift the ban on fund raising; he also invited Adams to St. Patrick's Day festivities at the White House.

Clinton believed that the peace process had reached an impasse over the arms issue. He was convinced that his earlier visa decision had been a catalyst in bringing about the cease-fire. The president felt that meeting Adams and allowing fund raising would persuade the IRA to remove its stockpile of weapons. He also hoped to encourage the British to begin ministerial-level talks with Sinn Féin.

On March 15, 1995, Adams launched the initial $200-per plate, Sinn Féin fund-raising dinner in New York.[11] He had earlier opened the first Sinn Féin office in Washington, intended as a bridgehead to powerbrokers on Capitol Hill. The climax of the visit came during a St. Patrick's Day luncheon hosted by House Speaker Newt Gingrich. President Clinton shook hands with Adams to the applause of assembled legislators. While this official acceptance by the leader of the world's remaining superpower was a crowning achievement for Sinn Féin, it came as a quid pro quo for progress in the decommissioning of IRA weapons.

Early in April 1995, in an effort to heal the rift in Anglo-American relations created by the "Adams Affair," John Major traveled to Washington to meet with Clinton. While acknowledging policy differences, the president emphasized that it was thanks to Major's "vision and courage" that the peace process was still alive. On April 24, the British government announced that a "sufficient basis" existed for ministerial-level talks to begin with Sinn Féin, implying that the IRA had given some ground on the surrender of weapons. As both sides prepared for talks, it seemed that Clinton policy initiatives had again helped move the peace process forward.

The Clinton administration has also tried to encourage reconciliation through the promise of financial and economic assistance. It is generally assumed that a strengthened economy, with more job opportunities and prosperity, would be an important element in an overall settlement of the Ulster conflict. Consequently, when the IRA cease-fire was announced, there was intense media speculation that White House officials were preparing a massive financial aid package. Some reports claimed that this

---

11. Chairde Sinn Féin later reported that $98,000 had been raised. As of April 1995, plans were being finalized for a multi-city US tour in which Adams was expected to net a huge financial windfall.

"peace dividend" could amount to direct assistance of $100 million to $200 million.[12]

On September 3, 1994, President Clinton interrupted his holiday on Martha's Vineyard to discuss financial assistance with Dick Spring, the Irish foreign minister. Spring later told reporters that "substantial sums would be forthcoming" from America. Later that month, John Hume also met Clinton to propose special terms of entry to the US for goods produced in the border region of Ireland.

It soon emerged, however, that direct US financial contributions would be constrained by budget limitations. When Clinton's package was announced in November 1994, the assistance to the International Fund for Ireland was raised by only $10 million to $30 million for 1996. Much greater focus was placed on encouraging private investment. In mid-December, as part of this effort, Commerce Secretary Ron Brown led a high-level American delegation to a "Forum for Investment" in Belfast. This conference was organized by the British government to explore schemes to invigorate the Ulster economy. Alan Hevesi, comptroller of New York City, sponsored the creation of Irish "Peace Bonds" that would be offered to American investors interested in channeling money into job-creation ventures. Other proposals ranged from the funding of a new "Presidents' Highway" linking Belfast and Dublin, to a vigorous new promotion campaign to attract American tourists to Northern Ireland.

On December 1, 1994, in order to coordinate all these propositions, Clinton appointed outgoing Senate Majority Leader George Mitchell as his special advisor on Economic Initiatives for Ireland. Since January 1995, Mitchell has been supervising preparations for a major international investment conference. This will be held in Washington in May and is expected to lure many new American businesses to Ulster.

The Clinton administration, through its concessions to Gerry Adams and its commitment to economic assistance, has become involved in the Ulster conflict on an unprecedented scale. The president's initiatives have given impetus to the peace process at vital stages. With these developments viewed as an important foreign policy success, and a re-election campaign looming in 1996, it seems certain that the American role in Northern Ireland will continue for the foreseeable future.

12. Douglas Jehl, "Ulster Truce Could Bring Dividend," *New York Times*, 3 September 1994.

Yet there are limits to what the Clinton administration can achieve. The only way that a lasting peace can be secured in Ulster is through reconciliation between the nationalist and unionist communities. Receptions and handshakes at the White House may advance political agendas but, as *Sunday Independent* columnist John A. Murphy bluntly commented, "The only handshake worth a damn in the end will be the one between John Hume and Jim Molyneaux."[13] As of April 1995, this rapprochement still seemed a long way off.

13. John A. Murphy, "Wiping All the IRA Atrocities Off Our Memory Map," *Sunday Independent* (Dublin), 19 March 1995.

BIBLIOGRAPHY

PRIMARY SOURCES

I. INTERVIEWS AND CORRESPONDENCE*

Daniel Berrigan, SJ: Peace activist; 26 April 1991.

Paul Brosnahan: Former executive member of the American Committee for Irish Freedom; 12 June 1989, 21 October 1989, 24 November 1989, 23 August 1993.

Joseph Clarkson: Head of the Registration Unit for the Foreign Agents Registration Act, US Department of Justice; 8 February 1989, 27 December 1989.

Robert E. Connolly: Author and Irish-American republican activist; 21 July 1990.

Tommy Corbett: Executive Member of the American Irish Republican Army; 14 July 1991.

Bernadette Devlin/McAliskey: Former member of Parliament and civil rights activist; 31 May 1989.

Tom Enright: Former treasurer of the American Committee for Irish Freedom; 14 November 1989, 4 December 1989, 1 February 1990.

Garret FitzGerald: Former Taoiseach of the Republic of Ireland; 19 December 1990.

Michael Flannery: Founder of Irish Northern Aid; 23 July 1991, 18 September 1992, 9 November 1992, 18 November 1992.

Brian Fleming: Republican prisoner, Federal Prison Atlanta; 8 October 1992.

Chris Fogarty: Vice-chairman of the Friends of Irish Freedom; 25 July 1992, 22 October 1992.

---

* In addition, there were many gunrunners and federal agents who spoke to me on the condition they remain anonymous.

Martin Galvin: Noraid Publicity Director; 14 November 1992.

Peter Gunning: Former Irish consul-general in Chicago; 13 July 1989.

Mrs. James Heaney: Wife of James Heaney, founder of the American Committee for Irish Freedom; 30 January 1990, 6 April 1990.

La Verne Hickey: Chair of the Institute for Economic Justice; 4 February 1990.

Rachel Hoffman: Director of American Protestants for Truth about Ireland; 30 November 1989.

Ted Howell: Director of Sinn Féin Foreign Affairs Bureau; 2 June 1992.

John Hume: Leader of the Social Democratic and Labour Party; 3 January 1989.

Senator Edward M. Kennedy: Leader of the Friends of Ireland in the US Congress; 28 March 1989, 16 April 1989.

Tom Lane: Noraid official in Chicago; 11 October 1990.

Michael Lillis: Former diplomat with the Irish embassy in Washington; 20 January 1994.

David McCalden: Founder of the Ulster-American Heritage Foundation; 7 July 1990.

Janet McIver: Former official with the British Information Service, New York; 2 June 1988, 26 November 1989.

Father Seán McManus: Director of the Irish National Caucus; 11 July 1991, 25 April 1995.

Dr. Conor Cruise O'Brien: Author and former Irish minister for Posts and Telegraphs; 15 October 1989, 1 November 1989.

Paul O'Dwyer: Founder of the American Committee for Ulster Justice; 15 May 1989, 21 June 1989.

Maureen O'Looney: Irish-American republican activist in Chicago; 21 July 1990.

Thomas P. "Tip" O'Neill: Former Speaker of the House of Representatives; 21 May 1991.

Robert St. Cyr: Former Member of the Executive of the National Association for Irish Justice; 26 May 1989.

John Taylor: Former Ulster Unionist member of the European Parliament; 5 January 1989.

Seán Prendiville: Former executive in the Irish Republican Clubs of North America; 6 January 1994.

Peter Robinson: Deputy leader of the Democratic Unionist Party; 28 May 1992.

II. COLLECTIONS

United States Government

1. Foreign Agents Registration Act Files: US Department of Justice, Federal Triangle Building, Washington DC

Alexander International Development Consultants: Registration no. 2706.

Irish Northern Aid Committee, File Section I and II: Registration no. 2239.

Jack Buttram, Inc.: Registration no. 3588.

The Friends of Fianna Fáil: Registration no. 3789.

2. Federal Bureau of Investigation Freedom of Information Files: FBI Building, Washington DC

Clan na Gael, no. 297, 641.

Defendants' evidence presented by the American Civil Liberties Union in Attorney General of the United States v The Irish People, Inc., no. 97–5299.

Irish Republican Clubs of North America, no. 270, 097.

Irish Republican Army (1970–89), no. 61—7606–633.

James Connolly Clubs, no. 270, 236.

National Association for Irish Freedom, no. 297, 650.

National Association for Irish Justice, no. 297, 648.

Noraid file, no. 296, 384.

3. Telegrams from US consul general in Belfast to State Department in Washington, 1970–1988. Linen Hall Library, Belfast.

4. US Government Reports

Congressmen Hamilton Fish and Joshua Eilberg, Northern Ireland: A Role for the United States. Report to the Committee on the Judiciary, 95th. Cong., 2nd Sess., August/September 1978.

Congressman Lester Wolff, Report on Trip to Northern Ireland. Hearing Before the Subcommittee on European Affairs. 92nd Cong., 2nd Sess., July 1972.

Department States Position on Irish Crisis. Department of State Bulletin, 20 March 1972.

Northern Ireland. Hearings Before the Subcommittee on Europe. 92nd Cong., 2nd Sess., 28 February to 1 March 1972.

President Carter States Policy on Northern Ireland. Department of State Bulletin, 26 September 1979.

Senator Claiborne Pell, Some Thoughts on the Situation in Northern Ireland. Report to the Committee on Foreign Relations. 97th Sess., 1st Sess., May 1981.

Senator George McGovern, Ireland in 1977. Report to the Committee on Foreign Relations, US Senate. 95th Cong., 1st Sess., August 1977.

Statements of the Ad-Hoc Committee on Irish Affairs in Congress. Congressional Record. 1979–92.

Statements of the Friends of Ireland in Congress. Congressional Record, 1981–92.

Statements on Northern Ireland from Congressmen Mario Biaggi, Hamilton Fish, Daniel Eilberg, Tip O'Neill, and Tom Foley. Congressional Record (House), 1968–92.

Statements on Northern Ireland from Senators Edward Kennedy, Chris Dodd, and Daniel Moynihan. Congressional Record (Senate), 1968–92.

United States Foreign Assistance Program and Aid to Ireland. Hearing Before the Committee on Foreign Relations. 92nd Cong., 2nd Sess., 10 April 1986.

Private

Collected Papers of James Heaney, Founder of ACIF.

Collected Papers of Paul Brosnahan, Executive member of ACIF.

Collected Papers of Paul O'Dwyer, St. John's University, New York.

Collected Papers of Sean Prendiville, Executive member of IRC.

Collected Papers on Northern Ireland of Professor Lawrence J. McCaffrey, Chicago.

Vanderbilt University T.V. News Archives on Northern Ireland, 1968–1992.

Collected Papers of the British Information Service, New York

H-Blocks: The Facts (1981).
Irish Terrorism's Overseas Supporters (1981).
Libya and the I.R.A. (1984).
Noraid and the Financing of Terrorism (1984).
Noraid and the Funding of the P.I.R.A. (1981).
The I.R.A. and Noraid (1983).
The I.R.A. and North America (1985).
The I.R.A. and Overseas Revolutionaries (1983).
The Irish Northern Aid Committee (1982).
The Provisional I.R.A. and Noraid (1984).

SECONDARY SOURCES

I. BOOKS, ARTICLES, AND PAMPHLETS

Adams, James. *The Financing of Terror*. New York: Simon and Schuster, 1986.
Alexander, Yonah, and Alan O'Day. *Terrorism in Ireland*. New York: St. Martin's Press, 1984.
Barron, John. "Breaking the I.R.A's American Connection." *Reader's Digest* 138 (March 1991): 65–71.
Barker, Godffrey. "Arms for Ulster: The Irish-American File." *The Spectator* (29 November 1975).
Bell, J. Bowyer. *The Secret Army: The I.R.A. 1916–1979*. Cambridge, Mass.: M.I.T. Press, 1980.
———. *The Gun in Politics: An Analysis of Irish Political Conflict, 1916–1986*. New Brunswick, N.J.: Transaction Books, 1987.
———. *The Irish Troubles: A Generation of Political Violence, 1967–1992*. New York: St. Martin's Press, 1993.
Bishop, Patrick, and Eamonn Mallie. *The Provisional I.R.A.*. London: Heinemann, 1987.
Bradley, James. "The Greening of America: Irish-American Lobbyists and Northern Ireland." *Irish Echo*, 15 December 1993.
Brown, Richard H. *I Am of Ireland*. New York: Harper & Row, 1974.
Brown, Thomas N. *Irish-American Nationalism, 1870–1890*. Philadelphia: Lippincott, 1966.
Brummer, Alex. "The Greening of the White House." *The Guardian*, 26 November 1985.
Burke, Father Maurice. *A Decade of Deceit: The New York Times and the War in Ireland*. New York: Noraid Publications, 1981.
Carroll, Francis M. *American Opinion and the Irish Question, 1910–23: A Study in Opinion and Policy*. New York: St. Martin's Press, 1978.
Charlton, Linda. "Irish-Americans are Aroused by New Troubles." *New York Times*, 16 August 1969.

————. "Biaggi, a Bronx Power, Has a Second Constituency in Northern Ireland." *New York Times*, 7 May 1978.

————. "Fund-Raising by a Group in U.S. Called Vital to I.R.A. Operations." *New York Times*, 23 September 1979.

Claibourne, William. "Cash is for the Bairns 'tis said, Not for Guns." *Washington Post*, 25 January 1976.

Clark, Dennis. *Irish Blood: Northern Ireland and the American Conscience*. Port Washington, N.Y.: Kennikat Press, 1977.

Clark, Liam. *Broadening the Battlefield: The H-Blocks and the Rise of Sinn Fein*. Dublin: Gill and Macmillan, 1987.

Collins, Tom. *The Irish Hunger Strike*. Dublin: Gill and Macmillan, 1986.

Connolly, Robert E. *Armalite and Ballot Box: An Irish-American Republican Primer*. Fort Wayne, Ind.: Cuchullain, 1985.

————. *The Connolly Report: An Irish-American Republican Reader*. Fort Wayne, Ind.: Cuchullain Publications, 1988.

Conroy, John. "The Irish Connection: Murder in Winnetka." *The Reader* (Chicago), 10 April 1992.

Coogan, Tim Pat. *The I.R.A.: A History*. Niwok, Col.: Robert Rinehart Publishers, 1993.

————. *On the Blanket: The H-Block Story*. Dublin: Ward River, 1980.

Corcoran, Mary. *Irish Illegals: Transients between Two Societies*. Westport, Conn.: Greenwood Press, 1993.

Crick, Bernard. "The Pale Green Internationalists." *New Statesman* 96 (7 December 1979): 888–96.

Cronin, Seán. *Washington's Irish Policy 1916–1986: Independence, Partition, Neutrality*. Dublin: Anvil Books, 1987.

Cullen, Kevin. "When Irish Eyes Aren't Smiling: The Conflict in Northern Ireland comes to Chicago." *Chicago Tribune Magazine*, 4 July 1993.

Davidson, Sara. "Bernadette Devlin: An Irish Revolutionary in Irish America." *Harper's Magazine* 240, no. 1463 (January 1970).

Deacy, Jack. "The I.R.A. New York Brigade." *New York Magazine*, 13 March 1972.

Dillon, Martin. *Killer in Clowntown: Joe Doherty, the IRA and the Special Relationship*. London: Hutchinson, 1985.

Donlon, Seán. "Irish-American Relations: Bringing Irish Diplomatic and Political Influence to Bear on Washington." *Irish Times*, 25 January 1993.

Duffy, P. G. *My Struggle for Irish Freedom*. Tacoma: AIRA Publications, 1986.

Farrell, Michael. *Sheltering the Fugitive? The Extradition of Irish Political Offenders*. Cork: Mercier, 1985.

————. *Twenty Years On*. Kerry: Brandon Books, 1988.

Farrelly, Patrick. "Blackmail: An F.B.I. and R.U.C. Attempt to Blackmail an Irish Emigrant into Becoming an Informer." *Irish Voice*, 1 September 1990.

Faul, Father Dennis, and Father Raymond Murray. *The Sleeping Giant: Irish-Americans and Human Rights in Northern Ireland*. N.p., 1979.

FitzGerald, Garret. *All in a Life*. Dublin: Gill and MacMillan, 1991.

Fitzpatrick, James. "The Irish-American and Sinn Fein." *Triumph Magazine* (October 1973): 13–16.

Flemming, Tom. "The Green Flag in America." *American Heritage* 30 (June/July 1979): 50–63.

Funchion, Michael. *Irish-American Voluntary Organizations*. Westport, Conn.: Greenwood Press, 1983.

Golway, Terry. "Irish-American Community Gets Close F.B.I. Surveillance." *New York Observer*, 17 August 1992.

Greeley, Andrew. *Irish-Americans: The Rise to Money and Power*. New York: Harper & Row, 1981.

Guelke, Adrian. "The American Connection to the Northern Ireland Conflict." *Irish Studies in International Affairs* 1, no. 4 (1984): 27–38.

———. *Northern Ireland: The International Perspective*. Dublin: Gill and Macmillan, 1988.

Healey, James. *The Northern Ireland Dilemma: An Irish-American Imperative*. New York: Peter Long, 1989.

Hickey, Neil. "Northern Ireland: How T.V. Tips the Balance." *T.V. Guide* (21 September 1981), 9–24.

Holland, Jack. *The American Connection: U.S. Guns, Money, and Influence in Northern Ireland*. New York: Viking, 1987.

Holland, Mary. "Carter, Kennedy, and Ireland: The Inside Story." *Magill* (1 October 1977).

———. "Kennedy's New Irish Policy." *The New Statesman* (11 May 1979): 678–79.

Howe, Russell W. *The Power Peddlers: How Lobbyists Mold America's Foreign Policy*. Garden City, New York: Doubleday, 1977.

Hume, John. "The Irish Question: A British Problem." *Foreign Affairs* 58 (Winter 1979/80): 300–313.

Kalb, Richard. "Unmasking the I.R.A.: The Propaganda War in America." *Conservative Digest* 9 (February 1983): 32–33.

Kelley, Kevin. *The Longest War: Northern Ireland and the I.R.A.*. Westport, Conn.: Lawrence Hill, 1982.

Kennedy, Edward. "Ulster is an International Issue." *Foreign Policy* 57 (September 1973): 57–71.

Kessler, Ronald. *The F.B.I.: Inside the World's Most Powerful Law Enforcement Agency*. New York: Pocket Books, 1993.

Loftus, John. *Valhalla's Wake: The I.R.A., M16, and the Assasination of a Young American*. New York: Atlantic Monthly Press, 1989.

Lynch, Eamon. "The State of the Irish Lobby." *Irish-America Magazine* (January 1995), 16–17.

McCaffrey, Lawrence J. *The Irish Diaspora in America*. Bloomington: Indiana University Press, 1976.

———. *Textures of Irish America*. Syracuse: Syracuse University Press, 1992.

McCarthy, John. "Northern Ireland: Irish-American Responses." *The Recorder* 2 (Winter 1986): 43–50.

————. *Dissent from Irish America*. New York: University Press of America, 1993.

McCluskey, Conn. *Up Off Their Knees: A Commentary on the Civil Rights Movement in Northern Ireland*. Dublin: Conn McCluskey and Associates, 1989.

McKinley, Michael. "Lavish Generosity: The American Dimension of International Support for the I.R.A." *Conflict Quarterly* 7 (Spring 1987).

McKittrick, David. "The Irish Connection." *World Press Review* 26 (November 1979): 25–29.

McManus, Father Seán. *The MacBride Principles: Genesis and History*. Washington, D.C.: I.N.C. Press, 1993.

Mallowe, Mike. "My Life and Times with the I.R.A." *Philadelphia Magazine* 64 (3 March 1973): 103–14.

Mansbach, Richard. *Northern Ireland: Half a Century of Partition*. New York: Facts on File, 1973.

Mount, Ferdinand. "The I.R.A. and the Barrooms of America." *The American Spectator* 13 (January 1980): 14–16.

Mullins, Emer. "The American Role in the Cease-Fire." *Irish-America Magazine* (November 1994), 16–17.

Murray, Hugh. "The Green and Red Unbending: The National Association for Irish Freedom from 1972–1975." *Journal of Ethnic Studies* (Summer 1975).

O'Donovan, Donal. *Dreamers of Dreams: Portraits of the Irish in America*. Bray: Kilbride Books, 1984.

O'Dwyer, Paul. *Counsel for the Defense: The Autobiography of Paul O'Dwyer*. New York: Simon and Schuster, 1979.

O'Malley, Padraig. *Biting at the Grave: The Irish Hunger Strikes and the Politics of Despair*. Boston: Beacon Press, 1990.

O'Neill, Tip. *Man of the House : The Life and Political Memoirs of Speaker Tip O'Neill*. New York: Random House, 1987.

O'Sullivan, Michael P. *Patriot Graves: Resistance in Ireland*. Chicago: Folletts, 1972.

Paletz, David. "The I.R.A., Red Brigades, and F.A.L.N. in the New York Times." *Journal of Communications* (Spring 1982).

Patterson, Henry. "Gerry Adams and the Modernization of Republicanism" *Conflict Quarterly* 10 (Summer 1990): 5-24.

Penn, Stanley. "Ulster Pipeline: How U.S. Catholics Help Their Brethren in Northern Ireland." *Wall Street Journal*, 12 October 1981.

Pogatchnik, Shawn. "Irish Expatriates Honor Heroes." *Los Angeles Times* (E, 1:4) 9 May 1991.

Powers, Charles. "New York Irish Aid: The Collecting o' the Green." *Los Angeles Times*, 12 January 1976.

Purdie, Bob. *Politics in the Streets: The Origins of the Civil Rights Movement in Northern Ireland*. Belfast: Blackstaff Press, 1990.

Quinn, Frank. "The Shadow of the Gunmen." *Irish-America Magazine* (January 1987): 18–20.

Raymond, Raymond J. "Irish America and Northern Ireland: An End to Romanticism?" *The World Today* 39 (March 1983): 106–13.

Reed, David. "Terror in Northern Ireland: The American Connection." *Readers Digest* 122 (April 1983): 163–64.

Ridgeway, James. "The Belfast Connection: Money and Munitions from New York are Helping the I.R.A. Lay Seige to London." *Villiage Voice* 39 (8 February 1994): 29–36.

Shannon, William V. "Northern Ireland and American Responsibility." *The Recorder* 36 (Fall 1975): 28–42.

Sheesgreen, Sean. "Missing the Story in Northern Ireland." *Chicago Journalism Review* 4 (20 November 1971).

Stone, J. L. "Irish Terrorism Investigations." *F.B.I. Law Enforcement Bulletin* 56 (October 1987): 18–23.

Tansill, Charles. *America and the Fight for Irish Freedom, 1866–1922: An Old Story Based Upon New Data.* New York: Devin-Adair, 1957.

Thatcher, Margaret. *The Downing Street Years.* New York: Harper Collins, 1993.

Thomas, Jo. "Bloody Ireland." *Columbia Journalism Review* 27 (May 1988): 31–37.

Thompson, Joseph. "U.S.- Northern Ireland Relations" *World Affairs* 146 (Spring 1984): 318–39.

———."The Anglo-Irish Agreement and Irish-American Politics." *Conflict* 7 (1987): 285–301.

Urban, Mark. *Big Boys' Rules: The S.A.S. and the Secret War Against the I.R.A..* London: Faber, 1992.

Ward, Alan. *Ireland and Anglo-American Relations, 1899–1921.* Toronto: University of Toronto Press, 1969.

Weinraub, Bernard. "I.R.A. Unit in the Bronx Linked to Flow of Arms." *New York Times*, 16 December 1975.

———."Split Among Irish-Americans Said to Cut Funds to I.R.A.." *New York Times*, 7 September 1979.

Weismann, John. "Buying Goodwill: Foreign Lobbyists and U.S. Television." *T.V. Guide* (25 November 1978): 30–35.

White, Barry. *John Hume: Statesman of the Troubles.* Belfast: Blackstaff, 1984.

Williams, Roger. "American Aid: Lifeblood for the I.R.A." *World Magazine* (24 April 1973): 28–32.

Wilson, Andrew J. "Irish-America and the Hunger Strikes." *The Recorder* 2 (Summer 1987): 14–31.

———."The American Congress for Irish Freedom and the Northern Ireland Civil Rights Movement, 1967–70." *Eire-Ireland* 29 (Spring 1994): 61–76.

———."The Conflict between Noraid and the Friends of Irish Freedom: Trends in Modern Irish-American Republicanism, 1980–92." Irish Review 15 (Spring 1994): 40–51.

Wright, Frank. Northern Ireland: A Comparative Analysis. Dublin: Gill and Macmillan, 1988.

II. VIDEO MATERIAL

The American Connection: Trial of Richard Johnson (BBC Northern Ireland: Spotlight, 1990).

Images of Ireland in Crisis: U.S. Television News Coverage of Northern Ireland (Private video of Joe O'Rourke, 1988).

Joe Doherty (New York: Celtic Videos, 1988).

Memorial Service for James C. Heaney (Private video of Tom Enright, 1986).

The Old Man and the Gun (WGBH Boston: Frontline, 1984).

A Turn to the Gun: The 1982 Trial of Michael Flannery (New York: Celtic Videos, 1985).

Unfinished Business: The Fight for the MacBride Principles (New York: Celtic Videos, 1993).

III. PRINCIPAL NEWSPAPERS AND MAGAZINES

1. American Newspapers and Magazines, 1968–1995

The Baltimore Sun
The Boston Globe
The Chicago Daily News
The Chicago Tribune
The Chicago Sun-Times
The Christian Science Monitor
The Detroit News
The Los Angeles Times
The New Orleans Times-Picayune
Newsweek Magazine
The New York Daily News
The New York Post
The New York Times
The Philadelphia Daily News
The Philadelphia Inquirer
The San Francisco Chronicle
The St. Louis Post-Dispatch
Time Magazine
The Wall Street Journal
The Washington Post
The Washington Star
U.S.A. Today

2. Irish-American Newspapers and Magazines, 1967–1995

ACUJ Newsletter: Monthly journal of American Committee for Ulster Justice, New York.

The Advocate: Weekly Irish-American newspaper, New York.

The American Gael: Monthly newspaper of Clan na Gael, Toledo.

American Irish Congress: Monthly newspaper of American Irish Congress, Long Island.

The A.P.E.C. Newsletter: Monthly journal of the American Political Education Committee, Stonybrook, New York.

The Boston Irish News: Weekly Irish-American newspaper, Boston.

The Felon: Monthly newsletter of the Irish-American Action Association, San Francisco.

The Gael: Monthly Irish-American newspaper, San Francisco.

The Harp: Quarterly newsletter of the Irish-American Labor Coalition, New York.

The Irish Activist: Monthly journal of the National Association for Irish Justice, New York.

The Irish Advocate: Weekly Irish-American newspaper, New York.

Irish-America Magazine: Monthly journal, New York.

The Irish-American News: Monthly newspaper, Chicago.

The Irish American Partnership Newsletter: Quarterly journal of Irish American Partnership, Boston.

The Irish-American Reporter: Bi-weekly newspaper of the American Congress for Irish Freedom, Buffalo.

The Irish-American Review: Monthly journal, New York.

The Irish-American Voice: Monthly republican magazine, Enterprise, Alabama.

The Irish Echo: Weekly Irish-American newspaper, New York.

The Irish Edition: Weekly Irish-American newspaper, Philadelphia.

The Irish Lobby: Monthly journal of the Irish National Caucus, Washington.

The Irish Newsline: Bi-monthly journal of the Irish-American Unity Conference, Washington, DC.

The Irish People: Weekly newspaper of the Irish-American Republican Movement, New York.

The Irish Rebel: Monthly newsletter of the Friends of Irish Freedom, Boston.

The Irish Voice: Weekly Irish-American newspaper, New York.

The N.A.I.F. Fact Sheet: Periodic newspaper of the National Association for Irish Freedom, New York.

The National Hibernian Digest: Monthly newspaper of the Ancient Order of Hibernians, New York.

The Rising of the Moon: Periodic newspaper of the Campaign for Ulster Justice, Boston.

Saoirse: Irish Freedom: Republican Sinn Féin monthly, New York.

The Sash: Periodic newspaper of the Loyal Orange Institution of America, San Francisco.

The Shillelagh: Monthly newspaper of the American Irish Republican Army, Philadelphia.

The Ulster-American Newsletter: Periodic journal of the Ulster American Heritage Foundation, Manhattan Beach.

3. British and Irish Newspapers and Magazines, 1968–1992

An Phoblacht/Republican News: Weekly newspaper of Sinn Féin, Belfast.
The Andersonstown News: Belfast, weekly.
The Belfast News Letter: Belfast, daily.
The Belfast Telegraph: Belfast, evening newspaper.
The Daily Telegraph: London, daily.
The Economist: London, weekly.
Fortnight: Belfast, monthly.
The Guardian: Manchester, daily.
Hibernia: Dublin, weekly.
The Irish Independent: Dublin, daily.
The Irish News: Belfast, daily.
The Irish Times: Dublin, daily.
Magill: Dublin, monthly.
The Observer: London, daily.
The Sunday Tribune: Dublin, weekly.

INDEX

Abzug, Bella, 93
Ackerman, Gary, 261
Adams, Gerry, vii, 19, 149–50, 227, 277, 279, 287n, 293; politicization of Sinn Féin, 198–200; attack on the Friends of Irish Freedom, 282; US visa, 295–96; US fund raising, 298–99
Ad Hoc Committee on Irish Affairs, 259, 269; formation and policies, 141–43; cooperation with Friends of Ireland, 287n; *see also* Biaggi, Mario
African Americans, 5, 18–21, 31, 33–35, 37, 41, 58, 275n
Agramonte, Edward, 91
Aguilar, Robert, 205, 259,
Airlee House Conference, 245n
AK-47 rifles, 209
Albanese, Sal, 274
Alliance Party, 79, 221
Allison, Michael, 117
Allport, George, 146
American Committee for Ulster Justice, 55, 58, 65, 78, 99
American Conference for Irish Studies, 166–67
American Congress for Irish Freedom, 22–26, 28, 40; links with Spanish government, 27–28; anti-investment campaign, 29; structure and ideology, 29–31; conflict with NAIJ, 37–38; conflict with Noraid, 48–49; and MacBride Principles, 269

American Association for the Recognition of the Irish Republic, 13
American Commission on Irish Independence, 12
American Friends of Irish Neutrality, 15
American Ireland Fund, 120–22, 154
American Irish Political Education Committee, 201, 268
American Irish Republican Army, 201–2
American Labor for Irish Freedom, 98
American League for an Undivided Ireland, 16, 56
American Protestants for Truth About Ireland, 268
American Repeal Association, 4–5
American Trade Union, 252
Amnesty International, 129, 155
Amon, Carol, 232
Anable, David, 88
Ancient Order of Hibernians, 23, 33–34, 98–99, 213, 215–16, 244; support for republican movement, 200–201
An Cumann Cabhrach, 43–45, 201, 281
Anderson, Jack, 173–74
Anderson, Robert, 235
Andersonstown News, 150
Anglo-Irish Agreement, 248–49, 253
An Phoblacht, 100n, 150
Armagh Women's Prison, 169, 177n
Armalite rifles, 87, 95, 208n, 231, 233, 263, 290
Aspin, Les, 88

Irish America and the Ulster Conflict, 1968–1995 was designed and composed in Times Roman with Perpetua display type by Books International, Norcross, Georgia; printed on 60-pound Glatfelter Supple Opaque Recycled and bound by Thomson-Shore, Inc., Dexter, Michigan; and designed and produced by Kachergis Book Design, Pittsboro, North Carolina.